Television Studies and Research on Series

Denis Newiak • Dominik Maeder •
Herbert Schwaab
Editors

Television Studies
and Research on Series

Theory, history and present of (post-)
televisual seriality

palgrave
macmillan

Editors
Denis Newiak
Brandenburg University of
Technology
Cottbus, Brandenburg
Germany

Dominik Maeder
Rheinische Friedrich-Wilhelms-
Universität
Bonn, Nordrhein-Westfalen
Germany

Herbert Schwaab
Universität Regensburg
Regensburg, Bayern
Germany

ISBN 978-3-658-42914-0   ISBN 978-3-658-42915-7   (eBook)
https://doi.org/10.1007/978-3-658-42915-7

This book is a translation of the original German edition "Fernsehwissenschaft und Serienforschung" by Denis Newiak, published by Springer Fachmedien Wiesbaden GmbH in 2021. The translation was done with the help of an artificial intelligence machine translation tool. A subsequent human revision was done primarily in terms of content, so that the book will read stylistically differently from a conventional translation. Springer Nature works continuously to further the development of tools for the production of books and on the related technologies to support the authors.

Translation from the German language edition: "Fernsehwissenschaft und Serienforschung" by Denis Newiak et al., © Der/die Herausgeber bzw. der/die Autor(en), exklusiv lizenziert durch Springer Fachmedien Wiesbaden GmbH, ein Teil von Springer Nature 2021. Published by Springer Fachmedien Wiesbaden. All Rights Reserved.

This Palgrave Macmillan imprint is published by the registered company Springer Fachmedien Wiesbaden GmbH, part of Springer Nature.
The registered company address is: Abraham-Lincoln-Str. 46, 65189 Wiesbaden, Germany

If disposing of this product, please recycle the paper.

Contents

Television Studies and Research on Series: An Introduction

Dominik Maeder, Herbert Schwaab, und Denis Newiak

During the conception of this volume, we as editors thought long and hard about the title: "Fernsehwissenschaft und Serienforschung" ("TV Studies and Series Reseach") was actually intended as a placeholder that should perhaps have been replaced by a more appealing, catchy title. There are plenty of examples of this in the literature on television series: *"Was bisher geschah. . ."* ("What has happened so far")[1] and *"Previously on. . ."*[2] were, for example, the undoubtedly concise titles of the first anthologies in the German-speaking world, which from 2008 onwards referred to the renaissance of the television series as a particularly 'temporalised' aesthetic form. This also made visible a more recent, heterogeneous research on series[3] that received aspects of seriality beyond television. In cheerful plurality, this

---

[1] Cf. Seiler (2008)

[2] Cf. Meteling et al. (2010).

[3] Cf. Blanchet et al. (2011); Kelleter (2012); Eichner et al. (2013) *Transnationale Serienkultur;* Lillge et al. (2014) Nesselhauf and Schleich (2014).

D. Maeder (✉)
Institut für Sprach-, Medien- und Musikwissenschaft, Rheinische Friedrich-Wilhelms-Universität Bonn, Bonn, Germany
e-mail: dmaeder@uni-bonn.de

H. Schwaab
Institut für Information und Medien, Sprache und Kultur, Universität Regensburg, Regensburg, Germany
e-mail: Herbert.Schwaab@sprachlit.uni-regensburg.de

D. Newiak
Brandenburgische Technische Universität, Cottbus-Senftenberg, Cottbus, Germany
e-mail: mail@denis-newiak.de

1

D. Newiak et al. (eds.), *Television Studies and Research on Series*,
https://doi.org/10.1007/978-3-658-42915-7_1

new series research was able to refer to the television series without having to take up the legacy of a decidedly television studies based preoccupation with seriality, whose paradigm had been the series broadcast on television.[4] Perspectives from literary studies, film studies, cultural studies, political science, popular culture studies, narratology, fan and participation studies, English studies/American studies, and other fields of research were thus able to work on the television series in a unquestionably productive manner, mostly in the form of anthologies, but along the line of their field of studies unburdened by the perspective of television studies. Some approaches even plead for the complete deletion of television from the terminological definition of the subject matter—the television series should thus become the medially indeterminate "audiovisual series".[5] One anthology even elevates the (quality) series in its title, half exclamatory, half questioning, to "Das andere Fernsehen" ("The other television")"[6] in general. As Michael Dellwing sums up on referring to the various collections of essays on television programs in *Reading Contemporary Television*, a clear foundation in theoretical approaches and methodological tools of television studies has become irrelevant in the current research on series.[7]

At the same time, however, in recent years the medial conditions of this separation of the series from television—DVD, file sharing, streaming—have not only been reflected upon by a distinct research on the series in media studies, but have also been seen as essential features of newer serial forms, precisely in the (explicit and implicit) negotiation of media transformations.[8] It would certainly no longer be possible to speak of a lack of theory in series research, but then it is no longer a matter of series analysis inspired by considerations of television theory, but rather of a genuine series theory that seeks productive connections to the theoretical fields of diagrammatics, systems theory, actor-network theory and governmentality research,[9] instead of limiting itself to the canon of television theory formation. However, it is precisely this connectivity of research on seriality, which is primarily

---

[4]Cf. as canonical texts of this 'first' television series research Hickethier (1991), Giesenfeld (1994).

[5]Kirschbacher and Stollfuß (2015), p. 27.

[6]Nesselhauf and Schleich (2014)

[7]Dellwing (2009), p. 239. For a critique of the *Reading Contemporary Television* series, see also Schwaab (2010).

[8]See, for example, Beil et al. (2016), Kelleter (2017) Maeder and Wentz (2013), Beil et al. (2017).

[9]See, for example, Wentz (2017), Kelleter (2014), Sudmann (2017), Maeder (2021).

oriented towards theories of series, to other descriptive languages of cultural and media studies that has been (partly) decisive for its success.[10]

Recent research on series thus draws on an affirmation of the not- or no-more-televisual series, to which the titles of publications that play with the characteristics of the serial bear witness. If we have opted here for a rather sober title, this means stepping back behind this—possibly premature—affirmation of a series detached from television. Rather, this volume aims to contribute to an active interrogation of the relationship between series studies and television studies against the backdrop of an unrelenting series boom as well as a fundamental technological change in the television dispositif. The conjunction of the two fields of research named in the title, which leaves their exact relation undefined, therefore seemed to us to be the most succinct paraphrase of our intention.

It is important to remember that televisuality is historically closely linked to various forms of seriality: in the design of its programming, the economy of its media production, and the ritualized form of its reception, television lives from repetition in series. In the television series, this coupling condenses into a genuine object form: through the reliable recurrence of familiar series characters, the mode of their cinematic and narrative procedures typical of each individual series, as well as the regularity and permanence of their availability, binding forces arise not only between the individual episodes of a series, but also between medium and audience,[11] through which the television series has become a model case for television theory itself.[12] Against the background of the emergence of research on series as an independent field of research outlined above, the historically close coupling of televisuality and seriality has increasingly weakened in recent years, both in terms of theoretical traditions and epistemologies as well as in relation to research programmatics: the unchanged high popularity of series and serial forms in media studies is thus contrasted by a comparatively low interest in the theorization of television.

This lack of interest raises problems because it seems so productive to think of seriality in terms of television. A brief look at some sections of the history of television research shows many impulses for research on series that have come from this field itself. This stretches back to early debates that predated the field of television studies, which only formed later, but which were critically concerned with television as a mass medium: Günter Anders, for example, while not explicitly

---

[10]Cf. Ernst and Paul (2015a, b), p. 16.

[11]Cf. Hagedorn (1988).

[12]Cf. the contribution by Denis Newiak in this volume.

relating his critique articulated in the 1950s to seriality, uses the term matrix to address the formative power of televisual patterns and repetitions that shape events and content.[13] Anders addresses this as an effect of the "Verbiederung der Welt"[14] (making the world mundane and trivial) which creates the familiar out of the unfamiliar and thus destroys any resistance of the world and therefore any possibility of (real) experience.[15] A similar critique is formulated by Theodor W. Adorno, who associates an affirmative function with the stereotypes and figures of repetition that dominate television.[16] These positions from the 1950s, both of which rarely deal specifically with specific formats of television, express the irritation about the unfamiliar, serial and newness of television. In his examination of 1950s television discourse in the United States, William Boddy makes clear that this perplexity was also mirrored by the television criticism of the time. This was, however, a reaction to a specific change in dominant series types—from the live drama of the anthology series, which due to its sources in theatre had cultural renown, to the filmed, episodic series that became popular, for example, as westerns from the mid-1950s onwards. Boddy quotes one critic as follows: "After the first show, I don't know what to say about a western or quiz show, and I don't know anybody else who does either."[17] This difficulty in finding words for the (new) seriality of the episodic in television is one reason for the problematic position of television in culture, which is met not only by a left-wing critique such as that of Adorno or Anders, but also by a conservative critique formulated by political institutions such as the FCC, the American programming regulator, and its head Newton Minow. He is best known for the dictum, formulated in 1961, that television was a 'vast wasteland' and that there was merely a parade of programmes such as Western, gangster and animation series, quiz shows, violence and boredom and formulaic comedies.[18]

This irritation with the serial, which is articulated in various ways as a critique of popular culture, is only belatedly processed by approaches influenced by cultural studies and above all by feminist-oriented television studies. Referring to *Crossroads,* a British melodramatic long-running series, Charlotte Brunsdon points out the extraordinary temporal and spatial design of this type of series in the early 1980s:

---

[13] Cf. Anders (2009), p. 110.

[14] Ibid., p. 113.

[15] Cf. Ibid.

[16] Cf. Adorno (2009), p. 62.

[17] Boddy (1993), p. 192.

[18] Cf. Thompson (1996), p. 26.

> There is no single linear time-flow. [...] In contrast with classical Hollywood cinema the temporal relationships between segments is rarely encoded. [...] Relationships between segments can be read as in most cases sequential or simultaneous. [...] The different present tenses of the narrative co-exist, temporally unhierarchised.[19]

Brunsdon emphasizes not only a temporal but also a spatial fragmentation in melodramatic formats and soap operas, which has implications for how stories are told in long running serials and what effects they have.[20] In the 1980s, Jane Feuer also highlights this idiosyncratic figure of a popular but little-recognized series type. She describes the long running serial melodrama as an extended middle that has no end, thus subverting the teleological form of classic cinematic narratives. There is no moral resolution or concluding assessment of a plot because it would contradict the nature of the long running serial melodrama to find an end.[21] Focusing on the serial and its effects, Feuer also challenges a distinction between the more progressively regarded sitcom of the time—liberal, feminist formats such as *The Mary Tyler Moore Show*—and the primetime soaps that were mostly regarded as conservative—*Dallas* and *Dynasty in* particular. She emphasizes that the sitcom, through its episodic resolution, is much more likely to be norm-setting than the primetime soap, which is geared towards endlessness and does not resolve the contradictions between different norms, thus challenging them, and must therefore be thought of as progressive in form.[22] Tania Modleski also emphasizes the consequences that serial forms have for American soap: "Tune in tomorrow, not in order to find out the answers, but to see what further complications will defer the resolutions and introduce new questions."[23] Endless complication means a permanent temporal delay, which creates spectators who are made to tolerate the experience of waiting.[24]

Feminist television scholarship discovers a complex temporality and spatiality, that offers a distinct perspective on the world, in serial formats that have received little recognition in cultural criticism. In fact, as Linda Williams notes, seriality is a form initially marginalized by television (primarily because the live dramas of the 1950s were regarded as unique events similar to musical and theatre performances): it has survived as a narrative form adopted from radio only in the genre of soap

---

[19] Brunsdon (1981), p. 34.

[20] Cf. Ibid., p. 35.

[21] Cf. Feuer (1984), p. 12.

[22] Cf. Ibid., p. 16.

[23] Modleski (2017), p. 63.

[24] Cf. Ibid.

opera, but through the principle of the melodramatic it is also present in other, episodic[25] or accumulative formats. "Scratch the surface of either the 'accumulative' series or mini-series, however, and melodrama is evident [. . .]."[26]

While the feminist re-reading of television series investigates what forms of experience are granted in different types of seriality, Umberto Eco argues that 'smart' recipients, who are regarded as cognitively active viewers, are also subject to similar effects of televisual seriality.[27] In his essay from the 1980s, Eco attempted to rehabilitate the serial as an artistic procedure with the concept of the art of repetition.[28] Many of his examples of specific manifestations of this repetitive art are taken from television. Series such as *Columbo*[29] or *Dallas*[30] provide different models of seriality that are linked to distinct forms of forgetting and remembering as well as the cognitive activities of the viewers and their pleasure in recognition or variation.

Omar Calabrese, to whom Eco refers, relates seriality back to an alternative understanding of art and takes an episodic series like *Bonanza* as a model for a special temporality of the series: "[. . .] *Bonanza* is archetypical in its ability to create a number of different time levels: a complete story in each episode, the open story of the series, and an intermediate model consisting of an open story lasting for a certain number of episodes".[31] Especially against the background of the contemporary dominant form of accumulative, or 'staggered' seriality[32] it is remarkable that Calabrese already speaks of a series that has a memory referring to *Bonanza*.[33] In doing so, he implies that viewers are also cognitively invested in tracing and breaking down this memory, and that their view of the characters changes as they watch more than one episode. What counts for his neo-baroque aesthetic as much as for Eco's art of repetition is that with each series or type of series, a new model is established that follows a tight set of rules as a virtuoso art of variation.[34]

---

[25] Cf. Williams (2018), p. 174.

[26] Cf. Ibid., p. 176.

[27] Cf. Eco (1989), p. 305.

[28] Ibid., p. 302.

[29] Cf. Ibid., p. 312.

[30] Ibid., p. 307.

[31] Calabrese (1993), p. 38.

[32] Cf. the contribution by Dominik Maeder in this volume.

[33] Cf. also Engell (2011) as a reading of series types based on theories of memory and cognition.

[34] Cf. Calabrese (1993), p. 40.

Calabrese's list of different models associated with series such as *Dallas, Ivanhoe*, or *Bonanza* is not at all interested in questions of narratology, the progression of plot or in investigating how a satisfying conclusion can be generated—but is interested in the serial form itself.

This insistence on a formal quality of the series that goes beyond a preoccupation with narration and progression distinguishes both approaches—Eco and Calabrese's engagement with the art of repetition and the feminist discussion of the forms of melodramatic series—from a current state of the art of research on the narrative complexity of series that has developed in relation to quality TV. Jason Mittell may stress that he personally prefers 'simple' series like *Everybody Loves Raymond* or *The Dick Van Dyke Show to* 'narratively complex' series like *24*, which have a clearly visible serial concept.[35] However, the unnecessary juxtaposition of narratively elaborate series and narratively conventional series[36] already sets a false tone that seems to understand the divergence only in terms of a divergence from a classic and normal form of seriality which, on close 'inspection, never existed but was 'complex' from the beginning.

The renunciation of this juxtaposition provides a perspective for investigating the series in television studies that raises a number of questions and problems: Are theories of television beyond the merely historical entanglement of televisuality and seriality still relevant for the study of contemporary series and serial forms? To what extent would the televisual be a possible point of reference for concepts of the serial even beyond television? Is there perhaps even a recursivity of television history, i.e. does the episodic of television, seemingly displaced by narrative progression, reappear in the form of the anthology series? Conversely, one can also ask how the conceptualization of television studies can react to the dissolution, transformation, and networking of media dispositives and their inclusion in a digital media ecology, the analytical penetration of which is precisely the aim of series research. How, then, does the study of televisuality benefit in turn from a conceptualization that refers predominantly to 'quality' TV, to the series offerings of HBO, Amazon, or Netflix, and to other post-televisual actors and media forms? How can an ignorance of television in research on series not only be problematized, but productively turned around? And how can theories of the serial possibly take the terminological repertoire of television theory beyond itself?

In doing so, we do not intend to uncritically continue the detachment of the series from television, nor do we want television studies to correct the supposed

---

[35] Cf. Mittell (2012), p. 99.
[36] Cf. Ibid., p. 97.

obliviousness in series research. Rather, we would like to openly question the relationship between the two approaches and thus enable and promote a mutual problematization of both series research, which occasionally follows its subject too affirmatively, and television studies, which sometimes fails to keep up with the significant technological and institutional transformations of its subject.

The contributions collected here explore this relationship in different ways and with different perspectives. Their common concern, however, is to question historically and typologically the connection (as well as, if necessary, the divergence) between televisuality and seriality and to outline, using concrete objects, how functional principles of television interlock with serialization processes or diverge from them.

To kick things off, Jana Zündel sheds a light on the changes to which television is exposed in the face of rapidly changing technical conditions. In meticulous detail, she shows that even in the age of Netflix and Amazon Prime, hardly anything has changed in the core televisual principles of the television series: Streaming services also conceive of their series as television series in a surprisingly conservative sense, retaining the unfinishable episode and season structure with its familiar distributive weekly and production-related annual rhythms, perpetuating and resurrecting established metatexts such as trailers, recaps, and commercial breaks, and striving to create an ongoing television experience despite (or perhaps because of) the fragmentary structure of their platform architecture, which, as an infinite *flow, is* intended to bind viewers to the devices (and subscriptions) as permanently as possible. Against this background, new products of streaming services appear as "overformed television", which simultaneously exaggerates and blurs the peculiarities of television, thereby propagating a new transmedial usage regime of endless "binge-watching" and yet can never dispense with a concept of the serial.

In her contribution, Christine Piepiorka examines transmedial forms of spatialization of serial narratives, which is associated with the extension to different media platforms. She attempts to classify these new spatialities with concepts from Deleuze and Guattari such as a 'notched space', which offers a model to describe a variable and constant spatial extension that nevertheless generates a closed cosmos, while the 'smooth space' generated by transmediality can be thought of as an expanding line that functions independently of the narrative anchor point. With such an approach, the article expands the vocabulary of a television scholarship interested in serial form and offers possibilities for thinking transmedial extensions beyond concepts such as participation that are dominant in convergence culture.

Stefan Borsos provides an insight into rather unknown territories of television history and recalls a now forgotten contribution to series research with William Steadman's monograph *The Serial* from the early 1970s. This examination of the 'serial eruptions' in the 1960s highlights how misguided the juxtaposition of classic series and the departures from this model in more recent series seems. In this decade, which has been neglected by television scholars, one can already find a multitude of 'deviations' from a type of series that never seems to have been fixed— psychological western series, series with accumulative character and memory, or, with *Peyton Place*, precursors of the primetime soap, already addressing an audience that was later taken over by Quality Television.

With a focus on the German-language television landscape, Florian Krauß then historizes the discourse on series quality and 'quality series'. Using the tools of production studies and on the basis of interviews with experts, Krauß thus works out how highly specific national programme structures, reception expectations and production cultures are seen by television producers as significant obstacles to the adaptation of a 'quality series' format based on the US model. Such obstacles are the focus on the non-serial individual televisual work, the orientation towards mass compatibility, the supremacy of directing and the interference of commissioning editors of the public and commercial television networks. The dispositif of television is also subject to a multiform change in Germany, which is establishing new networks, TV providers and production cultures, but, according to Krauß, these changes do not immediately render the long-lived institutional and personal production cultures of nationally organized television obsolete.

Inspired by sociological considerations, Denis Newiak's contribution deals with a constitutive loneliness of our lives in late modernity as a defining motif of many television series—and how televisual seriality makes this tendency to a growing social isolation more bearable at the same time. In a very detailed reading of the Netflix series *13 Reasons Why,* Newiak not only establishes many similarities between diagnoses of loss of community and orientation and motifs, scenes, and dialogues of the teen series, but above all describes how the series itself becomes an active and self-conscious medium not only of processing but also of compensating for loneliness: television series, according to Newiak, become the most important 'community factories' of late modernity precisely because of their serial character. The fact that the exemplarily examined series openly exhibits its serial construction on many levels (for example, when in the first season the main character Hannah creates her own series with cassettes) makes it a lucid examination not only of late modernity and its effects, but also of television itself, of serial narratives and how they affect society.

Sven Grampp then illuminates the double logic of televisual temporality by using Christmas episodes from television series of the 1950s to show how series and event intertwine in these 'special episodes'. Serial recurrence and eventful uniqueness are thus not mutually opposed modes of a temporal experience of the television program, but rather mutually related to each other. On the basis of this diagnosis of television series history, he then argues that such a simultaneity of festival and series also remains relevant for the post-televisual series design of streaming platforms: the reference to the yearly-cyclical extra-televisual event horizons that is fundamental for television is thus also inscribed in the temporal deep structure of television series beyond television.

Markus Kügle's contribution is dedicated to a different form of 'special episodes': with strong reference to psychoanalytic and post-structuralist film theory, he asks about the economy of desire of clip show episodes in which previously broadcast series material is re-contextualized and re-arranged for broadcast. On the one hand, Kügle works through the history of the clip show from the early cinema serial via the sitcom of the 1950s to current series of US provenance and, on the other hand, arrives at a theory of the clip show that sees in it not merely (but also) televisual surplus value production, but is able to read it as a symptom of a Lacanian logic of 'more than enjoyment' and thus of the television series in general.

Dominik Maeder then turns to televisual seriality of reality TV: like Kügle, he also emphasizes the economic foundation of serial forms and works out how contemporary series, through the media-historical transformation of first the introduction of the DVD and then streaming, introduce a third unit into the traditionally two-part organization of series and episode: the season. The 'season', according to Maeder, functions not only as a further, but as a formative principle for the organization of television serial narration. Maeder observes such a 'staggered seriality' not only in fictional series, but also in reality TV. Using *Germany's Next Topmodel* as an example, he shows how the casting format can be read and treated like a fictional series, as a staggered series whose time structures can be traced back to the basic unit of the season.

Also on the basis of *Germany's Next Topmodel* as well as on the political comedy programme *Neo Magazin (Royale),* Anja Peltzer then asks about the modes of time altered by the medium: if a television series can be called up, paused, slowed down and sped up at will at any time and practically at any place, what remains of the function of television as a "sozialer Zeitgeber" (a social agent that produces time, as Neverla calls it) that has structured the course of the day, week and year for half a century? In doing so, she shows how linear television formats, by absorbing new media, not only productively harness them for their own benefit, but also engage in a discourse about the nature of time organization in the age of ever-available, ubiquitous digital technologies constantly producing news. By taking up these non-televisual procedures, television offers a critical and sometimes normative perspective on how new media procedures reshape or subvert the serial principle of television. In the midst of a transformed media landscape of "social networks", media libraries and web offerings, Peltzer argues, television becomes the venue for negotiating new time regimes of the digital era by means of reality TV and entertainment shows.

Michaela Wünsch then takes a look at the 'prehistory' of seriality from the perspective of media philosophy. Taking up Eco's considerations mentioned above, Wünsch discusses seriality as a pre-industrial phenomenon that is inscribed in all art at the level of craft and technical production, its *technē*. Such a perspective of serial *technē* then opens up a media-theoretical perspective on language, writing, and image, as well as the relationship between repetition, difference, and imitation. The critique of a Platonic concept of image and writing articulated by Jean-Luc Nancy and Jacques Rancière, among others, amounts to the formulation of a concept of series that does not place art and technology in opposition to one another, but rather makes identity and difference legible as the result of different serialization pro-cesses. On the basis of *Breaking Bad,* Wünsch finally describes how such a differential seriality is caught up with in a media-reflexive way in terms of visual aesthetics.

With the rapid changes in the way television series are produced and received, the relationship between television and television viewers is also reshaping itself. At no time before has television wanted its viewers to be so actively involved in its series worlds, or as Kim Carina Hebben would say: Television now wants to *play* with us. In her contribution, she shows that television seriality and play are inextri-cably linked and dependent on each other, both of which live from the basic functions of repetition, variation and experimentation. As she demonstrates with *Black Mirror: Bandersnatch,* the game strategies escalate in transmedia television, which lets the viewers themselves become part of the series universe, for example by taking certain decisions from the characters or having to solve puzzles for them. The manifold interaction strategies of the new kind of television can perhaps be dismissed as gimmickry, but they fundamentally change the understanding of what can still be grasped under television series and television viewing at all: Is the viewer still playing with the series or has television long since been playing with the viewer? And how do the technical possibilities still to come change the television needs of the audience, which is increasingly being transformed into the playmate of its television set?

The Japanese anime series *Haha o Tazunete Sanzenri* (German title: *Marco*; English title: *From the Apennines to the Andes*, 1976), *Akage No An* (German title: *Anne mit den roten Haaren*; English title: *Anne of Green Gables*, 1979) and *Tanoshî Mûmin ikka* (German title: *Die Mumins*; English title: *Happy Moomin Family*, 1990), appear as an exact antipode to the fast-moving, impatient and excited streaming television of our time. Many people still remember these series from their childhood experiences of reception, but only a few may have been aware even then of the 'generous', almost wasteful way in which these animated series use the time of their viewers: While the sparse production method of 'limited animation' seemingly allows little movement to become visible in the images and seems to be predominantly a montage of frozen shots, the simple and comprehensible narratives are stretched as far apart as possible, so that hardly anything happens in individual episodes, or even over entire seasons (apart from extensive dialogue and landscape images), expressing their 'unlimited seriality'. For Schwaab, this contrast between spartan animation and overstretched plots constitutes a very special "configuration of the serial" in the anime series, which, especially in comparison to the contemporary series landscape, seems to have 'fallen out of time' in many senses.

This volume results from a workshop of the AG Fernsehen (Work Group Television) in the Gesellschaft für Medienwissenschaft (GfM, German Society of Media Studies), which took place at the Brandenburg Centre for Media Studies (ZeM) on 8 June 2018. The editors would like to thank all participants. We would also like to thank Tobias Emmerling for his great support producing the final version of the manuscript.

References

Adorno, Theodor W. (2009) Prolog zum Fernsehen. In: Grisko, Michael (Ed.) Texte zur Theorie und Geschichte des Fernsehens. Stuttgart, Reclam, pp. 52–64

Anders, Günther (2009) Die Antiquiertheit des Menschen. In: Grisko, Michael (Ed.) Texte zur Theorie und Geschichte des Fernsehens. Stuttgart, Reclam, pp. 101–121

Beil, Benjamin, Lorenz Engell, Dominik Maeder, Jens Schröter, Herbert Schwaab, Daniela Wentz (2016) Die Fernsehserie als Agent des Wandels. Münster, Litverlag

Beil, Benjamin, Herbert Schwaab, Daniela Wentz (Eds.) (2017) Lost in Media. Münster, Litverlag

Blanchet, Robert, Kristina Köhler, Tereza Smid, Julia Zutavern (Eds.) (2011) Serielle Formen. Von den frühen Film-Serials zu aktuellen Quality-TV- und Online-Serien. Marburg, Schüren

Boddy, William (1993) Fifties Television. The Industry and Its Critics. Chicago, University of Illinois Press

Brunsdon, Charlotte (1981) Crossroads. Notes on Soap Opera. In: Screen 22 (4), pp. 32–37

Calabrese, Omar (1993) Neo-Baroque. A Sign of Times. Princeton, Princeton University Press, pp. 27–46

Dellwing, Michael (2009) Serienforschung ohne Fernsehtheorie? Der Pragmatismus nonchalanter Neubeschreibungen in Reading Contemporary Television. In: Medien und Kommunikationswissenschaft 57, pp. 238–255

Eco, Umberto (1989) Im Labyrinth der Vernunft. Texte über Kunst und Zeichen. Leipzig, Reclam, pp. 301–324

Eichner, Susanne, Lothar Mikos, Rainer Winter (Eds.) (2013) Transnationale Serienkultur. Theorie, Ästhetik, Narration und Rezeption neuer Fernsehserien. Wiesbaden, Springer VS

Engell, Lorenz (2011) Erinnern/Vergessen: Serien als operatives Gedächtnis des Fernsehens. In: Blanchet et al (Ed.) Serielle Formen. Von den frühen Film-Serials zu aktuellen Quality-TV- und Online-Serien. Marburg, Schüren, pp. 115–132

Ernst, Christoph, Heike Paul (2015a) Einleitung. In: Amerikanische Fernsehserien der Gegenwart. Perspektiven der American Studies und der Media Studies. Bielefeld, Transcript Verlag, pp. 7–33

Ernst, Christoph, Heike Paul (Eds.) (2015b) Amerikanische Fernsehserien der Gegenwart. Perspektiven der American Studies und der Media Studies. Bielefeld, Transcript Verlag

Fahle, Oliver (2012) Im Diesseits der Narration. Zur Ästhetik der Fernsehserie. In: Kelleter (Ed.) Populäre Serialität: Narration—Evolution—Distinktion. Zum seriellen Erzählen seit dem 19. Jahrhundert. Bielefeld, Transcript Verlag, pp. 169–181

Feuer, Jane (1984) Melodrama, Serial Form, and Television Today. In: Screen 25 (1), pp. 4–16

Giesenfeld, Günter (Ed.) (1994) Endlose Geschichten. Serialität in den Medien. Hildesheim, Olms

Hagedorn, Roger (1988) Technology and Economic Exploitation: The Serial as a Form of Narrative Presentation. Wide Angle 10/4, pp. 4–12

Hickethier, Knut (1991) Die Fernsehserie und das Serielle des Fernsehens. Lüneburg, Zu Klampen

Kelleter, Frank (Ed.) (2012) Populäre Serialität: Narration—Evolution—Distinktion. Zum seriellen Erzählen seit dem 19. Jahrhundert. Bielefeld, Transcript Verlag

Kelleter, Frank (2014) Serial Agencies. The Wire and Its Readers. Alresford, Zero Books

Kelleter, Frank (Ed.) (2017) Media of Serial Narrative. Columbus, The Ohio State University Press

Kirschbacher, Felix, Sven Stollfuß (2015) Von der TV- zur AV-Serie. Produktions-, Distributions- und Rezeptionsformen aktueller US-Serien. merz. Zeitschrift für Medienpädagogik 4, pp. 21–28

Lillge, Claudia, Jörn Glasenapp, Elisabeth K. Paefgen, Dustin Breitenwischer (Eds.) (2014) Die neue amerikanische Fernsehserie. Von Twin Peaks bis Mad Men. Munich, Fink

Maeder, Dominik (2021) Die Regierung der Serie. Poetologie televisueller Gouvernementalität der Gegenwart. Bielefeld, Transcript Verlag

Maeder, Dominik, Daniela Wentz (Eds.) (2013) Der Medienwandel der Serie. Navigationen. Zeitschrift für Medien- und Kulturwissenschaften, 13 (1). Siegen, Universitätsverlag

Meteling, Arno, Isabell Otto, Gabriele Schabacher (Eds.) (2010) Previously on... Zur Ästhetik der Zeitlichkeit neuerer TV-Serien. Munich, Königshausen & Neumann

Mittel, Jason (2012) Narrative Komplexität im amerikanischen Gegenwartsfernsehen. In: Kelleter, Frank (Ed.) Populäre Serialität. Narration—Evolution—Distinktion, Bielefeld, Transcript Verlag, pp. 97–122

Modleski, Tania (2017) The Search for Tomorrow in Today's Soap Operas. In: Mendes, Kaitlynn (Ed.) Gender and the Media. Critical Concepts in Media and Cultural Studies, volume 2 Representing Gender. New York/London, Routledge, pp. 61–79

Nesselhauf, Jonas, Markus Schleich (Eds.) (2014) Quality-TV. Die narrative Spielwiese des 21. Jahrhunderts?! Münster, LIT Verlag

Nesselhauf, Jonas, Markus Schleich (Eds.) (2015) Das andere Fernsehen?! Eine Bestandsaufnahme des 'Quality Television'. Bielefeld, Transcript Verlag

Seiler, Sascha (Ed.) (2008) Was bisher geschah. Serielles Erzählen im zeitgenössischen amerikanischen Fernsehen. Cologne, Herbert von Halem Verlag

Schneider, Irmela (1995) Serien-Welten. Strukturen US-amerikanischer Serien aus vier Jahrzehnten. Opladen, Westdeutscher Verlag

Schwaab, Herbert (2010) Reading Contemporary Television, das Ende der Kunst und die Krise des Fernsehens. Zeitschrift für Medienwissenschaft 2, pp. 135–139

Sudmann, Andreas (2017) Serielle Überbietung. Zur televisuellen Ästhetik und Philosophie exponierter Steigerungen. Stuttgart, Metzler

Thompson, Robert J. (1996) Television's Second Golden Age. From Hill Street Blues to ER. New York, Continuum

Wentz, Daniela (2017) Bilderfolgen. Diagrammatologie der Fernsehserie. München, Fink

Williams, Linda (2018) World and Time: Serial Television Melodrama in America. In: Gledhill, Christine, Linda Williams (Eds.) Melodrama Unbound. New York, Columbia University Press, p 169–183rs, Günther: "Die Antiquiertheit des Menschen", in: Grisko, Michael (Ed.): *Texte zur Theorie und Geschichte des Fernsehens*, Stuttgart 2009, pp. 101–121

Series and TV Shows

Thirteen Reasons Why (Netflix 2017–2020)

Akage No An (Engl. title: *Anne of Green Gables*, Fuji Television 1979)

Black Mirror: Bandersnatch (Netflix 2018)

Bonanza (NBC 1959–1973)

Breaking Bad (AMC 2008–2013)

Columbo (NBC 1968–1978, ABC 1989–2003)

Crossroads (ITV 1964–2003)

Dallas (CBS 1978–1991)

The Dick van Dyke Show (CBS 1961–1966)

Dynasty (1981–1989)

Everybode loves Raymond (CBS 1996–2005)

Germany's Next Topmodel (ProSieben 2006–)

Haha o Tazunete Sanzen Ri (Engl- title: From the Apennines to the Andes., Fuji TV 1976*)*

Ivanhoe (ITV 1958–1959)

The Mary Tyler Moore Show (CBS 1970–1977)

Neo Magazin (Royale) (ZDFneo 2013–2019)

Peyton Place (ABC 1964–1969)

Tanoshî Mûmin ikka (Engl. title: Happy Moomin Family, TV Tokyo 1990*)*

Dominik Maeder Dr. phil., is a research assistant at the Department of Media Studies at the Rheinische Friedrich-Wilhelms-Universität Bonn, where he wrote his 2018 dissertation on "Die Regierung der Serie. Poetologie televisueller Gouvernementalität der Gegenwart" (The Reign of the Television Series. Poetology of televisual Governmentality) (Summa Cum Laude). In addition to his focus in television and series studies, he works on media of governance and media cultures of aviation. Selected publications: *Die Regierung der Serie. Poetologie televisueller Gouvernementalität der Gegenwart*, Bielefeld: transcript, 2021; "Serielle Anhänglichkeit: Sucht, Serie und die Ästhetik von Objektbeziehungen", in Montage/AV, vol. 27, no. 2, 2018, pp. 61–76; ed. (with Jens Schröter, Gregor Schwering and Till A. Heilmann): *Ambient. Aesthetics of the background*. Wiesbaden: Springer VS, 2018. Website: dominikmaeder.de.

Herbert Schwaab Dr. phil., teaches as a senior lecturer in the Department of Media Studies at the University of Regensburg. His research focuses on film philosophy and popular culture, sitcoms and reality TV, animals in animation, Japanese media culture, bicycle culture and the mediality of autism. PhD 2006 at the Ruhr University Bochum with a thesis on Stanley Cavell's philosophy of film. Important publications: Ed. (with Benjamin Beil, Daniela Wentz): Lost in Media. Münster: Litverlag, 2017; "Die schwierige Beziehung von Film und Sitcom," in: Thomas Morsch, Lukas Foerster and Nikolaus Perneczky (eds.): *Before Quality. Zur Ästhetik der Fernsehserie vor HBO, Netflix und Co.* Münster: Litverlag, 2019, 153–181; *Erfahrung des Gewöhnlichen. Stanley Cavells Filmphilosophie als Theorie des Populärkultur* (Experience of the Ordinary. Stanley Cavell's film philosophy as a theory of popular culture). Münster: Lit, 2010.

Denis Newiak Dr. phil., is researching at the Chair of Applied Media Studies at the Brandenburg University of Technology Cottbus-Senftenberg on expressions of loneliness in film and television and on theories of socialisation through television series. Further research interests: science fiction film, artificial intelligence and virtual language assistants, aesthetics of film music. Recent publications: *Loneliness in Series. Televisual Expressions of Modern Loneliness*. Wiesbaden: Springer VS, 2024; Denis Newiak and Anastasia Schnitzer (eds.): *Conspiracy Ideologies in Films and Series. Explanatory Approaches and Opportunities for Intervention*. Wiesbaden: Palgrave Macmillan, 2024. Website: denis-newiak.de

Television as a Plural and Transmedial Concept

Jana Zündel

Today's 'television' is highly diversified, be it technologically, economically or aesthetically. Linear and non-linear television, network and cable TV and streaming platforms exist side by side, their offerings forming a constant foil of contrast for one another. The continuous differentiation of distribution and reception possibilities of series formats not only calls into question their definition as *television* series. The ontological status of television itself is also up for debate: television cannot be described as a singular, congruent medium, but must be placed in the plural in view of the manifold dispositive orders through which series are received today: *the televisions*. Yet despite the progressive decoupling of series and television (as apparatus and institution on the one hand, and as pre-structured, receptive activity on the other), the new televisions remain committed to the programming logic of television and remediate its structural and textual principles. The streaming platform Netflix adapts the modularized performance as well as the reception-guiding textual strategies of television for its original and licensed series—and transforms them. Thus, episodes on Netflix are distinguished from one another by minimal yet recognizable interruptions; at the same time, these minimalized textual connecting pieces—similar to the *flow* typical of television—aim at a serialized reception. The object of the series then allows us to understand the transformation of television as a flexible, transmedial concept.

J. Zündel (✉)
Research Training Group "Configurations of Film", Institut for Theater, Film and Media Studies, Goethe University Frankfurt, Frankfurt, Germany
e-mail: Zuendel@tfm.uni-frankfurt.de

D. Newiak et al. (eds.), *Television Studies and Research on Series*,
https://doi.org/10.1007/978-3-658-42915-7_2

17

"Previously On": Questioning the Status of Television and Series

Are series still *television series*? Is television still *television* at all? In view of the migration of television content of all kinds to various web channels and the manifold viewing possibilities, the ontological integrity of the medium called 'television' is increasingly questioned. In this context, series are a predestined object for investigation: As a TV format that has been circulating in different media contexts for several decades now, they have seemingly become alienated from their primary medium. What the premium cable channel HBO once claimed in an advertising slogan ("It's not TV," 1996–2009), whereby the self-description as "not TV" seemed to refer in particular to its original series (including *Oz, The Sopranos, The Wire,* and many more.),[1] has evolved into an all-encompassing media cultural phenomenon in the wake of the long-standing Quality TV debate[2] as well as through new production and distribution mechanisms.[3] Today, a series narrative circulates on various distribution channels, on linear television, in media libraries and on streaming platforms, as well as in different forms of presentation, including the DVD format as a physically preservable publication of a partial work (season) or the complete work (complete series).[4] Series are thus not yet universally available, but they are much more accessible in terms of distribution. Although geo-blocking, licensing agreements and exclusive rights continue to restrict web affordances, viewers are no longer dependent on linear television programs in order to watch TV series.

The ubiquitous presence of serial content in our media culture is a consequence of the economic, aesthetic and narratological development of television series since 1997, through which the hybridization of television as a medium and institution can also be observed. The year 1997 marks the beginning of the commercial publication of series seasons on DVD and thus the widespread liberalization of serial reception.[5] Previously, series were ephemeral content in the linear programming flow of

---

[1] Cf. Rogers et al. (2002), p. 53.

[2] The "quality" label sought to distinguish certain fictional series from 'ordinary' television. See, inter alia, Blanchet (2010), p. 44.

[3] Cf. Lotz (2017b) o.p..

[4] Cf. Hills (2017), pp. 45–47; Mittell (2010), p. 136.

[5] Before the aforementioned upheaval, series were only released for individual reception to a limited extent through their more or less regular repetition on the respective station (so-called *reruns*) as well as through their syndication on international television markets. Their further exploitation took place exclusively within conventional television and its time-bound

television, to be received—whether on first broadcast or in reruns—*episodically*, always at a specific time on a specific channel. Today, they are available to a large extent on a wide variety of media channels and in different dispositive orders at any time. This is largely due to the intentional removal of series from the TV program—and their subsequent marketing as an independent 'work' in the form of the DVD boxset. Since the 2000s, a comprehensive economic 'afterlife' has been mapped out for television series, which today, in view of the web-based distribution of TV content, is divided into several secondary media existences beyond the original dispositif. Today, from the start of its production, a series' final separation from television is provided for within the systematic commercial exploitation up to and including DVD publication, and beyond that on legal streaming platforms.

Since 2014, the international streaming services Netflix and Amazon Video have been offering large-scale access to series content; they act as distributors of licensed formats and as producers of their own, exclusive series. As a final consequence, *straight-to-web-series*, who cannot be caught "on TV" at all, have entered the global television market. With these "streaming originals", the separation of serial formats from television seems to be complete, as they largely escape the narrative-economic and dispositive restrictions of program television. Their commercial value chain is shifting and shortening: many of these en-bloc-releases no longer go through the usual international syndication on television (e.g. *Stranger Things*, Netflix 2016–) or the season-by-season publication on DVD (e.g. *The Man in the High Castle*, Amazon 2015–2019). Accordingly, the contemporary television series is neither exclusively nor a priori 'at home' on conventional television. Their migration onto streaming platforms also means that the conditions of their reception are changing. Netflix and Amazon Video open up series to excessive modes of reception such as "binge-watching", which undermine the episodic concept of the television series and the programming logic of linear television.

The spatiotemporal dissolution of television series calls into question their status and that of television itself. Are series, released as entire seasons on Netflix, still *television series* in the conventional sense? Can streaming platforms still be subsumed under the collective term 'television' or must they be described as television-related forms of (re)presentation? What do we mean when we speak of 'television' today? Does the liberalization of television (series) reception entail the loss of definitional properties of television? Does television as a medium, as an institution and as an activity fundamentally change its form and function? Is what we call

---

program structures, and was only subverted by fan-driven practices such as VHS recording. A systematic removal of the series from linear television programming did not take place.

'television' today not so much a spatio-temporally fixed medium, but rather a multiform media concept?

From Television to *Televisions*

In order to approach these questions, it might be productive to dissolve the singular expression of 'television', for it is hybrid, heterogeneous and plural nowadays. Indeed, from a technological point of view alone, we are dealing with many different "tele-visions"[6]—linear TV programs, time-shifted on-demand offerings, content recorded on DVD and hard disk recorders; free-to-air channels, premium channels or subscription platforms. On the textual level, these media channels in turn produce different contexts that constitute the television series (as broadcasted programs, as DVD box sets, as retrievable data packages) and, from a reception-logical perspective, enable different ways of viewing (episodically or full-season, periodically or uninterrupted, casually or focused). On an economic level, too, in view of different broadcasting and business models (public service vs. commercial television, ad-funded free TV vs. subscription-based pay TV, etc.), television has long since ceased to be identical with itself—and possibly never was.

Nevertheless, television could previously be regarded as a stable, consistent medium or media system. This assumption only seems to have been permanently called into question by the move of its content to the World Wide Web and the progressive migration of serial formats. Indeed, numerous arguments can be found for defining streaming platforms and their in-house productions as "non-TV" and "AV series",[7] respectively. Thus, web channels forfeit television-specific, economic-institutional and dispositive characteristics such as periodicity, (economic) accessibility and inclusivity. Instead, they are characterized by "nonlinearity"[8] and "user specificity"[9]—properties that are not compatible with the linear program structures of classic television at first glance. Series available on Netflix or Amazon, in turn, exist as cultural commodities that individual viewers consciously seek out and select on the one hand, and as inexhaustible, arbitrary resources in an exorbitant supply structure on the other hand. Streaming also transforms the act of 'watching TV' from a spatiotemporally pre-structured, habitual everyday practice into an

---

[6]Cf. Lotz (2007), p. 78; Creeber (2009).

[7]Cf. Kirschbacher and Stollfuß (2015), pp. 21–28.

[8]Lotz (2017b) o.S.

[9]Ibid.

activity that is no less mundane, but now freed from the regulating power of a singular institution or apparatus. The reception of television series determined by the broadcaster in conventional television (weekly cycle, commercial breaks, breaks between seasons) rests more in the hands of the viewer when it comes to streaming media.[10]

The concept of television—especially in relation to series—can thus no longer refer to a concrete apparatus, a singular dispositif, a fixed institution or a pre-structured activity. Linear and non-linear program offerings, free and pay TV, streaming platforms and DVD boxes coexist as media contexts for old and new serial formats, their affordances standing in continuous contrast with one another and producing a vast, almost unmanageable supply of series. The continuous differentiation of distribution and reception options opens up new possibilities in terms of serial narration and dramaturgy. The television series of pay-TV providers are largely free from broadcasting restrictions regarding episode length, commercial breaks or weekly ratings warranting specific censorship. And the planned publication of series on DVD boxsets also generates creative, aesthetic and narrative freedom.[11] Against this background of a highly differentiated media landscape, it is no longer possible to speak of television as *such*. The multiple manifestations and textual constitutions of the television series, as well as their various dispositive framings or viewing possibilities, suggest a pluralization and flexibilization of the concept of television on a textual-pragmatic level. In the following, I consider Netflix's interface and playback mode[12] as representative for how streaming platforms adopt and modify television-specific principles of organization and structure.

---

[10] An exception are current, licensed TV series for which Amazon Video and Netflix have the international first publication rights (marketed as "Prime Exclusives" or "Netflix Originals"). New episodes of these series are released on a weekly basis (usually one day after the premiere on US television).

[11] Cf. Mittell (2010), pp. 141–142; Lotz (2017a), pp. 10–19. Not least, this fuels the discourse around supposed quality series that produce a different, supposedly 'better' television beyond economic and institutional constraints cf. Tryon (2015), pp. 104–116.

[12] The following discussion about Netflix and similar streaming services as a remediations of television is based on observations of Netflix Germany's interface and autoplay features as they present on the web browser or through Smart TV devices.

Streaming Platforms as Transformations of Television: On the Modification of Televisual[13] Principles on Netflix

Although the heterogeneous representations of a series on different distribution channels enforces its separation from conventional TV broadcasting, the basic *televisual* organization of the text remains: An audiovisual series, be it a production of public or pay channels or a "Netflix Original", is neither a closed nor a complete text, insofar as it was conceived for the respective (televisual) primary dispositif. Even in secondary distribution channels, series remain committed to the textual organization and programming logic of television in that they (1) continue to be presented by each distribution channel in distinct sub-texts (episodes), and (2) are surrounded by additional textual fringes such as recaps, preludes and credits, previews, trailers, flashbacks, (commercial) breaks, etc., as well as other possible 'programs', i.e. other series. In every media formation, a series is always embedded in some sort of "connective tissue".[14] On the one hand, this particular textual fabric distinguishes the episodes from one another by means of interruptions and inserts and, if necessary, also segments them intra-episodally. On the other hand, the "connective tissue" seeks to maintain viewing by means of precisely these little rupturing elements. All secondary representations of the series (TV reruns and syndications, DVD boxset, streaming publication) *remediate*[15] these televisual operations in a specific way, i.e. the modularization and segmentation[16] as well as the reception-guiding strategies of television. As series producers in their own right, streaming platforms—and Netflix in particular—turn out to be overformations of television that touch upon both dimensions of remediatization, *hypermediality* and *transparency*.[17]

---

[13] The term *televisual* is used here in the sense of 'television-like' or 'television-related'. It is not intended to refer to a particular aesthetic, as the term suggests, but to serve as an expression for inherent logics, strategies or operations that constitute television.

[14] Cf. Jacobs (2011), p. 260.

[15] Cf. Bolter and Grusin (2000).

[16] Cf. Ellis (1992), p. 51.

[17] Cf. Bolter (2007), pp. 27–28.

Hypermediality, or: Streaming Platforms as Overformed Television

Streaming services are *hypermedia,* as the organizational and structural principles of several media become visible there, a phenomenon dubbed as "hypermediacy".[18] Both linear, centralized television and the detemporalized, decentralized internet determine Netflix's interface: Televisual and web-specific text structures are co-present and interwoven here. Thus segments are the basic units of visual (re)-presentation of TV and streaming series as available commodities, and segmentation is the basic organizational principle on Netflix—as it is on classic television.[19] However, segmentation as a representational practice is modified by web interfaces according to the time-independent macrostructure of the internet.[20] Netflix transfers the chronological arrangement of program segments from linear television into the spatial arrangement of a seemingly inexhaustible assortment of goods. This is no longer arranged temporally, then, but inventoried alphabetically, thematically and by genre. Algorithms instead of program planners determine the offerings on every personal profile, when Netflix recommends further formats based on previously viewed series and films ("Because you watched xy"). Gerald Sim points out that Netflix's liberalization and individualization of television viewing is specious: the algorithms and the background data collection aim to navigate and manipulate the individual program as well as the reception strategies of the users in the interest of the platform,[21] for example by preferentially recommending Netflix's own productions and adapting their thumbnails to the previously recorded genre preferences of the respective user.[22] The attempt to pre-determine the individual viewer's selection and reception of serial content reveals the double legacy of streaming platforms: The strategy of permanently binding the viewer to a program, however predefined, is borrowed from television, yet it is now implemented with the means of the internet. The stringent succession of programs becomes an all-time juxtaposition of data packages, the fixed programming units become an infinite number of potentially and simultaneously available viewing strips.

In accordance with hypermediality, Netflix goes beyond conventional television: on the one hand, the platform produces a new, dispositively and temporally

---

[18]Cf. Bolter and Grusin (2000), p. 6.

[19]Cf. Ellis (1992), pp. 48–50.

[20]Adapted from Bolter (2007), p. 27.

[21]Cf. Sim (2016), p. 189.

[22]Cf. Jansen (2017) n.d.

unbounded experience of 'television'[23] and, on the other hand, a different conception of seriality, insofar as Netflix originals are perceived and measured in complete seasons from the outset, due to "binge-publishing".[24] Nonetheless, each serial offering remains segmentally structured. The square, tile-shaped arrangement of the available apps and products runs through all interfaces of streaming platforms and smart TV devices.

Moreover, Netflix is not only adapting programming structures under the auspices of Web 2.0, but is also renegotiating the cross-broadcasting competitive situation. Within this single platform, there is a high level of competition for attention, between films and series on the one hand and between in-house productions and licensed formats on the other. In addition, Netflix is only one provider among many streaming services due to its web presence as well as its integration in various smart TV applications. The already extraordinary competitive situation of regular television is exponentiated by the simultaneous and all-time availability of streaming content. The remediatization of television follows the ongoing hybridization of the medium, a co-presence of different media techniques and text types.[25] The underlying logic of segmental programming is potentiated across any distribution channels. On top of that, Smart TV and other streaming devices firmly tie the televisual competition to the domestic TV set, which now allows for the most diverse (media) reception practices. Switching between different channels or apps, a decidedly televisual operation, is just as possible as the continuous viewing of several series episodes. While streaming, the viewing practices intended on the production side are not only perpetuated, but other (fan) practices with regard to television series are also enabled, if not encouraged.[26] However, although streaming content is open to every mode of reception, Netflix's playback mode aims for continuous, excessive modes of reception such as "binge-watching".

---

[23]Cf. Bolter (2007), p. 26.

[24]Cf. Van Ede (2015), p. 36.

[25]Cf. Bolter and Grusin (2000), p. 6.

[26]Cf. Hills (2007), pp. 52–58; Mittell (2010), pp. 145–148.

Transparency, or: The Blurring of Televisual Program Connections on Netflix

In its autoplay mode, Netflix shows its *transparency*, meaning the tendency to mask or even "erase" the underlying medium of television.[27] When streaming several episodes in a row, televisual periodicity takes a back seat to continuous viewing: the now remaining 5-second interval between two episodes in a season-by-season release is so short that it might gloss over any other viewing preferences a user may have. Interestingly, this is realized via platform-specific paratexts, which are reminiscent of typical television program connections. Even during the former 15- to 20-second countdown[28] between two episodes of a *syndicated* series, Netflix re-arranged and remodeled these accompanying text segments, which John Ellis calls "interstitials."[29] The interepisodic splitscreen consisted of the following elements: A full-screen background image (usually a still from the current season or else a promotional photograph of the cast); a zoomed-out view of the closing credits in the upper left corner of the screen; a preview image for the next episode in the lower right corner, with three buttons positioned below it ("Back to Browse" to return to the main menu, "Exit Full-Screen View," and "More Episodes" to select another episode)[30]; a three-line synopsis of the upcoming episode to the left of the preview image (Fig. 1).

These seemingly marginal elements can be compared to "connective tissue" of television: The still is reminiscent of the broadcaster-specific background designs in program announcements, which often also integrate an image from the program in question (Fig. 2). The reduced view of the end credits remediates the televisual *bumper* at the end of a program, which often reproduces a short commercial and contains only a small part of the credits (Fig. 3). The preview image extends the typical television program note, which is inserted at the end of a program either as a one-liner *(stinger)* or as picture-text segment at the edges of the TV image. While this insert is accompanied by a short acoustic signal on many channels, it was

---

[27]Cf. Bolter (2007), p. 28.

[28]Until roughly 3 years ago, the countdown was 15s long when accessing Netflix content via an internet browser. In the context of the app integrated in Smart TV or on streaming devices, it was 20s. In the meantime, the countdown has been uniformly reduced to 5s for all series and in all apps, and the split screen has been replaced by other representations (see Figs. 4 and 5). Disney+ currently still uses a similar interepisodal countdown of 20s.

[29]Cf. Ellis (2011), p. 59.

[30]The "Exit Full-Screen View" option was only available when using Netflix via web browser.

Fig. 1 Netflix's former inter-episodic splitscreen on licensed series (described above), with adapted programming connections from traditional television (screenshot, Netflix Germany, Feb. 22, 2019)

presented on Netflix as an exclusively visual unit with web-specific functions. The time-related statement about the upcoming 'program point' ("Next Episode") was more precise due to the counted down seconds—compared to vague statements like "next up" or "following program" on a TV channel. The countdown also adapted another television insert, the bumper element before the final minutes of the program which counted down the time of the incorporated commercial, either by loading bar (Fig. 3) or by the second.

The previous Netflix splitscreen was already a synthesis and condensation of distinct program connections of linear television, which usually appear in the televisual flow at different times. Between the series episodes, they became part of the same textual intermezzo—just like the above-mentioned synopsis, itself a radically reduced form of the TV preview (also *promo* or *teaser*). The highly compressed, maximum 20-second trailer is a strategic programming element that usually shows some highlights from the next episode to attract new audiences and encourage loyal viewers to tune in again.[31] Substantively, an episode's promo merely conveys 'snippets' of the future plot, which are also potentially misleading

---

[31] Cf. Bleicher (2004), p. 250.

Fig. 2 Televisual model for Netflix's background image and announcement of the next episode, here for the new episodes of Grey's Anatomy, broadcasted on German TV channel ProSieben every Wednesday (Screenshot, YouTube, URL: https://www.youtube.com/watch?v=SJnmJAYlsa0, retrieved 25.09.2020. Image rights belong to ProSieben)

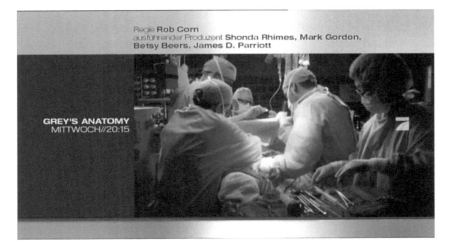

Fig. 3 Typical TV bumper at the end of ProSieben's Grey's Anatomy broadcast including a very reduced version of the end credits (Screenshot, YouTube, URL: https://www.youtube.com/watch?v=I47_14icbGY, retrieved 25.09.2020. Image rights belong to ProSieben)

due to the fast-paced montage. The preview is more of an appetizer and 'promise of upcoming attractions'.[32] Analogously, Netflix's synopsis is by no means a sufficient summary, but a sketchy, highly selective indication of plot. On a subscription-funded platform, this paratext admittedly seems obsolete, since Netflix and other streaming services do not (have to) attract viewers on a weekly basis. But the three-liner with selective details about the episode just about bridged the 15- to 20-second countdown—assuming the user waited for it in the first place. After all, the option to immediately start the next episode is ever-present and, considering the current 5-second countdown, even more pressing. Still, the stripped-down aesthetic of the preview in this former interepisode arrangement is significant: a standalone audio-visual unit shown *repeatedly* during the seven-day broadcast break is minimized to a three-liner seen *once* on Netflix right before the corresponding episode. The minimization of this promotional paratext, as well as the reduction and intermingling of the above-mentioned other segments, make the single episode less of a distinctive and anticipated event. The textual boundaries, marked by these very marginal phenomena, are blurred during streaming, episodes merge almost immediately into one another in the mode of "binge-watching"—which is entirely in the interest of the provider.

The remodelled paratexts mentioned here are an essential component of the flow of programming and the associated "nextness"[33] of television: they are a continuous reminder of subsequent broadcasts and thus of the endlessness of the full TV program. The above-discussed textual links are used to maintain the viewers' willingness to 'stay tuned' and thus to bind them to the respective channel.[34] At the same time, they are essential for our understanding of TV content and television as a medium:

> [. . .] interstitials have a key role for current viewers. They show how television regards itself (its brands); how it wants its programmes to be read (the trailers); [. . .] Interstitials, in short, are a series of distillations of television, and an internal meta-commentary on ordinary TV. In a world of multiple media opportunities, interstitials are little instruction manuals on how to read TV.[35]

It is the connective paratexts specific to television that create a program or an episode as a definable entity in the first place and at the same time prepare it for a

---

[32] Ibid., p. 255.

[33] Cf. Elrod (2019), p. 172.

[34] Cf. Ellis (2011), p. 99.

[35] Ibid., p. 90.

continuous flow.[36] The textual fabric of television continues to be used by Netflix in a diminished, yet recognizable form. Due to the publication of full seasons, these periodically recurring paratexts are now directly linked to the 'main text', the respective episode. Thus, they convey a different temporality of 'television', as well as a divergent experience of seriality, which is defined less by individual episodes than by entire seasons.[37] Also, due to their aesthetic and temporal diminution, the program-connecting elements described above can be grasped as *traces* of conventional television. As such, they continue to function as little "instruction manuals"[38] for 'perceiving' (online) TV content. But in doing so they guide us to a different form of serial reception. Whereas the original, televisual intertexts frame the series as an episodic one, Netflix adapts the "next" rhetoric to assert the opposite: the condensed and blurred paratexts aim to 'reprogram' the television viewer as a "media binger".[39]

This is even more evident today: While the end credits of licensed formats were previously 'allowed' to run for 15–20 seconds without any action on the part of the user, all closing credits are now automatically cut off after just 5 seconds, hardly giving the viewer enough time to intervene and select "watch credits". The opening credits of the subsequent episode are also skipped without further ado. This almost patronizing practice of the autoplay demonstrates Netflix's relatedness to broadcast television, where the closing titles are always "shunned and cut"[40] and where the opening credits may also be edited in some cases. Appearing as unnecessary voids and retarding moments in the linear programming structure,[41] likely prompting the viewer to switch, these potentially multivalent serial paratexts undergo various interventions from each media channel/televisual dispositif. Within these 'new televisions' called streaming platforms, (inter)titles and credits, although fully present, are once again marked as undesirable and dispensable. Netflix mimics the conventional editing practices of its 'media relatives', skipping any intermission caused by the closing credits in favor of excessive, seamless modes of reception—unless the user actively intervenes. Now, the televisual flow also aims at assembly-line like viewing. The aforementioned program connections are meant to bridge any

---

[36]Cf. Parr and Thiele (2004), pp. 261–282.

[37]Cf. Van Ede (2015), p. 36.

[38]Cf. Bleicher (2004), p. 250.

[39]Devasagayam (2014), p. 40.

[40]Mengel (1997), p. 241.

[41]Cf. Mengel (1995), p. 27.

'receptive voids' between shows or episodes.[42] Thus, 'television as we knew it' already promotes "binge-watching"—with one major difference: Usually, conventional TV channels contiously broadcast *heterogeneous* programs, i.e. independent, unrelated formats are to be watched one after the other. In contrast, streaming platforms like Netflix encourage the uninterrupted viewing of *homogeneous* programs, i.e. episodes of the same series. Here, the connective paratexts do not serve to reintroduce the viewer to the next episode and watch various other shows in the meantime, but rather to ensure that the user does not interrupt the viewing in the first place.[43] Netflix currently enforces this by eliminating all program connections inbetween episodes. In connection with the radical termination of the credits, only the buttons "Back to Browse",[44] "Watch Credits" and "Next Episode"[45] remain (Fig. 4). The background image only appears at the end of credits if the user chose to watch them (Fig. 5).

This process now erases the televisual fabric as far as possible, but in doing so pursues the same goal as the seemingly eliminated program connections, namely to keep the viewer engaged with the respective series. Thus, paradoxically, by eradicating certain textual elements of the underlying medium formerly known as television, the streaming platforms make their 'kinship' with it *transparent*. Over the course of its remediatization, 'old' television disappears in its aesthetic, dispositive or technological characteristics. All that remains—as a basic framework—are the reception-guiding logics and textual arrangements inherent to the medium. This inevitably affects our perception and understanding of 'new' streamed television.

---

[42] Cf. Bleicher (2004), p. 250.

[43] The automatic intertitle "Still Watching?" seems to confirm this. This one appears randomly during an episode, after several episodes have already been watched without interruption, and provides two or three options to choose from: to continue with the episode at the same point ("Continue watching"), to replay the episode from the beginning (only in the web browser) or to return to the main menu ("Exit"). This intertitle seems to counteract more absent-minded modes of reception, such as when viewers are tired, scrolling on their phone or leaving the room. This particular element of audience control does not exist in broadcast television. Here, the ideal of an observant and committed viewer emerges (cf. Tryon 2015, 112), who watches a series non-stop and with the utmost attention.

[44] This option only appears in the browser, namely as a back arrow in the upper left corner. In the Smart TV app, it can be selected at any time by pressing the back button on the remote control, but it is not visually displayed in the interface.

[45] The "Next Episode" button currently presents as a loading bar, as opposed to the 5 s countdown shown in Fig. 4.

Fig. 4 Premature termination of credits and elimination of televisual programming connections within Netflix's autoplay, described above (screenshot, Netflix Germany, Feb. 22, 2019). The current design of the "Watch Credits" and "Next Episode" buttons may differ

Fig. 5 Wallpaper and countdown as the only remaining program links between episodes which only present after watching the credits (screenshot, Netflix, Feb. 22, 2019). Current views may differ

Television as a Transmedial Concept of Audiovisual Text Organization and Reception Management

From a technological, institutional or dispositive-based perspective, the old and new televisions can hardly be reduced to a common denominator. Whether broadcast vs. web TV, free TV vs. pay TV, linear vs. non-linear TV offerings, or television as a periodic/episodic activity *(appointment TV),* in the form of switching/ zapping, in the mode of "binge-watching" or as a casual activity, and so on: Television is never the same, ever-changing and evolving as an object of study depending on the point of view (aesthetic, receptive, economic, societal or cultural). We are dealing with the most diverse forms *and* usages of the medium. However, a continuous conflict, between potential program control by recipients on the one hand and the attempt to instill a certain reception behavior through textual interventions on the other, is detectable in all televisions. The intentional 'program-ming' of a loyal, consistent, *serial* viewer through specific textual organization and segmentation seems to be the unifying 'idea' of all contemporary television.

A re-definition of television can therefore succeed from a text-pragmatic per-spective: Thus, conventional linear television and streaming platforms show their (distant) relatedness through the adapted, remodelled or eliminated connective paratexts and textual interventions, but even more so through their strategies of guiding reception. Basically, streaming platforms try to bind their users in the long run just as much as conventional TV channels want to bind their viewers. In this respect, interface design as well as Netflix's autoplay are geared towards continu-ously prolonging media consumption. These are televisual reception instructions that similarly neglect certain viewing preferences as well as patronize the viewer to a certain degree (despite all their programming and viewing choices). In this respect, streaming platforms are not without contradictions, as the liberalized (series) recep-tion is contrasted with updated viewing instructions and demands by the new televisions in the context of digital media culture:

> Technology may have freed us from the restraints on our viewing schedules placed on us by television networks, but it turned out to be a zero sum game; at the same time as one hand offered us freedom, the other was ensuring that we'd have to keep up to date and fall under an equally artificial schedule created by our online communities.[46]

---

[46]McMillan (2014), "Why Do People Still Watch Live TV?", n.d.

Therefore, the "binge-watching" mode favoured by Netflix and Co. does not open up unimagined 'consumer freedom'.[47] Instead, it is marked as a universally required reception practice and almost forced upon the users in order to shape them in the interests of these new televisions. The ideal viewer is—for broadcast and online televisions alike—a serial one, who is to be bound to the current program (heterogeneously or homogeneously) by connecting textual pieces or else by the lack of such. In this sense, 'television' can be renegotiated as a transmedially applied concept of textual organization and reception guidance, which seeks to bind audiences to audiovisual serial content in a specific way.

References

Blanchet, Robert (2010) Quality-TV: Eine kurze Einführung in die Geschichte und Ästhetik neuer amerikanischer TV-Serien. In: Blanchet, Robert, Kristina Köhler, Julia Zutavern, Tereza Smid (Eds.) Serielle Formen: von den frühen Film-Serials zu aktuellen Quality-TV- und Online-Serien. Marburg, Schüren, pp. 37–72

Bleicher, Joan (2004) Programmverbindungen als Paratexte des Fernsehens. In: Kreimeier, Klaus, Georg Stanitzek (Eds.) Paratexte in Literatur, Film, Fernsehen. Berlin, Erich Schmidt Verlag, pp. 245–260

Bolter, Jay David (2007) Remediation and the language of new media. In: Northern Lights: Film and Media Studies 5 (1), pp. 25–37

Bolter, Jay David, Richard Grusin (2000) Remediation: Understanding New Media. Cambridge, The MIT Press

Creeber, Glen (2009) Tele-Visions. An Introduction to Studying Television. London, British Film Institute

Devasagayam, Raj (2014) Media Bingeing: A Qualitative Study of Psychological Influences. In: DeLong, Deborah, Dawn Edmiston, Roscoe Hightower Jr. (Eds.) Once Retro Now Novel Again. Marketing Management Association, pp. 40–44

Ellis, John (1992) Fernsehen als kulturelle Form. In: Adelmann, Ralf, Jan O. Hesse, Judith Keilbach, Markus Stauff, Matthias Thiele (Eds.) Grundlagentexte zur Fernsehwissenschaft: Theorie—Geschichte—Analyse. Berlin, Erich Schmidt Verlag, pp. 44–73

Ellis, John (2011) Interstitials: How the 'Bits in Between' Define the Programmes. In: Paul Grainge (Ed.) Ephemeral Media. Transitory Screen Culture from Television to Youtube. New York, Bloomsburgy Academic, pp. 59–69

Elrod, James M (2019) Navigating the Nebula: Audience Affect, Interactivity, and Genre in the Age of Streaming TV. In: Participations 16 (2), pp. 167–195

Hills, Matt (2007) From the Box in the Corner to the Box Set on the Shelf. 'TV III' and the cultural/textual valorisations of DVD. In: New Review of Film and Television Studies 5 (1), pp. 41–60

---

[47] Cf. Sim: "Individual Disruptors and Economic Gamechangers", p. 193.

Jacobs, Jason (2011) Television, Interrupted: Pollution or Aesthetic? In: Bennett, James, Niki Strange, (Ed.) Television as Digital Media. Durham/London, Duke University Press, pp. 255–282

Jansen, Jonas (2017) Streamingdienst: So analysiert Netflix seine Nutzer. In: faz.net, 23.10.2017, https://www.faz.net/aktuell/wirtschaft/unternehmen/netflix-so-analysiert-der-dienst-seine-nutzer-15259930.html?printPagedArticle=true, Accessed 22 Feb 2019

Kirschbacher, Felix, Sven Stollfuß (2015) Von der TV- zur AV-Serie. Produktions-, Distributions- und Rezeptionsformen aktueller US-Serien. In: Medien+Erziehung 59 (4), pp. 21–28

Lotz, Amanda D. (2007) The Television Will Be Revolutionized. New York, New York University Press

Lotz, Amanda D. (2017a) Linking Industrial and Creative Change in 21st-Century US Television. In: Media International Australia 164 (1), pp. 10–20

Lotz, Amanda D. (2017b) Portals. A Treatise on Internet-Distributed Television. https://quod.lib.umich.edu/m/maize/mpub9699689, Accessed 22 Feb 2019

McMillan, Graeme (2014) Why Do People Still Watch Live TV? In: Time, 04 Apr 2014, https://time.com/12431/appointment-viewing-spoilers-live-tv/, Accessed on 22 Feb 2019

Mengel, Norbert (1995) Den Anfang macht die Ouvertüre. Entwicklung von Serienvor- und -abspännen: Vom 'notwendigen Übel' zum kreativen Freiraum—und zurück. In: Schneider, Irmela (Ed.) Serien-Welten: Strukturen US-amerikanischer Serien aus vier Jahrzehnten. Bielefeld, Transcript Verlag, pp. 19–41

Mengel, Norbert (1997) Gemieden und geschnitten: Vor- und Abspanne in den Fernsehprogrammen. In: Hickethier, Knut, Joan Bleicher (Eds.) Trailer, Teaser, Appetizer: zu Ästhetik und Design der Programmverbindungen im Fernsehen. Konstanz, UVK Verlagsgesellschaft, pp. 241–259

Mittell, Jason (2010) Serial Boxes: DVD-Editionen und der kulturelle Wert amerikanischer Fernsehserien. In: Blanchet, Robert, Kristina Köhler, Julia Zutavern, Tereza Smid (Ed.) Serielle Formen: Von den frühen Film-Serials zu aktuellen Quality-TV- und Online-Serien. Marburg, Schüren, pp. 133–152

Parr, Rolf, Matthias Thiele (2004) Eine ,vielgestaltige Menge von Praktiken und Diskursen'. Zur Interdiskursivität und Televisualität von Paratexten des Fernsehens. In: Kreimeier, Klaus, Georg Stanitzek (Eds.) Paratexte in Literatur, Film, Fernsehen. Berlin, Erich Schmidt Verlag, pp. 261–282

Rogers, Mark C., Michael Epstein, Jimmie L. Reeves (2002) The Sopranos as HBO Brand Equity. The Art of Commerce in the Age of Digital Reproduction. In: Lavery, David (Ed.) This Thing of Ours. Investigating The Sopranos. London, Wallflower Press, pp. 42–57

Sim, Gerald (2016) Individual Disruptors and Economic Gamechangers: Netflix, New Media, and Neoliberalism. In: McDonald, Kevin, Daniel Smith-Rowsey (Eds.) The Netflix Effect. Technology and Entertainment in the 21st Century. New York, Bloomsbury Academic, pp. 185–202

Tryon, Chuck (2015) TV Got Better: Netflix's Original Programming Strategies and the On-Demand Television Transition. In: Media Industries 2 (2), pp. 104–116

Van Ede, Esther (2015) Gaps and Recaps: Exploring the Binge-Published Television Serial. https://studenttheses.uu.nl/handle/20.500.12932/21554, Accessed on 22 Feb 2019

Jana Zündel Dr., studied Media Studies in Weimar and Bonn; Postdoc in the Research Training Group "Configurations of Film" at Goethe University; PhD thesis published as *Fernsehserien im medienkulturellen Wandel* (2022). Research interests: television studies, TV and streaming series, platform studies, meme studies.

Spatialized Transmediality: Processual Seriality

Christine Piepiorka

A viewer is in a room and consumes a television series. But here we don't mean the living room or something similar– no. A transmedia television series allows a viewer or an addressee to move around in a *series space of* his or her own—freely choosing which path to take at which time.

Television series advance to an overall transmediality, the narratives no longer unfold only temporally, but also spatially. This premise is accompanied by questions about how television series spatialize themselves across media boundaries and in what form temporality changes. Transmediality can be said to have a processuality that is connected to immanent seriality. Implications for the concept of seriality can also be assumed here, as well as indications of a diffusion or formation of television itself. In this way, questions are raised about the possibility of viewing the content as well as the terminology in a spatiotemporal context. In order to expand on the idea of transmediality as a description of the mediality of a series, this essay proposes to consider the series as both a temporal and a spatialized concept.

Based on current changes in US-American series productions since the 2000s, the transformations of serial narration on television open up a wide variety of perspectives on an object of research in media studies.This paper is based on Piepiorka's *Lost in Time & Space*[1] which further contours the research object via

---

[1] For the argumentation of the article as well as concrete parts of the text see Piepiorka: *Lost in Time & Space*. This is the subsumption and essence of the findings.

C. Piepiorka (✉)
Hochschule für Oekonomie und Management, Dortmund, Germany
e-mail: christine.piepiorka@fom.de

© The Author(s), under exclusive license to Springer Fachmedien Wiesbaden GmbH, part of Springer Nature 2024
D. Newiak et al. (eds.), *Television Studies and Research on Series*,
https://doi.org/10.1007/978-3-658-42915-7_3

a theoretical-conceptual development of a transmedial form of serial narration with the central categories of space and time. Likewise, in a broader contextualization of transmedia narrative, a questioning of traditional concepts such as that of seriality comes into focus. These may be symptoms of a fundamental paradigm shift in television's self-dramatization and the construction of the *spectator*. In what follows, the series *Breaking Bad* will serve as an example, but the theoretical coverage can be transferred to other examples and ultimately to transmedia television series in general.

Not All Series Are the Same: A Definition of Terms[2]

There is a great variance and inflation of terms in this field of research, so it seems fruitful to have a clear definition for a better understanding. Therefore the fact that we are making use of the terms of plot and story must be first clarified . This definition comes from the neoformalist approach of David Bordwell and Kristin Thompson, which was developed for film but has its origins in literary studies and the work of Gérard Genette. The concept will be adopted here for the subject of the series, since Kristin Thompson already proposes this transfer.[3]

The *plot* is to be understood as the presentation of the audiovisual elements.[4] The *story*, in turn, is the product of a cognitive process on the part of the viewer, in which the viewer forms the causal connections and the coherence of the story.[5] In the following, these terms and the concepts behind them will be used as a heuristic foil to describe transmedia series and the space-time constellations associated with them.

But before that, the term of *series* and further concepts related to it and which are used in this paper must be illuminated. It is thus proposed to speak not of television series, but of *series text* as a designation of the totality of all episodes and seasons of a series, regardless of the place of publication,[6] for example, of all episodes of the series *Breaking Bad*. The term *extensions* describes all elements belonging to the

---

[2]Cf. Piepiorka (2017), pp. 80–81.

[3]Cf. Thompson (2003), p. 19.

[4]Cf. Bordwell and Thompson (1979), p. 71.

[5]Cf. Bordwell (1985), p. 49.

[6]These are no longer necessarily broadcast and consumed on television; for example, *House of Cards* was first released on a streaming platform.

series. This term can then be further subdivided into *cross-media extensions*[7]—not extending the narration but repeating it in terms of content—and *transmedia extensions*[8]—extending the narration and thus the overall plot of the series text. Cross-media extensions for *Breaking Bad* are *graphic novels*, transmedia extensions are webisodes, online games,[9] a comic film[10] and *simulation sites*.[11] The *series* then refers to the totality of all parts: series text and cross- and/or transmedia extensions. The term can also refer to non-transmedia series, while the term *transmedia universe* recurs to the totality of series text, cross- and transmedia extensions as an overall plot, e.g. all elements of the series from comic to app. The *storyworld* is the world of the story emerging from the universe—which, from a neoformalist perspective, is an overall product of a cognitive process of the viewer emerging from the plot.

With reference to Henry Jenkins' reflections[12] on *media convergence*, i.e. media convergence under the sign of digitalization, and *participatory culture*, i.e. the inclusion of media users as committed participants, it is possible to think through the media-historical upheavals that form the precondition for transmediality. The notion of a transmedial universe takes into account the fact that the diffusion of narrative across different platforms is a form of spatialization. A transmedia television series narrates sprawlingly across media boundaries—the plot is retold on different media platforms such as websites, social media, print media and games, so that a continuation of the narrative takes place.

---

[7] See also *promotion paratexts* (Gray 2010) such as trailers of the series or *orienting paratexts* (Mittell 2015, 293).

[8] These are called *transmedia paratexts by* Mittell (2015) and *narrative expansions by* Gray (2010).

[9] E.g. *Interrogation: A Hank Shrader Game* (see AMC 2) and *The Costs of Doing Business: A Jesse Pinkman Game* (see AMC 3).

[10] This is a TEAM S.C.I.E.N.C.E. comic book movie drawn by protagonist Jesse Pinkman that narratively does not take on the world of the series text. Here, the characters of the series text are drawn as superheroes saving the world.

[11] *Simulation site is a* simulated, fictitious website; here: BetterCallSaul.com (see ABC 4).

[12] Cf. Jenkins (2006), p. 1 ff.

Space and Time in Series[13]

The profileration of series into other media results in a dissolution of the boundaries of narration and thus of the series itself across different media, but does that mean that the categories of time and space are already inscribed? A further question arises: Can transmedial universes be described as specific configurations of the aforementioned parameters of time and space?

A short survey of scientific and philosophical conceptualizations of time and space, will help to underline a performative and process-oriented notion of space as an inherent quality of time.[14] So how does the space and time of the series unfold within transmediality?

In contrast to ontological conceptualizations, however, the focus here is primarily one of media-aesthetics, oriented toward the description of interdependent spatial and temporal structures. The focus is not on a physical-material concept of space, but on a constructivist concept of space. For transmediality evokes a differentiated shaping of a spatiotemporality that always seems available to a potential recipient.[15]

Central to the development of a transmedial space/time concept are the reflections of Gilles Deleuze and Félix Guattari in *A Thousand Plateaus*, which draw an antagonistic, territorial concept of space by utilizing different types of spaces. The authors develop the spaces along different models: the model of technology, music, the sea, mathematics, physics and aesthetics or painting. The categorization of two types of spaces results from an exploration of these spaces: they make the distinction of a *striated (notched) space*, which is considered quantifiable, bounded and fixed, and a *smooth space* as open, infinite, mutating. This theoretical model proves compatible for the study of transmedia series, especially with regard to the interdependence of space and time.

The following explanations are ilusstrated in Figs. 1 and 2 for. However, these are not to be considered too separately, but are partly fluid, as the text will also show. Nevertheless, the illustration help to understand this discussion of striated and smooth space.

The striated space (cf. Fig. 1) can be compared with the transmedial extensions and therefore with the transmedial universe. This is closed and is divided according

---

[13] Cf. in detail Piepiorka (2017), pp. 80–81.

[14] Ibid., p. 83. A cursory overview is given here.

[15] Ibid., p. 92.

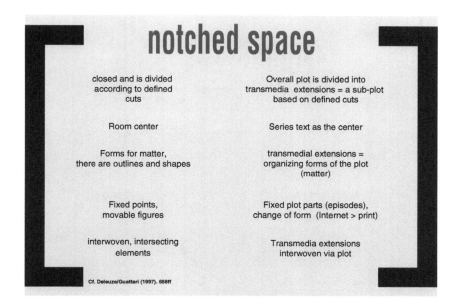

Fig. 1 striated space according to Deleuze/Guattari with the correspondences in the transmedial universe. (According to Piepiorka, Deleuze/Guattari: *Plateaus* & Piepiorka: *Lost in Time & Space*, own illustration)

to fixed striated,[16] which can be transferred to the transmedial: There exists an overall plot—the transmedial universe—which is divided into transmedial extensions and the series text itself. Each represents a sub-plot cut out from the overall plot. These range from books to the episodes themselves, comics, *webisodes, social media accounts, spin-offs*, games and *second screen applications*—to name but a few.

In most transmedia universes, there is a plot that provides a center; usually this is the series text such as *Breaking Bad*,[17] as the authors describe it for the striated

---

[16]Cf. Deleuze and Guattari (1997), p. 666.

[17]Jason Mittell describes this center in *Complex TV* as the *core text* from which *paratexts* emerge; there are also other centers, such as comics, from which transmedial universes can emerge, e.g. *Science Fiction* magazine as the origin of all media *versions of Superman* (comics, film, and current television series). *Breaking Bad* has no template, but is the original text of the narrative.

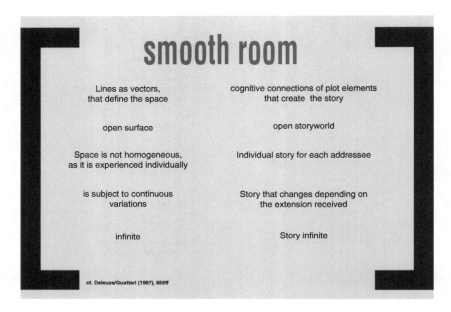

Fig. 2 Smooth space according to Deleuze/Guattari with the correspondences in the transmedial universe. (According to Piepiorka, Deleuze/Guattari: *Plateaus* & Piepiorka: *Lost in Time & Space*, own illustration)

space.[18] In a striated space, shapes organize matter (664); there are outlines and shapes (685). All transmedial extensions can be perceived as organizing forms of the plot—or, in other words, of matter—which take on certain outlines and forms in their own respective media-specific sub-plots. Thus, the respective episodes of the series text *Breaking Bad* are forms of the matter of the series narrative and are each sub-plots of the series text.

Such forms can be fixed points, but also movable characters (660) and stand out in the transmedial as fixed plot parts with, for example, the content of individual episodes. A transmedial extension can become mobile in the sense that a comic of the series appearing on the internet can become a print comic—thus *Breaking Bad* (2010–2013) became an (online) comic titled *All Bad Things* (2013). It changes

---

[18]Cf. Deleuze and Guattari (1997), p. 685; references in the following with the page number directly in the text.

form, even though the content can remain fixed. These moving elements can also be described by means of temporality, because a development or change always also indicates a temporal succession of occurrences.

The striated space is also defined by intertwined, intersecting elements (658). The transmedial extensions are also intertwined via the plot, each offering connection points to another extension. The production of the extensions, and thus their interweaving, is not simultaneous in time, nor is their reception. Thus striated space offers manifolds that are countable and thus metric and can increase or decrease (p. 669) just as extensions can have manifolds and increase the plot. The interweaving and connecting points can be the characters or else the narration. For example, some *webisodes* or even *minisodes* of the series *Breaking Bad* have narratological autonomy but are also connected via series characters. These are connections understood as parts of the *plot* that are not included in the series text. For example, a series of minisodes was released for *Breaking Bad* between seasons 1 and 2 meant as a narratological extension.[19] Similarly, an online application called the *Gale Boetticher Evidence File*, which was available on AMC's website,[20] works similarly. Here, you can look at a file which also plays a role in the series text. In the series text, Hank Schrader, who investigates the case, receives these same file documents, but they are not shown there in their entirety. In both examples, the transmedial extensions offer additional narrative information, so that the transmedial universe expands and the subplots are interwoven.

In summary, transmedial space, like striated space, interweaves variables and fixed points and orders different forms (663). Likewise, striated space exhibits a tendency toward homogeneity; the denser its mesh of elements, the denser the notch (676). A transmedial universe also exhibits this characteristic, as the narrative density can exhibit a more homogeneous overall plot through closely related extensions with the respective sub-plots. The spatiality of a transmedial universe is evident from this, as are the temporal dimensions, in that both the distribution and reception of transmedial extensions in striated space are temporally determined.

Smooth space (cf. Fig. 2), meanwhile, can represent story as a cognitive process that emerges from the transmedial universe with the representation of the overall plot. Thus, the characteristic of lines as vectors that define space is present (663): The lines are to be translated with the cognitive connections of plot elements that

---

[19]Minisodes titles and length: 1. *The Break-In (4:53)*, 2. *Good Cop, Bad Cop (2:56)*, 3. *Wedding Day (4:53)*, 4. *TwaughtHammer (4:17)*, 5. *Fallacies by TwaughtHammer (3:02)*, 6. *Marie's Confession (2:51)*.

[20]Cf. AMC 1.

create the story. For example, the aforementioned minisodes of *Breaking Bad* reveal plot lines that extend the *plot* of the series text and are motivated by the characters. This means that the recipient gets to know the protagonists through the extensions beyond the series text. Another example is the online game *The Interrogation: A Hank Shrader Game*, which focuses on one character. It introduces the recipient to *Hank* in 6 chapters. This expands the narrative and thus expands the storyworld space.

The space that is created thereby is also an open surface (666) and has no boundaries, no outlines or shapes, not even a center (684). Thus, the surface of the storyworld is open since each recipient can let the respective plot parts to his interpretation of the story emerge through subjective cognitive constructions. Therefore it has no concrete form since everyone can produce other cognitive connections, but also no centre since it emerges from all plot parts and does not necessarily have to have the series text as its center. Thus, a recipient can gain access through other plot parts—such as one of the online games—without first knowing the series text. This leads to another affinity of smooth space to transmedial space: space is not homogeneous because it is experienced individually (659). Even in the transmedial, the spatial is subjective for the individual recipient and always heterogeneous since everyone experiences the extensions in different orders and at different distances.

Ultimately, space does not connect antyhing fixed or mobile, but is subject to continuous variations (659). The storyworld is a cognitive product that continues to change depending on the received extension, as background information on events or character backstories are inserted and the previously cognitively developed story can be relativized, changed, or discarded. The recipient constructs the story in the course of its mediation, using given and not-given information to create a continuous generation, modification, and revision of inferences from the given information of the plot. These adjustments and changes of direction in smooth space arise from local operations in striated space (663): Thus, the local knowledge won from the the transmedial extensions can change the story and give it new directions. There is also a temporal variability when the story is constructed at a particular moment but is subjected to change by fresh expansions of the existing extensions. Thus, there is an affect-space that is determined more by events than by fixed properties (663–664). While the storyworld is determined by its plot-parts, it is also determined by cognitive reactions at the level of story-construction, which are characterized by changes in the plot-level. These circumstances characterize a smooth space that is subject to continuous changes of directions, clues, and approximations (683).

Thus, this space is also theoretically infinite and open in all directions, just as the storyworld can also be theoretically infinite, even if it is determined by the plot, since the spectator's construction can transcend it, for example in the form of fan fiction. For the storyworld, there is no duration of reception, because it emerges cognitively and is not limited in time. This proves the existence of a temporality in smooth space: there is a temporal sequence of events, such as successive reception, which gives rise to a storyworld, but also reformulates it again and again. It can be understood as a form of processuality.

In summary, the story of the transmedia series, which is subject to continuous variation and has a tendency towards heterogeneity, can be described as similar to smooth space. It is characterized by developments and mergers of all elements or all plot parts into one story (663); these represent a becoming and a process (684).

As a result, the following can be stated: It is crucial to bring together the theories of narration and its distinction between plot and story made at the beginning with the philosophical concepts of striated and smooth space. The distinction between plot as the audiovisually staged presentation of action on the one hand and story as the cognitive development of the entirety of a story on the other can be correlated here with the concepts of striated and smooth space. Individual extensions and various platforms such as websites, apps, etc. present the plot in the sense of a striated, i.e. limited and fixed, space, whereas the potential endless, mutating and dynamic storyworld can be understood as a smooth space.

Thus, not only a narrative space unfolds, but also a space that reveals a planar arrangement of parts that must be grasped in time. Thus, space and time in transmedia series are in synthesis with each other. Through their interdependence, they evoke a very specific constellation and ordering structure since they permeate all parts together and establish their existence in the first place.

Serial and Serialized Processes[21]

Hence a transmedial series exists through the existence of its extensions on the most diverse (media) locations, which ultimately evoke a space. These are in turn characterized by multipartiality, since there is usually never only one extension to a series text.

The concepts of Certeau[22] and Deleuze/Guattari[23] also always assume a plurality of points and elements in their conceptions of space. Elements of narration are thus

---

[21] Cf. Piepiorka (2017), p. 245 ff.

[22] Cf. Certeau (2006), p. 345 ff.

[23] Cf. Deleuze and Guattari (1997), p. 658.

distributed among these places, each of which represents a part of the series and can therefore be considered serialized. The extensions in themselves can each be counted as serial productions as the places in turn can consist of multiple parts. Thus, a *serialization of places* in transmedia series can be noted. The serial structure in general is always already intermedially conceived for continuation, also inside and outside the series text. Thus, transmedia extensions in space can unfold in the transmedia universe—a striated space emerges, with interwoven points between which intervals exist.[24]

The multi-part nature of both the series and the transmedia extensions describes an incompleteness that is oriented towards continuation. If something is continued, the existence of a following part is a condition. This serialization implies a temporality per se: the series is characterized by a succession of its elements, which are received successively.[25] One can thus also conclude a *serialization of time.*

In this context, serial unfinishedness is to be understood spatially and temporally, Because the ending of the narrative is continuously suspended.[26] Spatial proliferation is synonymous with temporal exploration by the recipient: This is a serialization of places and times. The result is a temporalized spatialization or spatialized temporality in series.

This serialization through the dissolution of transmediality ultimately has decisive *effects on seriality*: the mediality and seriality of a transmedia universe can be described as a process. A process is defined here as a procedure extending over a certain time in which something emerges or is formed.[27] Temporality is implied here since no process can take place without time passing.

The essence of the series itself Repetition and a procedure extending over time in which a story develops are essential to the series. Thus, by definition, it is a process.[28]

The creative power of the serial ultimately lies in the difference of the repetitions.[29] For the interval between the parts is synonymous with an act of

---

[24] Cf. Deleuze and Guattari (1997), p. 660.

[25] For example, an episode of a series text is received first, a blog mentioned in a dialogue is consulted, the next episode is received, and then the comic is read in order to follow up a plot line.

[26] Cf. Olek and Piepiorka (2012), p. 94.

[27] Cf. o.V. (2006), p. 636.

[28] Cf. Sielke (2012), p. 289.

[29] Cf. Blättler (2012), p. 75.

bringing forth, of becoming and growing.[30] Thus the difference of repetitions always produces something new and is therefore a creative process. Difference and repetition are represented in Deleuze as mutually generating processualities.[31] If a series consists of difference and repetition, the process is thus also an essential feature of the (media) locations. There is a simultaneous progress and regress, a juxtaposition of the modes of repetition and circling, and a spiral-like intensification (26f.), for repetitions have an inherent dynamism due to their temporal complexity (67). The repetitions of the series thus describe temporal complexities that are to be evaluated as processual.

The serial texts themselves represent this condition, they not only define a continuation of the narration, but also the seriality of its parts as episodes. Production and publication are usually successive, as is reception. This expands exponentially if one adds the transmedia extensions, which are also not created or received simultaneously.

The question of the processuality and thus also of the dissolution of transmedia narrative can be correlated with the question of the dissolution of traditional media dispositifs such as television. The transformation of a paradigmatically televisual form of narration in the proliferation of serial narration on different digital platforms leads to a performance of the televisual with new media-aesthetic strategies which stand under the sign of the transformations of the parameters of space and time examined here.

Once a Spectator: Now an Addressee[32]

These definitions also make clear that ther is a growing heterogemeity of the media which results from transmedia constructs. This results in different facets of the one who watches, reads, plays. Consequently, heterogeneous descriptions of the spectator like user, reader, player, are used. Similarly, neologisms such as *prosumer* or *produser* emerge in an attempt to find a fitting term for describing the ambivalent status of the spectator. The new conditions for the distribution and reception of transmedial content probably has effects for the study of the sprector in media theory. Assuming that previous concepts of transmediality have each presented isolated views or at least designations of the different facets of a recipient or have

---

[30]Cf. Engell (1999), pp. 477–478.

[31]Cf. Ott (2009), p. 26.

[32]Cf. Piepiorka (2017), p. 202.

only summarized parts of the same and thus deliberately omitted the subject matter, the following thesis is offered: The concept of the spectator is not an adequate concept in the context of transmedia series. Instead, the *concept of the addressee* is proposed, which can be 'transmedially' asserted across media.

Markus Stauff and other media scholars have suggested that the role of the spectator should be understood only within the media and not as a something outside media appropriating a media text.[33] Being inside the media is the essential part of an argument that comes into play here: it offers the possibility of arguing purely from the perspective of the media text– and indeed from the perspective of all media texts, including transmedia texts– it ist the text that provides us with clues and prompts.

Accordingly, information is contained in the media text or, more precisely, in the plot, or it is also withheld, leaving certain blank spaces that can be described as gaps.[34] However, these can also be solved by *cues*, which are to be understood as hints of information anchored in the text and which enable a classification of what is presented. Likewise, they evoke both concrete expectations and speculations regarding a future or past course of events.[35]

Even though this requires an interaction between the structure of the text and the activity of the addressee,[36] the cues and gaps are inscribed as addressings in the media texts. Thus, the spectator himself is inscribed in the aesthetics of media texts as a blank space, in that the text or its producers assume a spectator and address him. For the textual addressing anchored in the text remains and presupposes the addressee, whether the addressee acts by participating or not, as Holmes describes.[37]

These approaches apply to individual media, but can also be applied to a transmedial universe, insofar as narrative content and cues address the recipient on the various media platforms. Increasingly, strategies of cues for action are employed that ask viewers to transcend media boundaries while guiding them through the universe. As there exists a wide range of cues and action instructions in series, only a few of them can be referred to. The addressee receives instructions.

---

[33] Cf. Stauff (2005), p. 134.

[34] The gaps appear in various forms (cf. Bordwell: *Narration*, p. 55): *temporary; permanent* (they remain unresolved); *diffuse; focussed* (prompting assumptions or demanding information); *flaunted; supressed* (unrecognisable gaps).

[35] Cf. Bordwell (1985), pp. 27, 30, 48.

[36] Cf. Thompson (2003), p. 36.

[37] Cf. Holmes and Jermyn (2006), p. 49 ff.

These are possible paths, which he/she can follow to get to capture the overall plot or even to capture the transmedia universe. However, if these intratextual cues and subtexts do not reach the addressee, the addressing still remains in the text, even if it is not used: The media text inscribes the addressing, regardless of its use, so that the addressee is implied as a blank space. The media text, or rather the authors of the text, already imply this addressee by creating instructions for action. In this way, instructions are created for a dynamicprocess of constructing meaning by the addressee. Thus a temporal and spatial ordering strategy is suggested by the addressees, which can be understood as possibilities and not as obligatory. The result is an individual approach to the transmedia universe, in which each addressee *travels* different routes in space and time. The addressee can follow an individual route despite instructions for action by choosing other routes or following them in a different order than suggested—there are many options.

What Happened So Far: In Space and Time

Transmedial series exhibit a temporality and spatiality that can be described as interdependent. They offer an ordering structure within these categories, in which their existence originates in the first place. If the plot were not distributed temporally and spatially across (media) locations, there would be no transmediality and also no temporal coexistence of the individual plot parts. The question with such an observation is always how can it be described and understood.

Even if sample analyses have already been carried out elsewhere,[38] it is possible to conceive further research of transmedia series will offer further distinctions of a of space/time. Perhaps, just as Deleuze/Guattari suggest that there are other spaces for their way of thinking, new and distinctiveformations could be identified as a desideratum of future research. Likewise, the concept of the addressee needs to be examined in greater depth.

The development of media as well as their formats, their reception and their addressings is subject to a high dynamic and will always have to be looked at anew. Thus, the approach subsumed here could offer a fruitful proposal for ways of looking at the research object of the transmediaseries—as it currently exists:

A transmedial universe is a space with serialized places and equally serialized temporality, characterized by a juxtaposition of (media) places and a succession

---

[38] Cf. Piepiorka: *Lost in Time & Space*, p. 118.

through continuity and reception. Here, a serial processuality is present. Again and again and everywhere.

References

AMC 1: "Gale Boetticher Evidence File," ohne Datum, https://www.amc.com/shows/breaking-bad/exclusives/gale-boetticher-case-file, (Accessed on 04 Jun 2017)

AMC 2: "The Interrogation," ohne Datum, https://www.amc.com/shows/breakingbad/exclusives/the-interrogation (Accessed on 04.06.2017)

AMC 3: "The Costs of Doing Business," ohne Datum, https://www.amc.com/shows/breaking-bad/exclusives/cost-of-doing-business (Accessed on 04.06.2017)

AMC 4: "Better Call Saul," ohne Datum, https://www.amc.com/shows/better-call-saul/saul-goodman-esq/ (Accessed on 04.06.2017)

Blättler, Christine (2012) Serial Sixties auf Französisch—Zur Ambivalenz der Serie. In: Zeitschrift für Medienwissenschaft 2/2012, pp. 70–79

Bordwell, David (1985) Narration in the Fiction Film. Madison, University of Wisconsin Press

Bordwell, David, Kristin Thompson (1979) Film Art: An Introduction. New York, McGraw-Hill

Certeau, Michel de (2006) Praktiken im Raum. In: Dünne, Jörg, Stephan Günzel (Eds.) Raumtheorie. Grundlagentexte aus Philosophie und Kulturwissenschaften. Frankfurt, Suhrkamp, pp. 343–353

Deleuze, Gilles, Félix Guattari (1997) Tausend Plateaus. Berlin, Merve Verlag

Engell, Lorenz (1999) Fernsehen mit Gilles Deleuze. In: Fahle, Oliver, Lorenz Engell (Eds.) Der Film bei Deleuze—Le cinéma selon Deleuze. Weimar, VDG, pp. 468–467

Gray, Jonathan (2010) Show Sold Separately—Promos, Spoilers, and Other Media Paratexts. New York, New York University Press

Holmes, Su, Deborah Jermyn (2006) The Audience is Dead; Long Live the Audience! Interactivity, 'Telephilia' and the Contemporary Television Audience. In: Critical Ideas in Television Studies 1 (2006), pp. 49–57

Jenkins, Henry (2006): Convergence Culture: Where Old and New Media Collide. New York/London, New York University Press

Mittell, Jason (2015) Complex TV: The Poetics of Contemporary Television Storytelling. New York, New York University Press

Olek, Daniela, Christine Piepiorka. (2012) 'To be continued ... somewhere else!: Die Auswirkungen struktureller Räumlichkeit auf die Serialität im Kontext transmedialer Fernsehserien. In Spangenberg, Peter M., Bianca B. Westermann (Eds.) Im Moment des 'Mehr'. Jahrestagung der Gesellschaft für Medienwissenschaft, Münster: LIT Verlag, pp. 75–94.

o.V. (2006) Der Duden. Mannheim, Dudenverlag

Ott, Michaela (2009) Raum im Film—Spatial versus Topological Turn und der Standort der Kritik. In: Csáky, Moritz, Christoph Leitgeb (Eds.) Kommunikation—Gedächtnis—Raum. Bielefeld, Transcript Verlag, pp. 59–70

Piepiorka, Christine (2017) Lost in Time & Space—Transmediale Universen und Prozesshafte Serialität. Hamburg, Anchor Academic Publishing

Sielke, Sabine (2012) Joy in Repetition—Acht Thesen zum Konzept der Serialität und zum Prinzip der Serie. In: Kelleter, Frank (Ed.) Populäre Serialität: Narration—Evolution—Distinktion. Zum seriellen Erzählen seit dem 19. Jahrhundert, Bielefeld, Transcript Verlag, pp. 383–398

Stauff, Markus (2005) Das neue Fernsehen. Machteffekte einer heterogenen Kulturtechnologie. Münster, LIT Verlag

Thompson, Kristin (2003) Storytelling in Film and Television. Cambridge, Harvard University Press

Thompson, Kristin (1995) Neoformalistische Filmanalyse. In: montage/av 4/1, pp. 23–62

Christine Piepiorka Dr. phil., is Professor for Digital Media and Marketing, Hochschule für Oekonomie und Management, Dortmund. Before that she was Professor of Media & Communication and Vice Dean of the Department of Sport, Media & Communication at the University of Applied Sciences Europe. She studied Media Economics and Media Studies (M.A.) and holds a PhD in Media Studies from the Ruhr-University Bochum. She combines professional experience in TV and film production as well as marketing & PR, among others, with research interests in television economics and science, transmediality and augmented reality. Latest publications (excerpt): *Lost in Time & Space—transmedial universes and processual seriality.* Hamburg: Tredition, 2017; "YouTube in Serie—Serialität als Ordnungs-, Produktions- und *Rezeptionsprinzip*", in: Haarkötter, Hektor/Wergen, Johanna (eds.): *Das YouTubiversum—Chancen und Disruptionen der Onlinevideo-Plattform in Theorie und Praxis.* Wiesbaden: Springer VS, 2019, pp. 55–68.

'Serial Eruptions' in US Television from the Fifties to the Seventies

Stefan Borsos

If the daytime serial of television was stronger than might have been supposed at the beginning of the 1960s, the serial form had subtly taken over nighttime television as well.[1]

The Fugitive is a conspicuous example of how serial formats could be alternated—or, more precisely, blended—with spectacular success. In 1962, when continued drama was being given up for dead on the fiftieth anniversary of its birth, television producer Roy Huggins was telling ABC executives about an idea he had for a modern-day version of *Les Miserables* with overtones of *The Wandering Jew*. Reportedly without even a look at a finished script, the network representatives accepted Huggins' proposal, and *The Fugitive* went into planning.[2]

Long before the thread of *The Fugitive* was spun out, the program had imitators. One, *Run for Your Life* (1965–66), was certainly a legitimate variation: it was created by Roy Huggins. Instead of a doctor trying to find a murderer, Paul Bryan (portrayed by Ben Gazzara) was a lawyer racing to spend his last days in meaningful living, while a medical center labored to find a cure for the disease that otherwise would soon take his life. The next season a Quinn Martin character, David Vincent (Roy Thinnes), began his thankless battle to save the world from alien beings he alone recognized as *The Invaders*. Other serials emphasizing a search or race of one kind or another were *Hank* (1965), *Run, Buddy, Run* (1966), *Coronet Blue* (1967), *The Guns of Will Sonnett* (1967), and *The Prisoner* (1968).[3]

---

[1] Stedman (1971), p. 402.

[2] Ibid., p. 402f.

[3] Ibid., p. 404f.

S. Borsos (✉)
Institut für Medienwissenschaft, Ruhr-Universität Bochum, Bochum, Germany
e-mail: s.borsos@iffr.com

© The Author(s), under exclusive license to Springer Fachmedien Wiesbaden GmbH, part of Springer Nature 2024
D. Newiak et al. (eds.), *Television Studies and Research on Series*,
https://doi.org/10.1007/978-3-658-42915-7_4

All three quotes can be found in Raymond William Stedman's monograph *The Serials. Suspense and Drama by Installment* from 1971 and offer valuable clues for the history of series and seriality that would be worth pursuing. One might object, not without justification, that the book is completely devoid of references and footnotes, and that it offers no theorising whatsoever—even though Stedman received his doctorate in 1959 on the subject of daytime serial dramas in radio and television, and the book was published by a university press. Nevertheless, it is surprising that Stedman's work, precisely because it also takes a decidedly transmedial approach, has fallen into oblivion in the context of recent studies on television series and seriality, especially in the German-speaking research landscape. Even the extensive study by Vincent Fröhlich, which also has a transmedial perspective, draws on Stedman's work only occasionally, mainly in the chapters on cinema serials and soap operas.[4] The reason for this, apart from its lack of a strictly scholarly approach, seems to lie in current television series scholarship in general and in the discourse on the so-called quality television in particular. Symptomatic is a quotation from Christoph Dreher:

> Television series were memories of youth: Western series like *Bonanza* or *Laramie*, detective series like *Secret Mission for John Drake*, police series like *77 Sunset Strip* or *The Untouchables*, animal series like *Rintintin* or *Lassie*, thrillers like *The Fugitive* or *Mission Impossible*. They ran mostly on early evening programming or Sunday afternoons, were, as a core term of the television world goes, family-friendly, and had some obligatory characteristics: They were knitted according to a strictly observed pattern, that is, you reliably got the same thing over and over again, in variations, with plots completed within episodes. [...] These series basically reinforced two childish ideas: that nothing changes, everything stays the same, and that you live forever. The newer series of our time should fundamentally clear up both misconceptions.[5]

---

[4] Fröhlich justifies the omission of television series from the seventies to the nineties with the exceptional position of the 'continued narrative' in this period. Cf. Fröhlich 2015, p. 26; the fifties and sixties, which are also discussed here, are not mentioned at all.

[5] Dreher (2010), p. 23. In the original: "Fernsehserien waren Jugenderinnerungen: Western-Serien wie *Bonanza* oder *Am Fuss der blauen Berge*, Detektiv-Serien wie *Geheimauftrag für John Drake*, Polizei-Serien wie *77 Stunset Strip* oder *The Untouchables*, Tier-Serien wie *Rintintin* oder *Lassie*, Thriller wie *Auf der Flucht* oder Mission Impossible. Sie liefen zumeist im Vorabendprogramm oder am Sonntagnachmittag, waren, wie ein Kernbegriff der Fernsehwelt lautet, familientauglich, und hatten einige verbindliche Merkmale: Sie waren nach einem streng eingehaltenen Muster gestrickt, das heißt man bekam verlässlich immer Dasselbe, in Varianten, mit innerhalb der Folgen abgeschlossenem Plot. [...] Diese Serien bestärkten grundsätzlich zwei kindliche Vorstellungen: dass nichts sich ändert, alles bleibt wie es ist, und dass man ewig lebt. Mit beiden Missverständnissen sollten die neueren Serien unserer Zeit grundlegend aufräumen."

Currently, there seems to be just this consensus that the early 1980s mark a turning point in US television and television series history. In addition to Dreher, John Thornton Caldwell (1995) and Jason Jacobs (2001), among others, have argued for this historical caesura. This radical change is defined on the textual level by the overcoming of a previously dominant *zero-degree style*, which is replaced by a cinematic and videographic *televisuality*, as well as the form of the episodic series, whose 'return of the ever-same' is replaced by the contemporary *prime-time serial* through increasing serialization. In their critical examination of the discourse on quality television, Newman and Levine state accordingly:

> Since the 1980s, as we have seen, any highbrow brief for television's artistic respectability has made long-form, novelistic storytelling central to claims of legiti- macy. Taking a broad narrative scope and parceling out storytelling in regular installments function to elevate television above its historical status as intellectually worthwhile mass culture.[6]

While Caldwell devotes an entire chapter to television before 1980, Jacobs' and Dreher's remarks are limited to assumptions as well as youth and childhood memories. Dreher does concede that there were isolated series in earlier decades that broke with TV series standards, but he describes these 'early pioneers of the unusual' as 'entirely singular phenomena'. Indeed, the system of the major networks CBS, NBC and ABC presented itself in the 1960s at the height of its power: the introduction of the magazine format had largely wrested their influence from the sponsors, and the establishment of the episodic *telefilm* shot in Hollywood on 35 mm, which had displaced the more difficult-to-calculate live television dramas, gave them greater planning security. In a nutshell: hegemony.[7] "Yet the dawn of the 1960s," Mark Alvey points out,

> did not mark a point of closure and inertia for commercial television, but rather a transition into another stage of the medium's development, a stage characterized by continuing transformation and redefinition. Indeed, the new decade arrived on the heels of quiz show scandals, a perceived programming crisis, and mounting criticism from both inside and outside the television community. It was virtually inevitable that the industry would enter the new decade in a flurry of conscious and explicit change. The atmosphere of crisis and criticism intensified the creative and commercial stakes in an already competitive arena, and played into the industry's inherent quest for apparent novelty and regulated difference.[8]

---

[6] Newman and Levine (2012), p. 81.

[7] Cf. Mittell (2003).

[8] Alvey (1995), p. 34.

Related to questions of narrative structure and serialization, Caryn Murphy seconds:

> Episodic closure was an established convention of prime-time television by the early 1960s, and it was also supported by the increasingly profitable syndication market. During this decade, television writers and producers experimented with innovations in narrative in response to concerns about the quality of prime-time programming and as a method of encouraging audience engagement and habit viewership. Their innovations, including series with overarching plots, multi-part episodes and pure serials, necessitated a rethinking of prime-time screenwriting.[9]

Following reflections by Murphy, Alvey as well as Stedman, this rethinking also underlies the following remarks, which assume that, contrary to the established narrative of stasis and the image of the 'vast wasteland', the 1950s and, in particular, the 1960s and 1970s represent a distinctly dynamic, contradictory period, which can certainly be thought of as a phase of trial and experimentation, not least with a view to the definitive end of the live era (at least in the area of the fictional programming component) and the search for new forms of narration and presentation. Already in this period, the entire spectrum from anthology to episodic to serialized series is being explored and realized in very different configurations. A dichotomy of the two ideal-typical forms of episodic and serialized series is simply not present even in the US television of the fifties and seventies, which is often apostrophized as classical.

It is therefore not the intention to introduce new categories or concepts of seriality and serialization—Tanja Weber and Christian Junklewitz (2008, 2016) as well as Horace Newcomb (1985), Omar Calabrese (1992), Mark Alvey (1995), Robin Nelson (1997), Umberto Eco (2011), Greg M. Smith (2011), or Jason Mittell (2015) have all presented work that can be drawn on (to name just a few).[10] What is problematized instead are the often schematic historiographical models and overly linear-teleological conceptions of history that fail to do justice to the historical diversity and dynamism of the material. For example: Following Calabrese's study of the neo-baroque, Andrea Ndalianis identifies five prototypes of neo-baroque seriality in television. The underlying phase model, however, not only conceives the historical development of these prototypes as an evolutionary sequence (albeit with overlaps), but also allows only contemporary series the tendency "to blur the

---

[9]Murphy (2014), p. 382.

[10]See also the exhaustive table in Ursula Ganz-Blättler's study (Ganz-Blättler 2018), pp. 205–208.

boundaries by sharing characteristics with other prototypes".[11] The thesis put forward here, on the other hand, assumes that the serial narrative principles and types of television, however defined, not only occur simultaneously, but are also concretely realized at any given time as hybrid forms or, as Smith puts it, "are conceived as a constant maneuvering between the advantages and disadvantages of serial and episodic structures".[12] Accordingly, the following is intended to substantiate this historical and historiographical thesis with material, to trace serialization strategies in the diversity of their concrete articulations—and thus also to point out a glaring research desideratum, the rectification of which would not only straighten out a historically skewed picture of television series before the supposed quality revolutions, but also provide insights into the development of narrative, aesthetic strategies and also contribute to the understanding of recent series. Four points in time and thus case studies, for which I would like to use the Stedman's image of 'serial eruptions', will help to delineate the terrain of a serial panorama in the period under investigation. Inevitably, this will remain a sketchy idea, which, it is to be expected, raises more questions than it answers.

Prequel? *Lux Presents Wyatt Earp* and *Disney*

Whether we can already speak of one of the said serial eruptions in prime-time programming in the 1950s is difficult to answer definitely at the current state of research. Several examples, however, suggest that we can already speak of a pronounced variety of narrative combination strategies in this phase—and in the very TV genre that, in Caldwell's eyes, stands like no other for the worst characteristics of the episodic series before 1980: the *mindless* half-hour Western.[13] There are Disney's first live-action television adventures, all late offshoots of the *juvenile western,* as well as *The Life and Legend of Wyatt Earp*, shown on ABC from 1955 to 1961 and, together with *Gunsmoke* (USA 1955–1975), *Frontier* (USA 1955–1956) and the cornucopia of Warner series (the first to mention is *Cheyenne*, USA 1955–1963), one of the earliest examples of the televisual *adult western.*

As part of the anthology series *Disney Land* (USA 1954–1961), Disney presents Fess Parker as national hero Davy Crockett on five evenings starting in 1954, of which the first three episodes are only loosely connected, the other two, *Davy*

---

[11] Ndalianis (2005), p. 89.
[12] Smith (2011), p. 113.
[13] Cf. Caldwell (1995), p. 51.

Crockett's Keelboat Race and *Davy Crockett and the River Pirates* (both USA 1955, directed by Norman Foster), running as two-parters. Between 1958 and 1960, Robert Loggia took Crockett's place at irregular intervals as Westerner Elfego Baca. In addition to the tried-and-true form of the two-parter, Baca is given a professional career as a lawyer, so that here we can speak of tentative character development as we accompany the protagonist over several episodes as he studies, graduates and gets his first job.

In the course of the fifties, self-contained plots told over several episodes became a popular option for overcoming the limitations of the half-hour to one-hour time frame and, above all, for signaling the eventfulness and special nature of the broadcast. Especially the late live television dramas in anthology series such as *Kraft Television Theatre* (USA 1947–1958), *Playhouse 90* (USA 1956–1961), *Play of the Week* (USA 1959–1961) or *Sunday Showcase* (USA 1959–1960) are subject to a logic of heightening and surpassing, not least because of the then current trend towards all kinds of *spectaculars* and *specials*. In 1959, John Frankenheimer staged a three-hour version of Hemingway's *For Whom the Bell Tolls*, which was shown in two parts, while Sidney Lumet's adaptation of O'Neill's *The Iceman Cometh* (1960) ran to almost 4 h. But even in series that are otherwise largely episodic in structure, the multi-parter is establishing itself as a narrative convention in the serial repertoire. Thus, e a crime series like *The Lawless Years* (USA 1959–1961), which blithely alternates between anthological, episodic and serial approaches, presents the rise and fall of gangster Louis Kassoff (Paul Richards) in five half-hour segments. Finally, *Zorro* (USA 1957–1959) consists mainly of such episode-spanning stories.

Even the 1950s can be thought of as a constant negotiation of the serial form of the *telefilm*, which oscillates between the legacy of radio and the cinema serial and the conditions of the new medium always producing ever new hybrid forms in the process. As J. Frank MacDonald also notes, *Zorro's* cinematic models shine through abundantly in several ways.[14] When he writes of a "heritage of B Westerns"[15] in relation to the adventures, which are usually told over two to four episodes, he is primarily referring to the tradition of the cinema serial of the tennies and, later especially, the thirties and forties. In both cases, we are dealing with action and motion cinema aimed at a primarily juvenile audience, with a highly compressed story and plot. Unlike *Zorro Rides Again* (USA 1937, dir. William Witney, John English) or *Zorro's Fighting Legion* (USA 1939, dir. William Witney, John

---

[14] Cf. MacDonald (1987), p. 38f.

[15] Ibid., p. 38.

English), however, Disney's TV Zorro does not operate with the cliffhanger so distinctive of the serial form. Plots involving Don Diego de la Vega's uncle from Spain (Cesar Romero), who comes into conflict with Zorro because of his ever-changing plans to defraud him, or a deputy governor (Perry Lopez), whose tyranni-cal rule brings Zorro as well as other rebellious subjects onto the scene, are each told continuously over four episodes, but the individual episodes do not immediately follow on from the preceding one and are in turn narratively self-contained as episodic narrative units in their own right. The organization of the narrative strand around the super-villain 'The Eagle', whose feathered brotherhood wants to subju-gate all of Los Angeles, is somewhat reminiscent of the pigtail dramaturgy of the soap opera: After his plan seems to be foiled after four episodes and Zorro gets involved in other adventures in four more episodes, he returns at the end of the first season in the episode *The Tightening Noose* (USA 1958, director: Charles Barton), until the narrative strand reaches its conclusion in the season finale.

In any case, the narrative form chosen in the mid-fifties is surprising, since the adventures of serial heroes such as *The Lone Ranger* (USA 1938, directors: William Witney, John English) were adapted from serial to series for the new medium at an early stage and thus transferred into an episodic form (cf. *The Lone Ranger*, USA 1949–1957 or *Drums of Fu Manchu* (USA 1940, directed by John English & William Witney) vs. *The Adventures of Dr. Fu Manchu* (USA 1956)).[16] With its specific hybrid form of episodic and serialized series, *Zorro* occupies an intermedi-ate position here, serving as a model for later titles similarly related to the cinema serial, such as *Batman* (USA 1966–1968), *Lost in Space* (USA 1965–1968) and *Get Smart* (USA 1965–1970). The cliffhanger so emblematic of this form, weak in *Zorro*, comes back to the fore here as a stylistic device for narrative punctuation.

Whereas serialization, even in *Zorro*, only ever spans a few episodes, *The Life and Legend of Wyatt Earp* is fully serialized and tells a continuous story in terms of time, space, and characters, from Earp's first job as sheriff in Ellsworth (season 1), through his stops in Wichita (season 1) and Dodge City (seasons 2 through 4), to the day after the famous shootout at the OK Corral in Tombstone.[17] The narrator's

---

[16]The changes this 'flexible format' (Barefoot) underwent in the course of the media change are manifold: sometimes the number of episodes is reduced and cliffhangers removed, sometimes it is provided with a live framing or even edited into feature versions. Cf. Barefoot (2017), p. 174; Mathis (1999), p. 296.

[17]Unfortunately, there is currently no reliable information on the context of the production, in particular on the decision to tell the story in the form of a continuous series. Thus, one can only speculate whether the ending of the series in the sixth season was actually planned this way; the last episode rather suggests that season 7 would have begun with the start of the trial

voice, which contextualizes nearly every episode at the beginning, is visibly concerned with explaining plot connections with a gesture of historical authenticity. Particularly in the scene changes, emphasis is placed on clearly establishing the (new) space (even if they are admittedly the same backdrops on the studio backlot).

In *Wyatt Earp Comes to Wichita* (USA 1955, director: Frank McDonald, season 1, episode 5), for example, Earp (and thus the audience) is shown in detail where which shops and establishments are located on the main street when he enters the city. The serial memory claimed by Robert J. Thompson[18] or Robert Blanchet[19] for the newer quality series is surprisingly strong. In addition to the narrator, it is the characters themselves who recall earlier events. For example, shortly before leaving Ellsworth in the episode *Marshal Wyatt Earp Meets General Lee* (USA 1955, dir. Frank McDonald), Earp gives his young protégé Bat Masterson a hand on the way to completing his schooling. Reuniting in the episode *Bat Masterson Again* (USA 1956, Dir: Frank McDonald), Earp begins the episode by recounting how he last heard from Masterson in a letter about his progress in school. Shortly before his departure for the series' final major location, Tombstone, in *Dodge City Hall: Hail and Farewell* (USA 1959, dir. Frank McDonald), Earp recalls in a long flashback his gruff welcome to Dodge City (*Dodge City Gets a New Marshal*, USA 1956, dir. Frank McDonald) and his first encounter with his future deputy Shotgun Gibbs (Morgan Woodward) (*The Hole Up*, USA 1958, dir. Frank McDonald). Only the characterisation of the protagonist remains rather static, despite certain efforts at psychologisation, and admittedly there are episodes that have nothing to do with the Earp brothers' later arch adversaries, the Clanton family.

Remembering and Forgetting: On the Road with Dr. Kimble and Co

The trigger of the first serial eruption of the sixties, *The Fugitive* (USA 1963–1967), is also characterized by an arc of tension stretching over the entire series. Unlike *Wyatt Earp*, however, this narrative parenthesis not only forms a more or less coherent biographical slice, albeit with a growing focus on the confrontation with

---

against the Earp brothers. In any case, within the context of the otherwise almost exclusively episodic *adult-Western* wave of the late 1950s, *The Life and Legend of Wyatt Earp* is the odd one out.

[18]Thompson (1996), p. 14.

[19]Blanchet (2011), pp. 56–58.

the Clantons in the last two seasons, but also endows the main character with a quest motif and creates *suspense* through the premise of the chase plot, which can unfold over four seasons. *"The Fugitive* was," Alvey argues,

> a fascinating blend of anthology, series, and serial, balancing formula and variation, suspense tale and character study, melodrama and moral exploration, and marks a point of maturation and complexity for American television drama.[20]

In response to the programming crisis of the late 1950s, which threatened to become not only a crisis of quality and image but also an economic crisis in view of the dwindling ratings of the Western series that had dominated shortly before, the broadcasters tried out new narrative (hybrid) forms that sought to redefine the relationship between innovation and repetition and thus the relationship between episodic and serial components.[21] Following the discourse on these new series initiated in the industry magazine Variety, Alvey coined the term *semi-anthology* for *The Fugitive* and other examples of the late 1950s and early 1960s. In addition to other case studies discussed by Alvey, including *Naked City* (USA 1958–1963), *Route 66* (USA 1960–1964) and *The Defenders* (USA 1961–1965), *Wagon Train* (USA 1957–1965), *Outlaws* (USA 1960–1962), *Stoney Burke* (*USA* 1962–1963), *Breaking Point* (USA 1963–1964), *The Untouchables* (USA 1959–1963) and *Bus Stop* (USA 1961–1962) are also worthy of mention.

The spectrum of these *semi-anthologies* ranges from series such as *Outlaws* or *Breaking Point*, whose interest often focuses more on the guest stars than the supposed protagonists, to *Route 66*, which defines itself as a continuous story not only through its narrative arc and explicit two-parters such as *Fly Away Home* (USA 1961, directed by Arthur Hiller), but also through small, seemingly irrelevant details. Completely independent of the respective episode plots, Buz in *Sleep in Your Pillows* (USA 1961, dir. Ted Post, episode 18) and *An Absence of Tears* (USA 1961, dir. Alvin Ganzer, episode 19), for example, works as a cosmetics salesman while Tod attends a computer course at UCLA. "Other episodic serials of *The Fugitive* era," writes Stedman,

---

[20] Alvey (1995), p. 25.

[21] The supposedly obsolescent anthology also flourished, be it more typical examples like *Profiles in Courage* (USA 1964–1965) and *The Great Adventure* (USA 1963–1964) or more experimental ones like *The Richard Boone Show* (*USA* 1965–1966), which conceives of the format as repertory theatre, and *The Lloyd Bridges Show* (USA 1962–1963), in which leading man Bridges imagines himself as a reporter in all sorts of stories.

conveyed an impression of continuing narrative stronger than that found in like dramas of earlier day on both radio and television. The European air war seemed to progress with the successive episodes of *Twelve O'Clock High* (A Quinn Martin production), just as the ground war seemingly advanced on *Combat, Garrison's Gorillas*, and *The Rat Patrol*. Moreover, such shows as *High Chaparral, Julia*, and the amusing musical drama *That's Life* were clearly sequential in their introductory installments, something of a departure for episodic drama. While enjoyable independently, each unit of these programs carried added meaning for those who had seen what had happened before.[22]

However, the model that must be considered particularly effective in terms of negotiating narrative openness and closure remains *The Fugitive* at this point. In a New York Times article, television critic Val Adams even writes of a veritable wave of "run-run shows".[23] So while Dr. Richard Kimble is being chased across America by Lieutenant Philip Gerard in search of his wife's one-armed murderer, Shenandoah and Michael Alden go on a search for identity (*A Man Called Shenandoah* resp. *Coronet Blue*), grandson and grandfather follow in the footsteps of gunslinger Jim Sonnett (*The Guns of Will Sonnett)*, two teenagers travel a mysterious oriental India on the back of an elephant in search of their missing father *(Maya);* architect David Vincent, meanwhile, tries to stop an alien invasion *(The Invaders)* and the doomed Paul Bryan embarks on an uncertain journey through 1960s America after his diagnosis (*Run for Your Life)*.

All these series combine in different ways an overarching narrative thread with individual completed episodes.[24] Horace Newcomb introduced the term *cumulative narrative* for this form of negotiation between episodic and serialized series, which he sees realized for the first time with *Magnum P.I.* (USA 1980–88), and later also with *Cagney & Lacey* (USA 1981–88) and *Call to Glory* (USA 1984–85).[25] "One episode's events," he defines, "can greatly affect later events, but they're seldom directly tied together. Each week's program is distinct, yet each is grafted onto the

---

[22] Stedman (1971), p. 405.

[23] Cf. Adams (1966)

[24] Adams even reports on a planned series whose narrative construction is reminiscent of the miniseries form: In *The Long Hunt of April Savage,* the father played by Robert Lansing was supposed to find one of his family's eight murderers every six to eight episodes until he hunted down one after the other and the family was avenged. However, only the pilot was filmed (cf. Adams: "TV Heroes on the Run").

[25] Cf. Newcomb (1985), p. 24.

body of the series, its characters' pasts."[26] Newcomb emphasizes the extension of the narrative into the past (of the protagonists) and the resonance that events can have in later episodes[27]:

> The essential connections are not in the sequence of events, or in the causes and effects, but in their resonance. Each event reverberates with the harmonics of a hundred others. Tone and texture make the shows work, and liberate them from a repetitive style or motif. Seen in a first run or rerun, they are more like a mosaic or a tapestry than a series.[28]

Coronet Blue (USA 1967) and *A Man Called Shenandoah* (USA 1965–1966) must be considered particularly relevant with regard to the question of serial memory. Both protagonists lose their memory at the beginning of the first episode and suffer from amnesia throughout the series. The struggle between episodic and serial narrative principles thus not only takes place on the level of narrative operations, but is also negotiated on a textual level as a problem of remembering and forgetting. In the third episode of *Coronet Blue, The Rebels* (USA 1967, directed by Sam Wanamaker), for example, Arlen undergoes a series of experiments at a New York college that are supposed to reactivate his memory, but as a campus guard he is inevitably drawn between the fronts into the student protests. Arlen himself remains a kind of blank space, an outsider who serves as a projection screen for the social conflicts of the United States in the sixties. In order to maintain this function of Arlen for the series, the narrative has to constantly postpone finding further pieces of the puzzle, such as the meaning of the 'blue crown' conceived as a MacGuffin.

The titular protagonist of *A Man Called Shenandoah* (Robert Horton), on the other hand, is at first hardly distinguishable from other wandering TV Western heroes such as Jason McCort (Chuck Conners, *Branded*, USA 1965–1966), Josh Randall (Steve McQueen, *Wanted: Dead or Alive*, USA 1958–1961), William Colton (Lloyd Bridges, *The Loner*, USA 1965–1966) or Dave Blassingame (Brian Keith, *The Westerner*, USA 1960). And while the search for identity repeatedly leads to setbacks and thus narrative dead ends, Shenandoah becomes involved in side events and the episodic repeatedly gains the upper hand, there is nevertheless a development, the references to Shenandoah's past accumulate.

---

[26]Ibid., Although Newcomb uses similar attributions to characterize a number of adventure series as picaresque as early as 1974, including *The Fugitive*.Cf. Newcomb (1974), pp. 135–160, esp. 159–160), he does not revisit these ideas in the later text.

[27]Cf. Newcomb (1985), p. 24.

[28]Ibid. p. 25.

Probably due to the different generic contexts—spy on the one hand, western series on the other—*A Man Called Shenandoah* is more interested in providing the protagonist with an increasingly complex *backstory (wound)*.

In doing so, the series not only accumulates narrative information that at some point solidifies into a (admittedly always temporary) status quo and makes Newcomb's 'resonance' possible in the first place in later episodes, but also puts the identity and character of the hero up for debate time and again. Although questions raised are answered at the end of each episode if the corresponding assumptions turn out to be wrong, this 'what if', which is constantly in the room and is fired up again at the beginning of each episode, creates tension, not least because Shenandoah himself doubts his identity and considers it conceivable to be a cold-blooded killer or deserter. That's why Shenandoah's investigations sometimes land him abruptly in front of a court martial. In a way, the series can be read as an attempt to piece together the plot of the feature film *Shenandoah* (USA 1965, directed by Andrew V. McLaglen), which incidentally has no direct connection to the series, as a painful reminder of the dislocations and trauma of the American Civil War—*Past haunting the present.*

Highlight of the Sixties: *Peyton Place* and the Aftermath

"The memorable serial event of nighttime television in the fall of 1964, however, was *Peyton Place*,"[29] writes Stedman. In the research literature, this first attempt since the 1950s to tell a completely serialized story on two, later three evenings a week, finds little to no mention. Even Mittell, in his chapter on the influence of *soap opera* on *complex TV*, largely confines himself to reproducing Murphy's notes on the difficult genesis of the project and, consequently, the negotiations between producer Paul Monash, the broadcaster ABC, the censors and the consultant and soap grande dame Irna Phillips.[30] In contrast to the other two innovators discussed, *Mary Hartman, Mary Hartman* (USA 1976–1977) and *Soap* (USA 1977–1981), Mittell hardly addresses the textual level of the series—the serial eruption triggered directly by the series' success is played down.[31]

---

[29] Stedman (1971), p. 406.

[30] Cf. Mittell (2015), pp. 233–260, esp. 240–243.

[31] Cf. Ibid., The discourse developed by Murphy on the placing of the series between soap opera and television novel may be fruitful for Mittell's discussion of *complex TV*, but even in the early 1960s it is anything but new: *Hawkins Falls: A Television Novel* (USA 1950–1955),

In this context, *Peyton Place* (USA 1964–1969) is not only of interest because of its adaptation of the braid dramaturgy and 'paradigmatic complexity' characteristic of daily soaps[32] as well as a *long-take aesthetic*. The echoes of the series' success on both sides of the airtime divide in aesthetic terms have been very inadequately explored and understood. As Robert Jay,[33] but also Michael Z. Newman and Elana Levine have documented, the announcement and subsequent filming already trigger an extraordinary bustle of serial production. It is not surprising, then, when Peter Bart asks in his 1964 article title, "Will TV Serials Find Success?".[34] Partially or completely serialized examples such as *The Long, Hot Summer* (USA 1965–1966), *Our Private World* (USA 1965), *Bracken's World* (USA 1969–1970) and *The Survivors* (USA 1969–1970), but also unrealized projects such as *Jack and Jill* and the spin-off *The Girl form Peyton Place* can be understood as a direct result of the success of *Peyton Place*.[35] However: "None of these efforts had the staying power of *Peyton Place*, but," according to Newman and Levine, "their existence across the latter part of the 1960s points out one way in which serialized fare had a place in prime time television well before the Quality turn of the 1980s, even if that place was not especially valued either economically or aesthetically".[36]

Apart from these planned and realized *prime-time soap projects*, the popularity of *Peyton Place* also had an influence on other forms of *prime-time television*. Even the otherwise primarily episodic, male connoted spy adventures didn't escape the serialization boom of the sixties. *Blue Light* (USA 1966), for example, relies on a continuously told story in its first four episodes before switching to the selt-contained episodes of its competitors. In *The Man Who Never Was* (USA 1966–1967), US spy Peter Murphy (Robert Lansing) assumes the identity of his dead double and henceforth uses the rich playboy's façade for his espionage activities—in the season finale, he finally proposes to his wife, who noticed the hoax early on.[37] The most far-reaching influence, however, is to be found in those

---

which debuted as a one-hour programme on evenings but then moved to daytime program-ming as a 15-min soap, already bears this reference not only in its title but places it prominently in the *pre-title sequence*. Cf. also Stedman (1971), p. 354.

[32] Cf. Allen (1985), pp. 61–95.

[33] Cf. Jay (2009).

[34] Bart (1964), p. 61.

[35] Cf. Ibid.

[36] Newman and Levine (2012), p. 84.

[37] This partial serialization made it easier for the broadcasters to cut material for feature-length versions, which were particularly popular on the European market. *I Deal in Danger* (USA 1966), for example, consists of said first four episodes of *Blue Light, The Spy with the Perfect*

professional series for which Mary Ann Watson introduced the term *New Frontier character drama*.[38] In response to the quiz show scandals and the increasing criticism, even from the state, of the violence and commercialization of television, these doctor *(Dr. Kildare, Ben Casey, The Eleventh Hour, Breaking Point, The Nurses)*, lawyer *(The Defenders, Sam Benedict)*, teacher *(Mr. Novak, Channing)*, politician *(Slattery's People)*, and social worker series *(East Side/West Side)* not only continue the legacy of live television on a personal, thematic, and stylistic level, but also seek new paths between narrative continuity and flexibility, between standardization and innovation, and thus often fall into Alvey's category of *semianthology*. While most are cancelled by the mid-1960s, often after just one or two seasons, *Dr. Kildare* (USA 1961–1966) and *Ben Casey* (USA 1961–1966) use serialization strategies to breathe new life into their concepts.[39] "Both shows," writes Stedman,

> suddenly finding the going more difficult as they approached their fourth seasons, needed partial transfusions. Young Kildare's pattern of quick romances was broken, therefore, with a three-part series entitled "Rome Will Never Leave You." A Sally Benson script allowed Kildare (Richard Chamberlain) to visit Italy, fall in love with a titled signora (Daniela Bianchi) in the very garden set Leslie Howard and Norma Shearer had used in *Romeo and Juliet* (1936), and then step out of the girl's life so that she could carry out the wish of her dying father (Ramon Navarro) and marry a nobleman. Ben Casey, meanwhile, helped a lovely patient played by Stella Stevens come out of a fifteen-year coma and mature from the psychological age of thirteen to her real age of twenty-eight. Casey (Vince Edwards) achieved this goal in the first five episodes of the season, concurrently attending to other problems. The next year Dr. Casey was involved regularly in subplot serialization of this kind, while Kildare's shows became twice-a-week ultimate-conclusion serials, with story sequences sometimes running almost a month.[40]

Multi-parter were nothing new for *Dr. Kildare* since the third season, see for example *Tyger, Tyger* (USA 1964, R: John Newland episodes 16 and 17), but this initially rare practice becomes a clear trend in the following season. Finally, season 5, now in full color, is serialized under the influence of *Peyton Place*, airing twice a week as a half-hour series. With its stories told over two to seven episodes, *Dr. Kildare* in a sense returns to the format of *Zorro*. The most radical change,

---

Cover (USA 1967) and *Danger Has Two Faces* (USA 1967) were compiled from five and four episodes of *The Man Who Never Was*, respectively.

[38] Watson: *The Expanding Vista. American Television in the Kennedy Years*, 43f.

[39] Cf. Murphy (2014), p. 388; Bowie (2013).+

[40] Stedman (1971), p. 405.

however, is *The Nurses* (USA 1962–1965), which starts in 1962 as a one-hour prime-time series on CBS, is expanded by two male protagonists from 1963 under the title *The Doctors and Nurses*, and moves for the last season in 1965, finally, again under the original title (USA 1965–1967), to the daytime program of ABC as a daily soap.[41]

The extent to which *Peyton Place* had shaken up the prime-time landscape in the mid-1960s is underscored by the curious case of the Western series *The Travels of Jamie McPheeters* (USA 1963–1964). The first episode *The Day of Leaving* (USA 1963, director: Boris Sagal) ends with a veritable cliffhanger—whether the emergency operation that Dr. McPheeters (Michael O'Herlihy) performs in the last few minutes will be successful, the audience will only find out a week later, in the immediately following second episode *The Day of the First Trail* (USA 1963, director: Fred Jackman Jr.). Once the wagon train has started moving west, the series switches to a primarily episodic form with an occasional two-parter, but the continuous components remain stronger than in older competitors such as *Wagon Train* or *Rawhide* (USA 1959–1965), especially through the stable character personnel, e.g. in the form of the Kissel family. It is precisely this stability of the character personnel that causes plenty of confusion when the character of wagon driver Buck Coulter (Michael Witney) dies the series death in the episode *The Day of the Killer* (USA 1963, R: Walter Doniger) and is replaced by Linc (Charles Bronson) shortly after. Coulter's appearance in the following episode, whose fantastic plot turns out to be a fever dream of Jamie McPheeters (Kurt Russell), may yet be explained. Likewise the two-parter *The Day of the Pawnees* (Episode 14, USA 1963, R: Tom Gries, and 15, USA 1963, R: Fred Jackman Jr.), which is marked as a flashback by means of Jamie's voiceover. His later appearance at the end of episode *The Day of the Picnic* (Episode 22, USA 1964, R: Richard Donner), however, raises questions: how Coulter rose from the dead is not clarified. Whatever the reasons for this anything but smooth change of personnel, it underscores the

---

[41] Cf. Lamm (1995). The permeability of the boundaries between daytime and prime-time and their supposedly genuine narrative forms is also demonstrated by the daily soap *The Doctors* (USA 1963–1982), which was launched as an anthology format and only switched to serial narration roughly a year later (cf. Levien: "The Classic Soap Operas: The Doctors"). "A more detailed analysis," Levine pleads, "of the creative and economic exchanges between daytime and prime-time serialization would help us to better understand the degrees of influence in both directions between the 1950s and 1980s, as well as the ways that prime time's history of serialized narrative has developed from the 1990s on". Cf. Levine (2017), p. 107.

relationship between narrative, production and broadcast mode that is so precarious in serialized series, and which can lead to such aporias in programming.[42]

From Television Film to Miniseries: Serialization in the Seventies

Although the end of *Peyton Place* (1969)[43] and the failure of *The Survivors* put a temporary end to the serialization boom in the evening programme, serial components can be found in all kinds of formats and forms in the following decade: Series like *The Quest* (USA 1976), *Then Came Bronson* (USA 1969–70) or *Battlestar Galactica* (USA 1978–1979) tie in with heroic journeys à la The *Fugitive* and *Route 66*, two-parters are not uncommon even in anthology series like *Police Story* (USA 1973–1987). And while the attempts to establish a successful primetime soap failed several times with short-lived examples such as *Beacon Hill* (USA 1975), *Executive Suite* (USA 1976–77), *Big Hawaii* (1977) and *W.E.B* (USA 1978),[44] the primarily episodic *coming-of-age series James at 15* (USA 1977–1978) also marked the protagonist's aging visually, with the title in the opening credits of the birthday episode turning the 15 into 16. With *Cliffhanger* (USA 1979) there is even a *wheel show*,[45] which alternates between the serials *Stop Susan Williams, The Secret Empire* and *The Curse of Dracula*.[46]

---

[42] A similarly irritating example of this volatility is offered by *Hunter* (USA 1976) in the late seventies: In the pilot, James Franciscus plays a lawyer who was unjustly imprisoned and now, always pursued by mysterious killers, wants to take revenge on the person responsible, but in the first regular episode he appears as a secret agent of the US government. What the pilot had in mind is reminiscent of paranoid series like *The Immortal* (USA 1969–1971 or *Lucan* (1977–1978).

[43] The story returned to television for 422 episodes on NBC's daytime schedule as *Return to Peyton Place* (USA 1972–1974), followed later by two television movies (1977, 1985).

[44] Even the series *Dallas* (USA 1978–1991), which was decisive for the primetime soap opera of the eighties, is still strongly episodically organized in its pilot season.

[45] Although Hollywood's *telefilm* had already begun its triumphant march against New York's live anthologies with the *wheel show Warner Bros. Presents* (USA 1955–56) in the mid-1950s, the format initially fell into oblivion. Like the 'original', examples from the late 1960s and 1970s such as *The Name of the Game* (USA 1968–1971), *The Bold Ones* (*USA* 1969–1973), *The Men* (USA 1972), *Four in One* (*USA* 1970–1971) and *The NBC Mystery Movie* (*USA* 1971–77) were united by the concept of presenting weekly series under a single title. Similar to ABC/Warner Bros. launching the TV debuts of *Cheyenne, King's Row* and *Casablanca* in their *wheel show*, the broadcasters also use this form later to test new series over a limited period of time.

[46] Cf. also Newman and Levine (2012), p. 84.

The most important impulse for the broadcasters' serialization experiments came from two phenomena that at first glance seemed to run counter to one another, but which were intertwined: the television film *(telefeature)* and the miniseries. With the successive exploitation of the post-war film catalogues of the Hollywood major studios from 1961 onwards and the establishment of formats such as NBC's *Saturday Night at the Movies,* the feature film became a fixed component of network programming.[47] In the wake of a supply shortage and accompanying cost increases, growing censorship problems, especially with the broadcast of increasingly violent or permissive New Hollywood films, as well as a certain fatigue and saturation of the audience, the search for alternatives begins. Already with the 90-min Western series *The Virginian* (USA 1962–1971) and shortly afterwards with the first *telefeatures The Killers* (USA 1964, directed by Don Siegel, although released theatrically), *See How They Run* (USA 1964, directed by David Lowell Rich), *The Hanged Man* (USA 1964, directed by Don Siegel) and *Fame is the Name of the Game* (USA 1966, directed by Stuart Rosenberg), NBC tried out its own feature-length film formats in different broadcasting contexts. Finally, in the early 1970s, the television film was as much a fixture on the network's schedule as the feature film.[48]

These television films are usually one and a half to 2 h long, which is also the usual length for feature films, but *Vanished* (USA 1971, directed by Buzz Kulik) is the first television film to be broadcast as a two-parter because of its excessive length. The three networks finally receive the decisive push in the direction of miniseries from the new competitor PBS, which celebrates great success with miniseries bought in from Great Britain.[49] Newman and Levine explain:

> Yet serialized storytelling did begin to show some promise as both a commodity and a cultural marker during this period, in that during this time PBS began to air several serialized mini-series imported from Britain, among them *The Forsythe Saga* and *The Six Wives* of *Henry VIII.* The success of this programming led the American networks to program their own mini-series, which followed a serialized structure and form, albeit with a limited number of episodes. [. . .] With *Rich Man, Poor Man* and the mini-series that followed, a specific kind of serialization (adapted from a novel, historically

---

[47] Cf. Lafferty (1990)

[48] Cf. Edgerton (1991).

[49] Also worth mentioning are the two documentary or semi-documentary miniseries *Trial: The City and the County of Denver vs. Lauren R. Watson* (USA 1970, directed by Denis Sanders) and *The National Dream* (Canada 1974, directed by James Murral, Eric Till).

oriented, limited run) became a television institution, and a well-respected one, at that.[50]

From *Vanished* with a length of around 3 h, the first miniseries in the narrower sense is not far away. How fluid this transition is can be seen in the example of *The Blue Knight* (USA 1973, director: Robert Butler), which was broadcast in four one-hour episodes and at the same time shot as a feature film with partially different, cinema-quality footage.[51] But where NBC had distinguished itself as an innovator in the television film, this task was now left to its competitor ABC for the miniseries following *The Blue Knight*. *Qbvii* (USA 1974, director: Tom Gries), as well as *Rich Man, Poor Man* (USA 1976) and *Roots* (USA 1977) follow in quick succession; the latter's success finally establishes the new format and triggeres a veritable miniseries boom at the end of the 1970s.

Just how broad the range of serial forms can be within a single series is illustrated by the final case study, *How the West Was Won* (USA 1976–1979). Loosely based on the epic *Cinerama western* of the same name (USA 1962, R: John Ford, Henry Hathaway, George Marshall, Richard Thorpe), the series recounts the Macahan family's arduous journey west. The first incarnation is the two-hour *telefeature The Macahans* (USA 1976, Dir: Bernard McEveety), in a sense the pilot, followed by the first season, which aired in three episodes as a miniseries. Framed by three three-hour episodes, the story continues to be told as a serial, and the two-hour episodes of the third and final season finally oscillate between episodic series with serial elements and largely self-contained television films, which do, however, find time in episodes such as *Hilary* (USA 1979, director: Irving J. Moore) to tie in with plots and characters from the previous season. One could almost think that the series deliberately wanted to explore the entire spectrum of serial forms. Although writer and producer John Mantley's statements about the turbulent production and broadcast history[52] suggest that this maneuvering is the result of complex negotiations with the network, the series possesses a degree of self-reflection that makes such a reading at least not entirely absurd: At the end of season two, as the family begins the onward journey but instead of continuing directly toward Oregon, unceremoniously settles on a side trip to Yellowstone, daughter Laura (Kathryn Holcomb)

---

[50] Newman and Levine (2012), p. 84.

[51] The fact that IMDb lists *Vanished under* the category of miniseries, while *The Blue Knight is* classified as a TV movie, also underscores this impression, cf. https://www.imdb.com/title/tt0067926/?ref_=fn_tt_tt_8 resp. https://www.imdb.com/title/tt0069806/?ref_=fn_al_tt_4.

[52] Cf. Newcomb and Alley (1983).

comments, "We started out for Oregon over eight years ago and we're still nowhere near it."

To Be Continued. . .

The examples cited impressively underscore that questions regarding narrative form in general, and seriality in particular, reached a critical mass at the latest with the successes of *The Fugitive* and *Peyton Place*—and that serialization strategies were thus understood as a potential for innovation and a matter of distinction, despite the widespread soap/daytime stigma. It is neither splitting hairs nor an overemphasis of patterns of seriality, which Jeffrey Sconce speaks of in connection with cumulative storytelling in older series.[53] The all-encompassing dominance of the episodic form as 'amnesiac television' (Sconce), which is more claimed than proven, can hardly be maintained, or the other way round: one could rather speak of an ongoing crisis of the episodic series than of a monolithic stability that is only broken by recent series. Why this master narrative remains unquestioned even in recent and most recent research, for example by Linda Williams[54] or Gregory Mohr,[55] is inexplicable. A fundamental revision of the currently established research paradigm with the help of the material is therefore needed. Alvey is to be agreed with when he writes that

> any thorough understanding of television form will require solid historical ground-work. Without this foundation, arguments about contemporary texts will be tenuous, constructed in a historical vacuum, based on uncritical conceptions of earlier forms as static, conventional, and easily understood.[56]

Only when these foundations have been laid and one gets beyond reductionist, all too often mechanically and excessively used terms such as the 'Classic Network System', any 'Golden Ages' or strict epoch classifications and other arbitrary demarcations, a truetelevisual poetics can be considered. Only then can we seriously begin a work of reflection that, beyond all too deterministic economic-institutional explanations, asks to which social and cultural needs and problems these changing

---

[53] Cf. Sconce (2004), p. 98.
[54] Cf. Williams (2018)
[55] Mohr (2018) .
[56] Alvey (1995), p. 14.

serial arrangements react, which 'specific meanings are actualized', to paraphrase
Jens Ruchatz.[57]

References

Adams, Val (1966) TV Heroes on the Run. In: The New York Times, 27 Feb 1966, p. 335

Allen, Robert C. (1985) Speaking of Soap Operas. Chapel Hill and London, The University of
California Pres

Alvey, Mark (1995) Series Drama and the "Semi-Anthology": Sixties Television in Transition, unpublished dissertation. The University of Texas at Austin

Alvey, Mark (2000) The Independents: Rethinking the Television Studio System. In
Newcomb, Horace M. (Ed.) Television: The Critical View. New York, Oxford University
Press, pp. 34–51

Barefoot, Guy (2017) The Lost Jungle. Cliffhanger Action and Hollywood Serials of the
1930s and 1940s. Exeter, University of Exeter Press

Bart, Peter (1964) Will TV Serials Find Success? Tune in Again Next Fall for… In: The
New York Times, 26 June 1964, p. 61

Blanchet, Robert (2011) Quality-TV. Eine kurze Einführung in die Geschichte und Ästhetik
neuer amerikanischer Fernsehserien. In: Köhler, Kristina, Tereza Smid, Julia Zutavern
(Eds.) Serielle Formen. Von den frühen Film-Serials zu aktuellen Quality-TV- und
Online-Serien. Marburg, Schüren, pp. 36–70.

Bowie, Stephen (2013) Man. Woman. Birth. Death. Infinity. The dark medical drama *Ben
Casey. The AV Club.* https://tv.avclub.com/man-woman-birth-death-infinity-the-dark-
medical-1798239718, Accessed 9 Aug.2019

Calabrese, Omar (1992) Neo-Baroque. A Sign of the Times, Princeton, Princeton University
Press

Caldwell, John T. (1995) Televisuality. Style, Crisis, and Authority in American Television.
New Brunswick, Rutgers University Press

Dreher, Christoph (2010) Autorenserien—Die Neuerfindung des Fernsehens. In: Dreher,
Christoph (Ed.) Autorenserien. Die Neuerfindung des Fernsehens, Stuttgart, Merz
Akademie pp. 23–61

Edgerton, Gary (1991) High Concept, Small Screen. Reperceiving the Industrial and Stylistic
Origins of the American Made-for-TV Movie. In: Journal of Popular Film and Television
19 (1991), pp. 114–127

Eco, Umberto (2011) Über Spiegel und andere Phänomene, München, Hanser

Fröhlich, Vincent (2015) Der Cliffhanger und die serielle Narration. Analyse einer
transmedialen Erzähltechnik. Bielefeld, transcrip

Ganz-Blättler, Ursula (2018) Signs of Time. Cumulative Narrative in Broadcast Television
Fiction, Zürich, LIT Verlag

Jacobs, Jason (2001) Issues of Judgement and Value in Television Studies. In: International
Journal of Cultural Studies 4 (4) pp. 427–447.

[57]Cf. Ruchatz (2012), p. 80.

Jay, Robert (2009) Broadcast Twice a Week (or More). In: TV Obscurities, 2009. https://www.tvobscurities.com/articles/broadcast_twice_a_week, Accessed 9 Aug.2019

Lafferty, William (1990) Feature-Films on Prime Time Television. In: Balio, Tino (Ed.) Hollywood in the Age of Television. Boston, Unwin Hyman, pp. 235–256

Lamm, Bob (1995) Television's Forgotten Gems: The Nurses. In: Journal of Popular Film and Television 23 (2) pp. 72–79

Levien, Alisa (1997) The Classic Soap Operas: The Doctors. In: Abrams, Harry N. (Ed.) Worlds without End. The Art and History of the Soap Opera. New York, Harry N. Abrams Inc., pp. 138–139

Levine, Elana (2017) Historicizing the Influence of Soap Opera. In: The Velvet Light Trap 79, pp. 105–109

MacDonald, J. Fred (1987) Who shot the Sheriff? The Rise and Fall of the Television Western. Westport, London, Praeger

Mathis, Jack (1999) Republic Confidential Volume 1. The Studio. Barrington, Jack Mathis Adverising

Mittell, Jason (2003) The 'Classic Network System' in the US. In: Hilmes, Michelle (Ed.) The Television History Book, London, BfI, pp. 44–49.

Mittell, Jason (2015) Complex TV. The Poetics of Contemporary Television Storytelling. New York, London, New York University Press

Mohr, Gregory (2018) Slow-Burn-Narration. Langsames Erzählen in zeitgenössischen Fortsetzungsserien, Wiesbaden, Springer

Murphy, Caryn (2013) Selling the continuing story of *Peyton Place*: Negotiating the Content of the Primetime Serial. In: Historical Journal of Film, Radio and Television 33 (1), pp. 115–128

Murphy, Caryn (2014) The continuing story: Experiments with serial narrative in 1960s prime-time television. In: Journal of Screenwriting 5 (3), pp. 381–392

Ndalianis, Angela (2005) Television and the Neo-Baroque. In: Hammond, Michael, Lucy Mazdon (Eds.): The Contemporary Television Series, Edinburgh, Edingburgh University Press, pp. 83–101

Nelson, Robin (1997) TV Drama in Transition. Forms, Values and Cultural Change, Basingstoke, New York, Palgrave MacMillan

Newcomb, Horace (1974) TV: The Most Popular Art. New York, Anchor Press

Newcomb, Horace (1985) Magnum: The Champagne of TV?. In: *Channels* 3, May, June 1985, pp. 23–26

Newcomb, Horace/Robert S. Alley (1983) The Producer's Medium. Conversations with Creators of American TV, New York/Oxford, Oxford University Press

Newman, Michael Z./Elana Levine (2012) Legitimating Television. Media Convergence and Cultural Status. New York, London, Routledge

Ruchatz, Jens (2012) Sisyphos sieht fern oder Was waren Episodenserien?. In: Zeitschrift für Medienwissenschaft 7 (2)2, pp. 80–89

Sconce, Jeffrey (2004) What If?: Charting Television's New Textual Boundaries. In: Spigel, Lynn, Jan Olsson (Eds.) Television after TV: Essays on Medium in Transition. Durham, Duke University Press, pp. 93–112

Smith, Greg M. (2011) How Much Serial Is in Your Serial? In: Blanchet, Robert, Kristina Köhler, Julia Zutavern, Julia (Eds.) Serielle Formen. Von den frühen Film-Serials zu aktuellen Quality-TV- und Online-Serien, Marburg, Schüren, pp. 93–114

Stedman, Raymond William (1971) The Serials. Suspense and Drama by Installment. Norman, University of Oklahoma Press

Thompson, Robert J. (1996) Television's Second Golden Age. From Hill Street Blues to ER. New York, Syracuse University Press

Watson, Mary Ann (1994) The Expanding Vista. American Television in the Kennedy Years, Durham, Duke University Press

Weber, Tanja, Christian Junklewitz (2008) Das Gesetz der Serie—Ansätze zur Definition und Analyse. In: MEDIENwissenschaft 25 (1), pp. 13–31

Weber, Tanja, Christian Junklewitz (2016) Die Vermessung der Serialität: Wie Fernsehserien zueinander stehen. In: MEDIENwissenschaft 33 (1), pp. 8–24

Williams, Linda (2018) World and Time: Serial Television Melodrama in America. In: Gledhill, Christine, Linda Williams (Eds.) Melodrama Unbound. Across History, Media, and National Cultures. New York, Columbia University Press, pp. 169–183

Without Author (2019a) Vanished. In: IMDb 2019, https://www.imdb.com/title/tt0067926/?ref_=fn_tt_tt_8. Accessed 9 Aug 2019

Without Author (2019b) The Blue Knight. In: IMDb. https://www.imdb.com/title/tt0069806/?ref_=fn_al_tt_4. Accessed 9 Aug 2019

Series and TV Shows

A Man Called Shenandoah (ABC 1965–1966)
The Adventures Of Dr. Fu Manchu (NBC 1956)
Batman (ABC 1966–1968)
Battlestar Galactica (ABC 1978–1979)
Beacon Hill (CBS 1975)
Ben Casey (ABC 1961–1966)
Big Hawaii (NBC 1977)
Blue Light (ABC 1966)
The Bold Ones (NBC 1969–1973)
Bracken's World (NBC 1969–1970)
Branded (NBC 1965–1966)
Breaking Point (ABC 1963–1964)
Bus Stop (ABC 1961–1962)
The Blue Knight (CBS 1973)
Cagney & Lacey (CBS 1981–88)
Call To Glory (ABC 1984–85)
Channing (ABC, 1963–1964)
Cheyenne (ABC 1955–1963)
Cliffhanger (NBC 1979)
Coronet Blue (CBS 1967)
Dallas (CBS 1978–1991)
Danger Has Two Faces (20th Century Fox, 1967)
The Defenders (CBS 1961–1965)
Disney-Land (ABC 1954–1961)

Dr. Kildare (NBC 1961–1966)
The Doctors (NBC 1963–1982)
East Side/West Side (CBS 1963–1964)
Executive Suite (CBS 1976–77)
Fame Is The Name Of The Game (NBC 1966)
Four In One (NBC 1970–1971)
Frontier (NBC 1955–1956)
The Fugitive (ABC 1963–1967)
Get Smart (NBC 1965–1970)
The Great Adventure (CBS 1963–1964)
Gunsmoke (CBS 1955–1975)
The Guns Of Will Sonnett (ABC 1967–1969)
The Hanged Man (NBC 1964)
Hawkins Falls: A Television Novel (NBC 1950–1955)
How The West Was Won (ABC 1976–1979)
Hunter (CBS 1976)
The Immortal (ABC 1969–1971)
The Invaders (ABC 1967–1968)
James At 15 (NBC 1977–1978)
Kraft Television Theatre (NBC 1947–1958)
The Lawless Years (NBC 1959–1961)
The Life And Legend Of Wyatt Earp (ABC 1955–1961)
The Lloyd Bridges Show (CBS 1962–1963)
The Lone Ranger (ABC 1949–1957)
The Loner (CBS 1965–1966)
The Long, Hot Summer (ABC 1965–1966)
Lost In Space (CBS 1965–1968)
Lucan ABC (1977–1978)
Magnum, P.I. (CBS 1980–88)
The Man Who Never Was (ABC 1966–1967)
Mary Hartman, Mary Hartman (Tandem Produtions, 1976–1977)
The Men (ABC 1972)
Maya (NBC 1967–1968)
Naked City (ABC 1958–1963)
The Name Of The Game (NBC 1968–1971)
The National Dream (CBC Television 1974)
The NBC Mystery Movie (NBC 1971–77)
The Nurses (ABC 1965–1967)
The Nurses/The Doctors And Nurses (CBS 1962–1965)
Our Private World (CBS 1965)
Outlaws (NBC 1960–1962)
Peyton Place (ABC 1964–1969)
Play Of The Week (NTA Film Network 1959–1961)
Playhouse 90 (CBS 1956–1961)
Police Story (NBC 1973–1987)
Profiles In Courage (NBC 1964–1965)

QBVII (ABC 1974)
The Quest (NBC 1976)
Rawhide (CBS 1959–1965)
Return To Peyton Place (NBC 1972–1974)
See How They Run (NBC 1964)
The Richard Boone Show (NBC 1965–1966)
Rich Man, Poor Man (ABC 1976)
Roots (ABC 1977)
Route 66 (CBS 1960–1964)
Run For Your Life (NBC 1965–1968)
Sam Benedict (NBC, 1962–1963)
Trial: The City And County Of Denver Vs. Lauren R. Watson (National Educational Television 1970)
Saturday Night At The Movies (NBC, 1961–1978)
Slattery's People (CBS, 1964–1965)
Soap (ABC 1977–1981)
Stoney Burke (ABC 1962–1963)
Sunday Showcase (NBC 1959–1960)
Then Came Bronson (NBC 1969–1970)
The Travels Of Jamie McPheeters (ABC 1963–1964)
The Untouchables (ABC 1959–1963)
Vanished, (NBC 1971)
The Virginian (NBC 1962–1971)
Wagon Train (NBC/ABC 1957–1965)
Wanted: Dead Or Alive (CBS 1958–1961)
Warner Bros. Presents (ABC 1955–56)
W.E.B. (NBC 1978)
The Westerner (NBC 1960)
Zorro (ABC 1957–1959)

Movies

English, John/Witney, William (Regie): *Drums Of Fu Manchu*, USA 1940.
English, John/Witney, William (Regie): *The Lone Ranger*, USA 1938.
English, John/Witney, William (Regie): *Zorro's Fighting Legion*, USA 1939.
English, John/Witney, William (Regie): *Zorro Rides Again*, USA 1937.
Ford, John/Hathaway, Henry/Marshall, George u.a. (Regie): *How The West Was Won*, USA 1962.
Foster, Norman (Regie): *Davy Crockett And The River Pirates*, USA 1955a.
Foster, Norman (Regie): *Davy Crockett's Keelboat Race*, USA 1955b.
Grauman, Walter (Regie): *I Deal In Danger*, USA 1966.
McLaglen, Andrew V. (Regie): *Shenandoah*, USA 1965.
John Newland/Walter Doniger (Regie): *The Spy With The Perfect Cover* (USA 1967).
Siegel, Don (Regie): *The Killers*, USA 1964.

Stefan Borsos M.A., Studied Theatre, Film and Television Studies as well as Modern and Classical Sinology in Cologne; ongoing dissertation at the Institute for Media Studies, RUB on the topic of nation and gender in HK-Chinese Bond films of the 1960s and 1970s; research interests include Asian film, Hollywood (history), television (series) history of the 1940s to 1980s, seriality (history), media aesthetics, transmediality, transculturality, genre theory, cultural studies, post-colonial studies.

Historical Perspectives in the Industry Discourse on 'Quality TV'

Florian Krauß

Introduction

The terms 'quality TV' and 'quality drama', which media scholars in the German-speaking context have used repeatedly in recent years,[1] have been criticized for various reasons: among others, because of the elitist and judgmental tendency of these quality terms, their vagueness as well as their one-sidedness with regard to the heterogeneous, ever-transforming medium of television.[2] With its primary reference to changes in US television series since the 1980s and 90s,[3] many works operating with these terms also tend to neglect and omit other historical and national contexts—such as television fiction in the German-speaking world, on which this chapter focuses. In the German-speaking television industry, which leads in terms of the number of fiction productions in Europe,[4] but which has only been rudimentarily investigated lately,[5] a discourse on 'quality TV' drama and its

---

[1] Cf. e.g. Nesselhauf and Schleich (2016), Hahn (2013), Blanchet 2010).

[2] Cf. e.g. Dasgupta (2012), McCabe, Akass (2007). See on the heterogeneity of television Keilbach and Stauff (2011).

[3] Cf. e.g. Thompson (1996) and Schlütz (2016)

[4] Cf. Castendyk and Goldhammer (2012), see also interview 9 with Jan Kromschröder, producer and managing director of the production company Bantry Bay, Berlin, 2 Feb 2018.

[5] Cf. e.g. Klug (2016), Knöhr (2018) or Hißnauer et al. (2014) .

F. Krauß (✉)
Medienwissenschaftliches Seminar, Universität Siegen, Siegen, Germany
e-mail: krauss@medienwissenschaft.uni-siegen.de

© The Author(s), under exclusive license to Springer Fachmedien Wiesbaden GmbH, part of Springer Nature 2024
D. Newiak et al. (eds.), *Television Studies and Research on Series*,
https://doi.org/10.1007/978-3-658-42915-7_5

supposed absence in Germany has been going on for some time (and is linked to similar debates in the media public sphere).[6]

The term *quality TV*, which originated in the US television industry for programmes that address a narrowly defined, economically attractive target group,[7] is thus transferred to a different production context that is strongly shaped by public-service broadcasters. Although US-centeredness and a one-sided focus on the presence remain characteristic in this adaptation,[8] German television history and thus also the televisuality of the series become a topic on the margins.[9] It is precisely these television-historical features of the industry discourse on German 'quality TV' that my article traces. Following media industry and production studies,[10] the chapter concentrates on the perspective of the practitioners and views 'quality TV' less in terms of particularly 'good' programmes (i.e., programmes deemed valuable aesthetically or content-wise) and more as an industry discourse. In the following, I will discuss how central practitioners in TV drama development, in particular commissioning editors, producers and scriptwriters, negotiated television history in connection with the 'quality TV' drama.[11]

In the following analysis, history also encompasses the recent past, given the immense and quick transformations since the 2010s. The German television landscape has changed dramatically in the context of processes of digitalization and transnationalisation.[12] Recent 'quality TV' projects such as *Im Angesichts des Verbrechens* (*In the face of crime*, 2010, ARD et al.) were created in a still very different production and distribution environment than today.

Knut Hickethier's model[13] of the 'dispositif television' ('Dispositiv Fernsehen') provides a fruitful theoretical starting point for the analysis of this past, but also of the current television landscape. Conceiving television as an interplay of space, image, programme, viewer, politics and society as well as media institutions, the

---

[6]Cf. e.g. Schawinski (2008) DJ Frederiksson (2014).

[7]Cf. Feuer et al. (1984) Hißnauer and Klein (2012)

[8]Cf. Leder (2015).

[9]Cf. on similar television-historical argumentations in the feuilleton e.g. Diez and Hüetlin (2013).

[10]Cf. e.g. Krauß and Loist (2018) or Vonderau (2013).

[11]Interim results from the production study "'Quality series' as discourse and practice: self-theorizations in the German series industry" (Deutsche Forschungsgemeinschaft, German Research Foundation, 2018–2022).

[12]Cf. Krauß (2018a, b).

[13]Hickethier (1998); see on current changes in this dispositive of television Sudmann (2017), pp. 98–112.

model includes variability and transformations. Hickethier's model also helps to categorize the practitioners' arguments that will be discussed in the following. Among the various dispositif structures"[14] according to Hickethier, the TV professionals especially touched upon the levels of the *programme*, the *reception* and the *production*. The following chapter is divided into these three main points.

The practitioners dealt with the "media-industrial complex" particularly by negotiating production cultures. With *production cultures*, I refer to a key concept of *media industry/production studies,*[15] which refers to forms, networks and hierarchies of production under which media professionals work.[16] These production cultures—as will be seen—are shaped by national specifics.

At the same time TV fiction, and especially series from Germany, have traditionally been influenced by US and European productions to a great extent, for example through imports.[17] Moreover, television broadcasters and production companies are often integrated into transnational media corporations, which further complicates the notion of a clearly 'German', self-contained television industry.

By referring to a German (or, in many cases, de facto West German) television history, practitioners reconstructed the belonging to a national television industry and an "imagined community" in an increasingly transnational television landscape.[18] For all the imaginative work, this notion of a nation or a language space is at the same time based on 'real' national/German-speaking networks and projects. Many television fiction productions coming from Germany serve solely or primarily the DACH countries. With Switzerland, Austria, Germany, they already form a relatively large and economically relevant TV market.[19]

More recent approaches to 'high-end' or 'quality TV' dramas with serial storylines, with which producers also strive for transnational distribution or even include foreign liquidations in their budgets, represent exceptions and new developments in the German context, although some multi-part films (so-called

---

[14]Hickethier (2009), p. 272.

[15]Cf. among others Caldwell (2008), Banks et al. (2016), Krauß and Loist (2018) Medienindustrieforschung.

[16]Cf. Mayer et al. (2009), p. 2.

[17]Cf. e.g. Rohrbach (2009), Hickethier (1998), pp. 465–466. as well as Bleicher et al. (1993).

[18]Anderson (2005).

[19]Cf. Mikos (2016), p. 156 and Windeler et al. (2001), p. 106. See also interview 9 and interview 24 with Edward Berger, director *Deutschland 83,* Berlin (via Skye), 26 Nov 2018.

Mehrteiler, comprising two or three 90-min parts) were already shown abroad some years ago.[20]

The "exclusive informants"[21] of the 24 interviews used in the following were selected through different contemporary 'quality TV' drama projects.,[22] However, several of the interviewees were or are also working in other, supposedly less distinguished areas of German TV fiction such as the crime procedural or the daily soap. Having been active in the industry for decades, many interviewees also embody a piece of television history themselves. In this respect, they provide information about different times and facets of German-language television fiction.

According to a list from 2015,[23] by Barbara Thielen, Managing Director and Producer at the mainstream production company Ziegler Film, and Joachim Kosack, who works in a similar lead capacity at the UFA production house, four types of series in particular can be distinguished in Germany: first there is the daily soap, which is broadcasted every working day and produced 'industrially' with a strong division of labor[24]; secondly there is the "weekly", which consist of 26 episodes, or in some cases 50 episodes a year; and thirdly there are local season series that have fixed broadcasting slots, mainly in the prime time, and ideally consist of several seasons. They often revolve around one case in the main plot of each episode. Furthermore Kosack and Thielen mentioned the event or 'high-end' miniseries with a manageable number of episodes.[25] In the meantime, productions that fall outside these four segments have been supplemented by new providers such as Netflix, Amazon Prime or, on the public service side, Funk and ZDFneo. Furthermore, so-called *Reihen*, i.e. 90-min procedurals with only some serial elements, point to fluid boundaries between series and television films. The relevance of single TV films and procedurals with one main story per episode also

---

[20] Cf. Cooke (2016) and Dörner (2012).

[21] Bruun (2016).

[22] Selection based on the series *Deutschland 83/86/89* (2015–2020, RTL/Amazon Prime), *4 Blocks* (2017–2019, TNT Serie), *Die Stadt und die Macht* ('The city and the power', 2016, ARD), *Der Club der roten Bänder* ('Club of red bracelets', 2015–2017, Vox) and the TV film trilogy *Mitten in Deutschland: NSU* (*NSU German History X*, 2016, ARD). Complementary to the interviews, participant observations at the series-specific industry workshops *Winterclass Serial Writing and Producing* and *European TV Drama Series Lab* (Erich Pommer Institut, 2015–2018) were considered.

[23] Cf. notes on the *Winterclass Serial Writing and Producing*, Erich Pommer Institut, Film University Babelsberg Konrad Wolf, Potsdam, 2015.

[24] Cf. Kirsch (2001).

[25] Cf. also Krauß (2019a, b).

becomes apparent when we look at broadcasting slots, which underline the immense quantity of German-language and here above all public-service fiction. Such 'single pieces' were a crucial issue in the practitioners' negotiations of *programmes*, the component of the dispositif of television on which I will first concentrate. In addition to the television film as a central programme tendency, the TV professionals also dealt with former 'quality' work in German television history and with broadcasting slots as an important programme structure.

Programme Structures

Broadcasting slots are historically evolved structures of programming that continue to shape television professionals today and which, viewed with the actor-network theory, themselves represent a kind of actor.[26] The broadcasting slots are of immediate importance, first of all, through their connection with the administration of funds: in the case of public service broadcasters, it often still depends on the time slot from which pot of money a fictional production is financed. In the case of event programmes beyond established broadcasting slots or across them, often funds from different budgets have to be combined.[27] Against this background, it is plausible that many producers, despite today's possibility of online distribution, continued to uphold linearity and repeatedly demanded additional broadcasting slots for 'quality dramas' that they missed in the existing broadcasting schemes.[28]

Alongside the related diagnosis that "the linear [. . .] predominates",[29] or at least is highly relevant that of a caesura and a transformation is also to be found: "We stand on the ridge between linear and non-linear, we stand, so to speak, between the

---

[26]Cf. on a linking of television and actor-network theory, e.g. Teurlings (2013).

[27]Cf. e.g. Interview 15 with Johanna Kraus, commissioning editor, MDR, Berlin, 25 Oct 2018 and Interview [11] with Gebhard Henke, then Head of Programming, WDR, Cologne, 8 Mar 2018. See also panel discussion "Redakteur_innen in der öffentlich-rechtlichen Fernsehindustrie: Produktionskulturen und -praktiken", Jahrestagung der Gesellschaft für Medienwissenschaft 2018 "Industrie", University of Siegen, 28 Sept 2018.

[28]Cf. e.g. interview 3 with Ulrike Leibfried, freelance producer and former editor of RTL, Berlin 16 Jun 2016 or interview 5 with Bernhard Gleim, former editor, NDR, Hamburg, 1 Jul 2016.

[29]Claudia Simionescu in interview 18 with her and Harald Steinwender, commissioning editors, Bayerischer Rundfunk, Munich, 7 Nov 2018.

old and the new television",[30] stated for example (similarly to a number of televi-sion scholars[31]) Martina Zöllner, the head of the *documentary and fiction* program-ming department at the local broadcaster RBB—Rundfunk Berlin-Brandenburg, part of the ARD—Arbeitsgemeinschaft der öffentlich-rechtlichen Rundfunkanstalten (Consortium of the public-law broadcasting institutions). Fol-lowing her assessment, we are currently in a milestone moment of television history in which temporary dispositif structures of television such as the "temporal lineari-zation"[32] are in a state of flux. Historical perspectives became visible in the discussions of such a change and the former or previous characteristics of television. One commissioning editor also touched upon Raymond William's concept of *flow*,[33] demonstrating his knowledge in media/television studies to me, the scholar. Beyond the 'ordinary' television forming one flow, several practitioners turned to individual works in (West-) German history.

Serial Quality Programs in Television History

The practitioners particularly highlighted West-German 'quality dramas' from the 1970s and 1980s: for example *Acht Stunden sind kein Tag* (*Eight Hours Don't Make a Day*, 1972, ARD/WDR), *Rote Erde* ('Red Earth', 1983, ARD/WDR), *Heimat* (1984, ARD/WDR/SFB), *Monaco Franze—Der ewige Stenz* (*Monaco Franze—Eternal Dandy*, 1981–1983, ARD/BR) or the multi-part television version of the 'amphibian' film[34] *Das Boot* (1981/1985, ARD).[35] With such examples, the interviewees accentuated the former heterogeneity of TV drama in the (West-)

---

[30]Interview 16 with Martina Zöllner, Head of Programming, *Documentary and Fiction*, rbb, Berlin, 26.10.2018.

[31]Cf. e.g. Lotz (2009).

[32]Hickethier (2009), p. 286.

[33]Williams (1974).

[34]Cf. Rohrbach (2009). Günther Rohrbach, head of the television drama department at WDR from 1965 to 1979, referred to films that were intended from the outset for exploitation in cinema *and* television as "amphibious films". For various feature films (in addition to *Das Boot, for* example, *Der Baader Meinhof Komplex, The Baader Meinhof Complex*, 2008), there are also multi-part television versions with smooth transitions to the television series.

[35]Cf. e.g. interviews 5, 11 and 18 as well as interview 22 with Bernd Lange, screenwriter, Berlin, 21 Nov 2018.

German context[36] or the high budgeting of former productions.[37] Partly, the television professionals also criticized the historical amnesia and Anglo-American-centrism of the current discourse on 'quality TV' and opposed the impression that there is per se a quality deficit in German-language television fiction and, beyond the daily and weekly soap, no tradition of serial, cross-episode storytelling.[38] However, references to former 'classics' also served practitioners to classify the television fiction of the past as "a little further ahead", in the sense of being more courageous or relevant than the current or recent productions..[39] Linked to their retrospective view on German television history, the practitioners made out a "cultural change"[40] and "paradigm shift",[41] towards programmes, which increasingly oriented towards mass compatibility and only very little genres. The practitioners dated this narrowing, in which "pre-formatted broadcasting slots"[42] with certain 'colours' became decisive, above all in the 1980s and 90s,[43] when the advertising-financed broadcasters came up in German television and fundamentally changed the dispositif of television.[44] "Then came the private broadcasters and this unspeakable urge [of the public broadcasters] not to begrudge the private broadcasters any ground by lowering the level themselves",[45] criticised Hanno Hackfort, one of the three head writers of the recent 'quality TV' project *4 Blocks* (2017–2019, TNT Serie).

Gebhard Henke, head of the programming division of WDR—Westdeutscher Rundfunk (West German Broadcasting Cologne) until 2018, interpreted the shift towards "lightly entertaining formats" in the 1980s and 1990s transnationally, attributing it, among other things, to US imports: Through the big hits *Dallas* (1978–1991, CBS) and *Dynasty* (1981–1989, ABC), but also the high ratings for the first broadcast of *Pretty Woman* (1989)[46] on ARD's national programme Das

---

[36]Cf. interview 18.

[37]Cf. interview 23 with Gabriela Sperl, producer, Wiedemann & Berg, Berlin, 22 Nov 2018.

[38]Cf. e.g. interviews 5 and 18.

[39]Interview 4 with Martin Rauhaus, screenwriter, Berlin (telephone), 16 Jun 2016.

[40]Interview 11.

[41]Ibid.

[42]Interview 10 with screenwriters Bob Konrad, Hanno Hackfort, and Richard Kropf, Berlin, 14 Feb 2018.

[43]Cf. Ibid., and interview 11.

[44]Cf. Hickethier (1998), p. 414.

[45]Hanno Hackfort in interview 10.

[46]Cf. Backen (2008), p. 114.

Erste, "the sophisticated television play and also the sophisticated drama series went to the dogs, so to speak[.]"[47] Here, unlike in the current enthusiasm for US 'quality TV', US productions do not necessarily appear as a competing model of higher quality, but also as a potentially problematic influence, similar to earlier considerations: "At the time, US series were regarded exclusively as prime examples of the trivial and the ideological, especially by the feuilleton and media studies",[48] Dietrich Leder has summarized prevailing views from the heyday of *Dallas* and *Dynasty*.

The industry discourse on 'quality TV' also revolved around the past of US series and their influence on German-language television fiction when the practitioners, like various voices from academia,[49] television critic and feature pages,[50] noted a "qualitative leap"[51] of US productions in the 2000s and repeatedly cited well-known 'prototypes' that can now almost be called historical television, such as *The Sopranos* (1999–2007, HBO), *Mad Men* (2007–2015, AMC) or *Six Feet Under* (2001–2005, HBO). In respect to these shows, the practitioners did not only discuss innovations in dramaturgy and narration, but also addressed the broadcasting in linear, German-language television. In this context, these 'quality' serials were almost invisible or unsuccessful (measured by quantitative viewer ratings).[52] Commissioning editors from public-service fiction also diagnosed the more general disappearance of US series from the prime time and the early evening slots in Das Erste, the first channel by ARD, and in ZDF—Zweites Deutsches Fernsehen (Second German Television). This absence of US imports might have made the linear broadcast of more recent 'quality dramas' more difficult in the public-service programme.[53]

The interviewees highlighted other individual productions and phenomena from the young television past, mainly the German crime serials *Im Angesichts des Verbrechens* (*In the face of* crime, 2010) and *KDD—Kriminaldauerdienst* (*KDD—Berlin Crime Squad*, 2007–2009, ZDF),[54] but also the largely forgotten

---

[47] Interview 11.

[48] Leder (2015).

[49] Cf. e.g. Nesselhauf and Schleich (2016) and Ernst and Paul (2015).

[50] Cf. e.g. Diez and Hüetlin (2013) or Förster (2014).

[51] Interview 1 with Gunther Eschke, at the time of the interview Development Producer at Real Film Berlin, Berlin, 6 Oct 2015.

[52] Cf. inter alia Ibid., and interviews 5 and 16.

[53] Cf. e.g. Interview 5.

[54] Cf. e.g. Ibid., interviews 3, 18 and 9.

Sat.1 drama *Blackout—Die Erinnerung ist tödlich* (2006).[55] All these shows were former attempts from Germany to tie in with US 'quality TV' and to implement serial, 'complex' storytelling across several episodes or even seasons in the crime genre.[56] Sometimes, the producers also referred to individual serials with their own involvement, which contain at least some basic features of what they considered to be 'quality TV' ingredients (such as cross-episode storylines).[57] The practitioners were also interested in drama productions that, according to them, expanded broadcasting schedules, such as the Tuesday prime time slot for series on ARD's main channel Das Erste (see. *Weissensee*, 2010–, ARD/MDR),[58] or that were different from other series through their experimental character, such as the midlife crisis drama *Zeit der Helden* ('Time of Heroes', 2013, ARD/SWR/Arte), in which the time of the plot corresponded with the broadcast date.[59]

On several occasions, however, the interviewees tended to describe the television film as more experimental, whether in earlier productions such as *Das Millionenspiel* ('The Game of Millions', 1970, ARD/WDR) or in the present, just as they repeatedly emphasise the quality and continuing relevance of single TV films in German-language television fiction.[60]

The Television Film as a Central Programming Trend

"Why does one [. . .] actually despise the tradition of the television film, which the Americans [. . .] do not have at all? We have, so to speak, high quality [. . . .], which is not the same as bad, and series are not the same as good", argued Gebhard Henke.[61] The heyday of the television film and argumentation patterns according to which it is more progressive in form and content than the serial "long-form drama"[62] can also be found in other national contexts such as former British television.[63] But in the German-speaking market in particular, the development

---

[55] Cf. Schawinski (2008), pp. 96–119.
[56] Cf. Rothemund (2012).
[57] Cf. e.g. interview 5.
[58] Cf. interview 15.
[59] Cf. interview 16.
[60] Cf. interview 4.
[61] Interview 11.
[62] Creeber (2004), p. 1.
[63] Cf. Ibid.

does not seem to have proceeded as Robin Nelson describes it—away from the "television play" to the "flexi-narrative",[64] which mixes *serial* and *series*, and from here on to the "long-form high-end drama series".[65] Despite the sporadic crisis,[66] the television film continues to be present, anchored by diverse broadcast slots, and thus shapes the work as well as the argumentation of many television creators in Germany.[67] The single TV film is also inscribed in television fiction through the continuing tradition of the *Reihe*. The most prominent and popular example of such a hybrid form of television film and series, the only partially serialized *Tatort* ('Crime scene', 1970–, ARD/ORF/SRF),[68] was considered by several interviewees to be the 'quality TV' in the German/German-speaking context.[69]

Traits of the television film can also be seen in multi-part films (so-called *Mehrteiler*, comprising two or three 90-min parts). They point towards historically evolved programme structures, which numerous German 'quality TV' projects (such as *Ku'damm 56/59/63*, 2016/2018/2021, ZDF), in the tradition of the "historical-political event film[s]",[70] tie in with. The associated limitation of the number of episodes as well as the focus on historical themes and the event character are sometimes criticized,[71] just as various TV professionals generally regarded the 90 minute-long episodes between TV film and series as anachronistic, conservative, or as a provincial German *Sonderweg*.[72] The fact that the discourse on 'quality TV' in the German industry is interwoven with that on television films is also shown by the fact that, depending on one's point of view, the loss of meaning of the single TV film is feared, demanded or at least stated.[73] Jörg Winger, producer and writer of *Deutschland 83/86/89* (2015–2020, RTL/Amazon Prime), considered the "quality drama series [. . .] both creatively and economically"[74] superior and interpreted the long-standing tendency towards the single play in terms of cultural history:

---

[64] Nelson (2013), p. 26.

[65] Ibid., p. 27.

[66] Cf. Wiebel and Schneider (2018).

[67] Cf. e.g. interviews 11, 18 and 4.

[68] Cf. Göbel-Stolz (2016).

[69] Cf. interviews 3 and 15.

[70] Dörner (2012), see also Cooke (2016).

[71] Cf. interview 10 and interview 2 with Stefan Stuckmann, screenwriter, Berlin, 13 May 2016.

[72] Cf. in particular interviews 10 and 24.

[73] Cf. interview 6 with Jörg Winger, producer/showrunner, Berlin, 15 May 2017 as well as interviews 11 and 24.

[74] Interview 6.

> We [come] from a television film tradition, which has to do with the value pyramid in Germany [. . .] the cinema film was [actually always the supreme discipline], then the television film with some distance and then nothing for a long time and then the series as a commodity [. . .] if you sort it from E [E-Kultur, 'serious culture'] to U [U-Kultur, Unterhaltung, entearnment], clearly at the U [Unterhaltung, entertainment].[75]

Bernhard Gleim, a former commissioning editor at NDR—Norddeutscher Rundfunk (Northern German Broadcasting), a member of the ARD consortium, similarly noted a traditionally marginal role of the series compared to the TV film and saw the reasons for this in the "inability to integrate entertainment [into a cultural concept]".[76] The "German culture",[77] which the interviewee identified in this context, derived from its Anglo-American counterpart. Paraphrasing his former superior, he contrasted Goethe and Shakespeare:

> If you want to know what German television is like, then you have to look at what the two great classics [from] England and Germany look like. Goethe is educational theatre, so to speak, and Shakespeare integrates elements of popular theatre to a significant degree.[78]

According to Gleim, the low reputation of the television series stemming from this tradition was reflected in its former dominant environment, the public-service *Vorabend*, the access prime time, where in contrast to other public-service slots advertisement is shown. Series in this context offered advertisers "something like regularity",[79] but through the commercial background this segment of public-service drama was also outsourced to a certain extent. Internally at the public-service broadcaster, early evening commercial television had been described as a "hooker" who "goes out on the street so that the brother can study."[80] The brother—that's presumably the TV film on the main evening. In the saying, whose idiom seems to belong to a certain time and in which gendered production cultures are hinted at, the low status of the series compared to the television film once again came to light.

---

[75] Ibid.

[76] Interview 5.

[77] Ibid.

[78] Ibid.

[79] Ibid.

[80] Ibid.

In addition to the tendency towards the single TV film, the producers negotiated traditional narrative styles with regard to the programmes. Dramaturg and development producer Gunther Eschke attested to "German series" in comparison to contemporary US series "a consonance. You kind of think: they run like this, they don't get you fired up."[81] Similarly, editor Gleim attributed series from Germany to having served for a long time only the "viewers' need for harmonization".[82] The design of the fictional, serial program is connected with orientations towards the viewer, which in Hickethier's model decisively co-structures the television dispositif. In the following, I consider viewers primarily from the perspective of the producers: as their construction,[83] as target groups to be conquered and determined again and again, and as a central theme in their discourse on 'quality TV' in the history of television.

Viewers

Again and again, television professionals attributed the state of television drama to audience orientations in the past and present. Linked to the assumption that audience tastes have evolved historically is the discussion of the extent to which viewers can be 'educated'.[84] With regard to his (then) working environment, the ARD, the NDR editor Gleim emphasised above all the target group policy under Günther Struve (ARD's programme director from 1992 to 2008):

> Struwe countered the 14- to 49-year-old target group [...] with a look at the actual demographics in Germany [...] through the Degeto films on Fridays, the famous *Neubauer-Schinken* [Neubauer films] [...] this has also shaped the German series in a certain way. You can see that very clearly in the Tuesday slot. [...] the central pattern of this Tuesday series is that a middle-aged woman loses her husband and then has a new existence.[85]

In addition to the former program director, the statement contains other references to the more recent television past: to the long-time core target group of advertising-financed private television, 14- to 49-year-olds; to broadcast schedules, including

---

[81] Interview 1.

[82] Interview 5.

[83] Cf. Ang (1996 and 2001).

[84] Cf. e.g. interview 10.

[85] Interview 5.

the Tuesday night, to this day the only prime-time slot on ARD's national channel Das Erste for 45-minute series; and to Degeto television films. At times associated primarily with actress Christine Neubauer and melodrama, the ARD subsidiary Degeto was considered by the feuilleton to be a "Schnulzenfrabrik", a factory for weepies.[86] The corresponding valence is also noticeable in Gleim's talk of "Neubauer-Schinken", referring to films of low artistic value with the actor Christine Neubauer. The criticism thus also refers to 'female' connoted content and genres. Does Gleim continue the familiar pattern of devaluing 'female' culture here,[87] especially since he does not criticize the omnipresence of the crime genre (in contrast to other voices in Germany's feature pages and in the television industry[88])? More specifically, the interviewee referred to the tonality of ARD's Tuesday series, which has evolved in the course of time: These series have been shaped by productions such as the nuns' comedy *Um Himmels Willen* ("For Heaven's Sake", 2002–2020, ARD/MDR) or the subsequently broadcast weekly procedural *In aller Freundschaft* ("In all friendship", 1998–, ARD/MDR); according to Gleim, these series show "connections to the German Heimatfilm"[89] in post-war West Germany and primarily appeal to an older audience.

The dramaturge Gunther Eschke also dealt with past target group orientations, but his central point of reference were the advertising-financed channels, including his former employer Sat.1: "For far too long, there was such a focus on a main-stream, [...] a conservative basic approach, [...] it went well for a long time, ratings-wise. But at some point [...] not anymore",[90] he stated and problematized the US-centricity of the commercial mainstream channels in Germany the 2000s, after contrary developments in the 1990s[91]: In view of ratings successes like *House, M.D.* (2004–2012, Fox) or *CSI: Crime Scene Investigation* (USA 2000–2015), RTL and Sat.1 now relied primarily on U.S. imports, which are significantly cheaper than German originals commissioned to independent or affiliated production companies. However, procedurals with one case per episode, which work well in linear broad-cast,[92] became bit by bit more seldom in contemporary US drama. "At some point,

---

[86]Bergmann (2012).

[87]Cf. Hipfl (1995), pp. 155–156. See also interviews 4 and 11.

[88]Cf. Herzog (2012).

[89]Interview 5.

[90]Interview 1.

[91]Cf. Windeler et al. (2001), p. 96.

[92]Cf. Eschke and Bohne (2010), p. 141.

though, the supply broke off there [. . .] [in] this mainstream segment,"[93] Eschke
argued. His diagnosis points to transnational and economic aspects of the German
industry discourse on 'quality TV' drama as well as to influences by the historical
developments in US TV drama. The current need for German series results not least
from developments on the US market. In particular, practitioners from the commercial broadcasters, which at the time of the interviews still mostly focussed on a
'linear' distribution, described current US network series as meanwhile too 'niche',
too complex and serialized and partly also as too much oriented towards 'diversity'.[94] The latter point of criticism probably refers to the German mainstream
audience traditionally addressed by the commercial broadcasters: according to the
external attributions of the producers, which are only hinted at here, the German
majority is not very interested in the representation of certain minorities. Indeed,
several US hit series with a 'diverse' or specifically African-American cast were
hardly successful in the linear, 'free-TV' broadcasting in Germany.[95]

A lack of supply in German serials—as Eschke and other interviewees
suggested—also affected the creatives—whether because they and the emerging
talents have been neglected thanks to the temporary focus on US imports[96] or
because the mediocre quality of German-language television fiction has also left
its mark on the practitioners in a bad sense.[97] More generally, in their discourse on
'quality TV' drama, the TV professionals repeatedly touched on production in
addition to *viewers* and *programming*, the two decisive dispositif structures of
television according to Hickethier's model, and attributed current problems in
German TV fiction to historically evolved production cultures.

Production Cultures

The production culture that has developed over time in the script development for
TV in Germany generally consists of writers working on single scripts for episodes
or television films individually and independently of one another. They "sometimes

---

[93] Interview 1.

[94] Cf. protocol for participant observation at the series-specific industry workshop *Winterclass
Serial Writing and Producing of* the Erich Pommer Institut, Potsdam 2017.

[95] Cf. e.g. the ProSieben broadcasts of *This Is Us* (2016–2022, NBC) and *Empire* (2015–2020,
Fox).

[96] Cf. interview 1.

[97] Cf. interview 10.

write an episode for *SOKO* [a popular crime procedural with local spin-offs by public-service channel ZDF] or are on a children's series and so on,"[98] editor Gleim described the long-standing practice. Economically speaking, it is therefore necessary for the scriptwriters to work on different projects in parallel. Gleim explained:

> A writer who concentrates entirely on this work for a period of time—that would be necessary for such a writers' room—under [. . .] the guidance of a head writer [. . .]: That is very difficult to establish in Germany, also because of the production conditions for writers [. . .] one would actually have to pay the writers according to a different scheme[.]

The predominant and traditional scheme lies in the payment of individual scripts,[99] with the exception of alternative payment models for story editors in the daily or weekly soap production.[100] Beyond this specific production area, the writers' room, the collective script development under the leadership of a showrunner that characterizes the US series production,[101] is increasingly used, but often only in a rudimentary form.[102] Often, a collaborative series development through several writers over a longer period of time seems too costly,[103] and the historically developed way of writing TV drama in Germany is too divergent. Also, regarding writers and their remuneration, one can again find the tendency towards the 'single piece', which comes not only in the form of television films, but also in largely self-contained episodes (as in the *SOKO* format cited by Gleim, 1978–, ZDF). By contrast, writers' activities that span several episodes or follow the submission of a single script are often insufficiently remunerated or not planned in the production process.[104] Various practitioners linked shortcomings of scriptwriting in Germany when it comes to developing serial, cross-episode and character-centred storylines to the tradition of individual work.[105]

---

[98] Interview 5.

[99] Cf. also interview 10.

[100] Cf. Knöhr (2018) and Kirsch (2001).

[101] Cf. Phalen and Osellame (2012).

[102] Cf. Krauß (2018a, b).

[103] Cf. interviews 1, 3, 7, 24 and transcripts of the *Winterclass Serial Writing and Producing,* Potsdam 2017 and 2018.

[104] Cf. inter alia interviews 1 and 10. See also Schlütz: *Quality-TV als Unterhaltungsphänomen,* p. 85.

[105] Cf. esp. interview 5 and interview 8 with Benjamin Harris, head of the *Serial Eyes* programme at DFFB Berlin, Berlin, 8 Jan 2018.

In addition, the TV professionals regarded the ongoing relevance of the single TV film to be decisive for the important status of the director,[106] which historical studies on film and television production in Europe prove in general.[107] Winger argued, from his own position as a producer/writer, that "directors [. . .] wear the hat creatively in film. [. . .] You can't do that with a series and that's why we [. . .] haven't had quality series for so long[.]"[108] The diagnosis of a traditional production culture is accompanied here by the demand for change. More generally in the present, long-standing arrangements in production and project networks[109] of the German TV industry are now up for renegotiation.[110]

In particular, the strong editorial support from the broadcasters has been criticised publicly[111] and within the industry.[112] The traditional selection power of the broadcasters[113] and the supremacy of the public broadcasters, by far the most important commissioners, play a central role in this context. Several[114] practitioners regarded the federal structures of the ARD, which are rooted in the German history of television, as a particular challenge: they lead to slow processes and an often problematic polyphony in the production process. The "one vision"[115] associated with 'quality TV' is hampered by editorial guidelines on target groups, programme schemes and formulas, creatives complained.[116] The evil of 'editor's television' (*Redakteursfernsehen*) and the salvation of 'creative freedom' thus form central argumentation patterns and myths in the German industry discourse on 'quality TV' drama.

From concrete case studies and conversations with individual production participants, however, a more differentiated picture emerged, according to which

---

[106] Cf. interview 6.

[107] Cf. Kasten (1994) and Szczepanik (2013).

[108] Interview 6.

[109] Cf. Windeler et al. (2001).

[110] Cf. e.g. the initiative Kontrakt'18 and on this Gangloff (2016).

[111] Cf. Gangloff (2016).

[112] Cf. notes on the *Winterclass Serial Writing and Producing*, Potsdam 2015. See on industry discourses on the activities of editors also Krauß (2019a, b).

[113] Cf. Windeler et al. (2001), p. 102.

[114] Cf. Hickethier (1998), p. 64.

[115] Cf. Redvall (2013).

[116] Cf. inter alia interviews 1, 2 and 10 as well as Krauß: "Die Stadt und die Macht: A Production Study of a German mini-series".

commissioning editors fight for specific projects[117] or producers and creatives considered feedback from the outside to be quite enriching.[118] Some producers even gained positive aspects from the long-standing constancy of the editors in the public broadcasters; after all, this personnel continuity in the dispositif of television leads to a certain reliability, transparency and the option of linking up with past project networks,[119] unlike in the case of the new transnational SVOD providers, who often operate in a shielded manner. The "network of media institutions",[120] which, according to Hickethier, helps to structure the television dispositif, is becoming more heterogeneous in the present—as are the production cultures.

Outlook

In recent years, the TV landscape has transformed into a "multiplatform digital landscape",[121] which includes US-dominated SVOD and pay-tv providers, telecommunications companies as well as online services from established broadcasters. The circle of programme providers who broadcast fictional television series and therefore have them commissioned has therefore expanded considerably. Production companies and freelancers now potentially have more commissioners, distributors and financiers at their disposal, so that the long-standing "power asymmetry between broadcasters and producers"[122] is no longer equally valid. Power distributions are also shifting as new collaborations emerge, away from the 100 per cent financing through the commissioner and the so-called total buyout to the broadcaster.[123] In addition to unusual gatherings, as in the case of *Babylon Berlin* (2017–, ARD/Sky Germany), transnational networking can be detected (see e.g. the German-Romanian co-production *Hackerville*, 2018, HBO Europe/TNT Series).

However, long-standing production cultures, programme schedules and tendencies as well as target group orientations are not rendered obsolete ad hoc by new networks, new programme providers and individual 'quality TV' projects.

---

[117] Cf. interview 3, 6 and interview 17 with Florian Cossen, director, Berlin, 30 Oct 2018.

[118] Cf. notes of the *Winterclass Serial Writing and Producing,* Potsdam 2018.

[119] Cf. Windeler et al. (2001).

[120] Hickethier (2009), p. 279.

[121] Bennett (2016), p. 124.

[122] Windeler/Lutz/Wirth: "Netzwerksteuerung durch Selektion", p. 102.

[123] Cf. interviews 5, 11 and 16.

In view of institutional and personnel connections between 'old' and 'new' actors and the continuing importance of ARD and ZDF as central commissioners, it is rather obvious that historically grown dispositif structures continue to be formative. The danger of the 'quality TV' centricity lies in ignoring such traditions as well as a large part of German-language television fiction. Television films, hybrids of them and series as well as crime procedurals with one main case in each episode continue to occupy a central space in German TV drama. As "bread-and-butter series",[124] long and frequent running procedurals enable broadcasters and production companies to produce more cost-intensive 'quality' projects. The fact that the televisual (das *Televisuelle*) remains relevant is also emphasized by the practitioners when they repeatedly touched on television history in their current discourse on 'quality TV'.

References

Anderson, Benedict (2005) Die Erfindung der Nation. Zur Karriere eines folgenreichen Konzepts. Frankfurt a. M./New York, Campus

Ang, Ien (1996). Living Room Wars. Rethinking Media Audiences for a Postmodern World. London/New York, Routledge

Ang, Ien (2001). Zuschauer, verzweifelt gesucht. In: Adelmann, Ralf, Jan O. Hesse, Judith Keilbach, Markus Stauff, Matthias Thiele (Eds.) Grundlagentexte zur Fernsehwissenschaft. Theorie, Geschichte, Analyse. Konstanz, UVK Verlagsgesellschaft, pp. 454–483

Backen, Inga (2008). Theorie und Praxis des Kinofilmmarketing. Professionelles Marketing durch Produktions- und Verleihunternehmen. Berlin, Bertz + Fischer

Banks, Miranda J., Bridget Conor, Vicki Mayer (2016). Preface. In: Banks, Miranda, Bridget Conor, Vicki Mayer (Eds.) Production Studies, the Sequel! Cultural Studies of Global Media Industries. New York/London, New York University Press, pp. ix–xv

Bennett, James (2016) Public Service as Production Cultures. A Contingent, Conjunctural Compact. In: Banks, Miranda, Bridget Conor, Vicki Mayer (Eds.) Production Studies, the Sequel! Cultural Studies of Global Media Industries. New York University Press, New York/London, pp. 123–137

Bergmann, Jens (2012) Degeto Film: ‚Alles wird gut'. In: brandeins 14, no. 6, https://www.brandeins.de/magazine/brand-eins-wirtschaftsmagazin/2012/risiko/alles-wird-gut (Accessed on 04 Dec 2018)

Blanchet, Robert (2010) Serielle Formen: Von den frühen Film-Serials zu aktuellen Quality-TV- und Onlineserien. Marburg, Schüren

Bleicher, Joan Kristinl Rolf Großmann, Gerd Hallenberger, Helmut Schanze (1993) Deutsches Fernsehen im Wandel. Perspektiven 1985—1992. Siegen, Universität Siegen

---

[124]Interview 5, see also interview 9.

Bruun, Hanne (2016) The Qualitative Interview in Media Production Studies. In: Paterson, Chris, David Lee, Anamik Saha, Anna Zoellner (Eds.) Advancing Media Production Research. Shifting Sites, Methods, and Politics. Houndmills/Basingstoke/Hampshire, Palgrave Macmillan, pp. 131–146

Caldwell, John T. (2008) Production Culture. Industrial Reflexivity and Critical Practice in Film and Television. Durham, Duke University Press

Castendyk, Oliver, Klaus Goldhammer (2012) Die Produzentenstudie. Daten und Fakten zur Film- und TV-Produktionsbranche in Deutschland (Zusammenfassung). In: Funkkorrespondenz 50, pp. 3–14

Cooke, Paul (2016) Heritage, Heimat, and the German Historical 'Event Television'. Nico Hoffmann's teamWorx. In: Powell, Larson, Robert R. Shandley (Eds.) German Television. Historical and Theoretical Approaches. New York, Berghahn Books, pp. 175–192

Creeber, Glen (2004) Serial Television. Big Drama on the Small Screen. London, BFI Publishing

Dasgupta, Sudeep (2012) Policing the People. Television Studies and the Problem of 'Quality'. In: NECSUS. European Journal of Media Studies, 1, https://necsus-ejms.org/policing-the-people-television-studies-and-the-problem-of-quality-by-sudeep-dasgupta/. Accessed 04 Dec 2018

Diez, Georg, Thomas Hüetlin (2013) Im Zauderland. In: Der Spiegel 67, no. 5 (28 Jan 2013), pp. 130–133

DJ Frederiksson (Anonymus) (2014). "Die ausbleibende Revolution," https://d-trick.de/, 04 Feb 2014, https://d-trick.de/wp-content/uploads/die_ausbleibende_revolution.pdf (Accessed on 04 Dec 2018)

Dörner, Andreas (2012) Geschichtsfernsehen und der historisch-politische Eventfilm in Deutschland. In: Dörner, Andreas, Andreas Vogt (Eds.) Unterhaltungsrepublik Deutschland. Medien, Politik und Entertainment. Bonn, Bundeszentrale für politische Bildung, pp. 82–95

Ernst, Christoph, Heike Paul (2015) Amerikanische Fernsehserien der Gegenwart. Perspektiven der American Studies und der Media Studies. Bielefeld, Transcript Verlag

Eschke, Gunther, Rudolf Bohne (2010) Bleiben Sie dran! Dramaturgie von TV-Serien. Konstanz, UVK Verlagsgesellschaft

Feuer, Jane, Paul Kerr, Tise Vahimagi (1984). MTM. Quality Television. London, British Film Institute

Förster, Jochen (2014) Wir Serienmuffel. In: brandeins 16, no. 3, pp. 18–25, https://www.brandeins.de/magazine/brand-eins-wirtschaftsmagazin/2014/beobachten/wir-serienmuffel. Accessed 22 Jul 2019

Gangloff, Tilmann P. (2016) Die Angst der Redakteure. Warum es bestimmte Drehbuchideen hierzulande grundsätzlich schwer haben. In: TV Diskurs 77, pp. 102–107

Göbel-Stolz, Bärbel (2016) Once Upon A Time. Tatort, Germany's Longest Running Police Procedural. In: Powell, Larson, Robert R. Shandley (Eds.) German Television. Historical and Theoretical Approaches. New York, pp. 193–231

Hahn, Sönke (2013) Ich schaue kein Fernsehen, nur Qualitätsserien! Hintergründe eines kontroversen Begriffs und Beispiele qualitativer, serieller Produkte und Tendenzen aus Deutschland. In: Journal of Serial Narration on Television 2, pp. 11–26

Herzog, Katja (2012) Deutschland, deine Krimileichen. In: Institut für Medien- und Kommunikationspolitik (Eds.) Jahrbuch Fernsehen 2012, https://www.jahrbuch-fernsehen.de/datenbank/essays/2012/essay-2-katja-herzog.html. Accessed 04 Dec 2018

Hickethier, Knut (2009) Dispositiv Fernsehen. Skizze eines Modells (1995). In: Grisko, Michael (Ed.) Texte zur Theorie und Geschichte des Fernsehens. Stuttgart, J.B. Metzler, pp. 270–293

Hickethier, Knut (1998). Geschichte des deutschen Fernsehens (cooperation: Peter Hoff). Stuttgart, Reclam

Hipfl, Brigitte (1995) Zuschauen, Rezipieren, Partizipieren? Ein Forschungsbericht. In: Hipfl, Brigitte, Frigga Haug (Eds.) Sündiger Genuß? Filmerfahrungen von Frauen. Hamburg, Argument Verlag, pp. 148–171

Hißnauer, Christian, Stefan Scherer, Claudia Stockinger (2014) Zwischen Serie und Werk. Fernseh- und Gesellschaftsgeschichte im Tatort. Bielefeld, Transcript Verlag

Hißnauer, Christian, Thomas Klein (2012) Einleitung. In: Hißnauer, Christian, Thomas Klein (Eds.) Klassiker der Fernsehserie. Stuttgart, J.B. Metzler, pp. 7–26

Kasten, Jürgen (1994) Der Drehbuchautor in der Filmproduktion—Ein historischer Abriss und ein aktueller Ausblick. In: Berg, Jan, Knut Hickethier (Eds.) Filmproduktion, Filmförderung, Filmfinanzierung. Berlin, Edition Sigma, pp. 133–149

Keilbach, Judith, Markus Stauff (2011) Fernsehen als fortwährendes Experiment. Über die permanente Erneuerung eines alten Mediums. In: Elia-Borer, Nadja, Ralf Adelmann (Eds.) Blickregime und Dispositive audiovisueller Medien. Bielefeld, Transcript Verlag, pp. 155–181

Kirsch, Gunther (2001) Produktionsbedingungen von Daily Soaps. Ein Werkstattbericht. In: Montage AV 10, no. 1, pp. 45–54

Klug, Daniel (2016) Scripted Reality: Fernsehrealität zwischen Fakt und Fiktion. Perspektiven auf Produkt, Produktion und Rezeption. Baden-Baden, Nomos

Knöhr, Nathalie (2018) Neues aus der Soap Factory. Ethnografisches Forschen in der deutschen Fernsehindustrie. In: Navigationen 18, no. 2, pp. 7–25

Krauß, Florian (2018a) Im Angesicht der 'Qualitätsserie'. Produktionskulturen in der deutschen Fernsehserienindustrie. In: Navigationen 18, no. 2, pp. 47–66

Krauß, Florian (2018b) Showrunner und Writers' Room. Produktionspraktiken der deutschen Serienindustrie. In: montage AV 27, no. 2, pp. 95–109

Krauß, Florian (2019a) 'All is changing': Interview with Joachim Kosack on Deutschland83 and Transformations of the German TV Series Industry. In: SERIES. International Journal of TV Serial Narratives 5, no. 1, pp. 69–74

Krauß, Florian (2019b) Deutsche Fernsehfiktion und Redaktionsarbeit im Wandel. In: tv diskurs 23, no. 2, pp. 46–49

Krauß, Florian/Loist, Skadi (2018) Medienindustrieforschung im deutschsprachigen Raum. Einleitung. In: Navigationen 18, no. 2, pp. 7–25

Leder, Dietrich (2015) Als wäre es ein Weltwunder. Zur deutschen Begeisterung über die gegenwärtige Serien-Produktion in den USA. In: Medien Korrespondenz 24, 30 Nov 2015, https://www.medienkorrespondenz.de/leitartikel/artikel/als-waere-es-ein-weltwunder.html. Accessed 04 Dec 2018

Lotz, Amanda D. (2009) Beyond Prime Time. Television Programming in the Post-Network Era. New York, Routledge

Mayer, Vicki, Miranda J. Banks, John T. Caldwell (2009) Introduction. Production Studies: Roots and Routes. In: Banks, Miranda, Bridget Conor, Vicki Mayer (Eds.) Production Studies. Cultural Studies of Media Industries. New York, Routledge, pp. 1–12

McCabe, Janet/Akass, Kim (2007) Quality TV. Contemporary American television and beyond. London/New York, I.B. Tauris

Mikos, Lothar (2016) Germany as TV Show Import Market. In: Powell, Larson, Robert R. Shandley (Eds.) German Television. Historical and Theoretical Approaches. New York, Berghahn Books, pp. 155–174

Nelson, Robin (2013) Entwicklung der Geschichte. vom Fernsehspiel zur Hypermedia TV Narrative. In: Eichner, Susanne, Lothar Mikos, Rainer Winter (Eds.) Transnationale Serienkultur. Theorie, Ästhetik, Narration und Rezeption neuer Fernsehserien. Wiesbaden, Springer, pp. 21–43

Nesselhauf, Jonas, Markus Schleich (2016) Das andere Fernsehen?! Eine Bestandsaufnahme des "Quality Television". Bielefeld, Transcript Verlag

Phalen, Patricia, Julia Osellame (2012) Writing Hollywood. Rooms with a Point of View. In: Journal of Broadcasting & Electronic Media 56, no. 1, pp. 3–20

Redvall, Eva Novrup (2013) A European Take on the Showrunner? Danish Television Drama Production. In: Szczepanik, Petr, Patrick Vonderau (Eds.) Behind the Screen. Inside European Production Cultures. New York, Palgrave Macmillan, pp. 153–169

Rohrbach, Günter (2009) Das Subventions-TV. Ein Plädoyer für den amphibischen Film. In: Grisko, Michael (Ed.) Texte zur Theorie und Geschichte des Fernsehens. Stuttgart, Reclam, pp. 172–179

Rothemund, Kathrin (2012) KDD-Kriminaldauerdienst. Das Brüchige im Krimigenre. Berlin, Bertz + Fischer

Schawinski, Roger (2008) Die TV-Falle. Vom Sendungsbewusstsein zum Fernsehgeschäft. Reinbek bei Hamburg, Rowohlt

Schlütz, Daniela (2016) Quality-TV als Unterhaltungsphänomenen. Entwicklung, Charakteristika, Nutzung und Rezeption von Fernsehserien wie The Sopranos, The Wire oder Breaking Bad. Wiesbaden, Springer VS

Sudmann, Andreas (2017) Serielle Überbietung. Zur televisuellen Ästhetik und Philosophie exponierter Steigerungen. Stuttgart, J.B. Metzler

Szczepanik, Petr (2013) Wie viele Schritte bis zur Drehfassung? Eine politische Historiographie des Drehbuchs. In: montage AV 22, no. 1, pp. 102–136

Teurlings, Jan (2013) Unblackboxing Production. What Media Studies Can Learn From Actor-Network Theory. Amsterdam, Amsterdam University Press

Thompson, Robert J. (1996) Television's Second Golden Age. From Hill Street Blues to ER. New York, Continuum

Vonderau, Patrick (2013) Theorien zur Produktion: ein Überblick. In: montage AV 22, no. 1, pp. 9–32

Wiebel, Martin, Norbert Schneider (2018) "Man muss das System zum Tanzen bringen. Anmerkungen zur aktuellen Krise der fiktionalen Formate im öffentlich-rechtlichen Fernsehen. In: Medien Korrespondenz, 02 Aug 2018, https://www.medienkorrespondenz.de/leitartikel/artikel/man-muss-das-system-zum-tanzen-bringen.html. Accessed on 04 Dec 2018

Williams, Raymond (1974) Television. Technology and Cultural Form. London/New York, Routledge

Windeler, Arnold, Antje Lutz, Carsten Wirth (2001) Netzwerksteuerung durch Selektion. Die Produktion von Fernsehserien in Projektnetzwerken. In: montage AV 10, no. 1, pp. 91–124

Florian Krauß, Ph.D., research fellow at the University of Siegen, Germany, and visiting scholar at the universities Copenhagen, Bologna and Utrecht. He was previously a substitute professor in Media Literacy at the Technische Universität Dresden, a lecturer in Media Studies at the University of Siegen and research associate at the Film University Babelsberg KONRAD WOLF, Potsdam. He additionally works as a freelance script editor for Bayerischer Rundfunk (Bavarian Broadcasting), a member of the public-service ARD network. He is the co-editor of the anthologies *Teen TV* (2020) and *Drehbuchforschung* (*Screenwriting Research*, 2022). 2022 he received his 'habilitation' with the thesis *Quality Drama from Germany: Production Cultures, Narrative Styles and Television's Transformations* which will be published at Springer VS in 2023 and (in English) at Palgrave in 2024.

Television Series Against Late-modern Loneliness: Forms of Telemedial Communitization Using the Example of "13 Reasons Why"

Denis Newiak

For some time now, a striking preference for narratives and aesthetics of loneliness can be observed in serial fictional television entertainment—especially with the increasing popularity of streaming services such as Netflix and Amazon Prime. Numerous successful television series of the recent past are dominated by explorations of modern loneliness against the backdrop of increasing individualization, urbanization, and medialization, as they have decisively shaped life at least since the turn of the 1990s with the onset of late modernity: In the increasingly risky (Beck), accelerated (Rosa) and singularized (Reckwitz) societies of late modernity, communities have a hard time, so that the feeling of social disintegration and distance becomes a trademark of post-industrial 'highly developed' affluent societies.[1] While modernity can be characterised as an age of ever-increasing loneliness, the search for ways out of this 'social crisis' becomes a driving narrative and creative force in many art forms and not least in television series and the hyper-modernised characters who act in them. One need only think of the successful sitcoms of recent years, such as *The Big Bang Theory* (USA 2007–2019), *Two and a Half Men* (USA 2003–2015) and *How I Met Your Mother* (USA 2005–2014), which feed their cheerful narrative supply primarily from the countless (and only ultimately successful) efforts of their characters to establish sustainable relationships (in this case, partnerships) as a way out of their perceived loneliness. This paper will

---

[1] Cf. Beck (2007); Rosa (2013); Reckwitz (2017).

D. Newiak (✉)
Brandenburgische Technische Universität Cottbus-Senftenberg, Cottbus, Deutschland
e-mail: mail@denis-newiak.de

© The Author(s), under exclusive license to Springer Fachmedien Wiesbaden
GmbH, part of Springer Nature 2024
D. Newiak et al. (eds.), *Television Studies and Research on Series*,
https://doi.org/10.1007/978-3-658-42915-7_6

argue that television series at the same time actively produce their own specific communities—*in front of the screen.*

While the sitcom (and comic formats in general) are dominated by this pleasurable *communion* on 'eering ways', which requires loneliness as a dramaturgical premise and only resolves it in the finale, the characters in the contemporary drama television series of *Quality TV* usually go through an agonizing *loneliness* that becomes more and more crushing from episode to episode and hardly seems to stop in its tragic dynamic: In *Bates Motel* (USA 2013–2017), the world-famous up-and-coming motel manager, living in a tangled web of drug, arms and human trafficking, is left only with the 'emergency community' with *mother* as his only lifeline amidst increasingly complex and confusing late-modern conditions in the twenty-first century.[2] Similar forms of tragic spirals of late-modern loneliness (which not infrequently culminate in a catastrophic plot outcome) can be found not only in series of teen TV such as *The End of the F***ing World* (UK 2017–), *The Rain* (DK 2018–) and *The Society* (USA 2019–),[3] but across genres and audiences in formats ranging from *Breaking Bad* (USA 2008–2013) to *Designated Survivor* (USA 2016–2019) and *Black Mirror* (UK 2011–): Always dominant here, as Mácha identified it as early as 1968 as an "inner characteristic of industrial civilization," is an omnipresent and inescapable "sense of the individual existing in the web of social relations that are indifferent to him."[4]

Nietzsche was the first to anticipate the lonely consequences of modernization in their full scope: The growing complexity of the increasingly industrialized, urbanized, and technologized modern life challenged the hitherto unrestricted interpretive sovereignty of Christian morality as a whole, so that man at the beginning of modernity, while on the one hand gaining the freedoms arising with the secularized way of life, was at the same time exposed to a nihilistic deficit of meaning.[5]

The course of the twentieth century has, all in all, confirmed Nietzsche's interpretation of modernity as an epoch of growing loneliness: Rationalization and globalization, individualization and liberalization, medialization and digitalization are gradually dissolving the pre-modern communities of 'kinship, place and spirit' as Tönnies had described them in 1887, increasingly throwing modern man back on himself in a society driven by individual interests. [6]

---

[2]Cf. Newiak (2018).

[3]Cf. Newiak (2020).

[4]Mácha (1968) p. 294. My translation.

[5]Nietzsche ([1887] 1967) NF-1887,11[119]. My translation.

[6]Cf. Tönnies (1887).

For Fukuyama, modernity threatens to become the age of a Nietzschean "last man", who tries to make himself as comfortable as possible in his eternal lonely boredom,[7] but in fact, as Niethammer puts it, "threatens to become a degenerate, economically calculating, isolated and irresponsible individual"[8] For Bauman, as modernization progresses, society is increasingly transformed into a purely functional network of abstract relationships,[9] into a "swarm" of anonymous individuals, making them living in "times of staying together only 'until further notice' and as long (never longer) 'as the satisfaction lasts'."[10] For Giddens, traditional experiences of community such as the family, local togetherness, and transcendence increasingly dissolve in late modernity, leaving behind insecure individual subjects who hardly feel up to the demands of their life's reality.[11] While loneliness can generally be understood as "the agonizing awareness of an inner distance to other people and the accompanying longing for connectedness in satisfying, meaningful relationships",[12] in the following we will explicitly speak of *lonelinesses* in the plural in order to emphasize the multiplicity and complexity of the interlocking phenomena of modernization, which first lead to the typical late-modern "feeling of isolation and unbelonging",[13] which is articulated in television series.

This tendency of modernity to produce ever denser and harsher *lonelinesses* is also at the heart of four seasons of *13 Reasons Why* (USA 2017–2020): Hannah Baker, a student in a Californian high school, records on 13 sides of music cassettes her way of suffering. She narrates how she is subjected to constant meanness, bullying, and ultimately severe physical and sexual violence, in addition to age-typical and unavoidable misunderstandings and uncertainties. Through her 'Passion narrative', she is predominantly drawing a picture of a disoriented contemporary society, which is visibly overwhelmed by the specific challenges of modernization—with its tendency towards constant competition for wealth and relationships, the omnipresence of abstract communication technologies, the compulsion for spatial mobility and dynamically changing role expectations. Piece by piece, the last communities in the nuclear family, the clique and school collapse one after the other, not only for Hannah, but also for her classmates, teachers and

---

[7] Cf. Fukuyama (1992) p. 328.

[8] Niethammer, Dossmann (2000) p. 513. My translation.

[9] Cf. Bauman ([2003] 2014) pp. xi–xii.

[10] Bauman (2000) p. 41.

[11] Cf. Giddens (1991) pp. 33–34.

[12] Schwab (1997) p. 22. My translation.

[13] Adli (2017) pp. 228–229.

parents, until the resulting total abandonment in this narrative world offers only a seemingly logical way out: From the first cassette onwards, Hannah's suicide lies like a shadow of the highest possible loneliness over this television world, in which several tens of millions of people have probably participated at the same time in recent years.[14]

Dramaturgies of tragic loneliness and comic communion thus become the essential element of many serial worlds of contemporary television series.[15] But what is the origin of this increasing penetration of serial fictional television with questions of loneliness? Is the role of the contemporary television series exhausted in a 'neutral' representation of a general social change towards an increasingly isolated way of life in Western late modernity? Is the television series only a passive 'mirror of society'—or does television itself not rather actively participate in the processes of isolation and communalization? And if so, what exactly is the role and function of serial fictional television in this process?

Against the background of an intellectual history of modernity as an age of growing loneliness, television series such as *13 Reasons Why* can be seen as expressions of the processes of late-modern isolation alluded to. With the help of an interdisciplinary analysis along lines of discourse from television studies, media sociology, the sociology of knowledge, and social philosophy, however, I would like to show that the representations of loneliness produced by television series cannot simply be interpreted hermeneutically in a media-sociological sense as a "representation" of "excerpt[s] from social reality"[16] in which "social fears, desires, and interests are expressed".[17] Rather, within late-modern societies, television series themselves represent one of the most important instances that actively participate to a considerable degree in the modern processes of isolation and

---

[14]Official viewer figures are not available due to Netflix's corporate policy, but it is not disputed in the trade press that hardly any television series has attracted more attention and viewers in recent years than *13 Reasons Why*.

[15]The only exceptions are horror series such as *The Walking Dead* (USA 2010–2019, AMC), whose attractive horror arises precisely from the insurmountability of their structural loneliness and the resulting omnipresent danger, and daily soaps (which are losing popularity anyway in the age of streaming services), which, due to their 'endless' disposition, are dependent on a constant interplay between narratives of community and loneliness in order to maintain a sufficiently large supply of narration for its daily broadcast, which extends over decades, cf. Newiak, "Serial Horrors of Loneliness: The Impossibility of Communitization in The Walking Dead."

[16]Mikos (2010) p. 247. My translation.

[17]Balke (2015) p. 140. My translation.

communalization that are then aesthetically articulated in them. Whether in the form of collectively received, recited and revered cult series (Hills), through their seriality's predisposed ability to make social causation processes visible (Engell) and the production of temporal orders (Neverla), or through the behavioral offers they make for complex life situations in late-modern society (Hickethier): Television series intervene directly in the real-world processes of community *in front of the screen* through the mechanisms of community-construction inscribed in them. Thus, today more than ever, television series become an agency of 'substitute community', which provides a medially mediated 'makeshift community' and thereby enables the creation of meaning, everyday orientation and support in the advancing modernity as an age of social isolation. In this way, contemporary television series make it possible to successfully live through a late modernity in which certain isolating characteristics of modernity are only intensifying and traditional forms of community are systematically undermined.

This paper will show how television series, for example through the production of cults, rationalities, behavioural offers and time orders, participate in the *production of strong experiences of community*—you could also say an experience of 'social closeness' or 'human contact'—on which late-modern people depend in order to get through the loneliness that dominates their life reality. However, as an active motor of accelerated modernization, the television series thus creates its own preconditions in the first place, for this modernization goes hand in hand with a further increase in loneliness—and thus creates the need for ever stronger telemedial substitute communities, to which ever greater demands must be made in order to still be able to compensate for the escalating growing loneliness. The undeniable special status that television has occupied as a communication system within highly industrialized societies for half a century[18] up to present day is—as will be argued in the following—predominantly attributable to this unrivalled capacity for community production.

In the following, I would like to use the example of *13 Reasons Why to* show that contemporary television series not only visually and acoustically 'represent' the implied late-modern crisis of the social through telemedial aesthetics, but above all that *they themselves actively act as machines of substitute community*. While these provide a certain relief from the loneliness of modern life's reality, at the same time they only intensify the processes of modernization and, with the loneliness escalating as a result, make ever stronger substitute communities necessary— which, under late-modern conditions, can hardly be found outside serial television

---

[18]Cf. Sontheimer (1976) p. 162.

entertainment. *13 Reasons Why* unfolds a noteworthy self-referential game with the socializing logics of serial television fictions and their performance limits in a narrative-staging thicket of late-modern loneliness, which will be exemplarily examined in this paper. From this perspective, the series represents not only the processes of escalating social isolation in late modernity itself, but above all the modes of generating senses of community of television series, which are worked through autoreflexively in *13 Reasons Why* on the one hand, and at the same time are applied directly and effectively.

Dimensions of Community Production Through Serial Television

Serial fictional television, which continues to be the most broadly effective mass medium of late modernity par excellence, is today more than ever predominantly concerned with issues of loneliness—regardless of genre, target group and distribution channel. Hard to beat the tragic loneliness dynamic that befalls the main character of *13 Reasons Why*: Before her suicide, 17-year-old Hannah Baker records a series of audio cassettes, each of the 13 tape sides dedicated to a specific episode with a person from her social environment. According to Hannah's interpretation, her former (supposed) friends, casual acquaintances and the people in charge at school bear a more or less serious direct or indirect share of the blame for her feeling of total abandonment, which drives her to suicide in the first place: "The kind of lonely I'm talking about is when you feel you've got nothing left. Nothing. And no one." (S01E07M05) In keeping with Hannah's post-mortem novella, the tapes make their rounds among the 13 partial culprits, who are now confronted with their deeds and non-deeds—which, as expected, reveals a multitude of unspoken and hidden feelings, conflicts and intrigues, and provokes their public processing. In the face of the cassette series, the characters, who one after the other almost without exception turn out to be disoriented, deeply lonely souls searching for meaning, can no longer hide behind a mask of constant "I'm fine".

It is no coincidence that the series has its plot set in the world of experience of late-modern adolescents. For teenagers, the search for identity, belonging and extra-familial (couple) communities is not only a basic experience typical of their age. At the same time, adolescents are particularly exposed to certain modernization phenomena and thus to the feeling of loneliness. Twenge, for example, describes an increasingly tolerant and cosmopolitan, but also deeply insecure youth, who almost completely substitute direct social interactions with web-based communication and long above all for secure income and living conditions.[19] "Father, please bless and keep our children... Their world is darker than ours. And, Father, forgive us for what we've done to make it that way," prays a father after three seasons of lonely misdirection (S03E13M55), as the teenagers in *13 Reasons Why* barely manage to settle in between omnipresent observation techniques and exposure practices, an over-sexualization of their everyday interactions, the constant seduction to drugs and anabolic steroids, guns and violence, and an unbearable boredom of their suburban affluent world. In their pitiful attempt to adapt to late-modern living conditions, they thus expose themselves to the lonely forces of their present, which become the main narrative concern of the series and promise the television makers a virtually inexhaustible supply of narration and images.

But *13 Reasons Why* is not only an ideal example of the specific telemedial aesthetics and narrative worlds of late-modern loneliness in contemporary television series:[20] Rather, the series exerts a strong fascination and also a particular interest in television studies because it articulates *the central functions of television series in terms of their potential for community building:*

1. "Everything affects everything."[21]—Through the serially connected and systematically ordered cassette narration of their former classmate, the young people visualize that their own *actions are parts of chains of causation,* just as television series make the otherwise abstract and invisible social dependency relationships of late-modern social interactions vivid and demonstrate the causal order of actions in a social system.
2. "I could have done more."—The reenactment of what has happened and the revealed relationships of cause and effect allows for the re-evaluation of the characters' past individual decisions and a *play with decision-making options,* just as television series always require their audience to relate and question their own real-world decisions within social life to what is happening within the fictional world.
3. "You've been taking lessons."—"I've been watching Strictly Ballroom."—The cassette series, as well as the Netflix series itself, equally also offer an *archive of behaviors* that characters and television viewers alike can take advantage of in order to perform appropriate social interactions within complex late-modern

---

[19] Cf. Twenge (2017) p. 3.

[20] Cf. Newiak (2020).

[21] The quotes from this overview and the headings come from the characters in *13 Reasons Why* themselves, and will be detailly revisited below as articulations of the show's self-referential play on the community-building functions of television series.

living conditions and situations, making both series (regardless of the maturity of the listeners or viewers) important instances of socialization and thus progressive modernization of their audiences.

4. "Take me back to the night we met."—At the same time, Hannah's tapes function as a materialized cultural memory, as a repository of collective memories whose course can no longer be influenced, but whose serial narrative places the past, present, and future in a logical relationship to one another, thereby creating—like a television series—a *collective sense of the orderly progression and structure of time,* which is what makes meaningful social interactions within a community possible in the first place.

5. "You listen. You pass it on."—The concrete rules of use that Hannah envisions for her cassette series, intended to order collective use, as well as the emerging media appropriation practices (binge listening, reproduction, fan fiction) that ritualize serial reception, can be read as *'neo-religious' cult practices* that give the tapes the character of a mythically charged relic, which are only reinforced by the media-nostalgic aura of the analogue technology used, while fan cultures of collective worship also form around the television series itself.

6. "It's starting to make sense to me now."—Hannah's cassette narratives initiate an examination of the attribution categories of truth and fiction, and in the process produce their own concept of reality: just as television series can be understood as an important producer of social meaning, so too do the tapes *create a collectively shared consensus about the nature of social reality,* which—despite all its deficits as a fiction—still seems 'more real' than the fragmentary 'real' everyday individual perspectives of the subject. Through the serial principle of repetition, they create a sense of social order and collecitvely shared meaning.

7. "I think we should blame ourselves."—The positions developed by the tapes, the television series and television theory provoke questions about the influence and responsibility of individuals as well as media systems in a social structure. *13 Reasons Why,* following a public discussion of possible copycat suicides among teenagers, felt compelled to take various interventionist measures (both within and outside the diegesis) that, on the one hand, peculiarly exaggerate a possible negative social influence of television series, while at the same time problematically questioning the important community-building functions of serialized fictional television.

How the young people, through the serial cassette narration of their former classmate, begin to actively communicate with each other again, to interact and attempt to commune through a collectively shared horizon of causality, right decisions, appropriate action, memory and time, symbolic order, meaning and responsibility—in all these facets, the television series self-reflexively refers to the most important lines of discourse in television studies on the question of the extent to which television itself participates in processes of community formation. In doing so, television plays out its own modes of functioning, is preoccupied with itself in an almost narcissistic way, places its structural principles of action and their limits and contradictions at the centre of attention, while the solitary topics, narratives and characters seem to serve more as a backdrop for this autoreflexive play. To be sure, Hannah's tape narrative lacks the immediate visuality and vividness typical of television series, so the tape series cannot exude a televisual aesthetic of loneliness. However, with the serial nature of the 13 episodes, their vivid and meaningful embeddedness in the everyday lives of the show's characters, the practices of the tape series' usage, and the constant questioning of the veracity of Hannah's account, there remain enough parallels between the 13 tape episodes and the television series as a genre to allow for an insightful (if not exhaustive) autoreflexive examination of the communalizing agency principles of television series *through* Hannah's serial narrative. In the words of Kirchmann, one might say of *13 Reasons Why, "the TV program is the vividness of its own theory."*[22] Via the detour of the cassette season as a placeholder for television, which is otherwise absent from the series' world, the television series co-writes a philosophy of itself, which at the same time only makes a scientific theory of television tangible and possible: "[Media philosophy] is always already taking place, in the media and through the media. It can therefore only be encountered and uncovered there, in and on the media themselves."[23]

All of the indicated functional levels of television series, which become observable and verifiable in *13 Reasons Why,* can of course not be considered in isolation from one another, even if a scientific argumentation must attempt this for the purpose of a comprehensible approach through conceptual acuity. Thus, for example, the creation of time by a television series through the cultural memory stored in the media is dependent on ritualized repetition in the serial; at the same time, only this ritualized reception itself produces its own community experience through the production of cultural phenomena. The unifying element, however, between these various socially effective functional levels of television series remains *their shared capacity for building a sense of social closeness,* which fundamentally distinguishes them from other mass media systems of the present (the cinema, social media, etc.) and gives them a special position in modern societies. Television studies, which is

---

[22] Kirchmann (2006) p. 157. Emphasis in original. My translation.

[23] Engell (2012) p. 53. My translation.

also guided by the social interest in the (partly novel non-linear) forms of expression of television, must make it its task to strive for a unified theory of the social principles of the television series, to which this survey would like to contribute. This paper can only present excerpts from the extensive academic lines of discourse, which cannot claim to be exhaustive.[24] However, it seems central that television series hold together a society that is drifting apart and thus become the central collective lifeline in the age of loneliness.

"Everything Affects Everything."—Seriality, Causation Relations, Rationalization

Even the series title suggests that the focus of the plot is the search for the reasons behind the sudden death of California high school student Hannah Baker: Why did an outwardly vibrant young woman take her own life—and can that question even be answered after all?

The reasons for Hannah's decision initially remain opaque to the characters surrounding her. Even though individual characters become aware early on that they have not always behaved towards their classmate or protégé as would have been appropriate, hardly anyone believes that their own individual behaviour could actually be significant enough to provoke such fatal consequences like her suicide. On the contrary: There is a chronic fatalistic pessimism among young people that their own actions are in any case, all things considered, hardly likely to have any influence on the course of events around them. This powerlessness appears as an expression of a basic feeling, typical of late modernity, that in a world—with a practically infinite number of simultaneously acting participants in society and endless possibilities of shaping one's life—"[t]he technical complexity and the degree of interconnectedness of the world [have] increased to such an extent that direct cause-effect relationships can only be stated as an exception".[25] Late modernity comes with a suspicion that the fragmented and highly individualized way of life of individual members of society creates such unclear and convoluted interdependent relationships that, in Rosa's words, "social actors experience their

[24]This essay has been published in a shorter version earlier under the title "How Television Produces Invisible Communities in an Age of Loneliness. A Detailed Look at 13 Reasons Why", see references.

[25]Fabeck (2007) p. 137. My translation.

individual and political lives as fleeting and directionless, that is, as a state of frenzied stasis."[26]

Thus, the young people in *13 Reasons Why* torment themselves as representatives of the members of late modernity, because their existences seem dull to them and the individual scope for shaping them seems marginal: Time and again, the characters come up against the limits of their ability to actively influence their environment, such as when they try to hold the rapist Bryce responsible for his actions through legal channels—who then gets away with it after all: "Nothing does anything," Clay bitterly observes as Hannah's most important companion, as he fails despite the greatest individual sacrifice in his struggle against the inertia and blindness of late-modern automatisms and institutions (S02E11M38). While only the privileged elite of the school (the power-hungry competitive athletes and the prestigious wealthy) are aware of their power and are willing to act it out, most young people have long since lost the sense of a central social self-evident fact, namely "that I can have an effect on my fellow men, as well as that they can have an effect on me,"[27] that is, "that my actions, which I am able to conceive as typical actions, will have typical consequences," as Schütz characterizes it as the most important precondition for any form of social cohabitation.[28] A typical modern act is, for example, a traffic violation, which is typically punished by regulatory or criminal law, but in *13 Reasons Why*, time and again the young people get away with their missteps without sanction because of good relationships or caregivers concerned about their reputation. The characters experience their social environment as a mostly indifferent and faceless mass towards them, where occasional, superficial and trivial encounters take the place of stable and deep social relationships, creating a gnawing sense of "self-alienation and social alienation."[29]

The basic certainty and everyday experience, essential for the functioning of any form of social system, that individual actions entail concrete (if not always foreseeable) consequences, can easily be lost by the subject in view of the increasing unmanageability of social dependency relationships. In order to still be able to experience community as a living concept, regular self-assurance is needed under these conditions that society can still be shaped by individual actions. Hannah Baker takes on this role in the form of her serial cassette story: All the individual negative episodes in her life—the exposure after her first kiss, the dissemination of

---

[26]Rosa ([2013] 2018) pp. 64–65. My translation.

[27]Schütz, Luckmann (1975) p. 24. My translation.

[28]Ibid p. 37. My translation.

[29]Rosa ([2013] 2018) p. 141. My translation.

compromising images in social media, the circulation of rumours, lewd slurs, etc.—
form a web of causal relationships in Hannah's 13-part tale of woe to with an almost
inevitable outcome. In Hannah's story, every single social interaction leads to
consequences which can be spectated by the audience in front of the TV.

"Life is unpredictable, and control is just an illusion. . . . And sometimes all that
unpredictability is overwhelming. . . . And it makes us feel small and powerless,"
Hannah dictates into her tape recorder (S01E12M56), while she visualizes and tries
to order the dense network of her social interactions in a diagram (cf. Fig. 1). "And
once I took a look back and I finally understood how everything happened"
(S01E12M60)—Piece by piece, through her serial narration, Hannah works out a
logic of past events as a continuous narrative, although not without gaps. Shortly
before, she was still philosophizing with Clay (under the influence of drugs) about
the improbability of doing anything noteworthy at all in an infinite universe: "How
are we supposed to do anything significant? Anything that means anything?"
(S02E07M01)—But Hannah knows that "without you, without me, everything is
different." (S02E07M02) Together, they play out potential causation effects
between people around them and come to the crushing realization that "it's huge,
if you think about it." Even in their hallucinatory state, they are unable to conceptu-
alize this infinity, for in order to visualize the ways in which their marginal actions
entail socially relevant consequences, they lack a mode in this fictional world to
visualize late-modern life in its complexity and interdependence. In the series, the
young people are addicted to their smartphones, where superficial conversations
circulate via seemingly "social" networks as parallel monologues and incoherent
strings of potentially exposing photos—but they do not watch TV shows. In
Engell's sense, this would be the only chance to develop an understanding of the
principle of cause and effect, even under opaque late-modern conditions:

> In order for something to be made visible as the consequence of a cause and to become
> effective in its turn [. . .], it must be designated as the cause of a consequence, it must
> cause this consequence as a cause. In short: Only in seriality can there be causes and
> consequences and thus causality at all. Causality and seriality are indissolubly referred
> to each other.[30]

With reference to Peirce, Engell argues that it can be assumed that the world
fundamentally proceeds according to principles of causation, "but that causality,
on the other hand, in order to be recognizable and further processable, i.e. to be
effective in its turn, must remain or become a construction. Only as a construction is

---

[30] Engell (2003) p. 249. My translation.

Fig. 1 In preparation for her serial cassette narrative, Hannah sorts out the complex social causation network that barely fits on a page. (S01E11M49). Still from *13 Reasons Why*, Netflix 2017–2020. (© Paramount Television)

causality itself causal, e.g. for action."[31] It is precisely such constructions of causality that television series undertake, and because there are no TV shows in the world of *13 Reasons Why*, Hannah here takes on the thankless task of bringing rational order to the apparent chaos on behalf of television. As in a detective story, the schoolgirl takes matters into her own hands, she becomes a television detective in her own cause, and of necessity carries out her own "originator research",[32] thus creating—like the television series in which she lives—"a concept and a practice of causation and carries it out".[33]

Hannah is also sure in retrospect that there simply *must* be causal relationships—even if they are difficult to see through: "You've heard about the Butterfly Effect, right? . . . It's about how a tiny change in a big system can affect everything", she patiently explains to her listeners (S01E03M01). But this construct from theoretical mathematics not only seems improbable in itself, it also remains too abstract to be relevant to everyday life or even to guide action. While Hannah forensically

---

[31] Ibid. p. 248. My translation.
[32] Ibid. p. 251. My translation.
[33] Ibid. pp. 242–243. My translation.

reassembles and painstakingly reconstructs the strands of causality that are drifting apart, she, on the other hand, makes the difficult-to-fathom principles of causation of the social actions in her environment sensually perceptible and comprehensible again. In the style of a dramatist, she thus rescues the "belief, that the life of the individual really has a shape and a course, and that the determining forces can be identified",[34] as Goffman writes. Only this "belief" is what makes it possible to live in a community in the first place: Life in community must be perceived by individuals as capable of being shaped, so that they also feel bound to the collective mutual obligations and responsibilities.

Whether causal causes ultimately 'really' exist or whether it is merely a collective 'self-deception' necessary for survival that life is not controlled by uninfluenceable coincidences is ultimately irrelevant, because in order to be able to interact with each other in a socially meaningful way, the awareness of the influenceability of social actions is indispensable. A psychotherapist in the series puts it this way himself: "What happens to us, it may only have the sense that we make of it. But I do know that it's in telling the story that we learn who we are and maybe see who we might become." (S04E10M67)—Because it is precisely the contemporary quality television series of "Complex TV" that distinguish themselves by linking the actions of a fixed ensemble of characters within their vivid narratives to a "chain of events over time" and thus making them convincing,[35] they become the predestined venues for the late-modern uncertainty as to whether a life in community is still possible at all in view of its uninfluenceability. Only in the face of television series does our otherwise fragmented and seemingly random social coexistence still appear as a coherent fabric of mutual conditions, obligations and causes, in which actions entail consequences.

"I Could Have Done More."—Fatal Path Decisions

But this regained certainty about the effectiveness of social causal relationships in turn generates new nagging doubts, namely to what extent one's own actions meet the demands and requirements of the others, to what extent one's own past decisions were thus suitable for creating the basis for close relationships. "She was my friend. And I miss her . . . The worst part is there's nothing I can do. I can't save her; I can't bring her back. I'm completely fucking useless." (S01E09M38) When Clay Jensen,

---

[34] Goffman (2016) p. 598. My translation.
[35] Mittell (2015) p. 10.

perhaps Hannah's only real friend and almost-boyfriend, comes into possession of the tapes and becomes aware of the extent of Hannah's traumatic experiences, a sense of powerlessness and insignificance manifests itself in him: If the sudden death initially appeared as an impenetrable mystery, with the series of cassettes the links between cause and effect join to form a chain of meaningful causal relationships—but because it is no longer possible to intervene in the fatally flawed decisions in the reenactment, the outcome of the plot is ultimately beyond influence, the chance of establishing closeness for the time being lost. Even more so, the moments of obviously inappropriate decisions in certain life situations now appear as fateful moments that have triggered concrete courses of action that would only have led to the fatal outcome for Hannah. Confronted with Hannah's analysis, within the logic of the serial, the listeners see their own decisions as deficient because they entail consequences that lead to undesirable outcomes, in particular to ever new and even more crushing loneliness.

"One thing. If one thing had gone differently somewhere along the line, maybe none of this would have happened," analyzes the football talent Zach (S01E08M06), who is spoiled for success, but hardly any of the characters could fully assess the consequences of their actions and omissions at the moment of their actions. For the complexity of the unmanageable chains of causation remains impenetrable from the subjective perspective, which only contributes to the crushing loneliness of their late-modern existence. For Luhmann, it is a typical problem of large systems that the "long-term effects of decisions that can no longer be identified" are hardly transparent for the individual in view of the "over-complex and no longer tracable causal relationships", "although it is clear that without decisions such damage could not have occurred".[36] Because the future must "always remain a horizon of uncertainty",[37] but it must be the claim in a social contect to be able to shape the future through decisions and thus also to demand meaningful decisions from the individual, television, with its predisposition to deal with the social effects of causal relationships, has the task of transforming this typically modern "uncertainty into security".[38]

The playing out of certain key decisions therefore becomes, not without reason, the leitmotif of both the cassette and the television series itself, which not only undertake a 'root cause analysis' of the course of the fatal premise, but also implicitly contain alternative courses of action that would have made

---

[36]Luhmann (1991) p. 35. My translation.

[37]Luhmann (1990) p. 130. My translation.

[38]Ibid. My translation.

communalisation more likely. For example, the school counselor Porter regrets in court that he had not prevented Hannah, who was seeking help, from leaving his office in a state of dissolution after the failed consultation talk in order to offer her extensive help. While he imagines an alternative course of action in which he speaks to Hannah in an engaged and emphatic manner, conveys hope to her despite the hopeless situation and finally plucks the constantly ringing telephone from the line and tosses it aside, he tearfully confesses: "I could have done more. . . . I was just trying to do the right thing, I was following protocol. Protocol probably needs to change, but more importantly, Kevin Porter needs to change." (S02E09M33) Porter was only able to come to this admission, which gave him at least a little peace of mind, because Hannah's tape narration made him fully aware of the consequences of his own wrong decision to let the help-seeker leave the office without results. Even if the decisions can no longer be revised, the serial narrative gives justified cause for hope that future decisions might be made differently, that they might be suitable for curbing the loneliness of late modernity.

Clay also agonizes over his choices, which could have been made with less lonely effects. For example, the young man misses at least four opportunities to kiss Hannah Baker, who is obviously attracted to him, and thus to initiate a couple relationship. If the constantly changing role expectations, gender relations and performance requirements generate chronic decision-making uncertainties under late-modern conditions, the cassette series at least permits an examination of alternative courses of action. This play with possibilities, initiated by Hannah's narration, pervades the entire television series, in which decisions are repeatedly put to the test. Such a procedure appears to Kirchmann as a procedure typical of television series of a *"reflexive thematisation of alternative selection options in the narrative process itself*, in the form of alternative and at the same time antinomic plot designs within *one* narration".[39] If, in principle, every *"narrative can be understood as a fundamental operation with options at every branching point, as a technique of event selection"*, Kirchmann observes "a massive increase in [. . .] subjunctive narrative forms", especially for late-modern television.[40]

The question of what is the right decision in a particular late-modern life situation, i.e. one that is appropriate to the situation and promotes community, becomes increasingly challenging as modernization progresses, because the criteria and methods provided by modernity for systematic decision-making are not always functional and the number of decision options is practically unlimited. Moral

---

[39] Kirchmann (2006) p. 163. Emphasis in original. My translation.

[40] Ibid. p. 167. Emphasis in original. My translation.

criteria that emerged in relatively easily surveyable life conditions of pre-modernity, due to their rigid attribution criteria, completely fail as a method for decision-making in the face of the complexity and diversity of late-modern life situations, because they fail due to the multitude of morally ambiguous life situation.[41] Traditional forms of imparting knowledge for problem solving which is "institutionalized and routinely undertaken by certain role-players" of society[42] are thus reaching their limits. Modernity produces powerful institutions as a substitute, which order individual decisions as juridically permissible and impermissible on the basis of laws. However, according to Niethammer and Dossmann, it would overstrain the institutions of the administration of justice created as the 'last instance' if "the services to be rendered and conflicts to be regulated in the area of socio-cultural self-responsibility" were not also provided and clarified within the framework of the immediate "personal social relations" among one another.[43] Social systems are characterised by the fact that their members are also aware of the effects of their decisions beyond legal attributions and are also able to make decisions spontaneously and appropriately in the concrete moment.

Television series, in turn, take up decision-making situations in complex life situations that elude the traditional mediation of problem-solving by church, state and family. As a self-assurance of their capacity for "social self-organization,"[44] the significance of the reenactment of path decisions typical of contemporary television can hardly be overestimated for the reactivation of the feeling of being able to make effective and appropriate decisions at all within the complex circumstances of life. "I should have kissed her", Clay keeps reproaching himself. But even if it must remain uncertain whether his intervention could really have diverted the tragic course of the plot, the "talking in the subjunctive" typical of any television series at least allows for the soothing certainty "that everything could just as well have

---

[41] Although decision-making criteria of morality did not disappear completely with the onset of modernization, so that religious institutions continue to exist in some areas of late-modern societies, according to Niethammer, the "religious tradition reserves" have finally been used up in the course of a "continuing mobilization and medialization of everyday life in the modernization thrusts since the 1960s", so that, viewed from the perspective of society as a whole, pre-modern church morality hardly plays a role as a decision-making method anymore. Niethammer/Dossmann (2000) p. 420. My translation.

[42] Schütz, Luckmann (1975) p. 292. My translation.

[43] Niethammer, Dossmann (2000) p. 513. My translation.

[44] Ibid. My translation.

D. Newiak

been completely different or could have become completely different",[45] that is, that decisions in a social context always have effects, albeit occasionally unclear ones.

Due to the dramaturgical connotations, to what extent a course of action is staged as comic (community-building) or tragic (loneliness-producing), decisions can then be evaluated as desirable or undesirable on the basis of whether such decisions entail connecting or isolating consequences. It is through this multiplicity of possible path choices and assumptions about their consequences that the late-modern television series generates the "narrative complexity"[46] that makes it so attractive. If the series characters trapped in the diegesis are forced to settle their conflicts archaically on the football field, in the courtroom, or in the parking lot (occasionally with their fists) and to evaluate the quality of their decisions intuitively and only in the reenactment of unchangeable tragic courses of action, the television viewer is spared this: From a protected position of observation, the television series allows him to evaluate, on the basis of the recurring late-modern life situations shown and their variations of decisions, which of the courses of action shown are more suitable for community-building than others—and which have only intensified their loneliness.

"You've Been Taking Lessons."—"I've Been Watching Strictly Ballroom."—Telemedial Behavioural Propositions for Life in Late Modernity

One of the main features of the late-modern way of life is the exponential increase of possibilities for shaping one's life generated by a rapidly unfolding social change. Because the morality of fixed commandments and prohibitions stemming from pre-modern times is contraindicated for such rapid progress, secondary virtues ("Sekundärtugenden") such as discipline, politeness and honesty remain too general in their recommendations for action[47] and law and justice cannot directly keep pace with the changes taking place at all levels of society, the number of morally or legally unambiguous life situations continues to decrease with the growing complexity of social interactions. Thus, life in late modernity becomes a constant search for the 'right' behaviour in the "context of multiple choice", which decisively

---

[45] Kirchmann (2006) p. 171. My translation.
[46] Mittell (2006) p. 29.
[47] Cf. Lübbe (2003) p. 343.

shapes individual identity formation.[48] Although late modernity still has a remnant of at least partially functioning traditional socialization instances, it is at least questionable whether naturally tough democratic processes of political decision-making, traditionally rather inflexible institutions such as schools, parties and associations, and the core communities of marriage, parenthood and friendship, which are themselves struggling for survival, are suitable for making plausible and appropriate behavioral offers for the numerous new kinds of life situations.[49]

Serial fictional television is increasingly filling this gap, becoming an institution of the enculturation process that is available almost without restriction, universally understandable and permanently accessible.[50] For Hickethier, one of the central functions of television series, through the "portrayal of people in their behavior", is to "provide *models and patterns of behavior* [for] how to behave in the world in order to be successful (in a very broad sense)."[51] On the one hand, television assumes "very general *socialization functions* for adolescents", but at the same time it also influences "the adult audience in its orientation and behavior in the environment".[52] To this end, television series have their protagonists "act out behaviors and opinions of various kinds, which are juxtaposed and presented to the viewers on individual topics, and which must prove their appropriateness".[53] According to Hickethier, there is no "consistently fixed scale of values" for this assessment, but clearly predominantly those behaviours of "compassionate, socially acceptable values" appear to be more appropriate than those that are "marginal", "anti-social", "inconsiderate" or "emotionally cold"[54]—in short: isolating.[55]

By "offering and disseminating the behavioural models necessary for modernization",[56] television series are supposed to enable each individual "to live within society [. . .] because competent individuals are necessary for the continuation of a

---

[48] Giddens (1991) p. 5.

[49] Cf. Dant (2012) pp. 119–120.

[50] Cf. Gross and Morgan (1985) p. 223.

[51] Hickethier (2008) p. 53. My translation.

[52] Hickethier (2008) p. 54. My translation.

[53] Hickethier (1994) p. 67. My translation.

[54] Ibid. My translation.

[55] On the question of the aesthetic way in which certain courses of action are staged in television series as potentially communalizing and unifying, cf. Newiak: "Telemediale Narrative und Ästhetiken spätmoderner Vereinsamung am Beispiel von 13 Reasons Why".

[56] Hickethier (1994) p. 70. My translation.

complex society":[57] The constant changes within modernity require each individual to adapt to these new conditions so that interactions between the members of society remain possible and communities remain functional. Because, in turn, the individual members of society are interested in "becoming acquainted with the conditions and rules of society, its problems and considerations of solutions, at least to the extent necessary for them, in turn, to assert themselves somewhat successfully in that society",[58] television series continue to enjoy remarkable popularity to this day and, especially under late-modern conditions, assume an even greater importance because their modernizing power is even more urgently needed today in order to withstand the ever-increasing pace of modernization.

In order for this modernization process to succeed, the fictional life situations shown by television series must be sufficiently comparable with the real-world life experience of the television audience.[59] This is also the particular strength of contemporary TV shows. While the young people in *13 Reasons Why* intellectually understand what their teacher in communication class engagingly tells them about Bandura's theory of social learning (S01E03M25), the reality of their lives speaks a different language: The girls, for instance, feel pressured into a never-ending beauty pageant and find themselves among disoriented young men from whom social media, disproportionate wealth, and constantly available online erotica have weaned any sense of appropriate gendered behavior. Add to this alcohol abuse, STDs and the opioid epidemic, low-threshold access to anabolic steroids and guns, dysfunctional coping with rampant psychopathologies, and experiences of sexual violence. Within its fictional diegesis, the series takes a rather unequivocal stance on this: Finding their way in this world is largely left to the young people themselves—at least they cannot rely on adults constantly preoccupied with themselves and their own problems, on absent role models, or on authorities who have long since capitulated.

But they are not entirely alone. This becomes clearest in the episode of the *dance,* which is part of the core repertoire of youth series for good reason: Such rituals of initiating couple communities offer the prospect of suspending the automatisms of loneliness, at least for the time being, which makes them (just like the *party*) particularly appealing to young people. Social and couple dancing— historically an almost 'pre-modern' ritual of initiating relationships—becomes a rare opportunity to find each other. But what actually appears to be a standard

---

[57] Hickethier (2008) p. 47. My translation.

[58] Ibid. My translation.

[59] Cf. Hickethier (1992) p. 15. My translation.

situation of growing up remains alien to contemporary serial adolescents, on the one hand, because they are no longer used to participating in such a custom overloaded with physicalities and subtle forms of non-verbal communication, and on the other hand, because new rules of the game have long applied here, flasks are pulled out of jackets, compromising pictures circulate on cell phones, and social belonging depends on the availability of an SUV that smells like a new car. Clay visibly strains to find appropriate behaviors for this unfamiliar life situation. He therefore digs in his memory for fragments of behavior familiar from movies: "I'm not really sure how this is done... I don't know if people actually ask people this like 'in the world', but I'm just saying: I wonder if you wanna dance." (S01E05M30) After the hoped-for agreement, there is still fidgeting, as everyone does, but when the *slow song* plays, things become challenging: While the other young men have already 'positioned' their hands suspiciously low on their partners, Clay considers these unbridled advances inappropriate. The social reality of life surrounding him is apparently not a good role model for him. Of necessity, at this moment, he once again falls back on the extensive film knowledge he acquired as a temp at the local 'Crestmont' cinema: He looks deep into Hannah's eyes, places his hands familiarly and at the same time respectfully on her waist, and reminisces with Hannah about the romantic "old dance movies we play sometimes at the 'Crestmont'. Remember *Strictly Ballroom*?" (S01E05M34) The constructed fictions of the cult film, even if they seem ridiculous at times, are already enough at this point to navigate through this highschool dance evening (cf. Fig. 2), creating, as Hickethier would say, a "present range of behaviours that offer the spectator a *frame of orientation* within which he can move with some certainty".[60]

With this knowledge advantage, which is untypical of his age, he can just about manage the comparatively harmless couple dance situation—but it's not enough for a kiss again, and certainly not for the challenges that are yet to come. After becoming aware of his own behavioral deficits and their consequences in light of Hannah's serial tale of woe, Clay remembers the dance they shared to the melancholy strains of the series anthem *The Night We Met* and regrets his hesitancy to kiss. For the chance of closeness wasted in reality is followed by the biting awareness that the misjudgement based on ignorance and cowardice that night—with all its disastrous consequences—will not be able to be readjusted. To himself, the film-like reminders of a missed future may give only a brief ephemeral glimpse of the uncatchable missed communities—but to the television audience, hints of potentially appropriate behavior in complex life situations appear in these dreams.

---

[60] Hickethier (1994) p. 68. My translation.

Fig. 2 The knowledge advantage from the "old dance movies" saves Clay through the evening—but for the challenges of late-modern loneliness only TV shows hold suitable behavioral offers. (S01E05M35). Still from *13 Reasons Why,* Netflix 2017–2020. (© Paramount Television)

Television series would be uninteresting if the characters acting in them always displayed only appropriate behaviors and felt comfortable in them—rather, the television audience is also supposed to gain insights into the appropriateness of behaviors in late-modern life situations from possibly inappropriate behaviors, just as Hannah's listeners, in retracing the cassette series, slowly develop a feeling for which behavior toward the schoolmate would have been appropriate and inappropriate, which behavior should be imitated and which should be eliminated.

Thus Clay repeatedly comes up against his limits when it comes to finding his way in unfamiliar situations: As a young man, for instance, when a young woman who has just unambiguously given her consent to shared intimacy suddenly and abruptly rejects and shouts at you in defiance of all caution, should you give in to that young woman's insistent request that you leave the room, or would it be appropriate, perhaps even necessary, to at least demand an explanation? How does one deal—without losing one's mind—with the subsequent certain knowledge that this very same young woman has been the victim of a serious sexually violent crime, but that, in the absence of witnesses, there is little hope of a legal handling of the crime, threatening further crimes? And do you leave a heavily armed, life-weary classmate and his potential victims to the far-too-late and overwhelmed police, or do you attempt to intervene and protect victims and perpetrators alike from their deadly fate? Even if the fictional late-modern living conditions demand this of their characters, answers to these questions can hardly be demanded of anyone—not even of television, whose task cannot consist of presenting ideal-typical and patent solutions to even the most improbable variations of everyday occurrences. It can also be confidently demanded of an advanced television viewer that, in view of the obvious tendency of television series towards dramatisation, their claim to entertainment and the aesthetic connotations, he or she can assess that not every behaviour shown is worthy of imitation in itself and that television characters are instructive precisely because of their misjudgements, naivety and gaps in knowledge, since their behaviour must be measured not only against their own fictional circumstances, but also against the conditions of our own real world.

Instead of simply providing copyable instant behavioral patterns, television series rather shape a process of "permanent behavioral modeling of the participants" for the purpose of a successful and sustainable "modernization of society".[61] The fictional young people in *13 Reasons Why* then experience the same fate as the television viewers: It is precisely because the characters lack progressive, demanding, and modernizing media systems like television series in their world that the series narrative on the tapes, with its opportunities for behavioral modeling and offers for modernizing one's own behavior, assumes such great importance.

Of course, serial fictional television is not without competition, but feature films, for example, lack the ritualized, recurring appearance and the long playing time that are characteristic of television series, as a result of which extensive plot developments and narrative complexity can only unfold through the familiar habit of a fixed ensemble of richly detailed characters. The fragmentary, over-staged illusory worlds of "social media", which in any case play a dubious role in society (one need only think of manipulated elections, distorted ideals of beauty and excesses of malicious gossip[62]), cannot succeed in their brief passing in any case in presenting imitable complex behavioural options, let alone sustainable offers for the creation of meaning. Fictional television—even if it is always subject to certain ideological, material and narcissistic constraints as an entertainment medium subject to commercial rules—thus stands in late modernity between a multitude of still existing but dysfunctional instances of socialization as perhaps the only effective mass medium, which probably has the most promising role in the foundation of communities through modern behavioral offerings, without substituting the multifaceted structure of socializing influences.[63]

---

[61] Ibid. p. 71. My translation.

[62] As some examples of the extensive discourse on web loneliness, reference is made to van Dijck (2013); Vaidhyanathan (2018); Turkle ([2011] 2017).

[63] Cf. Dant (2012) pp. 144–145.

"Take Me Back to the Night We Met."—Time Foundations and Collective Memory

The nostalgic recollection of times past, which is itself forced by Hannah's cassette narrative, allows the acting characters as well as the television viewers to experience their world as ordered and susceptible to influence, to ascertain the appropriateness and inappropriateness of their own decisions, and to explore behavioral options. But this retracing of the past, of the missed moments of building a community and the awareness of one's own behavioural deficits, made possible by Hannah's narrative seriality, achieves even more: Serial fictions of television create a collective consciousness of time and community through the experience of a *shared history*.

While pre-modernity was dominated by a circular understanding of time linked to repetitive natural processes and beliefs, the transition to modernity is characterized for Anderson, using Walter Benjamins words, by the sense of a "homogeneous, empty time" of simultaneity, in which events do not take place in an orderly fashion but seemingly "by temporal coincidence" because they lack a goal direction as an ordering mechanism.[64] Only the synchronization of modern everyday processes through calendars and an ever more finely adjusted universal time allowed the organization of the increasingly complex social interdependencies in areas such as the industrial production of goods and trade, long-distance transport and science. Time, in Lübbe's words, becomes an important "medium of coordination of action",[65] through which a social systems coordinates itself and thus becomes capable of interaction. Nevertheless, the culturally constructed time system must remain an alien thing because it opposes the time sequences of nature, the body, and culturally and historically habitualized rituals. In late modernity, following Neverla, there is an additional "mixing, individualization and pluralization of time patterns":[66] The uniformly proceeding time as a collective experience threatens to break apart into a "polychronic time culture" of compressed individualized subject times.[67]

---

[64] Anderson (1983) p. 24.

[65] Lübbe (1997) p. 315. My translation.

[66] Neverla (2010) pp. 184–185. My translation.

[67] Thus, the abstract-linear time order of modernity is literally compressed into a point by late-modern technologies such as digital media: The Internet in particular is available virtually non-stop, generates an endless supply of signs without beginning or end, and demands constant presence and immediate reaction from the connected actors: in the course of modernization, *time, originally a medium of social action*, has thus become independent

Communities, however, need time because all human communication, practices of consensus building and conflict resolution, but also experiences of spiritual and physical closeness always have a temporal course. Communities need temporal margins because, according to Bauman, they are based on "biographies shared through a long history and an even longer life expectation of frequent and intense interaction".[68] For Rosa, on the other hand, late-modern time culture produces alienations from space, from things, from our own actions, from our fellow human beings, and also from time as a concept itself.[69] Thus, late-modern time culture is antagonistic to the principles and time needs of community formation— yet modernity, in order to defend its successes, is at the same time also dependent on a complex and dense time structure. Television, and television series in particular, play their part in managing this contradiction in everyday practice, without being able to resolve it entirely, by mediating between the two legitimate interests of time order: Television series create a collective sense of time in which communities can be created, and thus make possible the modernization processes within the accelerating social reality with its specific needs for temporal compression.

But how does television create this feeling of a time that runs evenly and corresponds to one's own subjective experience of time as a sequence of things? To begin with, the very narratives of the television series, with their causal-logical structure, are in Aleida Assmanns words as much "an essential form of the cultural construction of time as any other form of narrative (in novels, for example)", or to put it concisely: "Stories make sense of time."[70] In linear television, the program-ming of the broadcast schedule as a scheme of rhythmized (daily, weekly) recur-rence of certain programs, their characters, and narrative worlds articulates the fundamental reliability of social temporal processes.[71] Certain specials that recur in the course of a year, for example at the Christmas holidays, underline the ritual character that serial television shares with the social routine of life.[72]

Under late-modern conditions, however, and not least due to the widespread popularity of non-linear means of distribution, the time-founding functions of

---

and at the same time has become *an object of social action*", (Neverla 1992b, p. 53. Emphasis in original. My translation), see also Neverla 1992a.

[68] Bauman (2000) p. 48. Emphasis in original.

[69] Cf. Rosa ([2013] 2018) pp. 122–143.

[70] Assmann (1999) p. 15.

[71] Neverla (2010) pp. 27–28. These sequences are only interrupted by suspicious broadcasting failures and special broadcasts imposed by world events—which as exceptions then confirm the rule of the time order.

[72] Cf. Cavell (1982) p. 93. Cf. also Grampp's contribution in this volume.

television are undergoing rapid change, which are self-reflexively played out in a media-nostalgic manner in *13 Reasons Why*. Even though late-modern television lacks the process of programming, the core principle of serialization, the organization of narrative and reception as interconnected segments, remains. Hannah Baker's tapes also signal their episodic-serial character through their physical form of presentation: They enforce (not least through the map that she includes with her cassettes as a metatext, like a fanbox supplement) an orderly listening to one cassette side after the other, and are divided into narratively meaningful units that are nevertheless interdependent and refer to one another.[73] Little remains of the traditional time-ordering functions of linear television—but what survives is the possibility for the collective experience of time as the logical and future-directed sequence of shared fragments of events that necessarily lie in the past. Community, albeit invisible, is thus no longer created here merely through the immediate temporal simultaneity of reception,[74] but through the creation of *a shared history* that materializes itself in the serial narrative of Hannah's cassettes as in *13 Reason Why:* The series of cassettes they can access as a community reassures listeners that they are all part of a shared past—that their actions are not only causally and meaningfully interwoven, but that through the serial nature of Hannah's narrative they can also collectively access and appropriate it again and again. History means nothing other than sharing a common notion of the past and certain practices of reviving it so that it always remains part of the common present. While in late modernity the interest in shaping the future leads us through history, television series and their stories allow a recollection of *one* shared history.

---

[73] Nevertheless, the media use practices of the recipients differ considerably in some cases: Alex, for instance, listened to the entire series in one night and a total of two times ("Thought maybe I'd dreamed the whole thing", S01E03M39); Clay, on the other hand, who meticulously goes through each tape, retraces it at great emotional cost, and continues it in part in his own life's reality, would find such binge listening both too painful and too superficial; school president Marcus says he just didn't listen to the tapes at all, and the teacher of the communication course almost develops a kind of obsession ("I couldn't listen when they first came out, but now I just can't stop listening", S02E09M03). Although reception is occasionally still tied to certain everyday routines (Clay listens to the tapes before sleeping and after waking up, on his bike and in the car, at his desk and on the sofa), just as television viewers continue to enjoy watching their favorite series for breakfast and dinner, on weekends and holidays—participation in the series world is usually completely liberated in terms of time and space, as is typical of late modernity: Listening here is hypermobile, during the day and at night—and mostly experienced alone, just as smartphones with streaming apps are now standard equipment in subways, cafés, and occasionally in lecture halls.

[74] Cf. the description of the mass ceremony of newspaper reading in Anderson (1983) p. 35.

On the one hand, remembering what people have experienced together allows them, in Engell's sense, to place the past in a meaningful order, and the seriality of the narrative allows to acquire a sense of history in the logical course of narrative time, to reduce the complexity of what we have experienced to comprehensible dimensions, and thus to participate in history.[75] On the other hand, as Fabeck writes, history can only ever be comprehended and then written with a certain temporal distance: "The distance from events, which is their exclusive condition of experience, makes [history] possible in the first place. By contrast, the incessant transference of events into current information cuts off the bond with history."[76]—While the late-modern attention market makes topicality its currency, devalues the past, and thus builds up a distance to the past, the urge to repetition inscribed in the serial, which expresses itself in television series in familiar plotlines, characters, and aesthetics, allows for a particularly close bond to the past that can be strengthened ever further through renewed reception.

As Jan Assmann describes with the help of his concept of "cultural memory", every form of community is dependent, in the absence of a common "neuronal basis", on storing its shared identity-forming knowledge of history in reproducible form and on circulating and actively transmitting it through constant ritualized repetition.[77] Since late-modern societies lack pre-modern symbolic forms such as myths, sacred writings and relics to preserve their cultural memory, and since these would not even be able to comprehensively represent the complex late-modern reality of life, late modernity is dependent on finding its very own media for carrying and disseminating its history.[78] Despite increasing life expectancy, late-modern culture is more dependent than ever on institutionalized forms of collective memory that make it possible to pass on knowledge from one generation to the next, and even to update it within a generation due to rapid social change, i.e. to constantly modernize it and make it available to the social members. For this purpose, television series are the means of choice: Both series such as *13 Reasons Why* and Hannah's 13-part audio cassette series manifest the two crucial

---

[75] Cf. Engell (2011) p. 119.

[76] Fabeck (2007) p. 161. My translation

[77] Assmann ([1992] 2000) p. 89. My translation.

[78] For this reason, it can almost be understood as a sarcastic dig at his parents that Clay, in his search for a good excuse to continue dealing with the tapes, states that he still has to take care of the "Oral History Project" (S01E02) for school—for it is precisely modern and above all late-modern societies, in contrast to pre-modern societies that depended on oral tradition, that are able and also obliged to *materialize* their history in order to be able to permanently assure themselves of their common past.

safeguarding functions required to maintain a collective memory according to Aleida Assmann, namely "'safeguarding forms of duration' through storage techniques such as writing and image", as well as "'safeguarding forms of repetition' through performative media such as rites as forms of renewal, participation and appropriation".[79] One may watch television series alone—and yet one appropriates a communal cultural treasure that television secures and provides in duration and repetition. Accordingly, the late-modern television series has a special interpretative sovereignty over what becomes history and to what extent, "it makes the distinction between remembering and forgetting"[80]—and yet usually sides with remembering, because that is in its nature.[81] Just as every form of historiography simplifies, shortens, and idealizes the overwhelming complexity of the past into a representation that can be mastered by human beings, Hannah's history, too, despite all her efforts, is never able to grasp all the influencing factors, let alone reproduce them, yet it is precisely this reduction of an endless stream of events to something mentally manageable that makes the experience of shared history possible in the first place.

This remarkable function of the television series, to create forms of sociality through history as shared times, is also the basis of the striking media nostalgia that drives the protagonists of *13 Reasons Why:* The old-fashioned tapes express a longing for bygone times that seem attractive because (in accordance with the logic of modernization as an age of ever-increasing loneliness) close and warm communities must once have existed, they were only lost with late modernity. Nostalgia is the memory of an idealized history of communities that can no longer be achieved in the present. The physical materiality and haptic of the cassette tapes, the indexical inscription of Hannah's voice on the endless magnetic strip, the possibility of personal sharing and (temporary) possession of the shared treasure of history—all these possibilities for direct disposition of history establish a media nostalgia that has long since become an omnipresent stylistic device in many other

---

[79] Assmann (2006) p. 58. My translation.

[80] Engell (2011) pp. 124–125. My translation.

[81] The multitude of actors involved in the creation of television series, their artistic and economic interest in reaching a large audience, as well as the short feedback loops that on-demand video stores themselves make possible, just like the dynamic discourses on the Internet, hardly allow that aspects of history worth remembering could be accidentally 'overlooked' or 'forgotten'. In this way, television series differ fundamentally from the predominantly isolating "social media", which by their very nature tend to aim at fragmenting, obscuring, and ultimately erasing history.

television series such as *Stranger Things, Bates Motel*, and *Cobra Kai* as a promise of communities past.[82]

"Everything was better before", Clay comments as his buddy Tony slides another one of his mixtapes into the car radio—but Clay can only access that "before" with the help of the tapes' present: As Tony hands him a cassette with a copy of *The Night We Met*, Clay imagines a *better* past against the backdrop of Hannah's memories of them kissing. Rewinding through collective history makes it possible to retrieve moments of potential community: Even and especially if their chances of escaping the lonelinesses of late modernity were once missed in this moment, for Clay and his contemporaries the memory of their shared history remains linked to the hope that forming a vital community is thinkable after all— just as the television audience, in the face of television, envisions a future that hides communities that still seem impossible in the present.

"You Listen. You Pass It On."—Neo-religious Cult Communities

Closely linked to questions about the forms of sociality produced by the seriality through time and history are the cult practices by which Hannah's tapes, like the television series itself, are captured, unfolding their very own experiences of closeness, even perhaps transcendency. The way in which the young people in *13 Reasons Why* interact with Hannah's tapes and begin interacting with each other again through them is reminiscent of the highly ritualized collective worship practices of long ago pre-modern times:

---

[82] At the same time, the new type of television itself appears thoroughly nostalgic, since the designations for the usage techniques alone, such as *fast forward* and *rewind*—which enable navigation within the story, individual retrieval, without questioning the main direction of the course (there is no backward playback function)—refer to the buttons on a cassette recorder (also optionally called "radio thing", "boom box" or erroneously "obsolete", S01E01M13). They make it possible to experience that social time must always extend and cannot be compressed at will, that communities need time that can 'play out' in the logical course of things. Analogue music reproduction techniques are thus experiencing a revival for good reason, and not only in youth culture. While LPs hardly have an expiration date, especially in the professional music scene, Sony Walkmen, even (or especially) if they have heavy signs of use, are now being traded for several hundred euros.

- Before her death, Hannah gives very specific instructions on how to use her cassettes, setting explicit but comparatively easy-to-implement rules: "Rule number one: you listen. Number two: you pass it on. ... When you're done listening to all 13 sides... rewind the tapes, put them back in the box and pass them on to the next person." (S01E01M20) In the event that someone should disobey these strict instructions, she threatens the automatic release of the entire cassette series, which initially seems to be tantamount to eternal torment for the characters (who try to prevent this by all means).
- Hannah meticulously and imaginatively designs the box, the cassettes and their covers, as well as the enclosed city map by hand, decorating the everyday objects with ornaments and iconographic symbols, giving them their own distinctive aesthetic, making them an original one-off with a personal imprint and making them difficult to reproduce. In this way, Hannah gives the profane industrially produced cassette tapes the air of a sacred relic, which is only further mythicized through the ritualized use of the young.
- Regardless of Hannah's instructions for use, it is also the materiality of the cassettes that creates the compulsion to certain ceremonies and handling: They must first be inserted into a suitable device, carefully handled and stored, and passed around by hand in order to remain usable and survive time. The content and meaning of this 'holy' scripture is not immediately accessible, but only to those who have mastered the practices of use, who are willing to make the effort to handle it, and who can also decipher the content according to the instructions.
- Hannah's serial story, anecdotally composed of several individual narratives, develops a tragic, almost biblical dynamic, making her after a long and inexorable passion story of unbearable torment to a lonely martyr. She selflessly takes upon herself the guilt of the sinners surrounding her, thereby enabling them to recognize their transgressions with atonement and to come together again after the experience of loneliness—united by the common belief that Hannah's pain should not have been in vain. In this way, the individual episodic story of suffering becomes a universal narrative that seems to be inscribed with a universally valid knowledge of the world.
- In this, the tapes spoken by Hannah calmly, wisely and credibly have the status of an elegy, even a wistful sermon, in which the call to a new moral life is articulated. The voice resounds with the kind of omniscience one would hope for from one's counterpart in prayer, or at least confession—just as Hannah appears in Season 2 as an angel (albeit a rather intrusive one) who acts as a superhuman interlocutor for Clay. This presence, emanating from the sound of the disembodied voice, creates a 'togetherness in aloneness' as it applies to a believer's conversation with God.

– Thanks to the recording form, these prophecies can be repeated as often as desired and listened to regardless of location, which is how Hannah's admonishing words first find distribution and a hearing. This creates the possibility of reciting the text, reinterpreting it and giving it new meaning for one's own life situation. In the collective repetition of this 'Holy Scripture' and its constant interpretation, a special form of truth emerges that reaches beyond the immediate content of the text and can only exist because a community of believers attaches itself to it.

– At the same time, the cassette tapes (with a relatively long lifespan compared to CDs and certain data formats), as well as the incipient reproduction practices (backup copy at Tony's, upload by Clay), enable Hannah to achieve 'immortality' through the omnipresence of her story, which can no longer be erased. As a voice 'resurrected' from nowhere, a sacred, almost divine aura surrounds her, which is only enhanced by the comprehensively 'omniscient', almost prophetic nature of her narratives (cf. Fig. 3). By the time the tapes are buried in the series finale, the truth they have released has long since been duplicated in the minds of the faith community.

– While the tapes are initially intended only for a small circle of listeners, myths soon form around them in the school community, which then escalate with the publication of the recordings. Later, especially in the course of the court case in the second season, she takes on the role of an incarnation for certain complex contemporary discourses as an admonishing stalking and rape victim, which materialize in her as a person, which only further reinforces the myth surrounding her.

Without this list claiming to be exhaustive, it is obvious that Hannah's cassette series produces phenomena that also can be described for pre-modern script-bound monotheistic religions, such as Christian church morality. In this respect, the series itself refers to the diverse fan cultures and cult practices that surround mass media phenomena, and television series in particular. TV shows seem to be predestined for this—just think of the complex symbolic universes with their own language, morality and sacred texts, as they are produced by fans of the series *Star Trek* (the 'Trekkies'), and the bond between the 'followers of faith' that emanates from them.

The cult phenomena that emerge through Hannah's tapes in *13 Reasons Why* point to the multiple community-building functions of television series through the potential for meaning they offer, which springs from what Hills calls their expressions of

Fig. 3 The material presence of the tapes, releasing rituals of reception, transmission and storage, lends Hannah's serial narrative a spiritual aura. (S01E01M12). Still from *13 Reasons Why*, Netflix 2017–2020. (© Paramount Television)

"neoreligiosity".[83] Luckmann and Berger had described how societies depend on producing universally valid truths in order to interact and communicate meaningfully with each other on the basis of this shared understanding of the world: The fixed standardized stream of signs produced by religions, for example, creates a "symbolic universe" in whose order each individual is protected from the anomie of a loneliness of meaninglessness, can experience himself or herself as part of the larger whole, and can thereby experience transcendence.[84] Even if in the course of modernization strongly institutionalized, rigid and the society uniformly penetrating unitary forms of religion no longer played a greater role, the need for a world view as universal meaning system was not lost with it[85]—on the contrary: According to the needs of an increasingly free, highly differentiated and dynamically changing society the manifestations of the religious had changed, for instance by the emergence of a market of religions, the practice of religion moved into the non-public private sphere or religious topics were negotiated in the popular culture.[86] For Hills, television is predestined for the creation of such neo-religious experiences: Without the fan cultures generated by television being misunderstood as religion in the narrower, more traditional sense,[87] television generates various 'spiritual' practices of its own: it

---

[83] Hills ([2000] 2008).

[84] Berger, Luckmann (1967) p. 103.

[85] Luckmann (1963) p. 38.

[86] Luckmann (1967) p. 104.

[87] Hills (2002) p. 117.

creates specific forms of collective worship, canonization, and ritualization, thus transferring the procedures of institutionalized church religion into forms applicable to modernity.[88] Thus, for Gerbner and Gross, it is not surprising that while churches become empty, at the same time television habits even surpass the former attendance at mass in terms of religiosity.[89]

The ritualization practices that are released from televisual seriality and have a connecting effect as cult phenomena appear as typically telemedial. With Freud, part of the success of church religions lies in the fact that they make use of the human, quite natural[90] need for ritualized repetition practices.[91] Modernization and the secularization that begins with it initially create a chronic deficit of meaning because cultic acts no longer play a primary role in them. The routines (e.g. commuting between home and work), habits (e.g. brand loyalty) and compulsive actions (e.g. checking whether the door is locked) that emerge with modernity may help us not to get lost in the sheer infinity of possibilities for action, but they remain meaningless in themselves and do not come close to the meaning-giving and transcending power of pre-modern cults.

In *13 Reasons Why,* too, the characters' usual daily rituals seem increasingly purposeless, especially in view of the strokes of fate that seem to fall out of the blue one after the other: The communal meals (such as the obligatory breakfast, where no one listens to each other and the ignorant father prefers to sink into his iPad), the overstaged team-ball tournaments (which serve more to show off their athletes in the hope of a college scholarship than to strengthen the school community) and even the daily showers become more and more of a burden: "Look, I just. . . I turned the water on just now, and I thought about it all, the whole thing, taking clothes off, dealing with hair, and I just. . . I couldn't do it. . . . We shower, like, every day, and it's just, a lot." (S01E05M06) What everyday life has to offer here instills a certain amount of order, but hardly any communities, let alone transcendence. The ritual of listening to cassettes, on the other hand, is quite different: While the young people ritualistically listen through Hannah's tapes and pass them on, in times of social fragmentation they experience themselves again as part of a larger whole. For the

---

[88]Hills ([2000] 2008) pp. 137–139.

[89]Cf. Gerbner/Gross (1976) p. 177.

[90]Langer (1965) pp. 75–76.

[91]The strict regularity and punctuality with which prayers are said, Sunday sermons are delivered, and holidays are celebrated may outwardly appear with Freud as a pathological tendency to compulsive acts, but for Luckmann they are part of the "world view" produced by the religious, which enables its adherents to feel a sense of belonging to a comprehensive meaning-giving order and thus transcendence, cf. Luckmann (1967) pp. 55–56.

young people this is not easy to cope with (not least because this experience is accompanied by feelings of guilt). Some even resist the possibility that their lives, which seem so liberally formable and free of responsibility in an individualistic society, cannot simply be detached from all the contexts surrounding them—that the idea of a completely independent subject remains an illusion. The mythical reality content of the cassette series becomes the basis for new and urgently needed common communication, for new forms of close interactions, which only becomes possible again through the ritualized listening that Hannah had prescribed and that the serial medium itself demands.

Hickethier had already described for linear television that modernization goes hand in hand with an "individualization of media use", but that at the same time "more profound rituals can be established that have turned media use as a whole—and especially that of television—into a form of socialization of individuals."[92] *13 Reasons Why* demonstrates how the uniform ritualized practice of using the series becomes a prerequisite for the collective appropriation of the series text, which is then experienced as a shared reality as a result of communication. This shared ownership of truth allows young people to experience an unexpected community of meaning, just as viewers of series like *13 Reasons Why* become part of a world-spanning invisible community of truth at the moment of reception.

It is remarkable how the series heroes in the fictional world, just like the series viewers in front of the television screens, equally also make their own active contribution to the production of truth by producing text themselves: Television serials, through their narrative density and complexity, produce a "potentially infinitely large metatext",[93] which is expanded by fans through their own supplementary texts (characters, plotlines, backstories) into an independent universe of meanings.[94] What in reality is called "fan fiction" and has become a phenomenon surrounding every successful series production, not least due to the possibilities of exchange on the Internet, also plays out in *13 Reasons Why* when Clay decides to elicit an improbable confession of his deeds from the rapist Bryce and record it on the back of the seventh tape, i.e. as the 14th part. At the same time, first in conversations—in court, then after the publication of the tapes on the Internet—ever new meta-texts unfold, through which Hannah's tale of woe becomes an "inconclusive narrative"[95] and thus first becomes a "cult". Series thus establish an

---

[92] Hickethier (2008) p. 55. My translation.

[93] Gwenllian-Jones, Pearson (2004) p. xvii.

[94] Blanchet (2011) p. 40. My translation.

[95] Hills (2002) p. 143.

boundless universe in their admittedly finite stock of episodes, in which the characters and their actions are concretely located, but whose voids are filled by the fans with their own speculations, interpretations and fantasies. Together they imagine their own complete, from their point of view closed and consistent world that *makes sense*, what can be experienced as the basis for a functional community.

"It's Starting to Make Sense to Me Now."—Television as a Producer of Truth and Order

Television series thus produce communities of truth that are fed by the practices of their fans and the actual viewers. But TV series also produce truths and order of a more universal character that affects a society as a whole, holding it together and thus contributing to processes of socialization.

Truth as a binding consensus on the nature of shared social reality is a compelling prerequisite for people to be able to interact meaningfully with each other in a social context. Whereas, as has been shown, such universally valid knowledge was installed in pre-modern times by special institutions in a comparatively planned and controlled manner, modernity, on the other hand, is characterized by the diversification prevailing in it, by the fact that in it various relevant meaning-giving offers exist simultaneously and partly in competition with each other, which threatens the "promotion of community of meaning in communities of life"[96] and creates "the conditions for the emergence of subjective and intersubjective crises of meaning".[97] Because the permanence and reliability of the order of knowledge and values within modern societies always remain fragile, this is associated with a chronic uncertainty as to the extent to which the remaining members of society still feel committed at all to a concept of interconnecting universally valid truth. In an individualistic, liberal modern society, a lie is, for good reasons, only problematic in concrete special situations; nevertheless, a society remains dependent on a consensus about what is generally accepted as true and what is rejected as untrue.

Even the teenagers in *13 Reasons Why* don't really know what they can believe in anymore. Depending on how it benefits their own interests at the moment, everyone pretty much tells exactly what they want—what is true and what is not gradually becomes indistinguishable. This mode of uninhibited spreading of rumours, defamations and excuses only meets with bitterness with Hannah's series

---

[96]Berger, Luckmann (1995) p. 65.

[97]Ibid. p. 68.

of tapes: Even if in the end almost all members of the school community are aware that Hannah's stories correspond to the truth in their essence, some stick to the mode they have practised of defaming either the entire content or at least parts of the tapes as freely invented claims: Because Justin was incapable of protecting his girlfriend from being raped by Bryce (on whom he is materially and emotionally dependent), he convinces himself, and especially that very girlfriend, that everything actually happened quite differently than Hannah, who happened to be able to observe the event, had described it. The rapist himself also puts on a mask of sublime credibility for the trial and tells a freely invented story, behind which he tries to hide his own deep loneliness and whose absurdity is hard to believe and endure even for himself (S02E11). Because each individual has no direct interest in a concept of truth, from which the basic category of responsibility for every social cooperation would result, the most guilty ones systematically prevent their classmate Clay, who is working on a reappraisal of the events, from finding the truth until the end, which develops into an ever greater burden for the young people than their own misdemeanors and their consequences (the main theme of the third and fourth season). Only the consensus on truth they reach in the series finale becomes a hopeful outlook on a community that was still unthinkable in a world without the series.

That Justin, as well as the meddlesome school president Marcus, the over-involved Courtney, the voyeuristic photographer Tyler, and others, initially consider it at all realistic to be able to artificially withhold the truth about their own misdemeanors is rooted in a notable collective miscalculation, namely the strange underestimation of the ability of serial fictional narratives to appear vivid, logically plausible, and thus truthful. Of course, even Hannah's subjective 13-part narrative on tape can lay no claim to completeness or full accuracy of detail, which she herself even repeatedly addresses, and a certain appeal of the series also lies in the fact that the television viewer, as well as the characters in the diegesis, can never be conclusively sure whether the narratives of the two series are 'really' accurate at any given moment. Ultimately, however, the 13 cassette series episodes generate their own power of an unhidden reality that young people—lost among dubious 'photoshopped' images, petty pleasantries and the pressure to constantly stage themselves and their success—have long since become unaccustomed to. Because in the enigmatic world of *13 Reasons Why* (as in most dramatic television series of *Quality TV*) there are conspicuously no television series that could produce communities of meaning in the characters' universe, Hannah's cassette series creates a crushing honesty that becomes a burden for the young people, and for Clay in the second season even a pathological burden—but which ultimately appears as the last chance to overcome the late-modern lonelinesses of the individual characters and is therefore ultimately not really questioned by anyone.

Television viewers, on the other hand, can count themselves lucky that they live in a world in which television series exist, because for Keppler, with reference to Gehlen, television is becoming the central site of the mediation of meaning within late-modern societies: Television, as one of several "secondary institutions" organized by mass media, has the crucial role of "compensatorily taking the place of the disenchanted primary institutions of earlier times"[98] and substituting for their truth-giving effect. For Keppler, television has "long since become one among other authoritative *producers of meaning*,"[99] in that it provides television viewers with a sense of "what is historical, social, and cultural *present* beyond their own living environment." It provides them with "a more or less shared understanding of what is possible and impossible, alluring and repulsive, urgent or indifferent, here and now."[100] In a sentence: "In its continuous articulation and variation of what the current symbols of what is real and important are, television makes possible a collective consciousness of the present in modern societies, even beyond the boundaries of individual societies".[101]

Just as it is only the systematic reprocessing of what has happened in Hannah's serial narrative that gives young people a sense of what *really matters* in their present, of what is true and untrue, right and wrong, it is also the socially relevant and in this strength unrivalled achievement of television series that through them, as Hickethier writes, "in the presentation of media images, points of view, norms, values and knowledge are publicly communicated, whereby the medium of television makes an important contribution to the construction of a shared world among viewers". Television thus participates in the "constitutional process of social reality".[102]

Television series are thus not 'mirrors of society', but they themselves participate in a complex interdependent process of creating social reality.[103] Despite (or precisely because of) the highly individualized, globalized, and networked conditions of life, late modernity is also dependent on a more or less uniform canon of values and norms that makes it possible to predict the behavior of others to a sufficient degree, which makes social interactions within a complex society possible in the first place. Through the construction of generally valid self-evident

---

[98] Keppler (2010) p. 112. My translation.

[99] Ibid. p. 113. My translation.

[100] Keppler (2006) pp. 316–317. My translation.

[101] Ibid. My translation.

[102] Ibid. p. 96. My translation.

[103] Cf. Giddens (1991) p. 27.

truths, television series create what Berger and Luckmann see as a "minimum of mutual trust that must be presupposed for the existence of communities and thus of an entire society".[104] Even if distribution channels, aesthetics and usage practices are always changing, television series with their familiar characters, settings and props create the certainty that what was true in the last episode will also be true in the next, that the stability of reality can be relied upon. Television series often unfold their plot over a long period of time, which can span several decades, so that television viewers develop close parasocial relationships with their favorite characters, which allows them to partially predict the behavior of the series characters or at least to feel their motives, which then makes their behavior no longer seem arbitrary, but value-oriented and meaningful.[105]

Again and again, the young people in *13 Reasons Why* are plagued by the uncertainty that there are no longer any self-evident things in their lives, that even the most basic categories such as truth and untruth, right and wrong, love and resentment, which organize society, could become ineffective and meaningless: "Everything's broken. And I don't think any of it can be fixed." (S02E09M08) But through Hannah's series, bit by bit, they regain the confidence that even within their late-modern social reality, in which there hardly seem to be any certainties, there are universal concepts, binding criteria and clear rules, on the basis of which only community building becomes possible again (cf. Fig. 4). An inalienable, indisputable truth is thus inscribed in the cassette tapes as well as in the television series themselves: Although TV shows are freely invented texts, they give rise to an even *stronger* truth, a meta-reality that seems *more real* than the abstract truths of science or the subjective everyday perception of reality. The truths that television series produce through familiarity, order, and meaning are, all things considered, unassailable: No matter how much the insecure young people in *13 Reasons Why* resist the bitter truth—they cannot compete with the reality of serial narrative (even if it does not tell 'the whole story'). In this way, television series become perhaps the most important producer of security in a time of constant change that tends chronically towards uncertainty, an ontological lifeline through which communities can come together again.

---

[104] Berger, Luckmann (1995) p. 68. My translation.

[105] This is also one of the reasons for the conspicuous interest in sequel series such as *Bates Motel* and *Cobra Kai*, in which characters best known from cult films such as Norman Bates from *Psycho* and Johnny Lawrence from *Karate Kid* are released into a hyper-modernized reality in which they (like the audience) have to hold their own while all in all retaining the same character and nature traits and yet (as is only possible on television) remain forever recognizable.

Fig. 4 When confronted with the truth of the serial narrative, white lies become increasingly difficult to maintain, forcing a new community-building consensus about what is reality. (S01E12M22). Still from *13 Reasons Why,* Netflix 2017–2020. (© Paramount Television)

"I Think We Should Blame Ourselves.": Overestimating and Underestimating Oneself—Intervention Strategies in 13 Reasons Why

In the same way that *13 Reasons Why* plays out media-reflexively the extent to which television series participate in processes of community formation, the series provokes from the outset a very similar question about how mass media can or should be held responsible for their real-world interventions.

While the novel *13 Reasons Why* by Jay Asher was already a critical and popular favorite,[106] it was only the surprising success of the television series that led to an extremely controversial public discussion about the influence of television on the behavior of its viewers, especially in relation to minors. Parents, teachers and

---

[106] Asher (2008). Anyone wishing to purchase the current edition of the book on the US retail site amazon.com will see an unusual notice in the form of a banner: "If you are having suicidal thoughts, free and confidential support is available. Call the National Suicide Prevention Lifeline at 1-800-273-8255." Update: April 11, 2023.

psychologists raised concerns that the series could have a bad influence on young people and even incite them to suicide; in particular, the staging of suicide as a kind of vendetta would undermine the actually praiseworthy enlightening gesture of the youth series; some professional associations even called for a ban.[107]

Netflix felt compelled to place a variety of interventionist metatexts around the series: Inserts, text panels, and introductory clips warn against "Language, Sex, Drugs, Sexual Violence" and the thematization of "tough real-world issues" (S01E01M01). In short videos that precede the seasons, the actors hope for an open discourse on taboo problems of young people, refer to the telephone counselling service and the offers of help on 13ReasonsWhy.info.[108] The first three seasons are followed by a kind of '14th episode' entitled "Beyond The Reasons" with expert discussions between actors, series creators and experts, in which the central topics are worked through and the decisions of the characters are questioned and reflected.[109]

---

[107] This verified connection between reports and films about suicides and an increase in suicide rates or the number of cases of suicides with similar causes, known as the "Werther effect", was also the basis for numerous positions of interest groups and professional associations that warned of the dangers of the series. For example, the professional association of paediatricians and adolescent doctors demanded the "immediate cancellation" of the series (cf. Berufsverband der Kinder- und Jugendärzte (2017)). In the U.S., professional associations (including, ironically, the National Association of School Psychologists) also criticized the series as a possible trigger for imitative suicides. Recent studies show a correlation between the period of the series' release and a significant increase in suicide rates in the US (see Bridge, Greenhouse, Ruch et al (2019)) and recommend supervised viewing of the series for at-risk youth with suicidal thoughts, which provides an opportunity for sharing, as well as a high level of intervention among family and friends (Cf. Hong (2019)). On the limits of the Werther effect in *13 Reasons Why,* see also Wilson (2019) p. 204.

[108] On this website, sorted by country, national crisis hotlines can be found, a "conversation guide" as a PDF download, and, since May 2018, also six Youtube videos, each about one and a half minutes long, in which the actors in front of scenes of the series, like a video tutorial, offer help for certain problematic topics in the series (bullying, depression, drug abuse, gun violence, obtaining consent for sexual acts) as well as advice for a dialogue with teenagers ("You may wanna point out that some of the characters don't always make good decisions."). In three-minute featurettes, the performers express their excitement at having participated in a meaningful task, while also pointing out the public outreach opportunities. However, there is no imprint via which Netflix itself could be reached directly, for example to point out to the provider that some links do not work (as of January 19, 2021).

[109] One expert, for example, recommends not getting in the way of an "active shooter", as Clay is allowed to do in fiction, and talking down to him—even if, in case of doubt, this may not cost your own life but many others.

The amount and variety of metatexts arranged around a television show here because of its possible negative effects seems unprecedented. "Enjoy the show. Enjoy the conversation. And take care of each other."—That's what the performers wish their audience at the beginning of season three, before the show begins. But such forceful, almost insistent pleas can also be found within the diegesis: The characters don't just live out their ideas of a better life, they also formulate well-meaning but surprisingly explicit directives for action. They even address their unmistakable calls directly to their audience, such as when Clay leaves the school psychologist's office and speaks to him, almost directly into the camera, "It has to get better, the way we treat each other, look out for each other, it has to get better somehow." (S01E13M41).

In this multiplicity of obviously strained intervention efforts that are very atypical for television series, an astonishing mixture of boundless overestimation and at the same time suprising underestimation of the power of television and its audience is articulated: On the one hand, the television series—as public and scientific discourse also suggests—trusts itself to leave such an intense impression on the young people in front of the screens that in individual cases they would even do something to themselves. On the other hand, serial television also does not want to rely on the powerful socializing potentials typical of television series (of which it is obviously quite aware in its self-reflexive play) as a possible antidote—and in doing so risks neutralizing television's own important power of producing social cohesion. Whereas in the series the "suicide prevention" posters in the high school hallways are torn up by the angry characters and the phone counseling hotlines dutifully recited by the teacher are simply faded out behind Hannah's thoughts, *13 Reasons Why* surrounds itself with an arsenal of self-protective methods that only grow more extensive and problematic from season to season before the series creators seem to have made peace with themselves and their critics in the final season.[110]

This expresses a certain self-image of the television series: In the series, the characters share a collective guilt among themselves, without any individual factor being able to be singled out as the fatal cause of Hannah's inexorable process of isolation: "You think you could have changed anything. What does that make you? God?" (S01E11M41)—This is the question Tony asks his Clay, who is struggling with terrible feelings of guilt and who imagines that he has set in

---

[110]Perhaps the series managers are only acting for legal reasons at this point, in order to avoid a civil lawsuit (which is typically costly in the US), or they fear that interference or even restrictions could be threatened due to national youth protection laws.

motion a chain of tragic misfortunes through a regrettable but in itself trivial human error of judgement—but who first becomes aware, only through the cassette series, of the dense interweaving of causes and effects, options and offers for action, history and memory, beliefs and rituals, values and norms in a social context. The television series, on the other hand, allows itself, in Tony's words, to be burdened with a 'godlike' responsibility that rationalizes the complexity of social coexistence in terms of individual factors and thus at the same time over-simplifies it—and relativizes the diverse community-building functions of television series, which all in all do not tend to endanger social life, but rather to enrich it, and in late modernity perhaps make it possible in the first place.[111] A society that unilaterally attributes a systematic share of the blame for such tragic cases to its aesthetically sophisticated, narratively complex and discursively progressive television series, of all things, fails to recognize and endangers the important role of late-modern television series as perhaps the most important institution it has left to strengthen the binding force between the members of society as a whole.

"There's a Bond."—The Last Community

13 Reasons Why tells—as it is typical for contemporary TV series—about life in an age of increasing loneliness. Young people do a lot to escape the emptiness, anonymity and superficiality of high school, suburbia and smartphones, but all their hopes for a remnant of community remain unfulfilled: Just like the last places that promised community, such as cafés, cinemas and diners, the families, cliques and relationships of trust grind apart between money worries, competition and overstraining, until only the emergency communities—self-help groups, sports teams and parties—are left, where instead of trust, team spirit and exuberance, only envy, self-importance and excess await. In the course of the plot, even the last life rafts are washed away by the lonely forces of late modernity, because they either perish from their own basic contradictions or turn out to be ineffective and thus superfluous. Because the living conditions of their late-modern reality turn out to be unlivable for the young people, Clay sees in his nightmares a post-modern world that has collapsed in on itself, perishing from environmental destruction,

---

[111] As a counterpart to the Werther effect, the Papageno effect has been described, according to which the public discussion of suicide as a social problem, the identification of ways out and the diversity of causes can also reduce suicide rates, cf. Niederkrotenthale, Voracek, Herberth (2010) and Schnitzer (2020).

robotization, and resource warfare—and in which the young people are left entirely to their own devices: "Fighting an inhospitable world that took away their childhood. Having to become adults before their time, trying to take their world back." (S04E08M04).

Ironically it is the death of Hannah Baker, grown out of a late-modern abandonment that can no longer be increased, that becomes a turning point in the lives of the lonely, as a hope for the return of a sense of community arises again through her cassette series—*behind and in front of the screen*. In *13 Reasons Why,* the people are initially trapped in a world in which nothing and no one can show them how it might be possible to lead a meaningful life even under late-modern conditions and to counteract the loneliness: "I did the best I knew how. No one tought me better", a dying man regrets his wrong decisions as a father here, which can no longer be corrected (S03E13M62). New late-modern loneliness intrudes into the world of *13 Reasons Why* with each season, making real social contact seem unlikely. However, when fictional seriality finally enters their lonely TV-less world, their lives seem logically ordered again, positively changeable through appropriate behavior, connected by a shared history, collective memories—a common sense that makes communities shapable and livable again. The painful truth that Hannah's serial narrative unfolds seems at first to further tear apart the already isolated characters— but ultimately it is through this very series that the lonely slowly reunite, through which a foreshadowing of a sense of mutual responsibility, trust and, indeed, community, once again emerges. In the end, the completely exhausted characters, some of whom have been inadmissibly overworked and literally tortured by the series makers, can even bury the tapes, because both the television and cassette series conclude with what seemed impossible without Hannah: "We had to love each other at the end of it all." (S04E10M86, cf. Fig. 5).

In such a world, which television series present to us, communities are imaginable again—and thus they combat the nihilistic deficits of meaning of late modernity as an age of greatest loneliness with, of all things, their *own* modernity: Television series allow us—despite all tendency to dramatization, scandalization and simplification—to better cope with the challenges of modernity and to master its errors more securely, without questioning the obvious successes of modernization. With the help of television series, we can settle into modernity by providing us with new kinds of experiences of social closeness, while at the same time progressively modernizing ourselves more and more. However, this tendency toward further modernization potentially means only new, more oppressive lonelinesses— and it is unclear whether serial fictional television of the future will be able to counter them anymore.

Fig. 5 "For the first time I can remember, the town seemed small, tiny"—Hannah's serial narrative connects the disoriented characters to a community that promises at least temporary stability. Whether it will hold up against ever new late-modern lonely challenges, however, remains in question. (S04E10M87) Still from *13 Reasons Why,* Netflix 2017–2020. (© Paramount Television)

References

Adli, Mazda (2017) Stress in the City. Warum uns Städte krank machen und wie wir sie lebenswerter gestalten können. München, C. Bertelsmann

Anderson, Benedict (1983) Imagined Communities. Reflections on the Origin and Spread of Nationalism. London, Verso

Asher, Jay (2008) Thirteen reasons why. A novel. Princeton, N.J., Recording for the Blind & Dyslexic

Assmann, Aleida (1999) Zeit und Tradition. Kulturelle Strategien der Dauer. Köln, Böhlau

Assmann, Aleida (2006) Der lange Schatten der Vergangenheit. Erinnerungskultur und Geschichtspolitik. München. Beck

Assmann, Jan ([1992] 2000): Das kulturelle Gedächtnis. Schrift, Erinnerung und politische Identität in frühen Hochkulturen, München.

Balke, Gregor (2015) Episoden des Alltäglichen – Sitcoms und Gesellschaft. Eine wissenssoziologische und hermeneutische Lektüre. Weilerswist, Velbrück Wissenschaft

Barney, Darin (2010) The Network Society. Cambridge, Polity

Bauman, Zygmunt ([2003] 2014) Liquid love. On the Frailty of Human Bonds. Cambridge, Polity

Bauman, Zygmunt (2000) Community. Seeking Safety in an Insecure World. Oxford, Blackwall Polity

Beck, Ulrich (2007) Weltrisikogesellschaft. Auf der Suche nach der verlorenen Sicherheit. Frankfurt, Suhrkamp

Berger, Peter L., Thomas Luckmann (1967) The Social Construction of Reality. New York, Anchor Books

Berger, Peter L., Thomas Luckmann (1995) Modernität, Pluralismus und Sinnkrise. Die Orientierung des modernen Menschen. Gütersloh, Verl. Bertelsmann-Stiftung

Berufsverband der Kinder- und Jugendärzte (BVKJ) (2017) Kinder- und Jugendärzte fordern Verbot für Netflix-Serie „Tote Mädchen lügen nicht", Pressemeldung des Berufsverbandes der Kinder- und Jugendärzte, 06.07.2017. https://www.bvkj.de/presse/pressemitteilungen/ansicht/article/kinder-und-jugendaerzte-fordern-verbot-fuer-netflix-serie-tote-maedchen-luegen-nicht-der-be/. Accessed on 03.06.2020

Blanchet, Robert (2011) Quality TV. Eine kurze Einführung in die Geschichte und Ästhetik neuer amerikanischer Fernsehserien. In: Blanchet, Robert, Kristina Köhler, Tereza Smid et al. (Eds.) Serielle Formen. Von den frühen Film-Serials zu aktuellen Quality-TV- und Onlineserien. Marburg, Schüren, pp. 37–70

Bridge, Jeffrey A., Joel B. Greenhouse, Donna Ruch et al. (2019) Association Between the Release of Netflix's 13 Reasons Why and Suicide Rates in the United States: An Interrupted Time Series Analysis. In: Journal of the American Academy of Child and Adolescent Psychiatry 59, volume 2, pp. 236–243

Cavell, Stanley (1982) The Fact of Television. In: Daedalus 111, volume 4, pp. 75–96

Dant, Tim (2012) Television and the Moral Imaginary. Society Through the Small Screen. Basingstoke.

Engell, Lorenz (2003) Tasten, Wählen, Denken. Genese und Funktion einer philosophischen Apparatur. In: Münker, Stefan, Alexander Roesler, Mike Sandbothe (Eds.): Medienphilosophie. Beiträge zur Klärung eines Begriffs. Frankfurt a. M., Fischer-Taschenbuch-Verlag, pp. 53–76

Engell, Lorenz (2011) Erinnern/Vergessen. Serien als operatives Gedächtnis des Fernsehens. In: Blanchet, Robert, Kristina Köhler, Tereza Smid et al. (Eds.): Serielle Formen. Von den frühen Film-Serials zu aktuellen Quality-TV- und Onlineserien. Marburg, Schüren, pp. 115–132

Engell, Lorenz (2012) Folgen und Ursachen. Über Serialität und Kausalität. In: Kelleter, Frank (Ed.): Populäre Serialität: Narration – Evolution – Distinktion. Zum seriellen Erzählen seit dem 19. Jahrhundert. Bielefeld, Transcript, pp. 241–258

Fabeck, Hans von (2007) Jenseits der Geschichte. Zur Dialektik des Posthistoire. München, Fink

Fukuyama, Francis (1992) The End of History and the Last Man. New York, Free Press

Gerbner, George, Larry Gross (1976) Living With Television: The Violence Profile. In: Journal of Communication 26. Spring, pp. 172–199

Giddens, Anthony (1991) Modernity and Self-Identity. Self and Society in the Late-modern Age. Stanford, Stanford University Press

Goffman, Erving (2016) Rahmen-Analyse. Ein Versuch über die Organisation von Alltagserfahrungen. Frankfurt a. M., Suhrkamp

Gross, Larry, Michael Morgan (1985): Television and Enculturation. In: Joseph R. Dominick, James E. Fletcher (Eds.): Broadcasting Research Methods. Boston, Allyn and Bacon, pp. 221–234

Gwenllian-Jones, Sara, Roberta E. Pearson (2004) Introduction. In: Pearson, Roberta E., Sara Gwenllian-Jones (Eds.): Cult Television. Minneapolis, University of Minnesota Press, pp. ix–xx

Hickethier, Knut (1992) Die Fernsehserie – eine Kette von Verhaltenseinheiten. Problemstellungen für die Seriendiskussion. In: Beiträge zur Film- und Fernsehwissenschaft 33, volume 43, pp. 11–18

Hickethier, Knut (1994) Die Fernsehserie und das Serielle des Programms. In: Giesenfeld, Günter (Ed.): Endlose Geschichten. Serialität in den Medien; ein Sammelband. Hildesheim, Olms, pp. 55–71

Hickethier, Knut (2008) Fernsehen, Rituale und Subjektkonstitutionen. Ein Kapitel Fernsehtheorie. In: Fahlenbrach, Kathrin, Ingrid Brück, Anne Bartsch (Eds.): Medienrituale. Rituelle Performanz in Film, Fernsehen und Neuen Medien. Wiesbaden, VS Verlag für Sozialwissenschaften, pp. 47–58

Hills, Matt ([2000] 2008) Media fandom, neoreligiosity and cult(ural) studies, in: Mathijs, Ernest, Xavier Mendik (Eds.): The Cult Film Reader, Maidenhead/New York, Open University Press/McGraw-Hill Education, pp. 133–148

Hills, Matt (2002) Fan Cultures. London, Routledge

Hong, Victor et al. (2019) 13 Reasons Why: Viewing Patterns and Perceived Impact Among Youths at Risk of Suicide. In: Psychiatric Services 70, volume 2, pp. 107–114.

Keppler, Angela (2006) Mediale Gegenwart. Eine Theorie des Fernsehens am Beispiel der Darstellung von Gewalt. Frankfurt a. M., Suhrkamp

Keppler, Angela (2010) Variationen des Selbstverständnisses: Das Fernsehen als Schauplatz der Formung sozialer Identität. In: Maren Hartmann, Andreas Hepp (Eds.): Die Mediatisierung der Alltagswelt. Wiesbaden, VS Verlag für Sozialwissenschaften, pp. 111–126

Kirchmann, Kay (2006) Philosophie der Möglichkeiten. Das Fernsehen als konjunktivisches Erzählmedium. In: Oliver Fahle, Lorenz Engell (Eds.): Philosophie des Fernsehens. München, Fink, pp. 157–172

Langer, Susanne K. (1965) Philosophie auf neuem Wege. Das Symbol im Denken, im Ritus und in der Kunst. Frankfurt a. M., S. Fischer

Lübbe, Hermann (1997) Selbstbestimmung und über Fälligkeiten der Moralisierung und der Entmoralisierung moderner Lebensverbringung. In: Drehsen, Volker, Dieter Henke, Reinhard Schmidt-Rost et al. (Eds.): Der ‚ganze Mensch‘. Perspektiven lebensgeschichtlicher Individualität; Festschrift für Dietrich Rössler zum siebzigsten Geburtstag. Berlin/New York

Lübbe, Hermann (2003) Im Zug der Zeit. Verkürzter Aufenthalt in der Gegenwart. Berlin, Walter de Gruyter

Luckmann, Thomas (1963) Das Problem der Religion in der modernen Gesellschaft. Institution, Person und Weltanschauung. Freiburg, Rombach

Luckmann, Thomas (1967) The Invisible Religion. The Problem of Religion in Modern Society. New York, Macmillan

Luhmann, Niklas (1990) Risiko und Gefahr. In: Soziologische Aufklärung, Band 5. Opladen, Westdeutscher Verlag, pp. 126–162

Luhmann, Niklas (1991): Soziologie des Risikos. Berlin, Walter de Gruyter

Mácha, Karel (1968) Der einsame Mensch in der Industriezivilisation. In: Internationale Dialog-Zeitschrift 1, volume 3, pp. 291–297

Mikos, Lothar (2010) Fernsehen und Film – Sehsozialisation. In: Vollbrecht, Ralf, Claudia Wegener (Eds.): Handbuch Mediensozialisation. Wiesbaden, VS Verlag für Sozialwissenschaft

Mittell, Jason (2006) Narrative Complexity in Contemporary American Television. In: Velvet Light Trap 58, pp. 29–40.

Mittell, Jason (2015) Complex TV. The poetics of contemporary television storytelling. New York/London, New York University Press

Neverla, Irene (1992a) Der soziale Zeitgeber Fernsehen. Das elektronische Medium als Komponente und Agens der abstraktlinearen Zeit unserer Gesellschaft. In: Hickethier, Knut (Ed.): Fernsehen. Wahrnehmungswelt, Programminstitution und Marktkonkurrenz. Frankfurt am Main/Berlin, Lang, pp. 23–39

Neverla, Irene (1992b) Fernseh-Zeit. Zuschauer zwischen Zeitkalkül und Zeitvertreib. Eine Untersuchung zur Fernsehnutzung. München, Ölschläger

Neverla, Irene (2010) Medien als soziale Zeitgeber im Alltag: Ein Beitrag zur kultursoziologischen Wirkungsforschung. In: Hartmann, Maren, Andreas Hepp (Eds.): Die Mediatisierung der Alltagswelt. Wiesbaden, VS Verlag für Sozialwissenschaften, pp. 183–194

Newiak, Denis (2018) Nicht-Ort Bates Motel. Vorüberlegungen zu einer Ikonografie der Einsamkeit in der amerikanischen Moderne. In: VZKF Schriften zur Kultur- und Mediensemiotik 4, volume 5, pp. 79–122

Newiak, Denis (2019) Serial Horrors of Loneliness: The Impossibility of Communitization in The Walking Dead. In: ZER – Revista de Estudios de Comunicación 24, volume 47, pp. 51–64

Newiak, Denis (2020) Telemediale Narrative und Ästhetiken spätmoderner Vereinsamung am Beispiel von 13 Reasons Why. In: Krauß, Florian, Moritz Stock (Eds.): Teen TV: Repräsentationen, Rezeptionen und Produktionen zeitgenössischer Jugendserien. Wiesbaden, Springer VS, pp. 65–94

Niederkrotenthaler, Thomas, Martin Voracek, Arno Herberth et al. (2010) Role of media reports in completed and prevented suicide: Werther v. Papageno effects. In: The British journal of psychiatry: the journal of mental science 197, volume 3, pp. 234–243

Niethammer, Lutz, Axel Dossmann (2000) Kollektive Identität. Heimliche Quellen einer unheimlichen Konjunktur. Reinbek, Rowohlt Taschenbuch

Nietzsche, Friedrich ([1887] 1967): Posthumous Fragments (=NF). In: *Digital critical edition of the complete works and letters*, based on the critical text by G. Colli and M. Montinari, Berlin/New York, de Gruyter 1967–, edited by Paolo D'Iorio

Reckwitz, Andreas (2017) Die Gesellschaft der Singularitäten. Zum Strukturwandel der Moderne. Berlin, Suhrkamp

Rosa, Hartmut ([2013] 2018) Beschleunigung und Entfremdung. Entwurf einer kritischen Theorie spätmoderner Zeitlichkeit. Berlin, Suhrkamp

Schnitzer, Anastasia (2020) Aufklärung über Suizidalität im Jugendalter in der Netflix-Serie 13 Reasons Why. In: Krauß, Florian; Moritz Stock (Eds.): Teen TV: Repräsentationen, Rezeptionen und Produktionen zeitgenössischer Jugendserien. Wiesbaden, Springer VS, pp. 95–112

Schütz, Alfred, Thomas Luckmann (1975) Strukturen der Lebenswelt. Neuwied, Luchterhand

Schwab, Reinhold (1997) Einsamkeit. Grundlagen für die klinisch-psychologische Diagnostik und Intervention. Huber, Bern/Seattle

Sontheimer, Kurt (1976) Die gesamtgesellschaftliche Verpflichtung des Fernsehens. In: Brüssau, Werner, Dieter Stolte, Richard Wisser (Eds.): Fernsehen. Ein Medium sieht sich selbst. Mainz, v. Hase und Köhler, pp. 162–168

Tönnies, Ferdinand (1887) Gemeinschaft und Gesellschaft. Abhandlung des Communismus und des Socialismus als empirischer Culturformen. Leipzig, Fues

Turkle, Sherry ([2011] 2017) Alone together. Why we expect more from technology and less from each other. New York, Basic Books

Twenge, Jean M. (2017) IGen. Why Today's Super-Connected Kids Are Growing Up Less Rebellious, More Tolerant, Less Happy – and Completely Unprepared for Adulthood – and What That Means for the Rest of Us. New York, Atria Books

Vaidhyanathan, Siva (2018) Antisocial Media. How Facebook Disconnects Us and Undermines Democracy. New York/Oxford, Oxford University Press

van Dijck, José (2013) The Culture of Connectivity. A Critical History of Social Media. New York.

Wilson, Graeme John (2019) ‚None of You Cared Enough': The Problematic Moralizing of 13 Reasons Why. In: Popular Culture Review 30, volume 1, pp. 189–209.

Dr. Denis Newiak is researching at the Chair of Applied Media Studies at the Brandenburg University of Technology Cottbus-Senftenberg on expressions of loneliness in film and television and on theories of socialisation through television series. Further research interests: science fiction film, artificial intelligence and virtual language assistants, aesthetics of film music. Recent publications: *Preparing for the Global Blackout. A Disaster Guide from TV and Cinema.* Stuttgart: ibidem, 2022; "Fighting Conspiracy Ideologies: Learning from Pandemic Movies to Counter the Post-Factual", in Abraham, Praveen; Mathew, Raisun (eds.): *The Post-Truth Era. Literature and Media.* New Delhi: Authors Press, 2021. pp. 21–31.

Season Greeting's: Between Special Events and Repetition from Television to Streaming Platforms

Sven Grampp

Requiem for the Christmas Episode

"There's no room for Christmas on streaming TV"[1] was a headline in the German newspaper *Süddeutsche Zeitung* shortly before Christmas 2017. This does not mean that Christmas no longer plays a role in fictional series on streaming plattorms.[2] Rather, it's about *temporal* and *formal-aesthetic* aspects: "Streaming portals that publish entire seasons can't use *specials*."[3] Episodes that deviate significantly from other episodes of the same series in terms of formal aesthetics are obsolete because the link between individual episodes and their *seasonal* broadcasting has been broken. The *temporal* coupling of *specials* and extra-ordinary events or holidays (Christmas, Halloween, etc.) is thus invalid. In contrast to this, *special episodes* were broadcast in the classic television programme precisely at Christmas time, which often firstly took Christmas as their theme, therefore synchronising the internal time of the series and the external time of the recipients. Secondly, these episodes are in many cases specially designed to fit the 'holy season', i.e. they deviate significantly from the standard episodic model of a series in terms of form

---

[1] Schmieder (2017) my translation, SG.

[2] For example, the first season of the *Netflix* series *Stranger Things* ends exactly on Christmas.

[3] Schmieder (2017) my translation, SG.

S. Grampp (✉)
Institute of Theatre and Media Studies, Friedrich-Alexander University of Erlangen-Nuremberg, Erlangen, Germany
e-mail: sven.grampp@fau.de

and aesthetics, or are at least staged as a deviation from central parameters of a particular serial narrative.

In fact, this thesis seems quite plausible. If all episodes of a season are released at the same time, i.e. are permanently available to all subscribers from this point on and can thus be received individually at all possible times with varying duration and intensity: What added value should there then be in adapting the content, motif or even the formal aesthetics of individual episodes to the particularities of a seasonal outside time? After all, such an adaptation is based on the *synchronization* of the episode broadcasting event and the culturally and collectively traditional celebration event. Nevertheless, it seems worthwhile to examine more closely the thesis of the irrelevance of seasonal events and television programming conventions for post-television streaming plattform series formulated in the cited newspaper note. Ultimately, as I want to show, this 'requiem' for Christmas episodes, published just before Christmas, misses the crucial point of how post-television series actually deal with seasonal events.

Temporal Modes of Televisual Programming

After initial uncertainty, television was established worldwide in the second half of the twentieth century mainly as a programme medium.[4] The main characteristic of this programme medium is the *temporal* arrangement of its programme, which can be distinguished *into different modes of time structuring.* They create the programme *side by side* and *overlapping each other.* Four temporal modes relevant for the organization and reception of television can be distinguished, namely (1) the *linear,* (2) the *repetitive,* (3) the *cyclical* and (4) the *singular* mode (cf. Fig. 1).[5]

Two of these time modes, namely the *cyclical* and the *singular* mode, are primarily responsible for the identity of *series and special events.*[6] For this reason, I will only discuss these in more detail. *Series* in the sense relevant here are to be

---

[4]Cf. for example Zielinski (1989); Abramson (2003) on television as a programme medium; Hickethier (2010) pp. 153–156, 279–280.

[5]Cf. on the different time modalities of television already Neverla (1992) Kirchmann (2013) pp. 366–386.

[6]Of course, special events and series also participate in the linear programming mode, simply because they are part of the linear television time mode. And it is also true that when episodes or festival recordings are repeated, series and special events participate in the repetitive time mode. Nevertheless, their *central identity-forming* temporal signatures are to be found in the cyclical or singular mode.

time mode	characteristics	shapes
linear	broadcasting flow, directed towards the future	covers all programme elements, incl. teaser, recap, announcements, live cam, etc.
repetitive	identical repetition of a broadcast segment	programme repeats of series, films, interval fillers, etc.
cyclic	- return of the broadcasting slot - similar programme segments return	e.g., news formats, advertising, fictional series ↕
singular	extraordinary events	celebrations I specials, disaster reporting

Fig. 1 Own representation (SG)

assigned to the *cyclical time mode*. For television series—whether they are designed to tell a story arc across multiple episodes or episodically—are about a successive series of similar elements and thus about the recurrence of similar elements, that is, about repetition *and* variation of a basic narrative pattern, concept or setting. This *intrinsic cyclical* sequence is not necessarily, but quite often, connected with the fitting of the series into a rigid programme scheme, namely in such a way that individual episodes or seasons are broadcast *cyclically* interrupted by other programme segments.[7]

In contrast to this, the *special event* is to be assigned to the *singular* time mode. It is, after all—in this respect analogous to catastrophe reporting—an outstanding, unique or at least rarely occurring (media) event that temporarily suspends the usually very tightly knit corset of daily and weekly programming patterns in order to create the centre of media attention in the meantime.[8] Despite the exceptionality, it is nevertheless true that special events such as the Football World Championship or Christmas, which are broadcast and staged on television, are on the one hand *planned* in advance for the long term and on the other hand recur *cyclically*. In this

---

[7] Cf. concisely Hickethier (2010) p. 279 f.

[8] One only has to think of the temporary suspension of the usual programming schedule for major events such as the first manned moon landing, weddings of various royals, Football World Championships or even broadcasts for Christmas. These television special event are often accompanied by an overrun of the scheduled television time, the spontaneous scheduling of a live broadcast, extensive pre- and post-reporting, excessive advertising of the event or, in the case of television series, by an overlength of the episode and/or formal-aesthetic *special effects*. On the celebration as a televisual media event cf. Dayan/Katz (1994); on catastrophe or disruption as a media event, cf. Kirchmann (2010).

respect, the transmission of such special events as well participates in the cyclically schematized time mode of the television program. Insofar we can speak of a series of special events, or to put it even more paradoxically: of special events that return cyclically in a singular mode.

It is also true that series not only build successive identities and variability through their cyclical progression and broadcasting, but due to massive series competition and preceding episodes, it is probable and indeed common that series also operate with *strategies of overbidding*.[9] This ultimately means: Series participate in the singular time mode. At least in the course of many series, the aim is to offer something new, extraordinary, spectacular and surprising—again and again. One more paradoxically pointed: Series produce something even more singular in a cyclically recurring manner.

This very general structural interlocking of cyclical and singular time modes will be examined in more detail in the following using a very concrete phenomenon, in which the interlocking of series and special events is turned around even further: The *reentry* of the special events into the television series is to be investigated on the basis of various case studies. The question at stage here reads: How and for what purpose is the (Christmas) event virulent *in* fictional series as a *special episode?*[10]

---

[9]Cf. fundamentally Sudmann (2017). On this basis, Sudmann argues that in the more recent development of series there are no longer any *special episodes* at all and that basically only a serial logic of overbidding exists that makes individual *specials* needless or that *specials are* now inscribed in the series across episodes as a structural characteristic of permanent self-transgression. Sudmann writes: It is "no wonder that in times when the serial form of the episodic series hardly plays a role anymore, the practice of the Very Special Episode has also disappeared." (Ibid., p. 287, my translation, SSG) It has survived only in parody. This argumentation seems to me hardly plausible, if only against the background of *empirical* findings on the *Christmas Special episode*. Moreover, even if it were the case that there were only parodies of the 'very special show' (which is not the case), such a parody would still strategically remain a 'very special show', especially in the form of an 'anti very special show'. Furthermore, in my opinion, this line of argument ignores *intraserial* dynamics in the context of television as a programming medium and its connection to extraserial factors. Just as Christmas always returns, so too does the 'very special Christmas show', which as such in many cases year after year sets a (frequently similar) difference to other episodes of the same series.

[10]In the following remarks, I will refer exclusively to *fictional* series. Non-fictional series, such as documentary formats, probably follow different principles, which would certainly be worth investigating in more detail, but which will be left out here in order to be able to elaborate the connection between special events and series without running the risk of losing myself in differentiations and various relativizations. For the same reason, I will limit myself to *special episodes* about *Christmas*.

Christmas in TV Series

The cited article from the *Süddeutsche Zeitung* rightly points out that there are a large number of *special episodes* in the history of television series that were broadcast at Christmas. Several examples since the 1950s could be cited; many have already been the subject of research.[11] I will only go into a few of them in order to illustrate the range of different aspects that can be found in the design, location, and functionalization of Christmas episodes in the context of television programming.

The weekly domestic sitcom *The Adventures of Ozzie and Harriet* (ABC, 1952– 66), which centers on the everyday 'adventures' of the Nelson family,[12] features several Christmas episodes during its comparatively long run.[13] In the following I will concentrate on the episode *The Busy Christmas,* which had its television premiere shortly before Christmas on December 19, 1954 and was broadcast again eight years later, on December 24, 1962, with a new framework story. This repetion on Christmas Eve 1962 will be the focus of the following, since this broadcast has many aspects of a *Christmas Special episode* that can be found in various television series and variants to date.

Unsurprisingly, the episode *The Busy Christmas* is set at Christmas time and revolves around Christmas (or, more precisely, around Christmas preparations in a small US town: hanging lights, buying Christmas trees, etc.). Serial outside time and

---

[11]Cf. for example the monograph Werts (2006) or the study on the subversion of the *Christmas Special* by and in the *'Christmas Specials'* of so-called Post-Network Television by Hoffman (2017). For an intelligent and critical overview see: Longden (2019).

[12]For a concise overview, including basic data on the series, see Weisblat (2019).

[13]Just to name a few dates and episodes: In the first season, the episode *The Boy's Christmas Money* airs on 19.12.1952, then exactly seven days later, on December 26, 1952, the episode appropriately titled *Late Christmas Gift* is broadcast for its initial airing. In the second season, the episode *The Miracle* can be seen on 25.12.1953. Here, too, the title clearly refers to the Christmas season. In the third season, the episode *The Lost Christmas Gift* is broadcast for the first time on December 24, 1954. Incidentally, all the episodes listed are strictly fitted into the weekly broadcast mode. Here, then, from the outset, the supposedly 'outstanding' Christmas episode is, on the one hand, fitted into the more rigid cyclical programme scheme; even at holy time the 'profane' programme scheme is not broken up. On the other hand, the 'outstanding' episode is narratively synchronized directly with the outside time of the recipient and accordingly no difference is drawn on this level between a special series celebration time and the fworld of the recipients. At Christmas, as elsewhere during the year, the recipient should be able to 'enjoy' the cyclical recurrence of the series narrative, which is closely linked to his or her rhythm of life.

inside time are intricately intertwined when the episode airs in 1962—it airs on Christmas Eve, which is exactly when the series narrative ends. Moreover, the episode is marked as a special one on several levels: in terms of content, for example, a 'magical' event takes place for Ozzie. Miraculously, his lights, which he had installed unsucessfully on his house, do end up shining with unexpected strength. Likewise, Ozzie's failure to have purchased a Christmas tree ultimately dissolves into pleasant surprise. Furthermore, the viewers follow a comparatively long musical interlude at the end of the episode: Neighbors and friends pass by the Nelsons' house. They sing a choral song; the Nelsons join in, step out into the street, and become part of the choir that is about to leave for mass. This musical interlude on the street is unusual. On the one hand, it creates a thoroughly non-comedic situation within an otherwise permanently situation-comic Domestic Sitcom.[14] On the other hand, the living room, even the Nelsons' property, is left behind and the street becomes the setting, complete with camera movement that follows the chorus and points offstage. Location, chorus motif and camera operation cannot be described as anything other than extraordinary in the context of this Domestic Sitcom.

The Busy Christmas, however, is marked as a *Christmas Special episode* not only since the episode was broadcast on December 24, but also because this broadcast is situated beyond the normally strictly timed weekly broadcast mode of the series.[15] Furthermore, the episode is given a paratext in the 1962 broadcast— the viewers are directly addressed by Ozzie and Harriet Nelson at the beginning and end of the episode. They send Christmas greetings to their viewers. Thus, there is an explicit appeal to parasocial interaction that closely synchronizes intraserial televi- sion time and extraserial recipient time. During their Christmas greetings, the 1962

---

[14] Although it has to be put into perspective here: Song interludes (without *laugh tracks*) became a common motif in the later seasons, especially performed by Ricky Nelson, who also made a career as a singer beyond the series. Nevertheless, the choral singing on the street in *The Busy Christmas* remains exceptional.

[15] In fact, this is somewhat unusual – after all, as noted earlier, the episodes of this series are usually comparatively rigidly fitted into the weekly broadcast mode. This also applies to the first broadcast of the episode: there, the days before Christmas in particular are negotiated intradiegetically in order to synchronize the internal world of the series and the external world of the recipients. The next episode is then consequently titled *The Day after Christmas*. This episode premiered on December 26, in keeping with the weekly broadcast rhythm. This is exceptionally *not* the case with the repeat of the episode *The Busy Christmas* in 1962. The 14th season airs its last regular episode in 1954 on December 15 and does not resume until January 12, 1955. In between we find the repetition broadcast of *The Busy Christmas* – and insofar it fits not in the seven-day interval.

Nelsons explicitly think back to their Christmas in 1954.[16] At the end of the episode, their son Ricky sings a Christmas carol under the Christmas tree, which is considerably larger than in 1954, in the presence of his family for the viewers in front of the television screens. At Christmas 1962, the largely narratively linear progression of the series into the future is interrupted, and the repetition of the episode in the pre- and post-paratext is remembered as a series and life story that the protagonists share with the actors and the viewers.[17]

So what we have here is an extraordinary episode at and for Christmas, on at least five levels: (1) at the level of *paratextual* framing (direct address to television viewers, family gathering under the Christmas tree, including musical interlude by Ricky), (2) in terms of *content-narrative* (Ozzie experiences 'miracles'), (3) in terms of *formal aesthetics* (long passages of choral singing, lack of situational comedy and camera shots beyond the living room), (4) in terms of the *air date,* which *interrupts* the series' weekly *airing rhythm* precisely on Christmas Eve, and (5) the repetition of an episode that briefly *suspends* the *linear progression* of the Nelsons' serialized lives into the future.

In order to be able to grasp the connections between special event and series outlined here even more precisely and universally, a conceptual differentiation of the serial on the basis of various prefixes is proposed and their connection to the category of the special event is illustrated on the basis of *The Busy Christmas* (cf. Fig. 2).[18]

In The Busy Christmas, the Christmas feast is evidently *intraserially* virulent, or to put it more precisely: *intradiegetically,* the Christmas feast is the central event; all other events find their telos in it. On an *extradiegetic* level, Christmas is *ex negativo*

---

[16] On this practice of re-contextualizing an old episode, see also, for example, the Christmas episode of *Bewitched,* entitled *A Vision of Sugar Plums,* first broadcast on December 24, 1964, then provided with a new introduction and staged as a *flashback* a year later on December 23, 1965.

[17] Harriet appeals to the audience at the beginning, after Ozzie has announced that the repetition of an eight-year-old episode is now to follow: "[W]e warn you, just in case, we all look a little younger." This once again clearly synchronizes the differential marking of present and past with the physical aging process of the participants. At the end, Ozzie, also addressing the audience, visibly endeavors to incorporate the audience's hypothetical past: "[W]e are all [!] a few years older now." In a certain sense, an event is created in this case by means of repetition – the series event of a *special Christmas episode* is created through the identical *repetition* of a program segment on a holiday.

[18] Cf. on this kind of work with prefixes in the context of television series already Sudmann (2017) on interseriality: pp. 113–115, on intraseriality: pp. 200–203, on paraseriality: pp. 229, 289, on metaseriality: pp. 271–75.

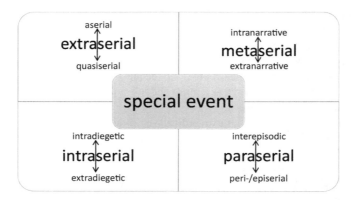

Fig. 2 Own representation

virulent in this episode[19]—after all, at the end of the narrative, the *laugh tracks* typical of sitcoms *and* ever-present in *The Adventures of Ozzie and Harriet* are excluded in favour of the singing of a emotional moved choir to mark the holy season.[20]

The category of *extraseriality* concerns first and foremost the broadcast period of the episodes and their relationship to the life of the recipients. On the one hand, the broadcast period can be arranged *quasiserially*. This is the case if the Christmas episode strictly corresponds to the weekly broadcast mode of the series. Or, on the other hand, the broadcast is *aserially* placed, i.e. the episode's broadcast takes place beyond the rigid programming scheme of a weekly broadcast. Both tendencies can be illustrated by *The Busy Christmas*: The initial broadcast is quasiserially fitted into the weekly broadcast corset *of The Adventures of Ozzie and Harriet:* The Dec.

---

[19] *Intradiegetic,* according to Genette, is to be understood as a narrative situation (here: Christmas) that is set in the world of the narrative. *Extradiegetic,* on the other hand, is a narrative situation that is set outside the world of the narrative (for example, music for the atmospheric background of the plot, without this music being part of the narrative world, i.e. it cannot be noticed by any of the actors in it; analogous to the musical accompaniment can be understood as the recorded laughter in a sitcom). Cf. on the juxtaposition of intradiegetic/ extradiegetic narration: Genette (1980) pp. 134–138.

[20] A positive example can be found in all the Christmas episodes where Christmas carols are played at the end without the protagonists (being able to) take notice of it, e.g. in *A Vision of Sugar Plums* of the series *Bewitched.*

19, 1956 broadcast comes exactly seven days after the final episode of the series.[21] The repetition of the 1962 episode, on the other hand, can be considered aserial in that it breaks the weekly broadcast pattern. Finally, the episode is broadcast with a new framing on December 24—and thus nine days after the last episode and nineteen days before the next one.[22] Thus, if in the first case the special event character of the episode is extra-serially reduced and thus synchronized with the recipients' 'everyday life', in the second case the special event character is specifically emphasized: The episode is broadcast directly on Christmas Eve and, appropriately for the holy season, the weekly broadcast cycle is suspended.

Paraserial elements can generally be distinguished with Gérard Genette into *peri-* or *episerial* and *interepisodic* aspects.[23] *Periserial* elements are those that are not themselves part of the serial narrative world, but are *materially* connected to

---

[21] For this quasi-serial broadcasting mode, reference could be made to *Special Christmas* episodes of many series; only the following episodes should be mentioned here: *Twas the Night Before Christmas* of the series *The Honeymooners* (first broadcast: December 24, 1955), *Twas the Episode Before Christmas* of the series *Moonlighting* (first broadcast: December 17, 1985), *Merry Little Christmas* of the series *House M.D.* (first broadcast: December 12, 2006).

[22] The marking of an aserial broadcast mode of a series is even more forced when the *Christmas Special* is completely decoupled from the season count and is broadcast at Christmas far after the end of the last season and far before the next season. See, for example, the broadcast and production practices of the series *Downton Abbey*. The first airings of all seasons end at the beginning of November; the *Christmas Special* premieres on December 25. Each subsequent season's airing, in turn, began the following September. To give just one more example: For the police series *Hubert und Staller* [*Hubert and Staller*], a *Christmas Special* was aired on December 19, 2018, titled *Eine schöne Bescherung* [*A pleasant surprise*]. The first broadcast date makes it aserial because the end of the previous seventh season already took place in March 2018; season 8 was again set for January 9, 2019 in a weekly broadcast rhythm. Incidentally, in the case of both *Downton Abbey* and *Hubert und Staller,* another feature of some *Christmas Specials* that can be tracked down (although not to be found in the case of *The Adventures of Ozzie and Harriet*) is *overlength.* In both cases, the specials are movie feature lengths (about 90 min.). The episodes of both series are usually about half shorter.

[23] The terms para-, peri- and episerial are based on the definitions and differentiation of paratext into peri- and epitexts by the literary theorist Genette, see Genette (2010) on peritext: pp. 17–37; on epitext: pp. 298–34. Peritexts are, for example, title, blurb, motto, notes. Epitexts are, for example, interviews, reviews of the text, colloquia on the text, advertising for the text. For a critique, modification and transfer of this concept to audiovisual media offerings, see Nitsche (2002) pp. 55–59.

it. A simple example of such a periserial element is the title sequence of a series.[24] After all, a title insertion is used to refer to the theme, in this case to the 'busy' Christmas, even before the narrative actually enters. Likewise, the direct address of the audience by the actors before the actual narration at the beginning, or Ricky Nelson's vocal interlude at the end of the episode after the conclusion of the narration of *The Busy Christmas*, can be determined as periserial elements.[25] *Episerial*, on the other hand, are phenomena that circulate *materially separate* from the series but are related to it. Interviews of the actors about the series or advertising trailers for the series could be mentioned here. In the case of *The Busy Christmas*, for example, the periserial appendix, namely Ricky Nelson singing, was episerially extended: The song performed in the episode was available for purchase—materially separated—as a record under the title *The Christmas Song (Chestnuts Roasting On An Open Fire)*.[26]

An *inter-episodic* approach puts into perspective the relationship *between individual episodes,* regardless of whether they are episodes of the same series or of different serial narrative worlds. Relevant questions here are whether individual episodes are similarly designed, in what way they deviate from one another, whether a development can be noted across several episodes, etc. In the present case, the focus is on the relationship between individual episodes. The difference to the episodes that are located in the temporal environment of *The Busy Christmas* is emphasized—after all, in this episode the recipients are directly addressed, an unusual choral sequence is inserted, the continuous narration is interrupted, and the difference between past and present is clearly marked by the explicit reference to the broadcast of a repetition. All of these are operations that are not found in the

---

[24]Countless examples could be cited. Just a small selection: *Merry Little Christmas* from *House, M.D.; Twas the Night Before Christmas* from *The Honeymooners; Twas the Episode Before Christmas* from *Moonlighting; Christmas Stories* from *The Simpsons; Schöne Bescherung* from *Hubert und Staller; Vanocé Anny Holubové* [*The Chrismas of Anna Holubová*] from *Žena za pultem* [*The Woman Behind the Counter*]*; and *The One with the Holiday Armadillo* from *Friends*.

[25]Such direct addresses to the audience at the beginning or end of an episode can also be found, for example, in: *Twas the Night Before Christmas* in the series *The Honeymooners; Twas the Episode Before Christmas* in the series *Moonlighting or A Vision of Sugar Plums* in the series *Bewitched*.

[26]This is a cover of a song by Nat King Cole first released in 1945.

episodes of *The Adventures of Ozzie and Harriet,* which are situated in the direct surroundings of the Christmas episode.[27]

Metaserial phenomena include all those phenomena that are *used to reflect on series and seriality.* The aforementioned reflection on the difference between the present and the past, which preceded the broadcast of *The Busy Christmas* in 1962, is an example of a *metaserial* functionalization of paraserial framing—on an *extranarrative* level. There, beyond the actual narrative, the relation of a repeated episode broadcast, cyclical recurrence of a fixed event, and the irreversible progression of the lifetime of the series' actors and viewers is considered.[28] A metaserial operation on an *intranarrative* level, however, is not to be found in *The Busy Christmas.* Although, there are many examples of this elsewhere.

To cite just one particularly impressive example of such an intranarrative meta-reflection of a series, let me take up a passage from a *Christmas Special* with the telling title *Das Größte Fest des Jahres* [*The Biggest Party of the Year*].[29] This *special* was first broadcast on the German TV Channel ZDF (Zweites Deutsches Fernsehen [*Second German Television*]) on Boxing Day 1991. In short episodes, it tells how families from five different ZDF series experience Christmas.[30] One of these episodes revolves around the experiences of the married couple Prof. Dr. Klaus Brinkmann and Dr. Christa Brinkmann, formerly Sister Christa Mehnert. The plot takes place, unsurprisingly, at Christmas, extraserially two years after the end of the series production, where the (basic) story of *Die Schwarzwaldklinik* [*The*

---

[27] A different example can be found in the episode *Twas the Episode Before Christmas* of the series *Moonlighting.* It is about an interepisodic relationship between *two* series. On the periserial level, the title *Twas the Episode Before Christmas* establishes an interepisodic connection to the episode *Twas the Night Before Christmas* of the series *The Honeymooners.* By changing the word *Night* to *Episode,* this also becomes a meta-serial reference to the broadcast conventions of series before/at Christmas.

[28] Likewise, it can be an implicit reflection of extraserial aspects when, as in the British *soap opera EastEnders,* for example, the Christmas episode is always precisely the one in which the worst things of the year happen – and thus the 'time of miracles' is anticyclically subverted.

[29] In this context, unusual camera operations at the end of an episode should also be mentioned, such as the camera shot at the end of the episode *Amends* of the series *Buffy the Vampire Slayer.*

[30] In detail, these are: *Zwei Münchner in Hamburg* [*Two Munich residents in Hamburg*], *Mit Leib und Seele* [*With Body and Soul*], *Forsthaus Falkenau* [*Forester's Lodge Falkenau*], *Der Landarzt* [*The Country Doctor*] and *Die Schwarzwaldklinik* [*The Black Forest Clinic*]. This 'anthology film' was later expanded into an irregularly broadcast miniseries (second episode first broadcast on December 23, 95, third on December 18, 2005).

Black Forest Clinic] was coming to a closure. In this particular case, the *Christmas Special* is a (short, one-off) inter-episodic continuation of *Die Schwarzwaldklinik* after its conclusion.

The story is quickly told: The Brinkmann couple is looking forward to a cosy Christmas evening for two. Gradually, however, many friends and (former) employees of the *Schwarzwaldklinik* unexpectedly come to visit. At the end of the episode, the small group gathers in front of a television set. The television programme announcer declares that the *Schwarwaldklinik* will now be repeated once again on Christmas Eve, "for the twenty-fourth time". The subsequent opening credits of the *Schwarzwaldklinik* creates the prelude to the closing credits of this *Christmas Special*. It is hardly possible to reflect the connection between an extraordinary holiday event and the repetitive series logic of the television program in a more intranarrative meta-serial way.[31]

The connection between series and Christmas is not only found in television series that are broadcast over several years or seasons, are designed to be open to the future, and accordingly already have an affinity to seasonal processes and events due to their running time and broadcast logic. Even for television series that are designed for few episodes and/or have a clear telos from the outset, the coupling of extra- and intraserial aspects can be virulent in view of seasonal events such as Christmas. In this context, we need only to take a look at the Czechoslovak series *Žena za pultem* (*The Woman Behind the Counter*) from 1977. The series consists of twelve parts, each of which is assigned a month. In strict chronological order, starting in January and ending in December of the same year, events and experiences are recounted that are related to the main character, Anna Holubová, a delicatessen saleswoman from Prague. In the opening credits, the number of the episode and the month in which it takes place are shown.

After the viewers have experienced with Anna Holubová a year-long cycle full of conflicts with employers, clients and children, and Anna's final separation from her husband, the series reaches its intradiegetic end on Christmas Eve in the episode *Vanocé Anny Holubové* (*The Christmas of Anna Holubová*). In accordance with the logic of the holiday, a harmonious communion takes place, including a new love for Anna. The last sequence, which leads into the end credits, is a camera shot of a prefabricated building front in Prague. In a long shot, Christmas trees can be seen

---

[31] An example of this can also be found in the series *Moonlighting*. In the episode *Twas the Episode Before Christmas,* a protagonist notices that a woman who left her child behind is named Marie. Three men from the Department of Justice search for the child. Their last names are King, King, and King. After the protagonist notices this as well, he formulates, "So? So? A woman named Mary, a baby, three kings? [. . .] I think we're trapped in an allegory."

shining out of the windows. Intradiegetically, Christmas Eve is the central telos in this series.[32] At this endpoint, the series 'says goodbye' with a metaserial twist—after all, the series is concluded there with a camera shot along a skyscraper façade, which is completely unusual for the entire twelve episodes. This makes it quite clear that the Christmas season has brought a harmonious time not only for the saleswoman Anna Holubová, but also for all viewers of this series. Fittingly, the premiere time period is chosen. Although it is the case that intradiegetically we follow twelve months in the life of a Prague saleswoman. Nevertheless the first broadcast is placed between 10.12 and 30.12.1977; thus begins at (pre-)Christmas time and closes at the end of the year, a few days after the story gets its closure intradiegetically. The entire series is ultimately to be understood extraserially as a television event at Christmas time, which intradiegetically culminates in Christmas Eve after the passage of a yearly cycle.[33]

Even series without this intradiegetic devotion to Christmas are relevant for the linking of series and Christmas. This is precisely the case when series are produced and broadcast especially for the Christmas season. An impressive example of this is the short, self-contained series broadcast on *ZDF* between Christmas and New Year from 1979 to 1995. Most of these series have nothing to do with Christmas in terms of content, but they are related to an extraordinary special season. Their implicit (holiday) recipients are oriented accordingly. These series are therefore quite rightly, albeit unofficially, referred to as Christmas series, even though their stories have nothing to do with Christmas.[34]

Cyclically, the form of such a Christmas series type has been returning to German television again and again for over three decades in a very special form: With few exceptions, new episodes of *Das Traumschiff* [*The Dream Ship*] are

---

[32] In The *Simpsons,* a Christmas episode does not mark the end of the series or season, but rather the beginning of the series. The first episode was released under the title *Simpsons Roasting on an Open Fire*, which is already a reference to Christmas on a paratextual level, as it is a reference to a Christmas song known in the USA as *Chestnuts Roasting On An Open Fire*. (A version of this song, is sung by Ricky Nelson in the 1962 Christmas *Special* of *The Adventures of Ozzie and Harriet*, as noted earlier). The first airing of this *Simpsons* episode was just before Christmas, on December 17, 1989. The content is about Christmas (Homer is worried that he won't get a Christmas bonus from his company). Later, the episode was also unofficially listed as *The Simpsons Christmas Special.*

[33] It would certainly be worthwhile to examine more closely why there were virtually no fictional series designed for an endless run in socialist countries and instead why series with few episodes and telos were preferred. For a critique of the ideology of the series as a form and expression of capitalist production values, see Steinmetz, Viehoff (2008) pp. 223–225.

[34] Cf. on these 'Christmas series' concisely Asia (2019).

broadcast on Boxing Day and New Year's Day. The extra-serial first broadcast and the intraserial destination of the *Traumschiff* are designed in an *anti-cyclical way:* In most cases, the voyages of the Traumschiff go to sunny climes, while the first broadcast of the episodes takes place in the cold season around Christmas. Here again the special event character of the *Christmas Special* was serialized into a cyclically recurring event—without being intraepisodically about Christmas.

What the many examples given of Christmas episodes and series from television history since the 1950s should show above all: In the history of series, a highly diverse interlocking of (Christmas) event and (television) series can indeed be observed. In the case of Christmas, this interlocking seems hardly surprising, not least because it is extraserially an outstanding event in the course of the year, which at the same time participates in the cyclical concept of time through its annual repetition. It is precisely because of this that Christmas structurally displays an affinity to serial and event-like representations, or more precisely: to their linking. It is this tension between singular and cyclical dynamics that is actually made productive in and through *Christmas Special episodes* and Christmas series for serial narration on television in intraserial, extraserial, metaserial and/or paraserial ways.

From this perspective, examining the interdependence between serial storytelling, specific episodes, broadcast in the televisual programming medium, and yearly cyclical events is indispensable for understanding the design of television series. The exclusion of extraserial aspects would render many aspects of serial storytelling simply incomprehensible. In the next step, I will explore whether and if to what extent the aspects and levels of the interlocking of series and (Christmas) event in traditional television programming could be made fruitful for the analysis of series productions of streaming platforms such as *Netflix,*

Post-Televisual Series and (Christmas) Events

For the sake of simplicity, I will only cover series produced and broadcast by the streaming service *Netflix.* The series examined also find common ground in the fact that all episodes of a season were made available simultaneously. This admittedly highly selective preliminary decision enables me to draw the difference as clearly as possible between television series that follow annual cycles in the initial broadcast of their episodes and streaming service series that do not seem to follow them.[35]

---

[35]Therefore, many examples have been omitted where the series are offered by streaming services, but not all episodes of a season are made available simultaneously. To name just a

After all, we are dealing—at least at first glance—with a very clear shift from the temporal paradigm of classic television programming to a spatial archiving of series in form of a digital database. In the following, I will undermine this seemingly clear contrast on different levels by using the example of a few *Netflix* series to show the extent to which these post-televisual series participate in televisual program operation logic, or how the latter are taken up by the former in a variety of ways.

The most obvious seasonally based adoptions of the (Christmas) festive season can be found at *Netflix* in the sphere of the extra-serial: For example, every year on the entrance page of the streaming service, the logo is graphically (re)designed according to the Christmas season. In this respect, a special time of the year is already referred to on the overarching platform level—analogous to studio decorations and graphic interludes of traditional television channels.

If *Netflix*'s Christmas broadcast date is associated with fictional offerings for which Christmas plays a central narrative and/or motivational role, then this is much more likely to be *movies* than series. In the run-up to Christmas 2015, for example, the film *A Very Murray Christmas,* which was accompanied by considerable advertising, was available exclusively on *Netflix.* The movie *A Very Murray Christmas* formally operates with something that is very often chosen as a genre mode for *Special Episodes* in series, namely a musical.[36] Formal conventions for *Special Episodes* are thus combined with an extra-series event to create the *'Special Movie'* for Christmas. In general, *Netflix* produces a comparatively large number of (Christmas) films for Christmas, makes them available at Christmas time, promotes them and adds a Christmas film category to the operating menu especially for this period.[37] Series that focus on Christmas in terms of content and/or motif, on the other hand, are hardly ever to be found.[38]

Even if on *Netflix* intradiegetically there are no series exclusively focused on Christmas, there are nevertheless considerable advertising measures on the occasion of Christmas that place *series productions* at the centre. For example, on Dec.

---

few examples of this: *The Handsmaid's Tale* (Hulu, since 2017, weekly), *The Romanoffs* (Amazon Prime, 2018, weekly).

[36] On the connection between series and musicals, see Boniberger (2013).

[37] See, for example, *Christmas Inheritance* (accessed: December 15, 2017), *A Christmas Prince: The Royal Wedding* (30.11.2018), *The Christmas Chronicles* (accessed: November 22, 2018). Here, *Netflix is continuing* a long tradition of the *Christmas movie* genre, which enjoys great transnational popularity, cf. Connelly: *Christmas at the Movies.*

[38] At least as far as the *Netflix originals* productions of the drama series and the sitcoms are concerned (I did not examine the children's or animation offerings in greater detail as a result).

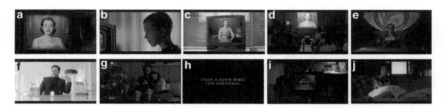

Fig. 3 (a–j) Still images from *Netflix commercials* at Christmas (2017) (© Netflix)

25, 2017, an advertisement was released offering a montage of various *Netflix* series. At the center is the first television broadcast of a Christmas greeting of the British Queen from the series *The Crown*. This series has been tracing the life of the real-life Queen Elizabeth over several seasons since November 4, 2016. The intraserial staging of the televisual Christmas greeting refers to the extraserially historically verified first live television broadcast from Buckingham Palace on December 25, 1957. This reenactment is assembled exactly 60 years after the actual television broadcast of the Christmas greetings with various scenes from other *Netflix* series and made accessible in the form of a commercial (cf. Fig 3a–j).

Montage and image editing suggest that the actors in this other series are watching the Queen's Christmas greeting on very different screens. Towards the end of the spot, a direct appeal is made to the viewer in capital letters: "ENJOY A ROYAL BINGE THIS CHRISTMAS", before the character Eleven from the *Netflix* series *Stranger Things* is shown sitting spellbound in front of a television set as she, the edit suggests, 'binges' *Netflix*. With this scene the viewer is guided to analogise the event of the Queen's live Christmas address with the possibility of 'binging' many episodes and series on *Netflix* at Christmas. The status of the live event at the *Christmas Special* event on traditional television is thus genealogically substituted by the event of excessive series consumption at the Christmas season on a streaming platform. In the case of the *Schwarzwaldklinik* episode described above, the self-ironic twist is that the *Schwarzwaldklinik* is broadcast on television on Christmas Day 'for the twenty-fourth time', meaning that the event of Christmas on television is every time a repetition of the *same*. The *Netflix* spot is exactly the opposite: The serial event on ('new') television at Christmas is stylized as an special event.

In *Netflix* series themselves, however, reflections of Christmas (episode) time can also be found starting from intradiegetic processes. Just to mention two examples: The second season of the series *Unbreakable Kimmy Schmidt* begins with a Christmas holiday scene that is abruptly cut short with the insertion "Three

Months Before." After that, events leading up to Christmas are dealt with. In episode 8 of the same season, we return to the initial situation. Here, Christmas turns out to be a fake Christmas, which Kimmy Schmidt wants to celebrate together with her friends, regardless of the date of the year. Thus, retrospectively, the Christmas episode and the Christmas season are intradiegetically decoupled, which can be interpreted as a metaserial commentary on the decoupling of the yearly cyclical fixation of certain events conventions and series narrative in the post-televisual series age. Underpinning this decoupling is the fact that the second season of *Unbreakable Kimmy Schmidt* was made available in the month of April. Since the described Christmas scene builds the prelude to this season, which is interrupted by the reference to the fact that what is now being shown is what took place three months earlier, we would be extraserially in the realm of Christmas, based on the extradiegetic information. But intradiegetically the characters are moving obviously through a New York summer.

And even more relevant in this context: On closer inspection of the eighth episode of the second season, the viewer can observe that the shots of the Christmas scene from the first episode, to which we now narratively return, are *not* only not identical to those of the eighth season, but moreover 'alternative facts' are presented there. The characters and objects are positioned (minimally) differently in relation to each other, and the dialogue differs (minimally) from that of the first episode (cf. the juxtaposition in Fig. 4a–b). Intraserial is thus marked here *en passant:* We are dealing with 'Fake Christmas' and *at the same time* with a fake repetition of 'Fake Christmas'. This means nothing other than we are not dealing with the repetition of an identical sequence, but with a *cyclical* return of the Christmas segment. Since Christmas always recurs cyclically, this measure turns the extraserial cyclical recurrence into an intraserial one. In *Unbreakable Kimmy Schmidt*, the overdetermined play with Christmas (episode) conventions thus leads to a metaserial decoupling of the series from extraserial factors—Christmas intraserially becomes 'Fake Christmas' (and can be celebrated at any time); intraserial references to the extraserial lead astray; the (yearly) cyclical return of Christmas is deleted through cyclical return of intraserial situations and events.

A second example in which Christmas plays a role intradiegetically can be found in the Netflix original *Stranger Things.* The first season ends intraserially exactly at Christmas, with a camera operation that has become topical to the conclusion of televisual Christmas episodes. This is a camera shot from the living room, where the family and friends are celebrating Christmas, to outside in front of the window, where family and friends can still be outlined against snow flurries, before the fade-out follows. This ending to the first season not only intraserially picks up on a Christmas topos of television series, but extraserially *inverts* the air date of

Fig. 4 (**a–b**) Still images from *Unbreakable Kimmy Schmidt* (2016), a. S02S01; b. S02E08 (© Netflix)

Christmas episodes. After all, the first season of *Stranger Things* was made available on July 15 pretty much *anti-cyclical* to the Christmas season. In that sense, we're dealing with the complementary strategy to the *Traumschiff* series. While there a ship sails anticyclically to summery climes at Christmas time, the viewers of *Stranger Things* can experience Christmas in the middle of the summer. In this respect, the same applies here as in the case of *Unbreakable Kimmy Schmidt:* the extraserial festival event of Christmas is suspended in an intraserial one, ironized metaserially.

Beyond all ironic references, however, the 'pure' *Christmas Special* episode also exists on *Netflix,* even though it is rare there.[39] Thus, almost one and a half years after season 1 of the series *Sense8,* a single episode was made available on December 23, 2016 under a title that in this context leaves nothing to be desired in terms of clarity—the episode is titled *A Christmas Special.* Many elements relevant to the classic televisual *Christmas Special* are invoked in this episode: Title marking, storyline at Christmas time, ending with a (Christmas) song and camera operations celebrating community at the end of the narrative, overlength. This *special* was paraserially advertised as the prelude to the second season of *Sense8,* which wasn't made available until nearly five months later. So this *Christmas Special* episode is basically extraserially an episodic foretaste as well as a serial promise of the new season, which was then still in the future upon release.

Regardless of the intraserial thematization of Christmas or the paraserial promotion of Christmas, the linking of Christmas and serial storytelling for streaming services such as *Netflix* at the level of extraserial *release* of series for Christmas would be obvious—analogous to televisual Christmas series. In my examination of the first season of *Netflix's* fictional *original series* released until February 2019, it is this obvious operation that could *not* be confirmed quantitatively. Instead of premiering at the turn of the year, many more series premiere in February or November of the same year (cf. Fig. 5). Therefore no statistical evidence can be found to suggest that the premiere of *Netflix* series are significantly clustered with the Christmas season, rather the opposite.[40]

Despite this quantitative insignificance, there are at least a few series for which the connection between the release date and the Christmas season is nevertheless relevant. A particularly interesting, because multi-faceted case offers the series *Black Mirror.* This is an anthology series, the first two seasons of which were broadcast by the British television station *Channel 4.* Episodes were shown at weekly intervals. To mark the series' 'farewell' from *Channel 4, a Christmas Special* was broadcast there on 16 December 2016, entitled *White Christmas.*

---

[39] Whether this will continue to have rarity value is hard to judge. At least two more *Christmas Special episodes* were released for Christmas 2018, which have extra-, para-, meta- as well as intraserial features of such a special. One is *Neo Yokio: Pink Christmas* (released on December 7, 2018, which is still nearly a year and a half after the first season of the animated series *Neo Yokio*). The other is the episode *A Midwinter's Tale* (released on Dec. 14, 2018) of the series *Chilling Adventures of Sabrina.* There, the time gap between the first season and the *Special Christmas Episode* is only about one month.

[40] All series from the drama, Marvel series and comedy categories that were made available on *Netflix* by February 15, 2019 (63 in total) were examined.

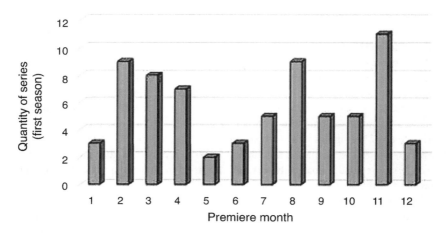

Fig. 5 Own representation

This episode was advertised as "Have yourself a dark and twisted Christmas". Since then, *Black Mirror* has been distributed by *Netflix*. According to *Netflix's* release practice, the episodes of the following seasons were made available at the same time.

A special feature in this context is the interactive film *Bandersnatch*, which was made available on *Netflix* after the fourth season. In *Bandernatch* the viewer has to make a decision every 90 seconds on average, which influences the course of the story and thus leads to very different narrative threads and times.[41] Viewers can thus watch a total of twelve different endings with nearly four dozen narrative threads that diverge from one another. Assuming a reasonably active recipient who pursues at least some of these possibilities, this interactive film is actually a series, since it emphasizes cyclical repetition and variation. In this way, this interactive film can be understood in a certain sense as a new season of the series *Black Mirror,* a season that admittedly has the peculiarity that it consists of a meta-episode, from which new internal episodes can be generated again and again.

Taking a closer look at the broadcast dates of the individual seasons (cf. Fig. 6), one can argue that the temporal *condensation* towards Christmas and the principle of the *Christmas Special* episode, which was already applied in the first season, was

---

[41] In total, there are five hours of film material available. Provided that the (interactive) viewer does not remain in a repetitive loop, this results in a maximum episode length of just under 90 minutes. Cf. the contribution by Hebben in this volume.

Distributor I Producer I Licensor	Season (Episodes)	Broadcast premiere I Date of access
Channel 4	1 (3)	4.12-18.12.2011 (weekly)
	2 (3)	11.02-25.02.2013 (weekly)
	(Special Episode)	16.12.2014
Netflix	3 (6)	21.10.2016
	4 (6)	29.12.2017
	[5] (Special Episode [Movie, interactive])	28.12.2018

Fig. 6 Own representation

at least taken up by *Netflix* in the broadcast of the fourth season and the interactive film—and applied there in an even *more condensed manner*. After all, Season 4 and the interactive film were put online at the time of the Christmas holidays, shortly before the turn of the year. The *Christmas Special* episodes of the television programme thus initially became the *Special (to) Christmas season*, which was then topped by a *Christmas Special meta-episode* in the following 'season'.

A very different *Christmas Special* is related to the *Netflix* series *House of Cards*. This 'Christmas greeting' comes from Kevin Spacey's *YouTube channel*. The actor, who played power-hungry politician and 46th U.S. President Francis 'Frank' Underwood from season 2 to 5, was unceremoniously banned from the series following allegations of sexual assault against colleagues. In the run-up to the sixth season, which has been accessible on *Netflix* since November 2, 2018, Frank Underwood's death was shared in a short trailer, while his tombstone can be seen. Nearly two months later, on December 24, 2018, Kevin Spacey, after nearly a year of not commenting publicly at all, released a three-minute video on his *YouTube channel* under the ambiguous title *Let Me Be Frank*. The actor works in the kitchen while he is talking towards the viewers (cf. Fig. 7).

Spacey is wearing an apron on which little Santas are depicted. In the context of the release date, the interpretation is obvious that this is about preparations for Christmas dinner or optionally the washing up afterwards. While Kevin Spacey works in a kitchen, he talks in his role as Frank Underwood about his supposed death in the series and at the same time always indirectly about the accusations of sexual assault against Spacey himself. In doing so, Spacey chooses a stylistic device that has become characteristic of the series *House of Cards,* namely the direct address of the audience by Frank Underwood. Depending on the interpretation or weighting, this video is a paraserial commentary on the series, specifically the supposed death of a main character, and/or a transmedia extension of the series after the official death of a series character.

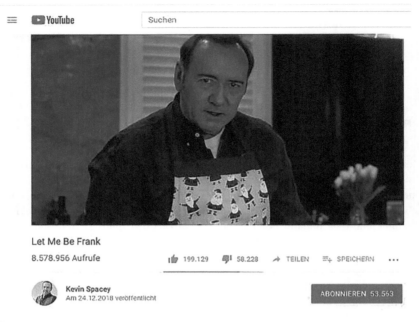

Fig. 7 Still image from Kevin Spacey's *YouTube channel*, Dec. 24, 2018, https://www.youtube.com/watch?v=JZveA-NAIDI (retrieved Jan. 07, 2019). (© Kevin Spacey)

But more interesting than the correct classification is probably the extraserial aspect—precisely on Christmas Eve this video is published, which is in terms of format, duration, media platform *aserial*: Against the backdrop of a *Netflix* series, which was broadcast simultaneously in seasons and was equipped with just under an hour of playing time per episode, Spacey chooses an unusual form and an unusual media platform for the celebration.[42] In this particular case, not only is the inside time of the series synchronized with the outside time of the viewers. In addition, a dramatic event in the life of Kevin Spacey, one that was at least decisive for his acting career and perhaps even ended it forever, and the death of the series

---

[42]The sexual assault allegations are reaching their (temporary) legal culmination in a court hearing. That hearing, set for January 7, 2019, took place just under two weeks after the video was released. Accordingly, the decision to release the video at Christmas is probably also related to this extraserial event.

character Frank Underwood (denied or reversed by Spacey in his video) are irritatingly blended into one another. Exactly on Christmas Eve, Spacey/Underwood thus spread the message of a double resurrection event.

Variations of the Christmas Episode

At the beginning, the hypothesis was formulated that the *special episodes* broadcast on television on a yearly basis are by no means obsolete in the age of streaming services, but rather remain virulent there on various levels. This assumption can be made more precise after a tour through various aspects of *Netflix* offerings. The *special episode* and its seasonal connection in traditional television programming can indeed be found in post-televisual series, but—in keeping with the logic of serial storytelling—in the form of a number of variations. Some of them I would like to recap:

Firstly, analogous to the Christmas TV studio settings, including matching graphic inserts from various TV channels, the festive season is marked in an extraserially aesthetic way, at least on the *Netflix* entry page, and *aesthetic practices* of television during the Christmas season are *imitated* accordingly.

In addition to such imitation, secondly, a *self-reflexive* and *media-reflexive decoupling* of the intra- and extraserial levels takes place on the basic of individual series offerings: Christmas in *Netflix* series does not primarily take place at Christmas, but at other times. This decoupling is often turned in a highly ironic media- and self-reflexive way, be it that Christmas in *Stranger Things* is made accessible anti-annually in midsummer or that in *Unbreakable Kimmy Schmidt* the celebration at Christmas turns out to be a 'Fake Christmas'.

Thirdly, with a few exceptions, no *Christmas Special* episodes can be found in *Netflix originals*. Instead, this streaming service focuses on its own *cinematic* productions for Christmas. On a *intermedially level,* this means: Instead of the *Special Christmas episode,* there is the *'Special Christmas movie'* on *Netflix.* Inter- and extraserial synchronization of a fictional event with the viewers' life culminates at Christmas on the streaming platform much more often in a film event and not in one of series.[43]

---

[43] The fact that the classic intradiegetic preoccupation with Christmas on *Netflix* is nevertheless assigned much more to the film than the series is evidence of a certain ironic or at least unexpected twist to the festive season: the very streaming service that stands for the

Fourthly: In the case described, in which a *Christmas Special episode* was actually produced by *Netflix*, this *special* is, strictly speaking, a prelude to the new season, a kind of 'pre-coupling'. Thus, the episode of the series *Sense8,* which was clearly marked as a Christmas *Special* by the title *A Christmas Special*, is retrospectively no longer explicitly listed as a *special,* but archived under the title *Happy F*cking New Year* as the first episode of the second season.[44]

Fifthly, series are to be found on *Netflix* that, while not featuring a *Special Christmas episode*, can be described as a *'Special Christmas Season'* on an *extraserial* level. While this strategy cannot be pinpointed across series as its central operation of the streaming service, still, there are some series that follow this logic, *Black Mirror* arguably being the most ambitious. After all, not only has season 4 been released there towards the end of the year, but so has the interactive film that follows a year later, with twelve different endings. *Black Mirror*'s release strategy reveals a *successive Christmas overbidding operation*: From the *Christmas Speical episode* to the *'Christmas Special season'* and ultimately to the *'Special Christmas meta-episode'*.

Sixthly, the decoupling of intra- and extraserial phenomena is also evident at the *paraserial* level. Primarily the advertising for *Netflix* at and short before Christmas makes it clear what Christmas is actually supposed to be about: The festive event consists of finally being able to watch extraordinarily long series, including and especially those without explicit diegetic reference to Christmas. The fact that the reenactment of the British Queen's historic Christmas address to the television audience in 1957 from the *Netflix* series *The Crown* was chosen as the advertisement for Christmas 2017, of all things, retains an *intermedial* punchline: What was once a live Christmas television event (and Christmas-themed) is now said to have mutated into a 'binge' event of post-television series consumption.

With regard to Kevin Spacey's *YouTube post* as series character Frank Underwood following a *Netflix series*, seventhly, a very special paraserial addition to the Christmas season can be located. 'Very special' implies, on the one hand, the ambiguity of whether it is a commentary beyond the series plot, or a transmedia extension of the serial cosmos, detached from the original media platform, creators and executives of the series *House of Cards*—or both. On the other hand, the event

production of serial pleasure like no other becomes extraserially at Christmas one thing above all, namely a (single) film producer and distributor.

[44] *A Midwinter's Tale* (accessible from December 14, 2018) For the *Netflix* series *Chilling Adventures of Sabrina,* the exact opposite can be marked – after all, there the special *A Midwinter's Tale* aired just under a month later than the first season, but is retrospectively made a part of the first season with the addition of *Chapter Eleven.*

spheres of the actor (thrown out from the series, accusations of sexual harassment) and his character (death) are crossed. Metaserial statements about the series character Frank Underwood and extraserial self-statements of the person Kevin Spacey in view of an upcoming court hearing are indistinguishably interwoven. In my view, the linking of a protagonist's sudden death due to an extraserial event, a transmedial extension of the serial narrative through a *YouTube* post on Christmas, and the simultaneous mixing of extra- and intraserial spheres of life testifies to one circumstance above all: the yearly cyclical event of Christmas and the associated synchronization of serial internal and external time of actors, characters, and viewers in television series such as *The Busy Christmas* have not entirely disappeared in the age of streaming services. Especially on the *periphery* of serial storytelling, the seasonally based (Christmas) celebration is still readily taken up for the strategic placement of very special *Season's Greetings*.

References

Abramson, Albert (2003) The History of Television, 1942 to 2000. Jefferson, McFarland

Asia (2019) „Weihnachtsschätze", In *Fernsehlexikon*. https://www.fernsehlexikon.de/tag/weihnachtsserien/. Accessed 4 Nov 2019

Boniberger, Stefanie (2013) Musical in Serie. Von Buffy bis Grey's Anatomy: Über das reflexive Potential der special episodes amerikanischer TV-Serien. Stuttgart, ibidem

Dayan, Daniel, Elihu Katz (1994) Media Events. The Live Broadcasting of History. Cambridge, Harvard University Press

Genette, Gérard (1980) Narrative Discourse: An Essay in Method. New York, Cornell University Press

Hickethier, Knut (2010) Einführung in die Medienwissenschaft. Stuttgart, J.B. Metzler.

Hoffman, Emily (2017) „Do they know it's Christmastime at all?: *Mad Men* and the dangers of seasonal nostalgia. In: The Journal of Popular Television 5 (1), pp. 69–81

Kirchmann, Kay (2013) Verdichtung, Weltverlust und Zeitdruck. Grundzüge einer Theorie der Interdependenzen von Medien, Zeit und Geschwindigkeit im neuzeitlichen Zivilisationsprozeß. Heidelberg, Springer

Longden, Kenneth (2019) 'Fuck you Santa'. Christmas Television – A Reckoning. In: CST online. Television Studies Blog December 22, 2017. https://cstonline.net/fuck-you-santa-christmas-television-a-reckoning-by-kenneth-longden/. Accessed 7 Jan. 2019

Nitsche, Lutz (2002) Hitchcock – Greenaway – Tarantino. Paratextuelle Attraktionen des Autorenkinos. Stuttgart, Weimar, J.B. Metzler

Neverla, Irene (1992) Fernseh-Zeit. Zuschauer zwischen Zeitkalkül und Zeitvertreib. München, Öhlschläger

Schmieder, Jürgen (2017) Im Streaming-Fernsehen ist kein Platz für Weihnachten. In: *Süddeutsche.de*, December 16, 2017. https://www.sueddeutsche.de/medien/tv-serien-an-feiertagen-im-streaming-fernsehen-ist-kein-platz-fuer-weihnachten-1.3793895. Accessed 7 Jan 2019

Steinmetz, Rüdiger, Reinhold Viehoff (2008) (Ed.) Deutsches Fernsehen OST. Eine Programmgeschichte des DDR-Fernsehens. Berlin, vbb

Sudmann, Andreas (2017) Serielle Überbietung. Zur televisuellen Ästhetik und Philosophie exponierter Steigerung. Stuttgart, J.B. Metzler

Weisblat, Tinky (2019) The Adventures of Ozzie and Harriet. U.S. Domestic Comedy: In: Museum of Broadcast Communication: https://www.museum.tv/eotv/adventuresof.htm. Accessed Jan 2019

Werts, Diane (2006) Christmas on Television. Westport, London, Praeger

Zielinski, Siegfried (1989) Audiovisionen. Kino und Fernsehen als Zwischenspiele in der Geschichte. Hamburg, Rowohlt

Movies/Series

A Christmas Prince: The Royal Wedding (Netflix, 2018).

A Very Murray Christmas (Netflix, 2015).

Bewitched (ABC, 1964–72).

Black Mirror (Channel 4/Netflix, since 2011).

Black Mirror: Bandersnatch (Netflix, 2018).

Buffy the Vampire Slayer (The CW/UPN 1997–2003).

Chilling Adventures of Sabrina (Netflix, 2018–20).

Christmas Inheritance (Netflix, 2017).

Das Größte Fest des Jahres [The Biggest Party of the Year] (ZDF, 1991, 1995, 2005).

Das Traumschiff [The Dream Ship] (ZDF, since 1981)

Der Landarzt [The Country Doctor] (ZDF, 1987–2013).

Die Schwarzwaldklinik [The Black Forest Clinic] (ZDF, 1985–89).

Downton Abbey (ITV, 2005–10).

EastEnders (BBC, since 1985).

Forsthaus Falkenau [Forester's Lodge Falkenau] (ZDF, 1988–2013).

Friends (NBC, 1994–2004).

Hubert und Staller [Hubert and Staller] (ARD, 2011–18).

House M.D. (Fox, 2004–12).

House of Cards (Netflix, 2013–18).

Law & Order: Special Victims Unit (NBC, 1999–2011).

Love Actually (GB/USA/FR, 2003).

Mit Leib und Seele [With Body and Soul] (ZDF, 1989–93).

Moonlighting (ABC, 1985–89).

Neo Yokio (Netflix, seit 2017).

Stranger Things (Netflix, since 2016)

The Adventures of Ozzie and Harriet (ABC, 1952–66).

The Christmas Chronicles (Netflix, 2018).

The Handsmaid's Tale (Hulu, since 2017),

The Honeymooners (CBS, 1955–56).

The Romanoffs (Amazon Prime, 2018).

The Simpsons (Fox, since 1989).

Unbreakable Kimmy Schmidt (Netflix, 2015–19).
Žena za pultem [*The Woman Behind the Counter*]] (ČST, 1977).
Zwei Münchner in Hamburg [*Two Munich residents in Hamburg*] (ZDF, 1989–93).

Sven Grampp is an associate professor at the Institute of Theatre and Media Studies, Friedrich-Alexander University of Erlangen-Nuremberg. Main research interests: Television series, media theory, space race. Publications (selection): *Marshall McLuhan. Eine Einführung*, Stuttgart: UTB, 2011; *Picture Space Race*, Berlin: Avinus, 2014; *Medienwissenschaft*, Konstanz/Munich: UVK, 2016; *Medienanalyse. Eine medienwissenschaftliche Einführung,* Munich: UVK, 2021; *Politische Medienikonografie. Eine Einführung zur Illustration*, Munich/Tübingen: UVK 2023 (in press).

The Clip Show as a Symptom of Surplus Value and More-Than-Enjoyment

Markus Kügle

Introduction

A clip show, clip show episode or retrospective clip show is the *special episode* of a series, be it on television or in the stream, in which the (re-)presentation of footage already used from the programme's own archive material takes place over long stretches. Various excerpts from previous episodes are loosely subordinated to a newly raised theme or question and declared as memories or flashbacks. The course of a clip show corresponds to the dramaturgical principle of a variety show. In most cases, a makeshift (newly filmed) frame story functions as an occasion of whatever kind (often poorly motivated) for a collective reminiscence by the characters of the *main cast*. Less frequently, the frame concept of a television show is used, in which—for example on anniversaries, the 200th episode—the *clips* are, as it were, moderated and played from outside the diegesis of the respective series universe. For a first approach, it is possible to divide the clip shows into intra- and extra-diegetic ones. Constellations designed accordingly could in principle contain (self-)reflexive potential, but in terms of viewing pleasure they are usually addressed to the most loyal fans among the viewers all those for whom being able to 'remember', i.e. which excerpt belongs to which episode, represents the special attraction of these episodes. There are no new insights into the situations seen, they are limited to pure self-reference—i.e. no deeper self-reflection. The clip shows thus have more the character and effect of a best-of album. Thus, in 'memory strategies' of this kind, the mythologies and, in the case of serials, the story arcs of the series in

M. Kügle (✉)

Institut für Medien- und Kommunikationswissenschaft, University of Mannheim, Mannheim, Germany

e-mail: Markus.kuegle@uni-mannheim.de

D. Newiak et al. (eds.), *Television Studies and Research on Series*,
https://doi.org/10.1007/978-3-658-42915-7_8

question remain untouched. We are therefore dealing with a significant disruption of the everyday series production. It acts against the logic of the respective series, i.e. how the episodes are to run. In the case of a *serial,* the general storylines are not followed up on, in that respect there is a short pause, so to speak. Even worse, the cliffhangers opened in the last episode do not find a resolution for the time being. The clip show willfully deviates severely from the series and how it offers alwas the same and standardized expiration of actions.[1] Therefore, the clip show episode must be assumed to be illogical, since the serial, which feeds on permanent continuity, is rigorously interrupted. Within the program course of the semiotic machine of television, however, it is logical, since the medium is fundamentally constituted by interruptions, as Raymond Williams has already described.[2] And there is also another sphere in which the concept of the clip show follows a logic of its own, but a definite one, and thus a clear goal: This is the sphere of the economic.

Now the spheres of the economic and the symbolic do not necessarily fit together, as Hartmut Winkler has already pointed out,[3] they are to be regarded as incommensurable. Nevertheless, they interact in a striking way, there is a lively exchange, and in the case of the clip show we are even dealing with a conjunction of these two fundamentally different spheres. The relationship between the economic and the symbolic should therefore be understood as an antinomy, or even more: as a paradoxical entanglement. This interplay is to be described by recourse to psychoanalysis for two reasons: On the one hand, the inner, unresolved contradictions are central to this discipline, on the other hand, psychoanalysis takes the basic assumption that unresolved contradictions do not inhibit the functionality of the respective process. Rather, it is assumed that this is the only way to achieve functionality.

Thus the clip show is understood as a symptom, as a special form of the symptom that Jacques Lacan and Slavoj Žižek call the sinthome. According to Žižek, it is "a certain signifier which is not enchained in a network but immediately filled, penetrated with enjoyment, its status is by definition 'psychosomatic', that of a terrifying bodily mark which is just a mute attestation bearing witness to a disgusting enjoyment, without representing anything or anyone."[4] This in turn leads to the question: what is it a symptom or sinthome of?

---

[1] David Marc has already rigorously broken this down to the following formula: "episode = familiar status quo → ritual error made → ritual lesson learned → familiar status quo." Marc: Comic Visions, pp. 190–191.

[2] Cf. Williams (2001)

[3] Winkler (2005), p. 50.

[4] Žižek (1991), p. 208.

More Then Worth Through Surplus Value: The First Clip Show in the Movie Serial

The concept of the clip show episode has already emerged in the field of cinema, more precisely in the field of movie serials. Thus, the clip show *is* the oldest form of a special episode in the serial. Its concept can already be found in the field of movie serials (or chapterplays), where it was invented or rather forcibly created in the mid-1930s under conditions that were unfavorable for production. The clip show must therefore be understood first and foremost as a symptom of an economic crisis.

Even if the audiovisual serial is considered to be part of television in many places, its roots lie in the cinema, or more precisely, in the pre program for the cinema. This movie serial is thus at the beginning of the mutually inspiring competition and interaction between these two audiovisual mass media. In nuce, it is a narrative that is generally told in 12–14 episodes, or reels or chapters. Performed at weekly intervals, the individual parts have an average length of 10–15 min—summa summarum (in the current understanding) a full-length film. Furthermore, the serial film is a child of the cinema of narrative integration, specifically of that era of cinema in which a change from attraction to narration took place from about 1907–1914.[5] The short films of early cinema gradually expanded, the film finally extending to a duration of 90–150 min. However, a shift from the 'attractive' one-reeler to the narrative, feature-length film could only take place in stages for a whole series of reasons (financial, production and marketing). One of these was the phase of the film serial: "In terms of production costs, serial films were comparable to standard short films; in any case, they cost considerably less than feature-length films."[6] Primarily for this reason, theatrical serials were shot primarily by smaller production companies such as *Republic Pictures Corporation, Kalem Company, General Film Company,* or *Mascot Pictures Corporation.* Officially, the 13 *Adventures of Kathlyn* (directed by Francis J. Grandon, USA 1913) can be considered the first serial film. Although a year earlier *What Happened to Mary?* (directed by Charles Brabin, USA 1912) had already been shown in 12 parts, but these were still self-contained episodes, whereas *Kathlyn* experienced a great adventure in India with 11 interruptions: "In addition to the entertainment value of a cinema of attractions, the serials offer the additional attraction of a continued, coherent story."[7] And this added attraction generated

---

[5] Cf. Gunning (1986), pp. 63–70.

[6] Hediger (2001), p. 64.

[7] Ibid., p. 71.

"benefits in distribution that were otherwise reserved for major productions: increased revenues, stronger audience loyalty to particular products, greater control of the theatrical market by distributors."[8]—in short, the possibility of an increase in value.

As early as 1913, the chapters of film serials were each provisionally ended with a cliffhanger,[9] so, for example, with *The Perils of Pauline* (directed by Louis J. Gasnier & Donald MacKenzie, USA 1914),[10] *The Exploits of Elaine* (directed by Louis J. Gasnier, George B. Seitz, Leopold Wharton & Theodore Wharton, USA 1914)[11] or in The *Hazards + of Helen* (directed by J.P. McGowan & James Davis, USA 1914), which even extended over 119 (!) chapters. Thus, these chapterplays proved to be successful both in the silent and later sound film era,[12] which is why they were still produced on a large scale until the end of the 1950s—i.e. far beyond the period of the mere change from short to feature-length films.[13] The film serial thus clearly emerged from an economic crisis. When it came to converting US production from short to feature-length films, a smaller-scale realisation (i.e. in individual film reels or chapters) proved to be a cheaper option Nevertheless, the production of chapterplays itself was not always free of budget problems, which eventually resulted in the clip show, primarily a trick or rather an economic strategy to make individual parts of the big whole even more cost-efficient. Thus, this venture obeyed the strict rules of the free market from the beginning and this in the sense of surplus value. According to Marx, surplus value is the decisive criterion for distinguishing productive from unproductive labour. There are three

---

[8] Ibid., p. 64.

[9] The year 1913 must therefore be assumed to be the birth year of the *moving picture series*, the same year, incidentally, in which assembly line production also began with the Ford Estate.

[10] Listed in 20 chapters.

[11] Performed in 14 chapters. Due to the high response continued with the ten-part *The New Exploits of Elaine* (directed by Louis J. Gasnier, George B. Seitz, Leopold Wharton & Theodore Wharton, USA 1915).

[12] The ten-part *King of Kongo* (directed by Richard Thorpe, USA 1929) is considered the first *serial film* with sound—not yet an *all-*, but at least already a *part-talkie*.

[13] The twelve-part *Panther Girl of the Kongo* (directed by Franklin Adreon, USA 1955), the twelve-part *King of the Carnival* (directed by Franklin Adreon, USA 1955) and the 15-part *Blazing the Overland Trail* (directed by Spencer Gordon Bennet, USA 1956) are among the last *serial films* produced. Nevertheless, the Golden Era of Chapterplays had already come to an end by the mid-1940s.

determinations of surplus value and the first two—the absolute and the relative—are of particular conciseness at this point:

> But we already know that the labor process continues beyond the point where a mere equivalent for the value of labor-power would be reproduced and added to the object of labor. [. . .] Through the activity of labor-power, therefore, not only is its own value reproduced, but a surplus value is produced. This surplus value constitutes the surplus of the value of the product over the value of the consumed product-formers, i.e., the means of production and the labor-power[14]

If workers are only worth 'their' money, then they are worth nothing to employers. Consequently, surplus value has to be fabricated—this is the absolute surplus value, absolute, since it does not cause extra costs. It is, according to Marx, "the substance of unpaid labour time".[15] Accordingly, the episode *Chapter Eleven: Agents of Disaster of* the cinema serial *Robinson Crusoe of Clipper Island* (directed by Ray Taylor Mack V. Wright, USA 1936), the first clip show ever, can be explained.[16] With a running time of 16 min and 22 s, this episode consists almost entirely of a montage of previous scenes and sequences from Chaps. 1 to 10. The reasons for this were of a purely economic nature, as the budget increased significantly in the course of filming. In order to be able to make the *serial* lucrative under the difficult conditions of the production, the screenwriter Barry Shipman created out of necessity that revision in the series, stretched the number of episodes and made *Robinson Crusoe of Clipper Island* in this way still profitable.[17]

> I call surplus-value produced by lengthening the working-day absolute surplus-value; surplus-value, on the other hand, which arises from the shortening of the necessary working-time and a corresponding change in the proportion of the two components of the working-day—relative surplus-value[18]

---

[14]Marx and Engels (1968), p. 223. In the original: „Wir wissen jedoch bereits, daß der Arbeitsprozeß über den Punkt hinaus fortdauert, wo ein bloßes Äquivalent für den Wert der Arbeitskraft reproduziert und dem Arbeitsgegenstand zugesetzt wäre. [. . .] Durch die Betätigung der Arbeitskraft wird also nicht nur ihr eigener Wert reproduziert, sondern ein überschüssiger Wert produziert. Dieser Mehrwert bildet den Überschuss des Produktenwerts über den Wert der verzehrten Produktbildner, d. h. der Produktionsmittel und der Arbeitskraft".

[15]Ibid., p. 16.

[16]Hise (1990), p. 41.

[17]Ibid.

[18]Marx and Engels (1968), p. 334. In the original: „Durch Verlängerung des Arbeitstags produzierten Mehrwert nenne ich absoluten Mehrwert; den Mehrwert dagegen, der aus der

What Shipman achieved after his officially paid working hours, the creation of an additional episode without additional effort, must be described as absolute surplus value. The clip show itself, on the other hand, must be described as a relative surplus value for *Republic Pictures*, since it emerged from the production without exceeding the budget. The *Chapter Eleven: Agents of Disaster* is therefore the surplus value of the serial film production *Robinson Crusoe of Clipper Island*—a very valuable value because it exceeds both its value in use and its exchange value. Because of this, the first clip shows were also known as economy chapters for a while. They, or their frame stories (if any!), are shot quickly and without additional effort—they are even more profitable than a bottle episode.[19] At *Republic Pictures*, Shipman's invention soon set a precedent, and hardly any of their *film serials* could do without an economy chapter, for which the name recap-chapter was soon adopted, probably to disguise the capitalist impetus. The next striking feature of surplus value corresponds to such a cultivation. For even if Marx clearly wanted surplus value to be understood as a "value newly created by the worker during the production process",[20] as "solidified labour",[21] which is able to distinguish itself by the fact that it costs "nothing to the owner of the whole product, the capitalist",[22] he could not avoid discovering another aspect in his market analysis of the Manchester Liberalism, which went beyond the mere exploitation of labour power: thus a part of the surplus value had to be unconditional

> [...] be transformed into capital instead of being eaten up as revenue. It must be transformed partly into constant, partly into variable capital. [...] The more highly developed production is, the greater will be the part of surplus-value which is transformed into constant capital, compared with the part of surplus-value which is transformed into variable capital.[23]

Verkürzung der notwendigen Arbeitszeit und entsprechender Veränderung im Größenverhältnis der beiden Bestandteile des Arbeitstages entspringt—relativen Mehrwert."

[19] With such 'episodes from the bottle', as with clip show*s, the* motto (or rather the dictate) is to produce as cheaply as possible, but there is no recourse to the use of *footage*. Savings are made in the areas of setting and cast. First, the episode is set in only one or two locations, using existing sets anyway in terms of *production design*. Secondly, the *dramatis personae* are reduced in a similar way. These economy measures give the *bottle episodes the* appearance of a chamber play.

[20] Marx and Engels (1968), p. 19.

[21] Marx and Engels (2010), p. 386.

[22] Ibid.

[23] Ibid. In the Original: "[...] in Kapital verwandelt werden, statt als Revenue aufgegessen zu werden. Er muß teils in konstantes, teils in variables Kapital verwandelt werden. [...] Je

The point is that the capitalists of *Republic Pictures* should invest the surplus value of the *economy chapters* in new film serial productions in order to generate further value. From the mid-1950s onwards, the chapterplay, this audiovisual form of storytelling and representation, migrated to television, which had by then advanced to become a mass medium. Explicitly at that time, serial entertainment on the US network stations was influenced stylistically and thematically by the film serials, which were produced for television in exactly the same way as they had previously been in the field of movie theaters. With one difference, however, because for Early Television, live performances were required.[24] It is also worth mentioning that *Republic Pictures* was one of the pioneers in that this film production company founded a subsidiary, *Hollywood Television Service,* which produced *serials* exclusively for television.[25]

In short: The clip show can thus generate surplus value for the series as a whole. And that is sorely needed, because the televisual series must prove its value again and again at certain times: that it is worth continuing to be produced. Thus, the principle of a clip show is used in order to be able to fulfill the quantity and quota of episodes ordered without additional financial expenditure, or to be able to invest more budget in the finale of the show. Therefore, most of these special episodes are from the production archive, however, no previously unreleased scenes and sequences are used. However, it took time for the clip show episode to become a staple in television series production. It was not until the end of the hegemony of CBS, NBC and ABC over the US airwaves that a high culture of clip show episodes emerged, because it was not until the end of the 1970s that US television entered a tangible economic crisis.[26]

---

höher die Produktion entwickelt ist, um so größer wird der Teil des Mehrwerts, der in konstantes Kapital verwandelt wird, sein, verglichen mit dem Teil des Mehrwerts, der in variables Kapital verwandelt wird." By constant capital is meant first and foremost the means of production, often machines, and by variable capital the human labour force.

[24] *Flash Gordon* (directed by Frederick Stephani, USA 1936), for example, was adapted for Television in 13 chapters, while *Buck Rogers* (directed by Ford Beebe & Saul A. Goodkind, USA 1939) was adapted in 12 chapters. *Buck Rogers* ran from April 15, 1950 to January 30, 1951 on ABC, *Flash Gordon* from October 15, 1954 to July 15, 1955 on DuMont Television.

[25] *The Adventures of Dr. Fu Manchu* (directed by Franklin Adreon & William Witney, USA 1956) was the debut of this series and was broadcast in 13 parts on NBC—from September 3 to November 26, 1956.

[26] Cf. Caldwell (1995).

Much More Than Worth Through Surplus Value? The Sheer Production Value of the Clip in the *I Love Lucy Christmas Show*

On Monday, December 24, 1956, the *Christmas Show of* the sitcom *I Love Lucy* (CBS, 1951–57) went on air at 9 p.m. as the eleventh episode of its sixth season.[27] After the *main characters* Lucy (Lucille Ball) and Ricky Ricardo (Desi Arnaz) put their son *Little Ricky* to bed, friends Ethel (Vivian Vance) and Fred Mertz (William Frawley) stop by and deliver the Christmas tree. While the living room is then festively decorated, the memories of bygone times come up. Looking ahead to Christmas Eve, Lucy and her husband Desi look back on years past, or rather episodes. Three 'Memoirs' are then presented, sequences from the episodes *Lucy Is Enceinte* (S02E10), *Lucy's Showbiz Swan Song* (S02E12) and *Lucy Goes to the Hospital* (S02E16). With a total length of 11 min and 10 s, these make up about a third of the 27-min episode. Thus, the *I Love Lucy Christmas Show* represents the first clip show in the television series. The fact that television had been a purely live medium up to that point was significant for this.[28] This was solely due to the lack of archiving options. If recordings were to be made (and not merely broadcast), the material resources of the cinema had to be brought to bear. This is not to say that Early Television did not record, but it was often done with inexpensive 16 mm film material that could be broadcast via *kinescope* or *telerecording* using a detour to screen projection. Of course, such an undertaking was not without loss of quality, which made it easy to distinguish between live and stored material. Only with the possibility of videography did the boundaries become increasingly blurred, prompting Stanley Cavell to state in 1982 that "'no sensuous distinction' between the live and the repeat, or the replay or the delayed"[29] could be established any more. Against this background, the clip show on television does not yet represent any surplus value (it appears in this form rather as a *sur-minus*); all this only developed later, when video storage options drastically reduced costs. However, it can be assumed as a symptom of a change in media, as well as a indicating the high popularity of this televisual series.

After 5 min the first clip is shown: While Fred Mertz is still struggling to trim the tree, Lucy and her husband are unpacking the Christmas decorations, reminiscing

---

[27] The episode is also one of the first *holiday special episodes*, but that aspect is left out here.

[28] Although only a mere coincidence, 1956 also saw the high-profile launch of the two-inch quadruplex (Mark IV) from Ampex, which enabled storage on magnetic tape. This ushered in the era of electronic storage and finally turned live television into a storage medium.

[29] Cavell (1982), p. 86.

together about what it was like when Ricky Ricardo heard the good news about his wife's pregnancy. So Lucy and Ricky think back to that moment when all this—which 'according to them' led to the current situation, the preparation of a celebration for the whole family—started, to the episode *Lucy Is Enceinte* namely. In the field of television series (or serials), such a principle was still new at that time. The fact that flashbacks or dreams could occur, temporarily interrupting the linear course of the plot, was already known at the time,[30] ... however, looking back on one's own series' past was a novelty.

The Early Television clip show must therefore be understood as a symptom of production value. The production value can be understood as a value inherent in the image, one that is capable of conveying a high level of production effort. At that time, this still consisted in the technical possibility of having footage, of having 'one's own archive material' at one's disposal and also being able to show it.[31] In the first *clip* of the *Christmas Show* we are dealing with such an *archival image*:

> The archival image can be described as a complex of signs, which on the one hand has its aesthetic marking and temporal location in the past, and on the other hand receives its spatiality in a different, often new media context[32]

The materiality of the media is particularly important at this point.. A distinction can be made between stock footage (or stock shots) and found footage,[33] i.e. officially registered and thus archived images and those that have been unofficially, mostly privately, stored. Steinle made out the "birth of the archival image in the 1950s",[34] according to which the *Christmas Show* must be seen as the 'midwife of the televisual archival image'—according to him, it would only have degenerated into a cliché from the 1990s onwards.[35] Moreover, the reasons for such recyclings "are manifold; discursive, narrative, aesthetic and economic motives are often

---

[30] E.g., in *I married Joan* (NBC, 1952–55), flashbacks were already used in the pilot, and in the episode *Dreams* (S01E11), according to the title, there were several dreams.

[31] Because whoever controls the past controls the future, as already George Orwell cynically wrote in the spirit of Stalin—or rather against it.

[32] Steinle (2005), p. 299. In the original: "Das Archivbild kann als Zeichenkomplex beschrieben werden, welches auf der einen Seite seine ästhetische Markierung und zeitliche Verortung in der Vergangenheit hat, und auf der anderen Seit+e seine Räumlichkeit in einem anderen, oft neuen medialen Kontext erhält."

[33] Cf. Zryd (2002), pp. 113–134.

[34] Steinle (2007), p. 276.

[35] Ibid., p. 281.

interlinked."[36] Archival images are thus characterized by high functionality, as well as immense connectivity for diverse discourses:

> An important aesthetic function is to provide temporality. In the montage, archive images often signal spatiotemporal leaps and serve as orientation. The reuse of the images can thereby use their inherent qualities or their familiarity for its own enhancement, be it in the form of an homage, or as an appropriation.[37]

Exact temporal localization, however, is seldom given. Thus—neither in the non-fictional nor in the fictional archive images—the exact temporality of the material, i.e. from when it originates (for example in the form of a text insertion) is not mentioned (just as little as the concrete origin).[38] They are only roughly classified (without original airing dates) and thus create a diffuse temporality which only allows a localization of the decade or at best the year. In this sense, the archive images in the *Christmas Show* indirectly indicate that they are from 5 years ago, but no more precise information is given.[39] Nor has any more data or facts been or will be provided in this regard in the extra-diegetic clip shows. Such a deliberately vague classification thus creates an unconscious appeal to viewers to have seen the episodes in question, to have remembered them, as it were. According to Steinle, *archival images* thus have three "medial-memory-cultural"[40] functions:

1. as *evidence in* the sense of a contemporary historical *document,*
2. as a reference to something past in the sense of a monument and
3. as an illustration without referential added value.[41]

---

[36] Ibid., p. 295.

[37] Ibid., p. 296. In the original: "Eine wichtige ästhetische Funktion besteht darin, für Zeitlichkeit zu sorgen. In der Montage signalisieren Archivbilder häufig raumzeitliche Sprünge und dienen der Orientierung. Die Wiederverwendung der Bilder kann dabei deren inhärente Qualitäten oder ihre Bekanntheit zur eigenen Aufwertung nutzen, sei es in Form einer Hommage, sei es als Aneignung."

[38] The credits always show the respective archives, but without any further information.

[39] The first *flashback* is from the episode of December 8, 1952, the second from the episode of December 22, 1952, the third from the episode of January 1, 1953. S02E10 was filmed on October 3, 1952, S02E12 on October 17, 1952 and S02E16 on November 14, 1952, while the *Christmas Show* itself, respectively the *frame story* was filmed on November 22, 1956.

[40] Steinle (2007), p. 262.

[41] Cf. Ibid. Emphasis added.

What this amounts to is, in semio-pragmatic manner, a "historicizing mode".[42] This one is characterized by the fact that " it points back along the timeline and refers to 'history' as a real enunciator."[43] This explains the special evidential power of archival images, the testimony and evidence that seem to be inherent in them and are not or must not be doubted. In "documentary discourse, archival images legitimize what is shown as an unquestionable 'That's how it was'".[44] The *archival images* thus have a special authority[45]—primarily in audiovisual memory, which has always been indispensably linked to illustrative pictorial evidence. In the case of the *Christmas Show,* this turned out as follows: In a television landscape in which archiving was not the order of the day around 1956, the birth of the archival image, the possibilities in this regard were suddenly defined. Because with *I Love Lucy* we are dealing with one of the rare series that were recorded from the first episode on high-quality 35 mm. The *executive producers* Lucille Ball and Desi Arnaz were instrumental in making the series appear of high quality (the reference point for a production value in terms of audiovisual material was then, as it still is today, the silver screen of the cinema).[46]

Primarily because of this, the series *I Love Lucy* was the first to be able to 'remember' itself. The original material was in impeccable condition—predestined for *re-runs* and various secondary uses in the syndication network.[47] This makes *I Love Lucy* one of the best-preserved series from the early days of television, which is probably one of the reasons why it is so well known (in the US) to this day.[48] The condition for this can be found in the area of media materiality—the clip thus functioned as a sheer production value.[49]

---

[42] Ibid., p. 263.

[43] Ibid.., p. 264.

[44] Ibid. Steinle refers here to what Roland Barthes calls *Ça-a-été,* which refers to a characteristic of photography. Cf. Barthes (1980), p. 120.

[45] Ibid.

[46] Among others, Karl Freund from Germany, a highly acclaimed *director of cinematography* who had already worked in the Cinema of the Weimar Republic, ensured this. Cf. Mills (2005), p. 39.

[47] Followed by the *intro*, the *recap* et cetera.

[48] When the TV is turned on in films like PRETTY WOMAN (directed by Garry Marshall, USA 1990) or in series like *American Gods* (Starz, 2017–21), *I Love Lucy* is already running. In *The Secret of Spoons* (American Gods, S01E02), it is also explicitly pointed out—by Lucille Ball, or resp. by Lucy Ricardo—that the "show shot in 35 mm".

[49] It seems almost ironic that the *I Love Lucy Christmas Show* in particular was considered to have been lost in the archives for a long time and was only broadcast again for the first time on

Stagnation! The *Clip* as a 'Souvenir Image'?

Everything that can definitely be quantified as surplus value in economic spheres, however, encounters considerable challenges in semiological spheres. All of a sudden everything is different here. Here the cards are reshuffled since the clip show must be deciphered as a harsh rupture, even as a disturbance, as it marks a striking time-out from narrative, content-related, thematic and aesthetic regularities of 'its' *televisual series* due to the frame story and clip aesthetics. This in turn leads to problems in the course of the respective series, since it is interrupted harshly—as emphasized by Doane, it has to be less about the "That's how it was" with the terms of Barthes and more about a "This-is-going-on!"[50] or even 'That's how it works!'. All this must follow the rules of a permanent "celebration of the instantaneous"[51] in other words.[52] A "sensory-motor linkage"[53] is required! The *clips* are boldly opposed to all of this, which becomes clear when, according to Deleuze, the *clip* is understood as a *souvenir image*.

So when a fragment from the episode *Lucy Is Enceinte* is shown in the *Christmas Show*, this functions as a sign primarily because of its presentation as a memory, as a *flashback*. In this respect, Deleuze has identified a special type of image in the third chapter of his *Cinema 2: L'image-temps* (1985), the "image-souvenir",[54] which has so far been translated as "recollection-image".[55] The *souvenir*, however, is not the memory (french: *mémoire*) itself, it is more a keepsake, a token of remembrance, at most the carrier of memories, the medial condition for, i.e. the formation that

---

December 18, 1989 (!), from 1990 even in a coloured version—that is, the archival pictures were left in black and white, only the *frame story* was coloured in.

[50] Doane (2006), p. 251.

[51] Ibid.

[52] A look at the history of US Television shows that even well into the 1970s, the *variety show* with its number dramaturgy was given preference over continuous series. For the *televison specials* or *spectaculars* could be sold to several advertisers at the same time, each 'number' being sponsored by a different company. Cf. O'Dell (1997), p. 2158.

[53] Deleuze (1989), p. xi.

[54] Deleuze (1985), p. 64.

[55] Deleuze (1989) translated by Hugh Tomlinson & Robert Galeta, p. 38.
The translation is somewhat unfortunate here, because the picture only becomes a 'Re-Collection' or even a Memory through its framework, its staging, its explicit setting in the scene.

triggers a memory, the frame condition or the object to which the ability to evoke a memory is attributed.[56]

This is why the french *image-souvenir* is translated at this point as *souvenir-image*. In terms of type, the *souvenir image* stands between the *movement-image* (*l'image-mouvement*)[57] and the *time-image* (*l'image-temps*).[58] According to Deleuze, the *flashbacks* in the clip show are characterized by the *reconnaissance*, meaning recognizing and also (automatic) recognition. This becomes apparent during the preparation of the *flashbacks,* that is, at the moment when the *flashback* as such is first configured accordingly: "it is generally indicated by a dissolve-link, and the images that it introduces are often superimposed or meshed. It is like a sign with the words: 'watch out! recollection' [*attention! Souvenir*]."[59] So, we are dealing here first and foremost with a conventional, extrinsic procedure.[60] Accordingly, when Lucy and Ricky reminisce, the transition is conspicuously ensured with a fade of a full 4 s (TC [05:38]-[05:42]), and in addition, a striking signaling occurs on the auditory level; here, the spherical sounds of a harp are heard to succinctly emphasize the change of levels. The *flashback* ends in a similar manner, but this time there are only 3 s of cross-fading (TC [09:13]-[09:16]). However, what also contributes to the idea and the meaning of a 'Watch out! Recollection' is a meticulous preparation at the level of dialogue.Thus Ricky muses on how both their lives have changed since "[Little] Ricky came along". As concise evidence of this, Lucy is able to immediately clarify the problem of even breaking the news of the pregnancy to her extremely stressed husband. "Don't you remember?" Because Ricky, who works as a nightclub singer, had barely had time for a quiet conversation, Lucy had virtually no choice but to break the news to him as part of his performance: "I gave a note to the maître d for you."[61] With this line of dialogue, the dissolve begins, creating a visually volatile transition, because next Ricky can be

---

[56] It is true that we are dealing here with a television series, but one that is very much oriented towards cinema in terms of materiality (35 mm) and staging: "Deleuze, the great film philosopher, failed to appreciate Television. He found nothing on Television comparable to the *mental image* in the cinema. [...]. Nevertheless, much of what Deleuze says about modern Cinema in his book *The Time-Image* does indeed, according to [Richard] Dienst, apply to Television." (Engell (2012), p. 199). Cf. moreover: Dienst (1994).

[57] Cf. Deleuze (1983).

[58] Deleuze (1985), p. 62.

[59] Deleuze (1989) translated by Hugh Tomlinson & Robert Galeta, p. 48.

[60] Deleuze (1985), p. 67.

[61] The term *maître d,* or *maître d'hôtel* is hardly used today, if it is, then only in the upscale gastronomy. It was/is used to describe the manager of a hotel restaurant.

seen on stage, the Big Band in the background, just at the moment when he receives the note in question:

> My Husband and I are going to have a pleasant event. I just found out about it today and I haven't told him yet. I heard you sing a number called "We're having a Baby, my Baby and me". If you will sing it for us now, it will be my way of breaking the news to him.

After the Song, during which Ricky finally recognizes who is meant, this *souvenir image* ends and the return to the present of the episode takes place, where it is immediately established by Lucy that this was 5 years ago. In this way, there is a declaration by means of perceptible signals (the cross-fade on the visual level, the sound effect, as well as the discussion of the situation on the auditory level), in order to not only initialize the *flashback,* but also to integrate it coherently into the theme and the course of the narrative. The *souvenir image* thus only becomes such through its embedding, it lives from its context, it is thus constituted from its edges or peripheries,[62] by means of the use of certain (according to Deleuze so called conventionalized to clichéd) signs. Despite the enormous temporal leap, however, the *souvenir image* in *I love Lucy* is more attached to the *movement image* than to the the *time-image*, that is, to the "sensory-motor schema"[63]: So the *souvenir images*

> [...] already intervene in automatic recognition; they insert themselves between stimulation and response, and contribute to the better adjustment to the motor mechanism by reinforcing it with a psychological causality. But, in this sense, they only intervene accidentally and in a secondary way in automatic recognition, whilst they are essential to attentive recognition: this latter comes about *through* them.[64]

The *souvenir image* would thereby be primarily subject to the succession logic of the plot. It ensures the progression of the linear narrative, ends in the present, so to speak, and in no way points beyond it, resuming where it began. In principle, we are dealing with Doane's *nowness,* a characteristic of television.[65] But this unconditional targeting of the present is further intensified by the fact that a clip show is ultimately distinguished by several different *souvenir images.* In Lucy's *Christmas Show* there were 'only' three, but since then there can be up to 14 in a half-hour

---

[62] Cf. Lehmann (2016), pp. 37–60.

[63] Deleuze (1989), p. xi.

[64] Deleuze (1989), p. 47.

[65] Doane (2006), p. 255.

episode of a series.[66] From time to time, it is no longer whole sequences that are represented, but rigorous montages of certain singular scenes. In such a case, a clip show can also consist of excerpts from up to 20 episodes, which means that the clip shows can sometimes even be double-length episodes.[67]

In such a constellation, we are dealing with a completely different form of progression or no longer progressing action. The gesture of pointing in and at actuality, which still existed in Deleuze in the case of a separate *souvenir image*, is transferred to the entire episode through the (re)performance of several *flashbacks*. In other words: the *flashbacks en masse* consistently deny the view forward. They vehemently mark a stagnation, a striking time-out. This is thus true not only for parts of the episode, not only for the entire episode, but even for the course of the series season.[68] And even if the sensory-motoric schema here consists merely of the principle of a number revue, it thus performs a form of linearity, a circular linearity, which deliberately offers no possibility of the series progressing. The clip show is therefore always tied to the respective here and now and proves to be almost hermetically sealed off from the outside (the rest of the series, the past episodes, as well as those yet to come).

Radical demarcations of this kind are therefore described by Deleuze as a relapse of images into clichés: "Thus the image does not cease to fall into the state of the cliché. Because it fits into sensory-motor sequences, because it organizes or induces these concatenations itself."[69] So we perceive only clichés because of those concatenations.[70] For the medium, such a strict denial of temporality seems counterintuitive and inefficient. The *clip* must therefore be seen here in terms of a symptom of stagnation. This is also supported by the fact that in the *Christmas Show,* as a special case, we are dealing with the most elaborate frame story in a clip show—never since then has so much fuss been made about the framing, which is decidedly designed for showing, indeed unwinding, *clips.*

---

[66] Exemplary of this: *The One With The Invitation* (*Friends*, S04E21)

[67] Exemplary for this: *Try To Remember—Part 1 & 2* (*ALF*, S01E16/E17), *The Clip Show: All About Rosey, Part 1 & 2* (*Roseanne*, S07E19/20), *The Clip Show/The Chronicle* (*Seinfeld*, S09E21/22).

[68] This is also supported by the fact that many clip shows *have* no serial nomenclature, no episode numbers.

[69] Deleuze (1985), pp. 32–33. [translation by the author].

[70] In the eighth chapter of *Cinema 1: The Movement-Image,* one can already find the idea of a bad repetition [*mauvaise répétition*], a repetition that is incapable of opening up future perspectives.

Over time, however, the proportion of clips in televisual series grew steadily, while the proportion of *frame stories* declined—both quantitatively and qualitatively. The increased emergence of extra-diegetic clip shows from the 1970s onwards is particularly impressive evidence of this. *The Best of All in* the *Family*, for example, consists of 87.2% already used footage, with a length of 50 min.[71] Henry Fonda, as the self-declared 'greatest fan', presented a total of 17 blocks of clips, 'his' share of which ultimately amounted to a length of 6 min and 40 s.[72] As a result, the frame stories *are* increasingly becoming mere cues, wraparounds, even in innerdiegetic clip shows. The high editing frequency of the clip aesthetic thus also has to cover up the dreariness of the *frame stories*, in which it was soon only a matter of marking a time-out, a state which was primarily intended to signal that the regular course of an episode of the respective series would not come about this time.[73] Holidays,[74] weddings,[75] accidents,[76] health emergencies,[77] even bureaucratic balance sheet measures[78] thus also always provide an 'Watch out! Recollection'. All this potentiates the aspect of stagnation, even justifies it, and strikingly marks a retrospective instead of a lookout into the future.

---

[71] The *138th episode Spectacular* (S07E10) of *The Simpsons* is a parody of the extra-diegetic *clips shows* in that it doesn't celebrate a round anniversary—the 138th instead of the 200th episode—and in that the opening credits already announce 23% *new footage*—which is a rarity, if not impossible, in the field of these *special episodes* from the 1980s on.

[72] Cf. moreover: *The 200th Episode Celebration of All in the Family* or *Cheers 200th Anniversary Special*.

[73] The clip show episode is also usually positioned at the provisional end, shortly before the end of the season, just before the winter or summer break—in the same manner as the *recap chapters* of the cinema serials.

[74] It's no surprise that most of these episodes can be found at Christmas, before the series' winter hiatus, near other holidays (Thanksgiving or Valentine's Day, for example), or near the end of the season, and therefore contain memorable, pithy, or even iconic clips.

[75] *The One With The Invitation* (*Friends*, S04E21) and *The One With The Vows* (*Friends*, S07E21).

[76] In *Shades of Gray* (*Star Trek: The Next Generation*, S02E22), Commander Ryker is in a coma and therefore 'remembers' previous episodes randomly and incoherently—similar to Mitch Buchannon in *The Chamber* (*Baywatch*, S02E17). Such an dramatic event also occurs on *Charlie's Angels* in the episode *Let Our Angel Live* (S05E17).

[77] In *Diary of a Young Girl* (*Family Ties* S02E21) Jennifer Keaton, the youngest daughter, has to undergo an operation soon and therefore starts keeping a diary in the hospital, which guarantees the opening of numerous *clips*. In *Hind-Sight* (*McGyver*, S06E21), it's the main character's fatherly friend who faces a similar situation.

[78] Sydney Bristow must undergo an FBI interrogation in *Q & A* (*Alias*, S01E17) and on *Nighthawks* (*Dead like Me*, S01E12), the Reapers have a self-assessment to write.

Stagnation as Surplus Value? The *Clip* as 'More-Than-Enjoyment'!

How do the spheres of the economic and the symbolic interact? How can the principle of the production of commodities be short-circuited with that of the production of meaning? And beyond: to what extent does the clip show represent an appropriate means, a mediating function?

With recourse to Lacan, a bridge can be built here using the term *plus-de-jouir*. The thesis here is: The desire [*désir*] of the subject is managed in a similar way to the economic creation of value within the framework of surplus value. At least that's how it should be handled. According to Lacan, *désir* emerged from a lack [*manque*], and therefore the subject defines itself through the *désir*. Lacan states that in the long run it is better for the constitution of the subject if the *désir* is never satisfied:

> So it would be fatal to assume that desire can be fulfilled or satisfied; on the contrary, panic arises not when we lack an object of desire, but when we come too close to it and are in danger of losing the lack, which would mean seeing the desire disappear.[79]

This *désir* is therefore to be understood as processuality, a permanently shifting search movement. Flexibility is ensured by the fact that this desire does not exist in advance, it must first be laboriously constructed under the influence of external factors, which makes it connectable to the media. Lacan himself described this in terms of *The Purloined Letter* (1844) by Edgar Alan Poe.[80] Peter Brooks transferred these assumptions to narratology, highlighting the purpose of the middle section of a classic three-act play as a construction of desire[81]; the second act thus functions as a postponement of desire. The production of dramaturgical tension, would thus be in line with Lacan's idea: "[W]hat does one enjoy if not that a tension is produced? That is the very principle of everything that has the name of enjoyment."[82] Žižek transferred this to cinema:

---

[79] Diefenbach (2002), p. 191. In the Original: „Es wäre also fatal anzunehmen, Begehren könne erfüllt oder befriedigt werden; ganz im Gegenteil taucht Panik nicht dann auf, wenn uns ein Objekt des Begehrens fehlt, sondern wenn wir ihm zu nahe kommen und des Mangels verlustig zu werden drohen, was bedeuten würde, das Begehren verschwinden zu sehen."

[80] Cf. Lacan (1966), pp. 11–61.

[81] Cf. Brooks (1980) Brooks (1984).

[82] Lacan (2013), p. 28.

> There is nothing spontaneous, nothing natural about human desires. Our desires are
> artificial. [. . .] Cinema is the ultimate pervert art. It doesn't give you what you desire.
> We have to be taught to desire.[83]

However, this must be revised, because the ultimate perverse art is the televisual
series. What this perversion consists of clarifies the *plus-de-jouir*: In English it is
often translated as surplus-enjoyment, but literally translated it is explicitly more-
than-enjoyment.[84] For desire, after all, must never be satisfied, otherwise it causes
frustration, up to and including (physical) pain[85] and, because of the basal condition
of transgression, establishes nothing less than a proximity to death. Since the
existence of the subject is based on desire, a final fulfillment of desires is equivalent
to the extinction of oneself. What is needed, therefore, is a pleasure beyond the
Freudian pleasure principle, which offers a support, even a (survival) strategy, by
delaying the desire of *désir*. In the case of a televisual series, this means succinctly
that when all questions have been resolved, the end is inevitably reached. The *more-
than-enjoyment* has to function primarily to avoid this. For televisual series consist
not only in the simple delaying of the desirable, furthermore in the radical
interruptus, but also in the fact that a (resolution) does not exist, indeed never
existed anyway. Schabacher stated the following in this regard:

> 'There is' not first a finished season (i.e. the entire work) that would then be aired, but
> rather the production process is caught up with the airing over the course of the season
> and is subject to constant readjustment—in look, mood, content direction—by
> broadcasters, advertisers, press, license dealers, as well as viewers and fans.[86]

The production of the (televison) series is therefore not done 'in one piece', but cut,
in separate stages, always threatened by ratings failure and the immediate cancellation that goes with it. As a result, no (television) series—whether series or serial,

---

[83] Žižek, in: *The Pervert's Guide to Cinema* (directed by Sophie Fiennes, UK/NDL/AT 2006).

[84] At this point, it is less about the excess. It's more about the 'more than', so much more, so
much beyond that the more becomes less. And from this less, more can then arise again, with
which the desire is maintained. To put it succinctly, it is first about chastity, renunciation,
austerity measures and conservation of resources.

[85] Cf. Lacan (1992), p. 194; Evans (2002), p. 93.

[86] Schabacher (2010), p. 29. In the original: „Es gibt'nicht zuerst eine fertige Staffel (also das
gesamte Werk), die dann abgesendet würde, sondern der Produktionsprozess wird im Laufe
der Season von der Ausstrahlung eingeholt und ist einer ständigen Rejustierung—in Look,
Ton, inhaltlicher Ausrichtung—durch Sender, Werbekunden, Presse, Lizenzhändler sowie
Zuschauer und Fans ausgesetzt."

whether on network TV, basic or premium cable TV, or in the streaming media—is conceived with a specific end in mind; instead, we are always dealing with new 'second acts' according to Brooks, which are also constantly haunted by interruptions—ad breaks, episode endings, post play features, (mid)season finales. In this way, desire is organized, because television desires the viewers' *désir*, if only for the sake of ratings. This is already founded in the nature of this mass medium:

> Endings on television are very rare. Almost nothing ends on television, at best it stops; and usually with a reference to how it will continue and when, what comes next, what can be expected in the next programme [...]. This is precisely why television is normally considered endless. Precisely because of this, it differs significantly from other media, such as film or books, which lead to a conclusion.[87]

Desire thus represents the permanent postponement of enjoyment, the production but not the release of tension, if the end, the conclusion, the resolution is seen as *jouissance*, as the satisfaction of desire. And the televisual series as an economic as well as symbolic construct complies dutifully with this Lacanian dictum.[88] For in serials as well as in *series*, the end is a difficult matter. On the one hand, each season must come to the end of its production cycle—also and above all with regard to secondary exploitation possibilities, for example the release on DVD. After all, tv series are not traded between different broadcasters, distribution companies or even streaming providers on an episode-by-episode basis, but rather in *seasons*. This is another reason why a not insignificant proportion of the conflicts and storylines raised in *serials* have to be resolved, usually in the form of a season finale, in which there should be no shortage of show (production) values or surprising plot twists. On the other hand, the end of a successful serial should only ever be a temporary one. Not all open questions are solved and if they are, new ones are raised at the same time.[89] There are so many content questions that make for open endings: from *Who shot J.R.?* and *Who killed Laura Palmer?* to *Who is Gossip Girl?* or *Who is*

---

[87] Engell (2006), p. 137. In the original: "Endsituationen im Fernsehen sind sehr selten. Fast nichts endet im Fernsehen, es hört allenfalls auf; und das meist mit dem Verweis darauf, wie es weitergeht und wann, was als nächstes kommt, was in der nächsten Sendung [...] zu erwarten ist. Eben deshalb gilt das Fernsehen normalerweise als endlos. Gerade dadurch unterscheide es sich doch signifikant von anderen Medien, dem Film etwa oder dem Buch, die auf einen Schluß hinausliefen."

[88] The answer to one question is given when another has already been raised.

[89] Unless it's a mini or (as it's called lately) limited series, precisely because a *limited edition* sounds and feels much more exclusive than a minimal version. Cf. *Picnic at Hanging Rock* (Showcase 2018) or *Maniac* (Netflix 2018). But as the second, third, and fourth seasons of the

Lady Whistledown? The most efficient televisual series result from impossible premises anyway, in the tradition of the outrageous events of the good old Novella. Premises, that make clear from the start that it can't possibly end well or even happily ever after, premises that are about delaying the inevitable ending episode by episode.[90]

And therein also lies the perversion of the clip show's *more-than-enjoyment.*[91] For in this it is a matter of

> [. . .] not about a more of enjoyment compared to a less, but rather about a surplus in the sense of a more-than-enjoyment and thus about a [. . .] dimension of the 'beyond', which—as radical irreducibility—sustains the movement of desire. The 'more' in more-than-enjoyment is [. . .] referring beyond in the sense of inconclusive chains of reference[92]

Production of 'senseless' surplus thus constitutes the Lacanian subject, for it would thus "be the 'effect' of discourse [. . .], but not its 'realization'. Discourse produces that *surplus of* the *plus-de-jouir.*"[93] Lacan once described this as *renonciation à la jouissance,* an official refusal, a renunciation of enjoyment, a relinquishment.[94] Accordingly, *renonciation* offers more *jouissance,* consisting of the constant delaying of the end, the resulting continuation.

---

original limited series *13 Reasons Why* (Netflix 2017–2020) show, even one is not immune from being continued.

[90] Cf. *Breaking Bad* (AMC 2008–13), *Suits* (USA Network 2008–2019) *Younger* (TV Land 2015–2019) or *Better Call Saul* (AMC, 2015–2022).

[91] The term formerly did not necessarily have a negative connotation, denoting a twisted or perverted state. From Freud onwards, it was conflated with sexual interests, but in doing so, surprisingly, quite without prejudice: perversion would be anything that has a connection to the sexual but does not serve the original purpose, i.e. procreation. Here again we have a curious case of the postponement of an inevitable. Cf. Freud (1989).

[92] Lummerding (2009), p. 201f. In the original:"[. . .] nicht um ein Mehr an Genießen gegenüber einem Weniger, sondern viel eher um einen Überschuss im Sinn eines Mehr-als-Genießen und somit um eine [. . .]n Dimension des 'Darüber-hinaus', die—als radikale Uneinholbarkeit—die Bewegung des Begehrens aufrechterhält. Das ‚Mehr'in Mehr-Genießen ist [. . .] Darüberhinaus- Verweisen im Sinn unabschließbarer Verweisketten."

[93] Soiland (2013), p. 143.

[94] Cf. Lacan (2006) The session of November 13, 1968.

Ever More-Than-Enjoyment: The Permanent Progress...

Thus, in the clip show we are dealing first and foremost with audiovisual surplus from the archive, which is of no use in terms of the sensory-motor schema. And in a manner similar to Marx's surplus value, this surplus may not be "eaten up" as "revenue",[95] must therefore be postponed as *désir*, if it is to continue with capitalist production as well as with the continued existence of the spectator subject or the televisual series. The surplus must be renounced, on both sides, for the sake of the continued existence of the thing—for Lacan, the pivotal point in such an allusion of surplus value was the feedback already mentioned: The transformation of surplus value into new capital, in order to be able to generate 'more value' in turn. And in this sense the clip shows function by celebrating renunciation. Such renunciation is not new, however, "that there is a discourse that articulates it, this renunciation, and which brings it to light."[96] The *more-than-enjoyment* in the form of the clip show thus strikingly demonstrates to us how a *renonciation* is capable of working. Contrary to Marx's surplus value, however, this ominous *plus* is not quantifiable in Lacan, as Lummerding notes:

> Lacan's more-enjoyment, like Marx's surplus value, implies an inevitable and necessarily incessant movement. Nevertheless, two different economies are addressed here. In contrast to the accumulation of capital in Marx, [...], more-enjoyment denotes the impossibility of a totality. For the [...] pointing out beyond a specific meaning [...] makes it impossible to conclude, complete or fix any specific meaning.[97]

The diffuse *more-than-enjoyment* that (post-)modern capitalism in particular produces extends into transcendence. Žižek explained it as follows using the example of Coca-Cola:

> [H]owever, it is precisely as such, as transcending any immediate use-value (unlike water, beer or wine, which definitely do quench our thirtst or produce the desired effect

---

[95] Marx and Engels (2010), p. 19.

[96] Lacan (2006), p. 6. [Author's translation].

[97] Lummerding (2009), p. 202. In the original: "Das Mehr-Genießen bei Lacan impliziert zwar ähnlich wie der Mehrwert bei Marx eine unumgängliche und notwendig unaufhörliche Bewegung. Dennoch werden hier zwei unterschiedliche Ökonomien angesprochen. Im Unterschied zur Akkumulation von Kapital bei Marx, [...], bezeichnet das Mehr-Genießen die Unmöglichkeit einer Totalität. Denn das [...] Über-eine-spezifische-Bedeutung-hinausweisen verunmöglicht [...] das Abschließen, Vollenden oder Fixieren jeglicher spezifischer Bedeutung."

of satisfied calm), that Coke functions as the direct embodiment of it: of the pure surplus of enjoyment over standard satisfactions, of the mysterious and elusive X we are all after in our compulsive consumption of merchandise. The unexpected result of this feature is not that, since Coke does not satisfy any concrete need, we drink it only as a supplement, after some other drink has satisfied our substantial need—rather, it is this very superfluous character that makes our thirst for Coke all the more insatiable [...]. Coke has the paradoxical property that the more you drink the thirstier you get, the greater your need to drink more—with that strange, bitter-sweet taste, our thirst is never effectively quenched.[98]

And just as Coca-Cola is about wanting to "drink the *Nothingness itself*, the pure semblance of a property that is in effect merely an envelope of a void"[99] in order to be able to continue drinking, televisual series are about successively delaying an end, about shipping the dissolution, or a promise of it, again and again, always anew into the transcended nothingness of the next episode. The following point is also relevant: the televisual series, like all media products, must not be understood as a material commodity, it is an immaterial one. This resolves Lummerding's objection. The accumulation of televisual capital takes place through a different system, that of Nielsen TV ratings. Because of this, the television series correlates much more directly with the impossibility of totality, which is always promised but ultimately never delivered. And thus capitalism succeeds in "making something accumulative, and thus the principle of its functioning, out of the fact that discourse demands of the subject a renunciation of enjoyment."[100] More than that, the end that no longer exists or never exists is successively delayed. This can be understood as exploiting negativity:

> One could therefore say that in capitalism, in addition to the separation of the worker from his knowledge and the appropriation of his labor, there is a third form of exploitation, which paradoxically lies in the exploitation of a negative [...].[101]

The clip show episodes must therefore not only be seen as less praiseworthy gap fillers. They mark a break, a breather in the course of the serials, whereby they are

---

[98] Žižek (1989), p. 22. Elsewhere, Zizek also explained the *plus-de-jouir* using the 'Kinder Surprise Egg': *The Pervert's Guide to Ideology* (directed by Sophie Fiennes, UK 2012).

[99] Ibid., p. 23.

[100] Soiland (2013), p. 143.

[101] Ibid. In the original: "Man könnte deshalb sagen, dass es im Kapitalismus neben der Trennung des Arbeiters von seinem Wissen und der Aneignung seiner Arbeit eine dritte Form der Ausbeutung gibt, die paradoxerweise in der Ausbeutung eines Negativen [...] liegt."

also able to mark a delay in the tension, to create a calm before the storm of the finale.

In the context of difficult production conditions, the clip show episode thus assumes an important function, especially when the industry is threatened by economic crises. Accordingly, this episode concept was widespread in the US television landscape of the 1980s and 90s, regardless of the type of series, especially shortly after the collapse of the hegemony of NBC, CBS and ABC. At the turn of the millennium, clip show episodes in their original form were used increasingly rarely, but this particular episode concept has not completely disappeared from the television flow since then. Rather, it was parodied here and there. For example, *Friends* (Fox, 1994–2004), *South Park* (Comedy Central 1997–present), *The Simpsons* (Fox 1989–present), *King of Queens* (CBS 1998–2007), and *Community* (NBC/Yahoo! Screen 2009–2015) all had clip show episodes on the air, but in an altered form that ran counter to their original concept. The episodes *The One with the Flashback* (*Friends*, S03E06), *City on the Edge of Forever* (*South Park,* S02E07), *Behind the Laughter* (*The Simpsons,* S11E22), *Dougie Houser* (*King of Queens,* S06E12) and *Paradigms of Human Memory* (*Community,* S02E21) played with the concept of the clip show, in that no original footage was used, but the 'memories' were alienated (or 're-shot') in terms of content, which indicates a reflexive attitude, a self-ironic approach to the episode concept.[102] And from the mid-2000s, this mode of a special episode was reactivated on a larger scale by the makers of the series *Lost* (ABC 2004–10)—with a total of 15 (!) extra-diegetic clip show episodes in six seasons.

With the concepts of surplus value and *more-then-enjoyment,* the essential characteristics of the mostly underestimated clip show can now be described on both levels, the economic as well as the symbolic—furthermore, a contouring of its considerable value, its function inside as well as outside the value-creation process in the context of the series (season) succeeds in this way: Economically, the clip show represents one, if not *the* surplus value in the field of series production; symbolically, it efficiently co-organizes the *désir* of the spectator-subjects.

---

[102] Another example of this is the episode *The Queen* (S01E07) from the serie *Castle Rock.* Here, the clips from the previous episodes are recontextualized from the point of view of a person with dementia.

References

Barthes, Roland (1980) La chambre claire. Note sur la photographie. Paris, Éditions du Seuil

Brooks, Peter (1980) Repetition, Repression, and Return: Great Expectations and the Study of Plot. In: New Literary History 11 (1980), H 3, pp. 503–526

Brooks, Peter (1984) Reading for the Plot: Design and Intention in Narrative. Cambridge, Harvard University Press

Caldwell, John Thornton (1995) Televisuality: Style, Crisis, and Authority in American Television. New Brunswick, Rutgers University Press

Cavell, Stanley (1982) The Fact of Television, Daedalus, Fall, Vol. 111, No. 4, pp. 75–96

Deleuze, Gilles (1983) Cinema 1: L'image-mouvement. Paris, Les Éditions de Minuit

Deleuze, Gilles (1985) Cinema 2: L'image-temps. Paris, Les Éditions de Minuit

Deleuze, Gilles (1989) Cinema 2: The Time-Image. Minneapolis, University of Minnesota Press. Translated by Hugh Tomlinson & Robert Galeta

Diefenbach, Katja (2002) Sehr rasch und nicht zu innig. Diesseits der Überschreitung. In: Baisch, Katharina, Ines Kappert, Marianne Schuller, Elisabeth Strowick, Ortrud Gutjahr (Eds.) Gender Revisited. Subjekt- und Politikbegriffe in Kultur und Medien. Stuttgart/ Weimar, J.B. Metzler, pp. 189–205

Dienst, Richard (1994) Still Life in Real Time: Theory After Television. Durham, Duke University Press

Doane, Mary Ann (2006) Information, Crisis, Catastrophe. In: Kyong Chun, Wendy Hui, Anna Watkins Fisher, Thomas Keenan (Eds.) New Media, Old Media: A History and Theory Reader. New York, Routledge, pp. 251–264

Engell, Lorenz (2006) Das Ende des Fernsehens. In: Engell, Lorenz, Oliver Fahle (Eds.) Philosophie des Fernsehens. Munich, Wilhelm Fink Verlag, pp. 137–153

Engell, Lorenz (2012) Fernsehtheorie zur Einführung. Hamburg, Junius Verlag

Evans, Dylan (2002) Wörterbuch der Lacanschen Psychoanalyse. Vienna, Turia + Kant

Freud, Sigmund (1989) Drei Abhandlungen zur Sexualtheorie. Frankfurt, S. Fischer Verlag

Gunning, Tom (1986) The Cinema of Attractions: Early Film, Its Spectator and the Avantgarde. In: Wide Angle 8 (1986), H. 3–4, pp. 63–70

Hediger, Vinzenz (2001) Verführung zum Film. Der amerikanische Kinotrailer seit 1912. Marburg, Schüren Verlag

Hise, James van (1990) Serial Adventures. Las Vegas, University of Nevada Press

Lacan, Jacques (1966) Le séminaire sur 'La Lettre volée'. In: Ecrits. Paris, Éditions du Seuil, pp. 11–61

Lacan, Jacques (1992) The Seminar of Jacques Lacan. Book VII. The Ethics of Psychoanalysis (1959–1960). New York, Norton & Company

Lacan, Jacques (2006) Le séminaire, livre XVI. D'un Autre à l'autre, 1968–1969. Paris, Éditions du Seuil

Lacan, Jacques (2013) Ich spreche zu den Wänden. Gespräche aus der Kapelle von Sainte-Anne. Vienna, Turia + Kant

Lehmann, Judith (2016) An den Rändern der Serie und des Quality TV In: Nesselhauf, Jonas, Markus Schleich (Eds.) Das andere Fernsehen?!: Eine Bestandsaufnahme des 'Quality Television'. Bielefeld, Transcript Verlag, pp. 37–60

Lummerding, Susanne (2009) Mehr-Genießen: Von nichts kommt etwas. Das Reale, das Politische und die Produktionsbedingungen—zur Produktivität einer Unmöglichkeit. In: Paul, Barbara, Johanna Schaffer (Eds.) Mehr(wert) queer—Queer Added (Value). Visuelle Kultur, Kunst und Gender-Politiken. Bielefeld, Transcript Verlag, pp. 199–210

Marx, Karl, Friedrich Engels (1968) Werke, Band 23, Das Kapital, Bd. I. Berlin, Dietz Verlag

Marx, Karl, Friedrich Engels (2010) Werke, Band 24, Das Kapital, Bd. II. Berlin, Dietz Verlag

Mills, Brett (2005) Television Sitcom. London, British Film Institute

O'Dell, Cary (1997) Special/Spectacular. In: Newcomb, Horace, Cary O'Dell, Noelle Watson (Eds.) Encyclopedia of Television (Museum Of Broadcast Communications). New York/London, Fitzroy Dearborn Publishers, pp. 2158–2159

Schabacher, Gabriele (2010) Serienzeit. Zur Ökonomie und Ästhetik der Zeitlichkeit neuerer US-amerikanischer TV-Serien. In: Meteling, Arno, Gabriele Schabacher, Isabell Otto (Eds.) "Previously On…": Zur Ästhetik der Zeitlichkeit neuerer TV-Serien. Munich, Wilhelm Fink Verlag, pp. 19–39

Steinle, Matthias (2005) Das Archivbild. Archivbilder als Palimpseste zwischen Monument und Dokument im audiovisuellen Gemischtwarenladen. In: MEDIENwissenschaft 3, pp. 295–309

Steinle, Matthias (2007) Das Archivbild und seine 'Geburt' als Wahrnehmungsphänomen der 50er Jahre. In: Müller, Corinna, Irina Scheidgen (Eds.) Mediale Ordnungen. Ordnungen. Erzählen, Archivieren, Beschreiben. Marburg, Schüren Verlag, pp. 259–282

Soiland, Tove (2013) Lacan und Marx: Das Subjekt und die Ideologie. In: Widerspruch: Beiträge zu sozialistischer Politik 32 (2013), H. 62, pp. 140–153

Williams, Raymond (2001) Programmstruktur als Sequenz oder flow. In: Adelmann, Ralf, Jan O. Hesse, Judith Keilbach, Markus Stauff, Matthias Thiele (Eds.) Grundlagentexte zur Fernsehwissenschaft. Theorie, Geschichte, Analyse. Konstanz, UVK Verlagsgesellschaft, pp. 33–43

Winkler, Hartmut (2005) Diskursökonomie: Versuch über die innere Ökonomie der Medien. Frankfurt, Suhrkamp Verlag

Žižek, Slavoj (1989) The Sublime Object of Ideology. London, Verso

Žižek, Slavoj (1991) The Truth Arises from Misrecognition. London, The Athlone Press

Zryd, Michael (2002) Found-Footage-Film als diskursive Metageschichte. In: Montage AV 11 (2002), H. 1, pp. 113–134

Markus Kügle , Dr., studied Media Studies at the Philipps-Universität Marburg, then worked at the Rheinische Friedrich-Wilhelm-Universität in Bonn, at the Pädagogische Hochschule in Heidelberg and at the University of Mannheim. His PhD-Thesis revolved around the question of how total social phenomena à la Marcel Mauss can be adequately conveyed in moving image and sound in documentaries since the 2000s.

On the Expulsion of Television from Television Series: Reality TV and Seasonal Seriality

Dominik Maeder

A Little Devoted and Sentimental: Serial Attachment in Reality TV

One of the most beautiful anecdotes of televisual series culture occured at the beginning of the tenth season of *Germany's Next Topmodel* in 2015. Juror Wolfgang Joop enters his second season as a member of the jury of the casting show, but does not join in the otherwise ostentatiously demonstrated anticipation of the new season:

> Every time I think of it, I think I see the old girls again. It's so funny. I guess I'm a little devoted and sentimental. I actually want to see everyone I've grown accustomed to now.[1]

What breaks through in Joop's anti-euphoria is nothing less than a figural series memory, which occurs here within the series and against the logic of the structural series memory.[2] It thus also works against the intention of the production, which is

---

[1] Wolfgang Joop, in: *Germany's Next Topmodel* S10E01 (ProSieben, 2006–) [translated from German].

[2] Cf. on the concept of serial memory formation Engell (2011). The concepts of figural and structural serial memory used here correspond in Engell to the concepts of the "operative memory of figures" and the "memory of the series" (p. 121). They are negotiated here under the common denominator of serial memory in order to emphasize their affiliation with serial logic.

D. Maeder (✉)
Independent Researcher, Bonn, Germany
e-mail: dmaeder@uni-bonn.de

entirely polarized towards a positive affective occupation of the beginning of the season. For instead of exhibiting the curiosity of beginning or the desire to begin again, this series memory primarily mourns the loss of the familiar series personnel, i.e. the contestants known from the previous season. If the logic of the season dictates the abandonment of a desire for repetition, the latent unwillingness to simply comply with the requirements of the serial logic persists in Joop's statement. He continues to be 'a little sentimental' throughout much of the opening episode: Not only does he persistently refuse to accept the tour bus—newly introduced for the tenth season—as a place to sleep, or prefers to sign autographs in the mall rather than recruit new contestants. Moreover, in response to Heidi Klum's leading question about whether he's excited before the first group casting, he gloomily replies, "[I'm] not really thinking anything right now."[3]

The *tabula rasa* of the beginning of the season is met by Joop with a melancholy that prescribes itself to a "serial attachment".[4] What is meant by this is a surplus of serial binding power owed to repetition, which usually takes effect on the part of series' recipients: Protests by series fans at the (fictional) death of popular characters are particularly prominent in this context, because they express an unwillingness to accept the change in serial formulaicity, the persistence of which is also a binding force that grows out of the repetitive structures of the series and still outlasts (serial) death. Joop's position in *Germany's Next Topmodel* can thus best be characterized as a fan of his own series: Sentimentally, he protests (if only through disgruntled disobedience) against the departure of the familiar series cast and may not even get involved with the new personnel. His second seasonhas so far also been the last in which Joop participated as a permanent jury member of the casting show.

Two things become clear from this anecdote: on the one hand, not only a non-fictional program like *Germany's Next Topmodel* can be described effortlessly with the terms of seriality studies. It is even possible to observe how serial logics in reality TV take on special propensities through the peculiarities of pseudo-documentary televisual access: the fact that with Joop's serial attachment a figural serial memory so blatantly contradicts the structural serial memory *on screen* would have been noticed as a contradiction in any mediocre fictional series and immediately eradicated from the script. Thus a special form of serial complexity emerges in

---

[3]Wolfgang Joop, in: *Germany's Next Topmodel* S10E01 (ProSieben, 2006–).
[4]Cf. Maeder (2018).

reality TV, which possibly diverges from the serial complexity of[5] fictional formats, but is not to be judged as inferior per se or even in principle. On the other hand, however, it becomes apparent here that the contrast between episodes and series, i.e. episodic and continuous seriality, is no longer decisive for contemporary reality TV. With the season a new serial organisational unit has risen to become the bearer of meaning, which has also become the decisive factor for fictional series.[6]

I will take up this double insight and first outline the difficult relationship between series research and reality TV. Not only does reality TV find itself at the opposite end of a cultural scale of values that is headed by 'quality TV' as the preferred research object of contemporary series research. The self-valorisation of seriality studies achieved through the academic nobilisation of the research object of the 'quality' series thus makes it necessary to radically exclude other serial forms of television from its discourse.[7] This expulsion of television from the television series,[8] forced by parts of seriality studies, also has ontological implications for the concept of the series: as will be shown, seriality studies has difficulty with an analytical approach to reality TV because it often misunderstands seriality as a genuinely narrative form. In this way, it denies itself access to non-narrative or only partially narrative serial forms, or is only able to identify these as derivative in relation to the supposed paradigmatic complexity of serial narration in contemporary series. This can be corrected with a concept of seriality as an operative principle, through which all forms of televisual seriality, and thus essential concepts of television theory, can be brought back into the discussion of seriality.

Subsequently, I will use the organizational feature of the season to argue for bringing reality TV and fictional series closer together through their seasonal organization and to determine common as well as divergent features of their serial structure with the concept of the seasonal series, whose emergence around 2000 has media historical implications. The aim is to show that the highly differentiated vocabulary for describing serial forms that seriality studies has produced can be applied much more broadly, and can certainly benefit from a link back to the basic concepts of television theory.[9]

---

[5]Cf. for the discussion of complexity the canonical book by Mittell (2015). However, this book deals exclusively with fictional formats in an abbreviation that is often characteristic of series research.

[6]Cf. e.g. O'Sullivan (2010).

[7]Cf. Schwaab (2010).

[8]See, for example, the coinage of terms by Kirschbacher, Stollfuß (2015).

[9]In relation to Let's Play videos I have already tried to show this elsewhere, cf. Maeder (2017a, b).

Only Mentioned in Passing: Reality TV and Seriality Studies

In their 2016 textbook on the television series, Markus Schleich and Jonas Nesselhauf begin with a definition of the term in which problems of series research that all too quickly distance themselves from television studies are condensed:

> Regardless of the medium, the structure of serially told stories is always the same: *a series consists of at least two parts of a narrative that build on each other in terms of content and establish a progressive continuation of the story (and thus of the narrative) through common themes or characters.*[10]

It is interesting to note here that even before the actual definition begins, the series has already been defined in a barely marked way: as a narrative form. While television series are unquestionably series with a narrative function, it seems more than problematic to make a reduction of the concept of series that commits itself exclusively to the narrative component. Doesn't the very syntagma of "serial narration"[11] call for a definition that would aim for a definition of the series independent of the narrative, in order to really understand what is actually serial about a serial narrative? Isn't the television series a serial organization that is already serial qua broadcasting slot, budgeting, production process, before any story is told? Shouldn't an analysis of the television series always begin with an attempt to describe it in the same way that serial mass production on the assembly line can be described, that is as the result of a complex, contingent production technology[12] for the generation of repetition and variation? And does a premature view of the series as a narrative form therefore not always already consider it from a temporal beyond, in which the product—the television series—is undoubtedly also narrative, but in which the seriality of the series "on this side of narration",[13] i.e. constitutively misses its analytical primacy over (but not outside of) narratives?[14]

The textbook does not ask itself these questions, but articulates with performative force and definitional gesture a pre-understanding of the series as a narrative form, which carries with it further, momentous implications. These include, firstly, the *indifference between media*, secondly, the *lack of history in the* concept of the series, and thirdly—and most importantly for this context—the *self-limitation* of

---

[10] Schleich, Nesselhauf (2016) p. 13 [translated from German].

[11] Ibid.

[12] Cf. on the assembly line Nye (2016).

[13] Fahle (2012) p. 169.

[14] Cf. also Maeder (2013).

series *analysis*, which makes the epistemological gain of reducing the series to a narrative form questionable.

The *media indifference* appears as a necessary consequence of a concept of narrative that conceives of narration as media-independent, transmedial. This tendency, inherent in a transmedial narratology, is not mere ignorance of mediality, according to Irmela Schneider, but systematic methodological privileging of the "narrative as deep structure",[15] whose "epistemological quasi-autonomy vis-à-vis the medium"[16] amounts to an independence of form from the medium, which seems at least debatable in terms of media theory.

Once conceived as independent of the material, symbolic and institutional conditions of the production of forms, i.e. transmedial, serial narration as a pure form also takes on a *transhistorical* character: compared to its deep structure, not only the medium but also time appears as a mere surface through which serial narration manifests itself as an "anthropological constant".[17] In this anthropological transfiguration of the series, history—in general, but also media and television history in particular—appears at most as the entelechy of serial self-realization: in the contemporary series, therefore, the series finally comes into its own. But why serial forms rise to become the leading cultural form precisely with industrialization—as the authors certainly concede—cannot then be conclusively deduced. The digital transformation of television is also not described in the specifics of its technical, discursive and imaginative form, but is presented as a "liberation from the fixed broadcasting scheme of linear television",[18] which ultimately leads to the release of unimagined serial complexity.[19] The fact that these—undoubtedly novel—serial time structures are themselves tied to the formation of viewers as subjects of selection—and thus to the contingent, historical formation of neoliberal governmentality[20]—remains unmentioned, as does the specificity of a digital mediality beyond the supposed liberalization ex negativo of television.

---

[15] Schneider (2010) p. 51.

[16] Ibid.

[17] Schleich, Nesselhauf´(2016) p. 13.

[18] Ibid., p. 75.

[19] Complexity has become the finer word for quality: Where the latter unambiguously invokes the register of evaluation and attribution, complexity, especially narrative complexity, appears as a quality that can be objectified in narrative studies, through which narratological series research is able to rise to the position of privileged discourse guardian of series quality and the habitual series distinction is academically nobilized as a "quality viewer" (Kumpf (2013), p. 347).

[20] Cf. Stauff (2005).

It is no coincidence that a specific *type of series* is subsequently designated as embodying the digital media entelechy of serial complexity: the contemporary, fictional, dramatic television series, especially of US provenance. *Soap operas*, the authors point out, can "hardly be described as complex, innovative and aesthetic forms".[21] However, the narratological reduction of the series through the focus on narration becomes clearest in the short chapter on quiz shows and reality TV. The authors concede that weather reports, sports shows and news are serially structured, but that they do not represent fictional narratives.[22] It is evident here that the series massively and fundamentally transcends the category of narrative. For the authors, however, this is not a reason to reflect on the self-induced confinement of the television series to narration, but to exclude all series that run on television—let us call them television series for the sake of simplicity—but do not represent fictional narratives, from an introduction that bears the title 'television series' after all.

This becomes even more complicated in the case of reality TV formats, which—as Nesselhauf and Schleich concede—do adapt features of serial narration in the narrower sense. It is interesting to note, however, that they pay little attention to the fact that reality TV is about television series that show characteristics of serial organization even on the level of narrative.[23] After a brief distinction between reality TV and scripted reality formats as well as a list of well-known shows, there is no discussion or example analysis of serial procedures in reality TV, but rather a reference to Jan Böhmermann's unmasking stunt in *Neo Magazin Royal* regarding the casting practices of *Schwiegertochter gesucht*, which exercises a reality TV critique based on production procedures.[24] Instead of an analysis, what we have here is culturally canonized criticism, whose status as a televisual practice itself is not reflected at all in the context of an entertainment show. Significantly, the sometimes precarious working conditions for screenwriters in the field of fictional series, for example, are not mentioned at all.[25] Instead, (fictional) series production is discussed under the signum of artistic creation, for which problems arise at most in the area of appropriate authorial attribution.[26] The one-sided slant in relation to reality TV culminates in the chapter's conclusion, which states without giving any

---

[21] Schleich, Nesselhauf (2016) p. 90.

[22] Ibid., p. 65.

[23] See on the basis of *Deutschland sucht den Superstar* Ganz-Blättler (2012).

[24] Cf. Schleich, Nesselhauf (2016), pp. 65–67.

[25] Cf. Henderson (2015).

[26] Cf. Schleich, Nesselhauf: Fernsehserien (2016).

further reason: "Such 'non-narrative cinematic forms' are, however, only condition-
ally comparable with series such as *The Sopranos* or *Tatort* and should therefore
only be *mentioned in passing*."[27]

But wouldn't the *conditional* comparability of two formats be of particular
interest for a comprehensive understanding of seriality, precisely because the
narratological corset becomes too tight to understand serial forms of organization
in their entirety? And could an understanding of seriality that is capable of grasping
all serial forms of television (and beyond) not also be fed back into an understanding
of narrative serial formats on *this side* of narrative, which could be read against a
completely different background but as phenomena of changing media cultures? It
is no coincidence that some of the most innovative seriality studies scholarship has
decidedly stepped back behind the paradigm of narrative in order to question serial
procedures and image logics, for example, with regard to their operative cognitive
function as diagrammatic forms, or to address them against the backdrop of
economic, discursive, and media dynamics of outbidding as the form and play of
logics of intensification, which can always be located trans-serially, for example in
architecture.[28]

For seriality studies, therefore, it seems appropriate to move all those supposedly
marginal serial formats on *this side* of narrative seriality into the center of analytical
efforts, in order to be able to fundamentally inscribe seriality as an economic,
epistemic, and affective form. By means of the serial, not least "the deep structures
of the techno-medial, economic and cultural conditions of modernity can be
recalled".[29] In the return to seriality on this side of the (narrative) series, however,
a dialogue with the basic concepts of television studies becomes necessary, in
which—even if not under the terms of serial narration—a reflection on processes,
procedures and forms of serialization has been taking place for a long time, for
example in the terminologies of segment (Ellis), *flow* (Williams) and genre
(Cavell).[30]

At the same time, however, it is also important for television studies to take into
account that the coupling of seriality and television is always already based on a
"'surplus' of the television series over television".[31] Attempts to contain the series

---

[27] Ibid., p. 67. [translated from German].

[28] Cf. Wentz (2017); Sudmann (2017).

[29] Ernst, Paul (2015) pp. 16–17.

[30] Cf. Adelmann et al. (2001). For an introduction to television theory that places the aspect of
seriality appropriately centrally, see Engell (2012).

[31] Ernst/Paul (2015) p. 12.

in terms of television studies are thus not only doomed to fail, but cut off the productive potential that series provide for thinking about televisual mechanisms, formats, and cultures. In series, an important but historically contingent feature of television is released for development in such a way that its momentum is able to design itself semi-autonomously via television. In this sandbox of seriality, which television series represent, one effect is that through the series it is possible to reflect on television and its media change.[32]

The Seasonal Series: About the Season as a Mesoserial Organizational Unit

It is precisely from this perspective that one can now also think about the season as a serial organizational unit. The season oscillates between a television studies perspective on cultural mechanisms of TV production and a narratological perspective on serial modes of narration.

For narratology, the season appears primarily under the concept of the '(story) arc', i.e. as the closing figure of a (story) arc, which takes the end of a season as an occasion to end (sub-)plots that are intentionally composed from the beginning of the season. These arcs not only give series coherence over the course of a season, but also bring about talk of serial complexity, insofar as the coordination of cross-episode storylines with simultaneous (partial) finality requires an increased complexity of narrative control logic that nevertheless still has to break down 'season arcs' into smaller units of "acts", "episodes" and "beats".[33] It is precisely the closing character of the arc that brings (seasonal) series close to an artisitic concept of opus. The nobilization of the series as an art form only seems to make sense against the background of an antiquated concept of art, but it leads to a fundamental misjudgment of the shift in narrative logic in the age of the series.

> Unlike practices of production and reception that are oriented towards the aesthetics of the work, popular series design themselves towards a constantly dislocated whole that enables the coherence of its parts without dominating it.[34]

---

[32]Cf. Beil et al. (2016).

[33]Newman (2016) pp. 23–24.

[34]Kelleter (2012) p. 27. [Translated from German].

Thus, the season de facto does not conclude the series, but is directed at its continuation. A continuation that aims at adding another story arc to the existing ones, thus continuing the series' season logic by way of repetition. The basic unit of repetition work within contemporary fictional series is thus not the episode, but the season, which, as the meso-level of serial organization, moves between the episodic micro-level and the 'whole series' as the macro-level:

> The thirteen-episode uninterrupted complete season provided, for the first time in American television history, a distinct narrative form, one that was large enough to occupy significant time and space, but not so large as to turn into vague sprawl.[35]

Where episodes increasingly flow into one another due to interwoven storylines, or at least where their boundaries are unclear and their internal dynamics sometimes heterogeneous, the series can no longer be defined as a form of repetition of episodic parts. Rather, the season functions as a "new and significant unit of meaning",[36] i.e. as the basic unit of the series' operative logic. This also corresponds to the distribution of series in seasons, instituted by DVD and taken on by streaming services. The consumption of seasons *en bloc* has since become the norm in 'binge watching' practices.

The current series thus gravitates in its (narrative) structural logic not around episodes, but around seasons, whose structure is meticulously planned, but which tend to become invariant as authoritative units: the fact that series are conceived, produced, distributed and received in seasons seems to have long since become a naturalized fact of series culture. Series are thus moving closer to (film) series, which is reflected in marketing by the introduction of numerical principles, among other things. *Netflix*, for example, aggressively promotes the individual seasons of *Stranger Things* as 'Stranger Things 2', 'Stranger Things 3', and so on. Although the parts are connected to each other, they do not result in a coherent work, but rather represent iterations of the blueprint of the first part, whose basic principles— such as the nostalgic aesthetics that define the cultural reception of the series, the exposed cinematic reference level, the basic plot, the genre markings in general[37]— are consistently repeated by the subsequent parts. There are certainly shifting effects and "overbidding dynamics" between the seasons,[38] but these are genuinely serial

---

[35] O'Sullivan (2010) p. 68.

[36] Ibid., p. 60.

[37] Wentz aptly calls this "mimicry [. . .] of '80 s media culture" (Wentz (2019) p. 441).

[38] Sudmann (2017) p. 14.

repetition derivatives, not planning results. The knowledge of how many seasons of a series there will be is not available for any planning in advance: series operate in a space of contingent connections and continuations, which may be filled with (art-like) intentions, but whose contours only emerge step by step as the seasons are passed through: There is no season that could not also have been the last.

Here, however, it becomes apparent that the narratological perspective on serial modes of narration must be framed by a television studies perspective on the cultural logics of series production, since without the limitations of the production side, the cultural logic of the series cannot be unlocked at all. Even before the season became the basic unit of serial narration, it had long been a televisual production category, which was therefore not *invented* by scriptwriters, but rather *found* by them. The televisual logic of the seasonal organization thus precedes the narrative logic of seasonal seriality. Accordingly, serial narration still means economy here as well. In O'Sullivan's definition quoted above, it is no coincidence that a quantitative definition—"large enough [. . .] but not so large as to turn into vague sprawl"[39]—of season-based serial narratives is featured prominently. Via the season, the dimension of the economic, which is fundamental to any determination of seriality, also reinserts itself into the contemporary series as a ghostly return of the repressed. For the season did not always serve television production as a unit of meaning, but has been as an internal organizational principle strongly adapted to the calendrical organization of time, while at the same time being relevant for the commercial internal organization of television financing (*sweeps/reruns*).[40]

If the *season* functioned as an organizing principle, but not as a basic narrative unit, this was initially due to the fact that television broadcasters deferred the *novelty value of* a series to its *habitual value and* thus dispensed with the marking of new episodes and their affiliation to a staggered production system. It appeared to be important *that* a certain series ran at a specific time slot (habitual value), but *which* episode it was—especially in the case of episodically organized series—was of secondary importance. Nevertheless, here too the season—for example in the case of the *cliffhanger* that spanned the summer break, or the *christmas episode* or the *clip show*[41]—sometimes produced effects of meaning and thus occasionally turned from an internal organisational principle into an explicit unit of meaning.

Viewed in the light of the season, the overabundant talk of narrative complexity increasingly loses its plausibility. The contemporary series instead appears as a

---

[39] O'Sullivan (2010) p. 68. [citation omitted by D. M.].

[40] Cf. Schabacher (2010) pp. 29–30.

[41] Cf. the contributions by Sven Grampp and Markus Kügle in this volume.

divergent serial form of organization that links the fictional series back to the non-fictional television series in a special way. For one thing, the boom in reality TV formats is also linked to the emergence of the season as an explicit unit of meaning for the serial organization of reality TV. Long-lived popular prime-time formats such as *Deutschland sucht den Superstar, Germany's Next Topmodel, Ich bin ein Star. . . Holt mich hier raus!* or *The Voice* call up the register of the season in their basic organisational structure to the effect that their episode-spanning narrative continuation is not calibrated for endlessness, but from the outset, for example through the number of participants and selection rules, for the finality of a season end, which provides the format's horizon of meaning. On the other hand, the emergence of season-based reality series also coincides historically with the boom in fictional series around 2000: The first season of *Big Brother* premiered in the Netherlands in 1999, the same year as *The Sopranos*, before being exported worldwide.[42] Subsequently, season-based serial forms of organization in both reality TV and fictional series become guiding cultural forms[43] of television production.

Wolfgang Joop's serial attachment to the past season of *Germany's Next Topmodel*, as described at the beginning of this article, can thus be attributed to a non-conscious analytical insight that makes reality TV formats addressable as seasonal serial forms. Reality TV can thus be placed in the context of a change of series logics to the unity of the *season*, which has been occurring across formats since 2000. In the case of *Germany's Next Topmodel*—which can stand pars pro toto for almost all casting shows—the season functions on the one hand as a *telos* of serial organization. In doing so, however, it does not set an ultimate goal, but a provisional one: to find/produce *the* 'Next Topmodel'. The fact that the series as a whole does not end with the season, however, owes much to a season-based logic of repetition that gives the show its title. The term '*next*' always implies sequence and

---

[42] Another point of reference would be *Survivor*, which starts in Sweden in 1997 as *Expedition Robinson* and is first adapted in the USA in 2000. However, this is not strictly about origins and filiations—although a direct path leads from *Survivor* to *Lost and* thus from reality TV to fictional series—but rather about the coincidence of season-based organizational forms of seriality across the threshold of fictional/non-fictional.

[43] What is meant here is not quantitative dominance: episodic formats retain their dominance across the various programme slots. Rather, seasonal series appear as a leading cultural form because, firstly, they become important discursive reference points for various debates—for example, about 'quality' TV and 'trash' TV; secondly, because they occupy a prominent position, *prime-time, in the* distribution economy of television; thirdly, because they serve television as experimental forms in which television redesigns itself as a convergent digital medium in the course of the 2000s and 2010s.

succession and constitutively leaves the total duration of the series open, since a successor always remains conceivable from the series logic—which here also corresponds to the logic of the fashion industry. While the season has a strong finality, a 'season arc', the title-giving search for talent indicated that the entire series remains indefinite, continuable.[44] At the same time, however, the season-bound finality also becomes productive on the inter-episodic level, i.e. the organization of the relationships between individual episodes. For example, the singular of the title stipulates that there is exactly *one* winner to be chosen per season, for which a multitude of young women contend at the beginning of the season. The logic of the season thus suggests the rough order of a selection process, which peels the singular winner out of the multitude of contestants. In a first step, which usually comprises the first episode(s),[45] the multitude—usually several thousand female applicants—is initially reduced to a manageable cast number, varying between 12 and 24 participants, by means of preselection, rapid mass casting, etc. This initial reduction of the number of participants is then carried out by the jury. It primarily serves the possibility of serial memory formation: Viewers and jury alike are able to build up familiarity with the participants, through which the figures become recognizable, identifiable characters through familiarization and immersion. Thus, a *series cast* is created at the beginning of each season, which then goes through the process of *character development*, at the end of which there may be serial attachment to the protagonists.

However, this character development also represents the narrative hook of the format: *Germany's Next Topmodel* is, at its core, a *coming-of-age narrative* that turns (notoriously so-called) 'girls' into young women who know how to confidently deal with the institutionalized male gaze of the fashion industry and capitalize on it as entrepreneurs of themselves.[46] This process is both enabled and limited

---

[44] Here lies a significant difference to the mythological exaltation of the principle of staggered seriality, which promises the definiteness of the totality of serial organization. This promise, however, can only ever appear as an irredeemable promise, which, in the case of a series finale that may occur, leads to countless problems and tends to bring dissatisfaction among mythologically oriented series fans. Using *Lost* as an example, cf. Maeder: "Economies of Contingency". It is no coincidence that series production has largely turned away from such *myth arcs*.

[45] Over the course of its 14 seasons to date, the format has used various methods, which I cannot discuss in detail here.

[46] The latter point is often the (ideology-critical) focus of reality TV research, which for its part seeks too little connection to the formalistic vocabulary of series research and looks directly at content and staging. Above all, a particular complexity of non-fictional formats emerges here, which cannot seamlessly ascribe their characters to these narratives, but must at

by the season: In the end, the top model is a form of female subjectivity that combines attractiveness, success and self-determination, but in this it also knows no logical progression. The 'top model' marks the zenith of this specific female subjectification, which is unsurpassable, simply 'top'.

Ultimately, however, the serial logic of continuation determines the inter-episodic order of the reality series, which leads from the applicant plural to the singular, also as a competitive selection process that progresses with each episode. Typically, one contestant is eliminated per episode until only three finalists remain by the season finale (which, as a live show, occupies the space of a double episode). The act of selection thereby represents the climax of each episode, so that even the intra-episodic order is still shaped by the logic of serial continuation. However, the format can be quite flexible in shaping these selection rules. For example, the selection process can be suspended for one episode, only for several contestants to be eliminated at once at a later date. Similarly, four finalists can be nominated instead of the usual three. Variation at the level of rule design ensures unpredictability, which is eminently important intraepisodically for the intensity of tension in the selection process.

In any case, the central role that the season plays as an organizational unit for the casting show becomes apparent: as a 'season arc', it defines a partial finality of the 'next' that can be re-iterated across seasons. It enables a large series cast that undergoes a reduction over the course of the season, which is shaped interepisodically as a competition. This competitive principle still has an effect on the intra-episodic dramaturgy and thus institutes a quasi-institutional selection pressure, which can be experienced by both participants and viewers as an intensity of tension. The 'character arc' of the participants corresponds to a *coming-of-age narrative* that runs towards the vanishing point of a female subject becoming a 'top model', who proves resilient to this intensified selection pressure. The narrative internal organization of *Germany's Next Topmodel* can thus be given a series-analytical description thanks to a cross-format concept of seasonal seriality, which operates in terms of serial organization and thus provides a common vocabulary for discussing both fictional and non-fictional formats.

Above all, however, this can be linked back to the production and thus the media-specific level: The economic advantage of the season as a meso-unit between series and episode lies on the one hand in being able to achieve cohesion and tension effects that bind viewers to the medium over longer periods of time and produce

---

times reckon with unforeseen ambivalences, volts and turnarounds that repeatedly set limits to straightforward storytelling—see Joop's melancholia.

television events in the form of season openings and finales that guarantee attention peaks. On the other hand, however, the season still allows enough flexibility to enable a series-typical feedback between production and reception, which strengthens popular segments and weakens disliked ones from season to season. This can also be interpreted in terms of media competition, especially with regard to the internet, which slowly became the leading medium at the end of the 1990s: In the face of the considerable techno-medial shortening of feedback intervals between production and reception on the net (up to the abolition of the difference in Web 2.0 as of 2003), television accepts longer feedback intervals in the form of the mesoserial organisational principle of the season. Yet it increases medial binding effects via the content cohesion of season-based progression as well as event qualities which, thought of in a media-differentiated way, produce selective peaks of attention not only for the individual series, but always also for the medium itself.[47]

Instead of being 'only mentioned in passing', non-fictional seriality therefore belongs rather at the centre of series-analytical descriptions that strive to think of the expulsion of television from the television series not as the transcendence of the series over television, but as the digital-media reconfiguration of televisual seriality.

References

Adelmann, Ralf, Jan O. Hesse, Judieth Keilbach, Markus Stauff, Matthias Thiele (2001) (Ed.) Grundlagentexte zur Fernsehwissenschaft. Theorie – Geschichte – Analyse, Konstanz, UVK

Beil, Benjamin, Lorenz Engell, Dominik Maeder, Jens Schröter, Herbert Schwaab, Daniela Wentz (2016) Die Fernsehserie als Agent des Wandels, Münster, LITverlag

Engell, Lorenz (2011) Erinnern/Vergessen. Serien als operatives Gedächtnis des Fernsehens. In: Blanchet, Robert, Kristina Köhler, Tereza Smid, Julia Zutavern (Eds.) Serielle Formen. Von den frühen Film-Serials zu aktuellen Quality-TV- und Online-Serien. Marburg, Schüren, pp. 115–132

Engell, Lorenz (2012) Fernsehtheorie zur Einführung, Hamburg, Junius

Ernst, Christoph, Heike Paul (2015) Einleitung. In: Ernst, Christoph, Heike Paul (Eds) Amerikanische Fernsehserien der Gegenwart. Perspektiven der American Studies und der Media Studies. Bielefeld, transcript Verlag, pp. 7–34

Fahle, Oliver (2012) Im Diesseits der Narration. Zur Ästhetik der Fernsehserie. In: Kelleter (Ed.) Populäre Serialität: Narration – Evolution – Distinktion. Zum seriellen Erzählen seit dem 19. Jahrhundert. Bielefeld, Transcript Verlag, pp. 169–181

---

[47] This is being overtaken with the penetration of television by the net, i.e. streaming.

Ganz-Blättler, Ursula (2012) DSDS als Reality-Serie. Kumulatives Storytelling ‚on the go. In: Frank Kelleter (Ed.) Populäre Serialität: Narration – Evolution – Disktinktion. Zum seriellen Erzählen seit dem 19. Jahrhundert. Bielefeld, transcript Verlag, pp. 123–142

Henderson, Felicia D. (2015) Options and Exclusivity: Economic Pressures on TV Writers' Compensation and the Effects on Writers' Room Culture. In: Alvarado, Manuel, Milly Buonanno, Herman Gray, Toby Miller (Eds.) The SAGE Handbook of Television, London u.a. (2015), S. 183–192

Kelleter, Frank (2012) Populäre Serialität. Eine Einleitung. In: Kelleter, Frank (Ed.) Populäre Serialität: Narration – Evolution – Disktinktion. Zum seriellen Erzählen seit dem 19. Jahrhundert, Bielefeld, transcript Verlag, pp. 11–46

Kirschbacher, Felix, Sven Stollfuß (2015) Von der TV- zur AV-Serie. Produktions-, Distributions- und Rezeptionsformen aktueller US-Serien. In: *merz. Zeitschrift für Medienpädagogik* 4, pp. 21–28

Kumpf, Sarah (2013) Ich bin aber nicht so ein Freak. Distinktion durch Serienaneignung. In: Eichner, Susanne, Lothar Mikos, Rainer Winter (Eds.) Transnationale Serienkultur. Theorie, Ästhetik, Narration und Rezeption Fernsehserien. Wiesbaden, Springer, pp. 347–366

Maeder, Dominik (2013) Transmodalität transmedialer Expansion. Die TV-Serie zwischen Fernsehen und Online-Medien. In: Navigationen. Zeitschrift für Medien- und Kulturwissenschaften 13:1, pp. 105–126

Maeder, Dominik (2017a) Kohärenz, Permutation, Redundanz: Zur seriellen Ökonomie des Let's Plays. In: Ackermann, Judith (Ed.) Phänomen Let's Play-Video. Entstehung, Ästhetik, Aneignung und Faszination aufgezeichneten Computerspielhandelns. Wiesbaden, Springer, pp. 71–83

Maeder, Dominik (2017b) Economies of Contingency. Lost, Dschungelcamp, and the Governmental Poetics of Being Cast Away. In: Beil, Benjamin, Herbert Schwaab, Daniela Wentz (Eds.). Lost in Media, Münster: LitVerlag, pp. 74–96

Maeder, Dominik (2018) Serielle Anhänglichkeit: Sucht, Serie und die Ästhetik von Objektbeziehungen. In: Montage AV 27:2´, pp. 61–76

Mittell, Jason (2015) Complex TV. The Poetics of Contemporary Television Storytelling, New York/London, NYU Press

Newman, Michael Z. (2016) From Beats to Arcs: Towards a Poetics of Television Narrative. In: The Velvet Light Trap 58, pp. 16–28.

Nye, David E. (2016) America's Assembly Line, Cambridge/London, MIT Press

O'Sullivan, Sean (2010) Broken on Purpose: Poetry, Serial Television, and the Season. In: Story Worlds: A Journal of Narrative Studies 2, pp. 59–77.

Schabacher, Gabriele (2010) Serienzeit. Zur Ökonomie und Ästhetik der Zeitlichkeit neuerer US-amerikanischer TV-Serien. In: Meteling, Arno, Isabell Otto, Gabriele Schabacher (Eds.) Previously on... Zur Ästhetik der Zeitlichkeit neuerer TV-Serien. München, Königshausen & Neumann, pp. 20–39

Schleich, Markus, Jonas Nesselhauf (2016) Fernsehserien. Geschichte, Theorie, Narration. Tübingen, A. Francke Verlag

Schneider, Irmela (2010) Medien der Serienforschung. In: Meteling, Arno, Isabell Otto, Gabriele Schabacher (Eds.) „Previously on..." Zur Ästhetik der Zeitlichkeit neuerer TV-Serien. München, Königshausen & Neumann, pp. 41–60.

Schwaab, Herbert (2010) Reading Contemporary Television, das Ende der Kunst und die Krise des Fernsehens. In: Zeitschrift für Medienwissenschaft 2:1, pp. 135–139

Stauff, Markus (2005) Das neue Fernsehen'. Machtanalyse, Gouvernementalität und Digitale Medien. Münster, Lit Verlag

Sudmann, Andreas (2017) Serielle Überbietung. Zur televisuellen Ästhetik und Philosophie exponierter Steigerungen. Stuttgart, J.B. Metzler

Wentz, Daniela (2017) Bilderfolgen. Diagrammatologie der Fernsehserie. München, Wilhelm Fink

Wentz, Daniela (2019) Stranger Things (2016). In: Fahle, Oliver et al. (Eds.) Filmische Moderne. 60 Fragmente. Bielefeld, transcript Verlag 2019, pp. 439–444

Dominik Maeder, Dr. phil., is an independent researcher. His PhD thesis deals with the poetics of governmentality in contemporary fiction and non-fiction television series. Selected publications: *Die Regierung der Serie. Poetologie televisueller Gouvernementalität der Gegenwart*, Bielefeld: transcript, 2021; "Serielle Anhänglichkeit: Sucht, Serie und die Ästhetik von Objektbeziehungen", in *Montage/AV*, vol. 27, no. 2, 2018, pp. 61–76; ed. (with Jens Schröter, Gregor Schwering, Till A. Heilmann): *Ambient. Aesthetics of the background.* Wiesbaden: Springer VS, 2018. website: dominikmaeder.de.

Evidence in Series? Time and Reality References of Serial Television Formats on Digital Platforms Using the Example of *Germany's Next Topmodel* and *Neo Magazin (Royale)*

Anja Peltzer

Introduction: Are the Days of Television Over?

The most significant achievements of television have to do with time. Time, according to Mary-Ann Doane, is even the essential category of television, its foundation, its structural principle and its constant reference.[1] Television is "completely anchored in time and to be worked out by means of time".[2] This becomes obvious when looking at the programme structure of television, which, at the latest with the establishment of "stripping"[3] in the 1990s, has completely committed itself to the linear principles of seriality, regularity and repetition. This strong regimentation of time in the programming of television had the effect that looking at the television set was like looking at the clock: if daily soaps or daily talks were on, one was in the afternoon program, if feature films or elaborate entertainment shows were on, it was already evening, and if one came across a documentary about the life of hippos at night, one was certainly already in the midst of just that. Men and women kept to the 'television times' at which they gathered in front of the

---

[1] Cf. Doane (2006) p. 102.
[2] Doane quoted from Engell (2012) p. 150.
[3] Bleicher (2001) p. 508.

A. Peltzer (✉)
Institute for Media- and Communication Studies University Mannheim, Mannheim, Germany
e-mail: anja.peltzer@uni-mannheim.de

© The Author(s), under exclusive license to Springer Fachmedien Wiesbaden GmbH, part of Springer Nature 2024
D. Newiak et al. (eds.), *Television Studies and Research on Series*,
https://doi.org/10.1007/978-3-658-42915-7_10

television: the daily *news* [D since 1952, Das Erste] at 8 p.m., *Lindenstraße* [D since 1985, Das Erste] on Sunday evening at 6.50 p.m., *Tatort* [D/AT/CH since 1970, Das Erste] on Sunday evening at 8.15 p.m., etc. In this way, television established itself as a "social zeitgeber",[4] provided orientation and became a structuring factor in the everyday life of many of its viewers.[5]

But it is precisely this binding nature of fixed times that seems to have become obsolete today due to digital possibilities: streaming platforms, media libraries as well as the landing pages of individual programmes create freedom for the viewer in terms of the question of 'what' 'when' 'where' and 'how' can be watched. The times of television both as a massive, technical apparatus and in its function of ordering the processes of everyday life seem to be over.

Despite all the prophecies of doom, however, this article is based on the thesis that television is not at a disadvantage in relation to the digital competing offerings, but rather opens up a transmedial space of experience precisely through its exposed link with digital possibilities, which corresponds in many ways with the everyday culture of its viewers. By implementing the decentralized infrastructures and the constant offer of real-time communication of social media in its daily programming, television thematizes and reflects the current change of medial references to time and reality in the course of digitalization. When a TV show like *Circus HalliGalli* [D 2013–2017, ProSieben] puts a fax machine on stage with a request for participation, or when *Neo Magazin (Royale)* [D since 2013, ZDF/ZDFneo] regularly parades the supposed 'digital citizen', but also when *Germany's Next Topmodel* [D since 2006, ProSieben] provides its viewers with status updates of its contestants every 60 min via social media, then the two central figures of time in television—"-live as a specific organization of simultaneity and the series as a specific organization of the passing and continuation of time"[6]—not only become visible in the course of their digital transformation, but are also simultaneously and normatively framed and released for critical reflection.

This article focuses on the transformations of time and reality references in serial television formats through the dramaturgical integration of social media. The three leading questions are: (1) How do the references to time in serial television formats change through the use of social media? (2) Do the references of the televisual to the extra-filmic reality change through the use of social media? (3) What is the position of television in contemporary societies with regard to its reality-forming character?

---

[4] Neverla (1992) p. 59.

[5] Cf. Meteling, Otto, Schabacher (2010), p. 7.

[6] Engell (2012) p. 150.

Because it is of course true that 'good old' television is under pressure to move if it wants to remain of public relevance[7] and not lose the young target group to the permanent option of social media.[8,9]

While questions about temporality are primarily posed to the so-called Quality Series, for which the operation with a complex temporality is almost constitutive,[10] this article explores these questions in serial formats that have already established themselves in linear television under the 'dictates of the quota' and which in the meantime—without having left the terrain of analogue television—use the digital possibilities in a significant way. This applies, for example, to the casting show *Germany's Next Topmodel* and the late-night show *Neo Magazin (Royale).*[11] In the following, both shows will be read as examples of serial television formats in the digital transformation and will be the focus of the analysis presented here. Admittedly, there are considerably more formats in current television programming that not only present themselves 'also' in social media, but also use them constructively to explore the dramaturgical boundaries of their own genre anew (e.g. *Tagesschau, hart aber fair* [D since 2012, WDR], *Berlin Tag & Nacht* [D since 2011, RTL II]). However, the present selection is supported on the one hand by the fact that both programmes began to use social media very early, and on the other hand by the fact that the comparison of the two different formats also legitimises cross-genre statements about the integration of digital possibilities in serially structured television programmes.

However, before the results of the analysis are presented, it is necessary to offer the basics, i.e. in a first step I will briefly discuss the relationship between television and time as well as the modifications of this relationship through digital transformations (Chap. 2). Subsequently, I will demonstrate these modifications by means of two case studies (Chap. 3), before concluding with three remarks on the temporality of digital television and its reality-forming character (Chap. 4).

---

[7] Cf. Schrape (2015) pp. 199–211.

[8] Cf. Schmidt, Taddicken (2017) pp. 3–22.

[9] Cf. Engel, Breunig (2015), p. 312.

[10] Cf. Meteling, Otto, Schabacher (2010) p. 7.

[11] Neo Magazin Royale went on air in 2013 with the title Neo Magazin. Since 2015 it has had the title Royale and is also broadcast in the main ZDF programme, which has led to a new season count. In this text, the episodes are listed according to their publication either as Neo Magazin (seasons 1–3) or as Neo Magazin Royale (seasons 1–4). If all episodes of the format are meant, then we are talking about Neo Magazin (Royale).

Polychronic Seriality? On the Relationship Between Social Time and Televisual Seriality in Everyday Life

The question of the relationship between time and television in the course of digital transformations is of a fundamental character; its actual telos is the determination of the role of television for the social construction of reality. As basal as the conception, experience, and organization of time are to the construction of a shared reality, it is not inherently given. Time must first become determinable so that it can serve as a "frame of reference"[12] for social interactions but also for collective ordering processes. Time, with Elias, is to be seen as a "social construct, a system of symbols and references that emerges in human interaction and at the same time serves to coordinate interpersonal interactions."[13] So, as differently as time may be experienced in the subjective experience of people, it is nevertheless to be understood in the "dimension of action [...] as a knowledge element of the lifeworld [Lebenswelt]".[14] Consensually agreed divisions of time are a prerequisite both for the coordination and ordering of social coexistence and for the ordering of individual identity formation processes. Every society forms its own specific time culture, which is related, among other things, to the respective form of time determination, but also to the communicability of time.

The media of a society, especially television with its 24-h programme flow, are closely involved in the construction and experience of such a time culture. They objectify and represent the time order of a society and can thus assume the function of a social 'Zeitgeber'.[15] Similar to the church or the employer, to cite two other examples of social Zeitgebers, the media structure socially shared time. However, while the newspaper is opened once or a movie is watched once, the flow of television is potentially always available in the present tense. For a temporally determined beginning and a temporally determined end, as is constitutive, for example, for watching a film,[16] there is no counterpart for the programme flow of television. It ultimately consists of time divisions of a "world time" accessible to everyone,[17] which can then be referred to in human interaction within one's "own

---

[12]Elias (1984) p. 41.
[13]Neverla (2010), p. 184.
[14]Ibid., p. 185.
[15]Cf. Ibid., 187 f.
[16]Cf. Seel (2013) p. 136.
[17]Nowotny (1989) p. 20.

subjective local time".[18] It is precisely this linking of the media and the social present, however, that is the basis of television's socially formative power: "It is this interweaving that places the often quite scattered presences of the media reality in the context of a social reality (...), that is, ultimately: providing multiple possibilities of reassuring oneself of the reality of a world common to many or all in the partial reality of life of individuals and collectives".[19] Media experiences may not infrequently involve enormous spatial distances, but the experience itself remains bound to the world time of a shared present. For the experience of a shared world, the synchronization of time in the form of a world time, as a frame of reference and orientation founder, is as much a compelling prerequisite as it is its result. The technical communication media—smartphones, tablets, PCs, web-based services, films, newspapers and television—all correspond to this idea of a shared time and form their specificities precisely through their reference to this idea of time: the omnipresence of potential real-time communication, for example, in the so-called social media, as well as the continuous reliable programme flow of linear television.

The fictional, narrative television series in particular is a child of the linear flow of television and is closely related to the serial principle of television. Knut Hickethier emphasizes the productive fit between series and television as a happy coincidence for television in the 1950s, which was still in its infancy:

> With their extensive narrative volume, series correspond not only to television's growing demand for programmes, but also to its serialised programme structure. The periodic or serial offer structure (which is expressed in the programme in fixed, recurring programme slots) leads to the increased production and broadcasting of fictional series in addition to the fictional single film.[20]

In addition to these economic considerations to increase efficiency, the great potential of viewer loyalty to a particular series and thus to the corresponding channel also helped the series to achieve its lasting popularity in everyday television.[21] As early as 1987, Umberto Eco noted for the 'new' phenomenon of the television series that "the [series] text [adopts] the rhythms of the same 'everydayness' in which it is produced and which it mirrors".[22] While live broadcasting

---

[18] Ibid.

[19] Keppler (2006), p. 42.

[20] Hickethier (2001), p. 197.

[21] Cf. Wedel (2012) pp. 22–27, p. 22 f.

[22] Eco (1987) p. 105.

particularly emphasizes the timeliness of the snapshot and the simultaneity of event, presentation, and perception, the series, with its weekly or even daily rhythm of broadcasting, brings out the sense of time in linearity and duration. Both the serial structure of television and the television series make time experienceable by establishing an inseparable link between "time and its outside."[23] For example, if one has to wait a week for the release of the next episode of a series, then time becomes almost painfully tangible, depending on one's expectations. In the case of the television series, the interweaving of media and social reality thus takes place on both a thematic and a structural level. Through the series' reliable return to the screen at a certain point in time, it not only structures time, but also inserts itself into everyday routines characterized by repetition.[24] The latter in particular coincides with the spirit of the series, for which the repetition of familiar elements is also constitutive: characters, settings, problems and solution strategies, the dramaturgical rhythm of the individual episodes, right down to the use of music, are repeated in every series to a reliable degree of variation. According to Angela Keppler, this repetitive character of television series is not a well-kept secret; rather, it is the basis for the pleasure that series give their viewers, and it is ultimately also the basis for the familiarity that television viewers develop with the series' worlds of meaning.[25]

Neither the serial structure of television nor that of the television series is, however, an invention of television, but rather these were prepared by previous serially structured products of (popular) culture (e.g. by the form of serial novels, cinema film series, but also radio series) as well as by the rhythmisation of everyday life in the course of industrialisation, and have then become further established in direct response to the viewing behaviour of their audience. Seriality as a mode of organization can be understood as a nexus between social everyday life and the media flow of television—on the one hand, because our everyday life is structured much more by routines and repetitions than one is perhaps sometimes willing to admit, and on the other hand, because the temporality of television corresponds directly with the time culture of its society. In this respect, the television series can also be understood as "a typical expression of modern culture [precisely] because it is *serial*."[26]

---

[23] Fahle (2010) p. 242.

[24] Cf. (2012) Die Fernsehserie, ihre Form und ihr Wissen—Ein kurzer Überblick, p. 30.

[25] Cf. Keppler (1995), p. 85.

[26] Schröter (2012) p. 29.

However, if today the television series with its fixed broadcasting rhythm no longer represents the status quo, but rather stands for "the dynamisation of time at the centre of series aesthetics",[27] then the question arises, on the one hand, as to which are the daily routines into which these flexible series viewing habits fit, and on the other hand, for which culture they are thus a typical expression. One thing is certain: the digitalization of television has the potential to fundamentally change the time references of television and thus also the role of television as a producer of meaning and provider of orientation.[28] Essential characteristics of television such as linearity and flow seem to become obsolete with the digitization of television. While the flow of television has corresponded very well with the notion of an abstractly linear 'world time', the "contemporary time culture [...] is characterized by contradictions, homogeneity is juxtaposed with heterogeneity",[29] which leads Irene Neverla to speak of a "polychronic time culture".[30] If television is therefore first and foremost a medium of its time culture, then this change should also be reflected in its structure and products. It was precisely this question of how time becomes visible in serial television formats that have embraced digital possibilities that guided the product analysis, the results of which will now be presented in the following chapter.

Evidence and Irritation in the Digital: Two Case Studies on the Temporality of Serial Television Formats in Digital Cultures

Television's interventions with the possibilities of digital cultures can take on completely different forms. While here, for example, we can also think of the algorithm cultures[31] that calculate further series suggestions for their customers in the background of the interfaces of Netflix and Co., in the following I will pursue this transmedial shoulder-to-shoulder on the material-semiotic level of the televisual. The focus will be on established television genres that are characterized by the dramaturgical integration of social media and the potential commissioning of the sociomedial practices that accompany it. These are thus televisual products that

---

[27] Fahle (2010) p. 231.

[28] Cf. Keilbach/Stauff (2011) pp. 155–182.

[29] Neverla (2010) p. 185.

[30] Ibid.

[31] Cf. Seyfert, Roberge (2017)

extend the ongoing serial principle by the decentralized structures of digital cultures, by the possibility of real-time communication, by the possibility of remediation of content, and by the potentially ubiquitous availability and network character of social media.[32] Such a fundamental expansion of dramaturgical possibilities raises not only the question of the change in television's references to time, but also of the change in television's references to reality: for the interweaving of media and social reality is rooted in the reference to the same time horizon. In this context, *Germany's Next Topmodel* and *Neo Magazin (Royale)* were examined as examples. Although both formats offer many possibilities for analysing the interplay between television, digital change and time, I will focus here only on a selection of significant aspects. I will start with *Germany's Next Topmodel*, a format of the reality TV genre, which started very early a successful connection with social media and the real-time communication that goes along with it.[33]

Case Study I: More Authenticity Through Real Time? On the Temporality of Serial Formats Through the Integration of Social Media Using the Example of *Germany's Next Topmodel*

The casting show *Germany's Next Topmodel* has been broadcast on the German private television channel ProSieben in prime time since 2006 and is the German adaptation of the US original *America's Next Top Model* (USA since 2003, UPN). Season after season, *Germany's Next Topmodel* offers its young contestants the 'unique' chance to be chosen by Heidi Klum as 'Germany's Next Topmodel'. Whether they have what it takes, 'Heidi's girls' have to prove in different tests, usually in more or less fancy shootings. In the end, a jury—led by Heidi Klum— decides who has to 'go home' and who can stay and hope to be crowned a 'top model' in the end. While the first season had to limit itself to 10 episodes, the last three seasons have had 16 episodes each to find Germany's next top model. The show is always broadcast in the first half of the year and culminates in a rather opulently staged finale, which is broadcast live. The basic structure of the format thus follows the serial principle, in that the current episode is broadcast once a week on linear television, but lives from the principle of real time. For within this de facto time span, the show promises, the next top model will be found, which will eventually culminate in the live show that the individual episodes work towards.

---

[32] Cf. Lievrouw and Livingstone (2006).

[33] Cf. Würker (2013).

The fact that the show is largely pre-produced is, in turn, not publicly addressed in any form.

At the latest since the twelfth season (10.02.–25.05.2017), the casting show is increasingly embedded in social media. The show can now be followed not only on television or on the landing page of ProSieben,[34] but also on the various channels of social media. On the one hand, you can apply to be a contestant on the show via Twitter and Instagram (e.g. via the hashtag #IchBinGermanysNextTopmodel2017, which, however, earned more scorn than applications), and on the other hand, the contestants receive a Facebook and Instagram account, among other things, via which they can interact with the viewers of the show—always assuming that the viewers also decide to 'follow' the contestants. The show's own YouTube channel, which is supplied with plenty of content in the form of YouTube-compliant clips, has already been available since March 5, 2013. It is also possible to subscribe to *Germany's Next Topmodel*'s WhatsApp newsletter, which seems to address two key concerns by promising to (1) keep you 'always up to date' and (2) provide 'exclusive insights' into the *Germany's Next Topmodel* universe. In the twelfth season, for example, the format populated the various social media channels with such intensity that viewers connected to the show, depending on how many of the contestants they ended up following, received messages about 'Heidi and her girls' on their smartphones every hour on average. The WhatsApp newsletter checked in at least once a day over the course of this season, and usually no later than eight o'clock. However, in the fourteenth season, the broadcast rhythm of the WhatsApp newsletter drastically reduced. Thus, although the newsletter was used as early as January 17, 2019, to promote the fourteenth season. However, the publication rhythm of the WhatsApp newsletter has reduced to more like once a week on average. Even though the presence of the format via WhatsApp has significantly reduced, the liaison of serial communication and supposed real-time communication that the show has entered into through the WhatsApp newsletter, but also through the playout of photos, clips, polls and statements via social media such as Instagram, Facebook and Twitter, remains. Traditional linear television, this much can already be said at this point, is therefore by no means being replaced by social media, but—on the contrary—it is expanding its offerings. In the case of reality TV, it can also be shown that the transmedial expansion of the programme to include the structures of the social web not only entails a spatial, content-related and temporal expansion of the televisual, but also an expansion of cinematic authentication

---

[34] https://www.prosieben.de/tv/germanys-next-topmodel

strategies, which plays a central role particularly with regard to the specifics of the genre of reality TV.

The genre 'reality TV' consists of a mixture of fictional and non-fictional elements. It is important to note that this mixture is not a blurring of the line between the fictional and the non-fictional, but that the mixture results in an essential entertainment value of the genre.

> The audience is not fooled or deceived, it is entertained with the dramaturgically forced errors and confusions in the lives of real people. (. . .) The special gesture of reality TV – and the special *thrill* for its audience – on the other hand lies in the *game* with *factual* joys and hardships sparked by its constitutive marks of authenticity.[35]

For the genre, the game with the boundaries of fiction and documentary can thus be described as quite constitutive. This game is now being significantly expanded by the possibilities of social media. Through transmedia storytelling via Instagram and the like, the format can now—beyond the usual procedures of the reality TV genre—produce understandings of reality and thus extend the "*game* with *factual* joys and hardships sparked by its constitutive markers of authenticity"[36] to the terrain of social media as well. For example, in the thirteenth season, the candidate 'Klaudia with K' chats in her first video on her YouTube channel of the same name about why she is ultimately no longer a contestant on *Germany's Next Topmodel* (Figs. 1–3) and, looking directly into the camera via the corresponding video title "Warum ich nicht mehr bei *Germany's Next Topmodel* dabei bin" (Why I am no longer a contestant on Germany's Next Topmodel),[37] promises nothing less than to now talk 'turkey' about her time on *Germany's Next Topmodel* beyond the terms of the television format. Both Klaudia's communicative gesture and the media framing through YouTube stylize this video as the supposed backstage of the television format *Germany's Next Topmodel.* I understand the backstage with the sociologist ErvingGoffman as the place "where the impression created by the representation is consciously and naturally refuted [and] (. . .) illusions and impressions [are] openly developed"[38] and where one can "drop the mask, deviate from the textbook, and fall out of character."[39] However, the genre framework of reality TV, which is also present in this YouTube clip solely through the character 'Klaudia with K', does not

---

[35] Keppler (2015) p. 159.

[36] Ibid.

[37] https://www.youtube.com/watch?v=So8vLM2VeI0&t=2s

[38] Goffman (2003) p. 104.

[39] Ibid., p. 105.

Figs. 1–3 Stills from the transmedia network of the casting show *Germany's Next Topmodel* (season 13, 2018)

allow for such a reading of the backstage, so that the question also arises here: How actually to distinguish the fictional from the non-fictional? The same is repeated on Instagram, for example, when contestant Zoe from the same season ventilates her anger about the comments and loyalty of fans with another fellow contestant in an Instagram story, directly addressing viewers with the comment "you don't know what goes on behind the scenes" (Figs. 1–3/First week of April 2018). Here, in addition to the contestant's direct gaze into the camera, the format of the Instagram story, the tinny, amateurish tone of the story, the shaky camera, and the contestant's rather euphoric manner of speaking imply the communicative gesture of an authentic, because immediate and spontaneous statement, which at the same time, however, must also be called into question due to the ambivalent genre framework with regard to such a reading.

This relationship is certainly taken to the extreme with Zoe's Facebook post on 22 April 2018 (Figs. 1–3): The candidate is sitting on a picnic blanket in the greenery above Schönbrunn Palace in Vienna and wants to share with her viewers, by means of a short clip, what she is carrying in her backpack. Once again, the young candidate directs her gaze directly at the camera and now turns her supposed innermost thoughts inside out: In addition to her passport, Zoe confesses in the video, she always has her Canon camera with her, which, she says, is almost more important to her than her own passport. If the brand of the camera was not understood correctly, so you can read it again unproblematically in the hashtags to the post:

What do you always have with you? What should never be missing in your handbags? Lately I've been carrying the #canoneosm100 with a case that matches my outfit. This way I can always capture special moments spontaneously ☺ https://bit.ly/2HDBa70 #liveforthestory #deinstyledeinestory #gntm Canon Germany Canon Austria.[40]

Taken to the extreme, this appears to be an attempt to profit from the format's indecision between fiction and documentary. Similar to influencers, advertisers rely on the supposed credibility and authenticity of the candidates among the primarily young target group. However, the high credibility in this framework is not so much attributable to Zoe as a person, but rather to the media framing of her appearance in social media. Christian Meyer and Christian Meier, for example, show that "quasi-simultaneous pointing communication via WhatsApp and similar instant messaging services [. . .] through its immediacy [creates] the fiction of a shared everyday life closer to interaction and [endows] it with more direct vividness and proximity to experience."[41] Closeness to experience, in turn, corresponds above all with live communication, broadcasting in 'real time'. Media products that are broadcast live represent an intensified form of presence, since not only the presence of the screening coincides with the presence of the viewer, but also the duration of the event shown coincides with the presence of the screening and the viewer. By also interacting with its viewers via social media, *Germany's Next Topmodel* can communicate with its audience in supposed real time and establish a supposed live character around the serial broadcast dates during the season on ProSieben. Communication in real time as well as the additional communicative offers in the gesture of direct addressing intensify the feeling of 'being there' and the 'thrill' of deciding what can still be classified as "real" and what can just "no longer" be classified as real. For one effect of this narration and publication in real time via social media is an increased interweaving.

However, this entanglement is not to be understood as a dissolution of the boundary between reality and mediality, but rather as a reflexive game with this boundary. The supposed evidence of social media becomes part of the game about the status of the factual that is constitutive for the genre of reality TV. The genre concept of reality TV does not allow for a naïve realism regarding media representations of reality. This reflexive game is centrally related to the experience of time, as it is constitutive for television and especially for the television series. For while the classic television series has inserted itself into a linear, successively proceeding everyday life and thus reproduced it, the transmedial space of

---

[40] Facebook post on Zoe. Topmodel. 2018, April 22, 2018.

[41] Meyer, Meier (2017) p. 90.

experience and action of the casting show *Germany's Next Topmodel* establishes a polychronic culture of time around the weekly broadcast episode of the show. What is repeated here in this concept, above all week after week and day after day, is the unpredictability of the format's playouts in social media and the equally unpredictable self-disclosure of the format in the real everyday life of its viewers that accompanies it. In this concept, the reliability of the series is transformed into the unpredictability in series. Through the unpredictability of the playouts, but also through the staging of supposed real-time communication, the format establishes different levels of time and thus also levels of reality, which not only enriches the genre-typical game of the supposedly real with further variants, but the format also releases the media-cultural habitus of its viewers, who are also present as actors in the transmedial experience space of the casting show, for reflection.

Case Study II: Reflection in Real Time: On the Temporality of Serial Television Formats on Social Media Using the Example of *Neo Magazin (Royale)*

Neo Magazin (Royale) is a format that almost seems to be about the question of 'contemporary television':[42] On the one hand, Jan Böhmermann's show repeatedly puts the social-forming effect of television to the test with various actions, e.g. when the editorial team successfully infiltrated two actors on the German Reality-TV Show *Schwiegertochter gesucht* [Daughter-in-law wanted] (D since 2007, RTL) (*Neo Magazin Royale* season 02/ episode 11; 12.05.2016)' when Böhmermann read out the poem about Turkish President Recep Tayyip Erdoğan entitled 'defamatory criticism' on the show (*Neo Magazin Royale* season 02/episode 09; 31.03.216) or when the editorial team caused a stir with their supposed confession video about the extended middle finger of Greek Finance Minister Yanis Varoufakis (*Neo Magazin Royale* season 01/episode 07; 19.03.2015). On the other hand, the show uses social media itself in different ways. For example, the show is always first offered online in the ZDF Mediathek, before it is then broadcast on Thursdays at 10.15 pm on ZDFneo and, since February 2015, also on Friday nights in the main ZDF program.

---

[42] *Neo Magazin* was already awarded the Grimme Prize in 2014 for its willingness to experiment with social media. In 2017, the show *Neo Magazin Royale* received, among others, the *Golden Camera Digital Award* in the category #ViralerClip for the video *BE DEUTSCH* (season 02/episode 14; 02.06.2016) and in 2019 again the Grimme Award for the show *Lass dich überwachen! The PRISM IS A DANCER Show* (Season 04/Episode 10; 05.04.2018).

The show is also represented on zdf.de with its own show page (https://www.zdf.de/comedy/neo-magazin-mit-jan-boehmermann). In addition, *Neo Magazin (Royale)* is also present on the common platforms of digital communication: Twitter, Snapchat, YouTube, Facebook, Instagram. But social media are also used in the programme itself, e.g. through the hashtag of the week, which can then be used to tweet about the respective programme. The hashtag of the week is found as part of a hashtag conference, in which anyone interested can participate via Periscope. Unlike the conventional hashtags of television shows, the hashtag of *Neo Magazin (Royale)* does not contain a reference to the show, but rather the goal is to announce a hashtag that has not been tweeted about beforehand. The hashtag, e.g. #hitzekindofmagic [Hitze means heat and is spelled similar to "it's a"] (*Neo Magazin Royale* season 05/episode 16, 13.06.2019), is then announced via social media and as a welcome in the show by Böhmermann himself. So in the case of *Neo Magazin (Royale)*, the connection to the show can only be made by those who currently watch it or are connected to it via social media. Through this 'disguised hashtag', *Neo Magazine (Royale)* builds an 'insider knowledge' that excludes those who are neither networked with the show nor watching. This supposedly purposeful restriction of the audience represents an ironic sideswipe in two directions. On the one hand, the 'camouflaged hashtag' alludes to its own placement as a niche format, perceived only by a small sworn community beyond a quota reality. On the other hand, the 'camouflaged hashtag' ironizes the use of hashtags to television shows as a supposedly unrestricted mouthpiece into the digital world, as a saving link between digital natives and classic television (#LateNightBerlin, #hartaberfair, #tagesschau etc.). The decisive factor for accessibility, according to the statement of this staging of the broadcast hashtag as a whispering post of a transmedial television, is not the medium, but the content. With regard to the time references of the format, what is special about the hashtag of the week is that this extends the serial and pre-produced television format of the late-night show by the possibility of real-time communication parallel to the broadcast and elevates the actual live-on-tape broadcast as part of the Twitter network to a live event. I will return to this significant interweaving of television time and social time via the integration of the broadcast into the structures of social media at the end of this analysis.

Social media and the practices associated with them thus appear in many ways in *Neo Magazin (Royale)*: on the one hand, through how the programme presents itself on the platforms, on the other hand, through how the possibilities of digital communication itself are used in the programme, and finally, also through how content from the new media becomes the thematic object of the programme itself. The latter is the subject of several programme sections, which become part of the programme on an irregular basis. The section *PRISM is a Dancer* has been a fixed

Figs. 4–6 Stills from *Neo Magazin* (D, ZDF/ZDFneo, Season 01/Episode 01; 31.10.2013)

part of the show since its first broadcast (*Neo Magazin* season 01/episode 01; 31.10.2013) and is still used again and again today. In the section, content published by the studio audience on the Internet (tweets, websites, YouTube clips, Facebook entries, auctions, etc.) is made the thematic subject of the show. Whereas in the world-famous PRISM programme the digital communication of more or less everyone was recorded, here the focus is very specifically on the digital footprints of the studio audience, which are immediately revealed on television by 'whistleblower' Böhmermann (Figs. 4–6). Crucially, viewers in the studio of the broadcast know nothing about what may have been found out about them, nor what will actually be used in the section. During the taping, viewers are then confronted with the editors' findings. This significant visualization of temporality through the immediate reenactment of already past digital missteps in the broadcast moves the *PRISM is a Dancer* rubric into the research focus of this analysis. The starting point is the first issue of the rubric from the first broadcast of *Neo Magazin* (Season 01/Episode 01; 31.10.2013). In this issue, there are three studio guests: Nina Kristin Svenja is approached about a photo of herself with Gundula Gause and Claus Kleber (both are news presenters on German television), which she published on her Facebook profile (Figs. 4–6). Pascal Haube is quizzed about, among other things, his interests 'friends and drunken parties', which he has stated on his gamer FM profile. Finally, the online auction at kalaydo.de by viewer Julia is brought up, in which she offered a leaded glass window for sale. The host now pulls it out from under his desk. The *Neo Magazin team* bought the piece themselves for €50. Whenever the camera turns to the studio audience during this section, the image appears filtered in red and is framed by a computer-animated graphic that seems to reveal various fictitious information about the audience (Figs. 4–6).

When the viewer Nina is asked about the photo of herself with Claus Kleber and Gundula Gause and Pascal about his statements at gamer-FM,[43] screenshots of the

---

[43] Gamer-FM was an online radio station by gamers for gamers and is no longer online. However, there are still a few shows of the radio station on soundcloud.com to listen to, see https://soundcloud.com/gamer-fm

corresponding internet finds are mounted in the shot-counter-shot procedure, with which the conversations between the exposed and Böhmermann are presented. In the case of Nina, it is her Facebook profile, which also contains the aforementioned photo with the two moderators of the German News Show *heute journal*, which then becomes the central object of the conversation and the scene (Figs. 4–6). The screenshot fades in several times to fill the screen and can actually be seen for longer than the two participants in the conversation themselves. By means of this montage technique, the content from social media is integrated into the representational logic of the show. In the case of the third candidate, the viewer Julia, the transfer of content from social media into the television programme goes one step further. Here, too, the candidate is first confronted with the editorial team's find in form of a screenshot. A sales campaign on kalaydo.de is shown, in which Julia is hawking a leaded glass window. Viewer Julia, incidentally, shows no interest in participating in the game, let alone answering Böhmermann's questions. Even when he asks if the leaded glass window is still available, she remains stubbornly silent. But Böhmermann is not deterred, reaches under his desk and brings out said lead glass window to give it back to Julia.

This last variant, of not only fading in digital messages from viewers via screenshot, but also having them themselves perform 'live' in the show in some form, is increasingly developed in the further editions of the section: For example, a viewer's band was given a second chance in the form of a spontaneous live performance—of course only after the YouTube video was shown in detail in the show, in which the singer repeatedly failed with the self-written lyrics during a performance (*Neo Magazin Royale* season 02/episode 12; 19.05.2016). Another time, viewer Vanessa Schäfer was confronted with the answers she posted about herself on the website ask.fm. The confrontation ultimately took the form of a typical TV quiz show titled *Find Yourself and be that.* The title is also a find from the viewer's online content (*Neo Magazin Royale* season 02/episode 07; 17/03/2016). Such digital missteps by the audience are so numerous that *Neo Magazin Royale* has been broadcasting PRISM specials at irregular intervals since June 2017 (Season 03/Episode 18; 08.06.2017; Season 03/ Episode 32; 30.11.2017). In the guise of a TV show à la Wetten *Dass…?* (D/A/CH 1981–2014, ZDF/ORF/SRF/MHOCH2 TV), the studio audience is then paraded in rows for 45–90 min. Since November 2, 2018, *PRISM is a Dancer has* even been presented in the form of a stand-alone TV show under the title *Lass dich überwachen! The PRISM is a Dancer Show* aired on ZDF (Season 01/Episode 01; 02.11.2018; Season 01/Episode 02; 31.05.2019).

Comparing these cases, a pattern becomes clear: the omnipresent and supposedly 'virtual' social media are here, literally, translated into action. The viewers' digital actions are translated into face-to-face interactions, albeit in the televisual logic of the late-night show genre. The re-enacted missteps of the viewers thus provide 'good old' television with plenty of scene material. The translation of viewers' stagings in social media into television's forms of staging has several effects: On the one hand, *Neo Magazin (Royale)* invites its candidates to face-work with the confrontation and, in doing so, not only creates media-reflexive moments, but on the other hand, it also creates the live moments that are as characteristic as they are important for the television genre of late-night shows, in which spontaneity and staging have an equal effect. The clou of this media charade is that at the moment of the performance of the online content, it is precisely television that presents itself as the place where event and presentation coincide, and not the social media, which actually stand for the possibilities of real-time communication. The 'old medium' of television thus not only benefits from social media, but thanks to social media can also distinguish itself as the more 'social' and 'immediate' medium.

Neo Magazin (Royale) also shows that social media do not mean the end for television, but that they represent a conceptual extension for television, both on a technical and on a content level. In particular, the communication situation of media product and viewer experiences a significant shift through the use of social media in *Neo Magazin (Royale)*. However, this shift does not point in the direction of the popular and optimistic concept of the 'produser',[44] which would like to see the user on an equal footing with the television producers, but rather in the direction of an enlightened and reflexive approach to (social) media on the part of both the users and the producers. For *Neo Magazin (Royale)* not only makes its own viewers the target of ridicule, but at the same time engages in an ironic game with the traditional forms of serial television entertainment. In this way, a new style of media entertainment is introduced, in which an offensive self-reference of media presentation takes the place of the serial principle of 'repetition in moderate variance'. The various time references of the format are particularly constitutive for this offensive self-reference. For both the integration of the show into the structures of social media and the reenactment of past missteps on digital terrain in real time on television ultimately display in particular the significant entanglement of media time and social time. Finally, the *way* social media is used in *Neo Magazine (Royale)* reveals at least two things about our everyday lives. One: With the self-evidence with which the new (and old) media are used in our everyday life, the reflection of how we deal with them should also become self-evident. For another: Television may change in

---

[44] Cf. Jenkins (2006).

the modes of its broadcasting and use, but its function as a seismograph of social processes remains unaffected.

Conclusion: Time and Reality References of Serial Television Formats in Digital Cultures

Based on Eco's thesis that television series integrate themselves into the rhythms of everyday life, which they also reproduce, two questions in particular were open at the beginning of this article: What are the everyday rhythms into which the series concepts linked to social media fit, and for which time culture are the transmedial series formats thus a typical expression? And how do references to time and reality become visible in serial television formats that have embraced digital possibilities? At the end of this article, these can now be answered as follows:

1. Through the networking of serial television formats with social media, a significant expansion of television takes place in terms of content, space and time, beyond an episode-centred broadcast rhythm. In the case of *Neo Magazin (Royale)*, for example, a transmedial format architecture is emerging via the 'hashtag of the week', which networks the programme itself with digital media cultures and thus supplements the originally serial television format 'late-night show' with further communication offerings, certainly also in real time. According to Umberto Eco, the everyday routines into which the serial inscribes itself and which it also reproduces are no longer those of a linear, successively ordered everyday life, but those of a polychronic time culture of digital contemporary societies. While, for example, the unique selling point of an animated series such as The *Simpsons* [US since 1989, FOX] is precisely that it is "removed from time",[45] the transmedial serial formats are characterized by a temporalization that is dedicated to immediacy and liveness, whereby time becomes affectively perceptible and the format is anchoredin the 'here and now'.
2. Television's socially formative impact is rooted in its reference to the same time horizon as its viewers. According to Angela Keppler, this common vanishing point is the basis for the interweaving of the media and the social present. The dramaturgical use of social media consequently leads not only to a change in television's references to time, but in particular to a change in the references to reality of television itself. As television has left behind its traditional place in the

---

[45] Fahle (2010) p. 239.

domestic closet and now meets its networked audience on their own smartphones, it is not only omnipresent in the actual everyday life of its viewers, but also benefits from the promise of digital communication to create "through its immediacy the fiction of a shared everyday life"[46] and to make it more interactive. The lynchpin of transmedia series is no longer the reliably recurring broadcast date of the current episode, but the networked smartphone of its viewers. The digital outer space of these transmedial formats, beyond the dramaturgically designed playout of the broadcasts in the social media, becomes an intermediate space in which media and real actions intersect, so that this transmedial setting always also offers the reflection of one's own time culture and one's own media habitus.

3. In the digital age, serially organised television is therefore not at a disadvantage compared to the so-called social media, but has become the new paradigm of the knowledge order in the digital world precisely through its interventions with the social media and their time structures. Television provides knowledge for a life in the digital transformation both through the integration of social media in its diverse formats and through the various forms of thematization of digitalization in its broadcasts.[47] This updates the orientation function of television for the members of its society—and does not make it obsolete. For by trying out and reflecting on the possibilities of digital change in its various formats, television invites its viewers to do the same. The irritation of the leading medium is an irritation of the culturally familiar aspects of a society and thus an opportunity for reflection and the acquisition of digital literacy on the part of both media production and reception.

References

Bleicher, Joan Kristin (2001) Mediengeschichte des Fernsehens. In: Helmut Schanze (Ed.) Handbuch der Mediengeschichte. Stuttgart, Alfred Kröner Verlag, pp. 490–518

Doane, Mary-Ann (2006) Information, Krise, Katastrophe. In: Fahle, Oliver, Lorenz Engell (Eds.) Philosophie des Fernsehens, München: Willhelm Fink Verlag, pp. 102–121.

Eco, Umberto (1987) *Streit der Interpretationen*, Konstanz, Universitätsverlag

Elias, Norbert (1984) Über die Zeit. Frankfurt a. M., Suhrkamp.

---

[46]Meyer/Meier: "Epistemic Regimes of New Media. A Cultural Sociological Perspective on Digital Image Communication", p. 90.

[47]Cf. Hörning (2017): *Wissen in digitalen Zeiten*, pp. 69–86.

Engel, Bernhard, Christian Breunig (2015) Massenkommunikation 2015. Mediennutzung im Intermediavergleich. In: Media Perspektiven 8, pp. 310–322

Engell, Lorenz (2012) Fernsehtheorie zur Einführung. Hamburg, Junius

Fahle, Oliver (2010) Die Simpsons und der Fernseher. In: Meteling, Arno, Isabell Otto, Gabriele Schabacher (Eds.)'Previously on'. Zur Ästhetik der Zeitlichkeit neuerer TV-Serien. München, Wilhelm Fink Verlag, pp. 231–242.

Goffman, Erving (2003) Wir alle spielen Theater: Die Selbstdarstellung im Alltag (1959), München, Piper

Hickethier, Knut (2001) Film- und Fernsehanalyse, Stuttgart, J.B. Metzler

Hörning, Karl Heinz (2017) Wissen in digitalen Zeiten. In: Allert, Heidrun, Michael Asmussen, Christoph Richter (Eds.) Digitalität und Selbst – Interdisziplinäre Perspektiven auf Subjektivierungs- und Bildungsprozesse. Bielefeld, transcript, pp. 69–86

Jenkins, Henry (2006) Convergence Culture: Where Old and New Media Collide, New York, New York University Press

Keilbach, Judith, Markus Stauff (2011) Fernsehen als fortwährendes Experiment – Über die permanente Erneuerung eines alten Mediums. In: Borer, Bohrer, Samuel Sieber, Georg Christoph Tholen (Eds.) Blickregime und Dispositive audiovisueller Medien, Bielefeld, transcript, pp. 155–182

Keppler, Angela (2015) Das Fernsehen als Sinnproduzent: Soziologische Fallstudien. München, de Gruyter

Keppler, Angela (2006) Mediale Gegenwart. Eine Theorie des Fernsehens am Beispiel der Darstellung von Gewalt. Frankfurt a.M., Suhrkamp

Keppler, Angela (1995) Person und Figur: Identifikationsangebote in Fernsehserien, In: montage/av 4 (2), pp. 85–100.

Lievrouw, Leah A., Sonia Livingstone (2006) Handbook of New Media: Social Shaping and Consequences of ICTs. London, Sage

Meteling, Arno, Isabell Otto, Gabriele Schabacher (2010) Previously on. In: Meteling, Arno, Isabell Otto, Gabriele Schabacher (Eds.) 'Previously on'. Zur Ästhetik der Zeitlichkeit neuerer TV-Serien. München, Wilhelm Fink Verlag, pp. 7–16.

Meyer, Christian, Christian Meier (2017) Epistemische Regime der neuen Medien. Eine kultursoziologische Perspektive auf digitale Bildkommunikation´. In: Navigationen 17 (1), pp. 77–94

Neverla, Irene (1992) Fernseh-Zeit. Zuschauer zwischen Kalkül und Zeitvertreib. Eine Untersuchung zur Fernsehnutzung. München, Öhlschläger

Neverla, Irene (2010) Medien als soziale Zeitgeber im Alltag: Ein Beitrag zur kultursoziologischen Wirkungsforxsschung. In: Hartman, Maren, Andreas Hepp (Eds.) Die Mediatisierung der Alltagswelt. Wiesbaden, Springer

Nowotny, Helga (1989) Eigenzeit: Entstehung und Strukturierung eines Zeitgefühls. Frankfurt a.M., Suhrkamp

Seel, Martin (2013) Die Künste des Kinos. Frankfurt a.M., Suhrkamp

Seyfert, Robert/Roberge, Jonathan (2017) Algorithmuskulturen – Über die rechnerische Konstruktion der Wirklichkeit, Bielefeld, transcript

Schmidt, Jan-Hindrik, Taddicken, Monika (2017) Entwicklung und Verbreitung sozialer Medien. In: Schmidt, Jan-Hindrik, Monika Taddicken (Eds.) Handbuch Soziale Medien. Wiesbaden, Springer VS, pp. 3–22

Schrape, Jan-Felix (2015) Social Media, Massenmedien und Öffentlichkeit: Eine soziologische Einordnung. In: Imhof, Kurt, Roger Blum, Heinz Bonfadelli et al. (Eds.) Demokratisierung durch Social Media?: Mediensymposium 2012. Wiesbaden, Springer VS, pp. 199–211

Schröter, Jens (2012) Die Fernsehserie, ihre Form und ihr Wissen. Ein kurzer Überblick. In: tv diskurs 62 (4), pp. 28–31.

Wedel, Michael (2012) Der lange Weg zur „Qualität". Zur Geschichte des Serienformats in Film und Fernsehen, In: tv diskurs 62 (4), pp. 22–27.

Würker, Sascha (2013) Die Verschmelzung von Fernsehen und Social Media als Erfolgskonzept am Beispiel von ‚Berlin – Tag und Nacht'. Mittweida,

TV Shows

America's Next Top Model (USA seit 2003, UPN)
Berlin Tag & Nacht (D seit 2011, RTL II)
Circus HalliGalli (D 2013–2017, ProSieben)
Germany's Next Topmodel (D seit 2006, ProSieben)
hart aber fair (D seit 2012, WDR)
Lindenstraße (D seit 1985, Das Erste)
Neo Magazin Royale (D seit 2013, ZDF/ZDFneo)
Schwiegertochter gesucht (D seit 2007, RTL)
Tagesschau (D seit 1952, Das Erste)
Tatort (D/AT/CH seit 1970, Das Erste)
Wetten Dass. . .? (D/A/CH 1981–2014, ZDF/ORF/SRF/MHOCH2 TV)

Internet Sources

„#hartaberfair", *Twitter*, https://twitter.com/hashtag/hartaberfair?src=hash, (Accessed on 02.09.2019)

„#IchBinGermanysNextTopmodel2017", *Twitter*, https://twitter.com/hashtag/ichbingermanysnexttopmodel2017?src=hash. Accessed 2 Sep 2019

„#LateNightBerlin", *Twitter*, https://twitter.com/hashtag/LateNightBerlin?src=hash, (Accessed on 2 Sep 2019)

„#tagesschau", *Twitter*, https://twitter.com/hashtag/tagesschau?ref_src=twsrc%5Egoogle%7Ctwcamp%5Eserp%7Ctwgr%5Ehashtag. Accessed on 2 Sep 2019

„ask.fm", https://ask.fm/. Accessed on 2 Sep 2019

„gamer-FM Hear The Game", *Soundcloud*, https://soundcloud.com/gamer-fm, (Accessed on 02.09.2019)

„Germany's Next Topmodel", *ProSieben*, https://www.prosieben.de/tv/germanys-next-topmodel, (Accessed on 02.09.2019)

„Germany's Next Topmodel – WhatsApp", *ProSieben*, https://www.prosieben.de/tv/germanys-next-topmodel/whatsapp. Accessed on 2 Sep 2019

„Klaudiamitk", *YouTube*, 11.05.2018, https://www.youtube.com/channel/UCQ3xmulF54mTsWGfVCRqbqQ. Accessed on 2 Sep 2019

„Neo Magazin Royale", *ZDF*, https://www.zdf.de/comedy/neo-magazin-mit-jan-boehmermann. Accessed on 2 Sep 2019

Zoe.Topmodel.2018", *Facebook*, 22.05.2018, https://www.facebook.com/215616889011537/videos/246198479286711/. Accessed on 2 Sep 2019

Anja Peltzer is researching media studies at the University of Mannheim. Her main research interests are: Film and Television Analysis, Aesthetics and Politics of Digital Communication, and Qualitative Methods of Social Research. Most recently published: ‚Oh mein Gott Druck is so raffiniert!' Repräsentation und Rezeption von Sozialen Medien im Alltag Jugendlicher im Funk Format Druck. in: Stock and Kraus (eds.). *Teen TV: Repräsentationen, Lesarten und Produktionsweisen aktueller Jugendserien.* Wiesbaden: Springer VS, 2020, pp. 219–253 (will be published in English by Springer in 2024).

Relational and Differential Seriality

Michaela Wünsch

The approach that there exists a prehistory of seriality that will be explored in this paper is based on the idea formulated by Umberto Eco or Richard Dyer, among others, that seriality does not only become virulent with technical reproducibility and serial capitalist production and distribution, but has "always" shaped art and culture:

> It's clear that humans have always loved seriality. Bards, jugglers, griots and yarnspinners (not to mention parents and nurses) have all long known the value of leaving their listeners wanting more, of playing on the mix of repetition and anticipation, and indeed of the anticipation of repetition, that underpins serial pleasure.[1]

Umberto Eco points out, based on television series, that art has always been serial. He understands seriality as a very broad category, "or as another term for an art of repetition,"[2] which encompasses both television series and Greek tragedy.

Dyer's and Eco's approach that the arts have always been serial are taken here as a suggestion to elaborate on how philosophy has discussed, circumscribed, and aesthetically evaluated aspects of the serial before a clearly defined concept of series associated with media could emerge. This exploration is intended to complement the concept of the serial and offer new perspectives on television and series such as *Breaking Bad*.

---

[1] Dyer (1997) p. 14.
[2] Umberto Eco (1989) p. 302.

M. Wünsch (✉)
Heinrich-Heine-Universität, Düsseldorf, Germany
e-mail: Michaela.Wuensch@hhu.de

D. Newiak et al. (eds.), *Television Studies and Research on Series*,
https://doi.org/10.1007/978-3-658-42915-7_11

241

(Perceptual) Aesthetics

Eco points out that it was only in modern aesthetics that art, which has since been valuated by the degree of novelty, was distinguished from craft, whereas in classical aesthetics the 'serial' execution of a previous pattern was also judged to be artistic:

> The same term *(technē, ars)* was used to denote the activities of a barber or shipbuilder as well as the work of a painter or poet. Classical aesthetics was not concerned with innovation at any price. Even in those cases where the modern sensibility delighted in the revolution wrought by a classical artist, contemporaries appreciated the opposite aspect of his work, that is, his respect for preceding models.[3]

Seriality as a mode of production in the sense of craftsmanship was valued precisely as such as a skill. The medial aspect of craft or artistry would be the material that brings something to view.[4] It mediates between the viewer and the object. However, this materiality tied to mediation was by no means purely positively determined or unproblematic, nor can we exclusively assume such 'equal treatment' of craft and art as Eco posits.[5] To illustrate this problematic, two examples will be taken: the use of *technē* in relation to writing and Plato's allegory of the cave. With Jean-Luc Nancy and Jacques Rancière, Plato's critique of writing and the image as repetition and mimesis will be questioned, to elaborate in the final move how writing and image also leave behind this Platonic discourse in *Breaking Bad* and how the series performs a self-assertion of both the image and things.

---

[3] Ibid., p. 301 f. In the German translation: "Der gleiche Terminus (technē, ars) wurde benutzt, um sowohl die Tätigkeiten eines Friseurs oder Schiffsbauers wie auch die Arbeit eines Malers oder Dichters zu bezeichnen. Die klassische Ästhetik war nicht auf Innovation um jeden Preis bedacht. Selbst in solchen Fällen, in denen sich die moderne Sensibilität an der Revolution erfreut, die durch einen klassischen Künstler bewirkt wurde, schätzten die Zeitgenossen den entgegengesetzten Aspekt seines Werkes, d. h. seinen Respekt vor vorangehenden Modellen."

[4] Mersch (2006) p. 13.

[5] Cf. on this also Martin Seel (2003): "Finally, as far as aesthetics is concerned, with the medial techniques art has acquired a highly changeable material, which once again makes it clear that in art it is never the material alone that matters, but operations with the materials—and that it is the wide scope of these operations that forms the+ actual medium of the respective arts." Seel (2003) p. 11. In the original: "Was schließlich die Ästhetik betrifft, so ist der Kunst mit den medialen Techniken ein höchst wandelbares Material zugewachsen, an dem einmal mehr deutlich wird, dass es in der Kunst nie auf das Material allein, sondern au Operationen mit den Materialien ankommt—und dass es der weite Spielraum diese Operationen ist, der das eigentliche Medium der jeweiligen Künste bildet.

Technē includes not only the artifice mentioned by Eco, but also calculating and writing, "which, situated between artifice and technique, leaves undecided what consequences and effects it produces."[6]

However, Jacques Derrida has already pointed out that Plato's writing has to do with both craft and the serial in the sense of (technical) repetition: Writing can do nothing but (repeat itself), "always signify[ing] the same thing (*semainei*)."[7] From this follows a definition of writing that repeats without knowing.[8] It is anti-substance, non-being.[9] Plato's reproach against writing, and thus against medial techniques as pure (automatic) repetition, goes even further: it robs the subject of memory and will "create forgetfulness".[10]

If one follows the idea that Plato's critique was directed against technology rather than against writing,[11] this raises the question for Derrida's or Jean-Luc Nancy's deconstructive reading of Plato, of what reevaluations are to be drawn from the non-being and non-knowing of technology and what this might mean for the concept of the serial.

Erich Hörl points out that Nancy also thinks of the place of technology as insubstantial, "as a supplement of nothing".[12] According to Nancy an emptying of meaning takes place through technology, which, however, only exposes meaning as such: "In Nancy, technology appears as the denaturing event par excellence, which first and foremost exposes meaning as such. Without technology, there would have been no entry into the order of sense and no sense of being at all."[13]

This sense, however, is "neither directional nor significant"; the "event of technique" rather opens up a space because sense is lacking in it.[14] If technique is constitutive of sense, it is also and in a special way for the arts, which are first understood as techniques.

---

[6]Mersch (2006) p. 33. In the original: „[...] die, zwischen Kunstfertigkeit und Technik angesiedelt, unentschieden lässt, welche Konsequenzen und Effekte sie zeitigt."

[7]Jacques Derrida (1995) p. 73.

[8]Ibid., p. 83.

[9]Ibid., p. 78.

[10]Mersch (2006) p. 32.

[11]Ibid., p. 33. In the original: „Die Technik erscheint bei Nancy als das denaturierende Ereignis schlechthin, das zuallererst den Sinn als solchen freistellt. Ohne Technik würde es überhaupt keinen Eintritt in die Ordnung des Sinns und keinen Sinn von Sein gegeben haben."

[12]Hörl (2010) p. 137.

[13]Ibid., p. 142.

[14]Ibid.

In doing so, Nancy, like Eco, questions the separation of art and technique, rejecting not only topics of originality but also the distinction between truth and deception, *simulatio* and *dissimulatio*, "as it has run through Western thought and dominated the philosophy of art since Plato."[15]

Nancy's concept of the technical maybe becomes clearer in his discussion of cinema (and the gaze): According to Nancy, film is not concerned with representation, but with the axiomatics of the cinematographic gaze (*regard*) as a reference (*égar*) *to* the world and its truth. This gaze is determined by the technical dispositif of the cinema as a situation in the cinema hall.

> So it is the room itself that becomes the site or dispositif of the gaze, a showcase to see – or rather: a box that is a gaze or that establishes the gaze, a peephole to denote an opening designed to allow observation [...]![16]

The emphasis here should be on opening, because—in contrast to other uses of the concept of the dispositif as constituting in the sense of a constricting formation— Nancy describes dispositif as an opening onto a space or a world. Accordingly, cinema is not concerned with representation or spectacle, but with the opening of a gaze to a real.

In doing so, Nancy also moves to the opposite position of Plato's allegory of the cave. Therefore for Nancy, truth or knowledge does not lie outside the image that deceives the reality it recreates, but is found in the medium as "an artificial intelligence of sense, the sense conceived and grasped through art and as art, i.e. techné."[17]

Nancy criticizes Plato's critique of the deceptive and oblivious effect of the image and the path to truth juxtaposed with it as violent:

> Throughout its history, philosophy has embraced the violent emergence of truth. (Already it was she who forced Plato's prisoner to come out of his cave, only to blind him with the sun).[18]

---

[15] Mersch (2006) p. 23.

[16] Nancy (2005) p. 13. In the German translation: "Es ist also der Saal selbst, der zum Ort oder zum Dispositiv des Blicks wird, ein Schaukasten, um zu sehen—oder eher: ein Kasten, der ein Blick ist oder den Blick herstellt, ein Guckloch, um eine Öffnung zu bezeichn en, die dazu bestimmt ist, eine Beobachtung zu erlauben [...].!"

[17] Hörl (2010) p. 141.

[18] Jean-Luc Nancy (2000) p. 86. Cf. also Nancy (2012), p. 42. In the German translation: "Während ihrer ganzen Geschichte hat sich die Philosophie des gewaltsamen Auftauchens der

If truth is located beyond the image, the true must forcibly invade being. But the critique of the non-truth of the image, according to Nancy, fails to recognize the (violent) self-assertion of the image, which results from a rivalry with things.

> This is what we have to deal with. Not with the mimetic character that *doxa* first associates with the term 'image', but rather with the fact that the image, even the mimetic one, must be valid through itself and for itself, since otherwise it threatens to become nothing but a shadow or a reflection, but not an image.[19]

According to Nancy, the image is an imitation of a thing only insofar as it competes with it: it exhibits the thing, not only *presenting* and deforming it, but also showing what and how it is, making it a subject. This also constitutes the monstrosity of the image, since it exhibits and deforms at the same time.

Jacques Rancière has also stressed that the (serial) images of cinema suspend the old mimetic order because it poses the question of mimesis at its root—the Platonic rejection of images, the opposition between sensually perceptible copy and intelligible model. For him, cinematographic images are themselves things, "they bring plastic, signifying elements into play in such a way as to create a shared sensorium of words, rhythms, ciphers, and images: an anti-Cartesian 'I feel'".[20]

(Cinematic) images unite thinking and non-thinking, sensual perception and intelligibility. According to Rancière, television in particular not only fulfils what film lags behind, but also an essential feature of the relationship between thought and art in the aesthetic regime:

Wahrheit angenommen. (Schon sie war es, die den Gefangenen von Platon zwang, aus seiner Höhle hinauszukommen, um ihn dann mit der Sonne zu blenden)."

[19] Ibid., p. 87: In the original: "Damit müssen wir uns befassen. Nicht mit dem mimetischen Charakter, den die Doxa zuerst mit dem Begriff ‚Bild' verbindet, sondern vielmehr damit, dass das Bild, selbst das mimetische, durch sich selbst und für sich selbst gelten muss, da es sonst droht, nichts als ein Schatten oder ein Reflex zu werden, aber kein Bild". Nancy adds in parentheses, "Incidentally, philosophical antimimetism treats it as a shadow or reflex. But this very resistance to the self-assertion of the image and in the image, to the pure pictoriality of the image, shows perhaps conversely how sensitive it is to it." In the German translation: "Übrigens behandelt der philosophische Antimimetismus es als Schatten oder Reflex. Gerade aber dieser Widerstand gegen die Selbstbehauptung des Bildes und im Bild, gegen die rein Bildlichkeit des Bildes zeigt vielleicht umgekehrt, wie sensibel er für diese ist."

[20] Schwarte (2011) p. 356. In the orinal: "sie bringen plastische, bedeutsame Elemente so ins Spiel, dass ein gemeinsames Sensorium der Worte, Rhythmen, Chiffren und Bilder entsteht: ein anti-Cartesianisches 'Ich fühle'"

It is much more fundamental, much more ironic, an optical machine that eliminates mimetic deviations and thus realizes in its own way the panesthetic project of a new art of [immediate sensual presence].[21]

Breaking Bad is regarded as a series that uses camera techniques to direct a particular gaze at things, but also at the equipment, style and form. The final part of the text asks whether this procedure can be read as this immediate sensual presence assigned to television by Rancière. Although on the narrative level *Breaking Bad* is much concerned with the fact that circumstances are not as they seem—in particular the fact that Walter White, a teacher with cancer, is secretly manufacturing crystal meth and selling it in ever-increasing quantities—the camera suggests that things and objects are as they are. Their texture and color become superficial. At the same time, they also have the ironic features Rancière alludes to, such as the hat White acquires, the precise look of vegan bacon, his initially bland beige-grey clothing matched by his car, later replaced by a garish pink sweater. On the one hand, this focus points to the seriality of everyday goods and things, but it also potentially conveys them in their sensual presence. This issue will be explored in more detail in the final part of the text.

Philosophy of Language

Various approaches of media theory and media philosophical genealogies agree that the examination of language and writing forms an essential part of media philosophy and reflected philosophically on language and writing before media philosophy existed.[22] As an example, Johann Gottlieb Herder's philosophy of language will be singled out here and applied to a possible concept of seriality, since it analyzes not only writing, but language as a whole, and thereby recurs to a moment of repetition.

In this way, he points far ahead of the media-theoretical approaches of the twentieth century. However, Herder does not base his model on the classical system

---

[21] Rancière (2015) p. 33. The passage in the square brackets is my translation, since the word presence is missing in the German translation, it simply says of the "immediately sensual".

[22] As a representative example, Reinhard Margreiter is quoted here as saying that "every medium is a kind of 'language' or 'writing'". Margreiter (2003) p. 158. Frank Hartmann notes that not every philosophy that has language as its theme is also a philosophy of media. See Hartmann (2000) p. 294. Even if, of course, by no means everyone adheres to a language-oriented concept of media, the philosophy of language is at least considered a precursor, as the following quotation also shows.

of rhetoric, as it was common at the time, but rather on the possibility of experiencing the world. It is not the idea or the conception that generates the word, but the word that generates the thought: Herder thus inaugurates a conception that will reach from Wilhelm von Humboldt to Nietzsche to Heidegger and that identifies language as the medium of all thought. For the first time, mediality is thought of as a constituent.[23]

Herder develops a model according to which language emerges mimetically through phonetic imitation; he thinks language from the primacy of the voice. In relation to seriality, it is interesting that the step to meaning does not take place via representation, but via the detour of repetition. "Herder knows that no relation of representation can succeed that is not embedded in a genuine iterability."[24] He thus discovers a "decisive principle of the mediality of all sign processes: to be repeatable."[25]

When it comes to repetition in oral language, we seem to be back to Richard Dyer's notion of seriality, the fairy tales, bards and jugglers. According to Herder, incarnation (of the infant) begins with language acquisition; under "family language" he includes "songs of their fathers, songs of the deeds of their ancestors the treasure of their language and history and poetry, their wisdom and encouragement, their lessons and games and dances."[26] This language based on repetitiveness, however, differentiates itself into an "infinite field of diversities."[27] In both Dyer and Herder, the serial forms of cultural techniques are thought of as "universalization, routinization, ritualization, habit formation, ... in short, *repetition.*"[28]

Friedrich Nietzsche's formula of 'eternal recurrence' also suggests habit, equilibrium and similarity by association, but must be interpreted differently.[29] Moreover, while Herder still focused on the idea of the 'origin' of language, Nietzsche, as is well known, dealt with concepts of the mask and deception. He advocated the non-originality of language, whose mediality he addressed as one of the "first media

---

[23] Mersch (2006) p. 39.

[24] Ibid.: In the original: „Herder weiß, dass kein Abbildungsverhältnis gelingen kann, das nicht in eine genuine Iterabilität gebettet ist."

[25] Ibid.

[26] Herder (1966) p. 103. In the original: "Lieder von ihren Vätern, Gesänge von den Taten ihrer Vorfahren der Schatz ihrer Sprache und Geschichte und Dichtkunst, ihre Weisheit und ihre Aufmunterung, ihr Unterricht und ihre Spiele und Tänze."

[27] Ibid., p. 105. It would go too far at this point to criticize this differentiation for its connotations of the concept of nation and associated racism.

[28] Krämer (2003) p. 86.

[29] Cf. Deleuze (1992) p. 22 f.

theorists".[30] His famous sentence that "our writing utensils [work] with our thoughts"[31] already reflects the proximity between writing techniques, the written and the (serially) printed that emerged with the typewriter. But Nietzsche does not postulate a technical a priori, he elevates the deceptive, simulating level of language to its principle and does not criticize it. For him, the production of meaning is only possible through persistent paraphrases, transferences and displacements, i.e. the formation of metaphors.[32] Metaphor formation means a transference in which something is, as it were, repeated and transformed,[33] a process through which not only the distinction between original and reproduced and 'inauthenticity' becomes obsolete, but also meaning cannot be definitively fixed, but is postponed, as Derrida also noted following Nietzsche's "styles".[34] Nietzsche can thus be made useful for a media philosophy of the serial that does not grasp media determinatively as a technical a priori.

Deleuze's concept of repetition without an original event, that produces series and serials, is also inspired by Nietzsche. He writes on Nietzsche:

> Everything has become a mirage. For by mirage we must not understand a mere imitation, but rather the act by which still the idea of an archetype or a privileged position is contested, overthrown. The mirage is an instance that includes a difference within itself, as (at least) two divergent series on which it plays its game, without any resemblance, without there being henceforth the existence of an original and an image.[35]

Following Nietzsche, Deleuze inverts the opposition of original and copy, truth and deception, by setting the supposedly secondary as primacy. Even more: difference in repetition produces a series. The serial principle of repetition and variation is

---

[30] Kittler (1986) p. 124.

[31] Nietzsche: *Briefwechsel*, quoted from Kittler (1986) p. 293.

[32] On the (serial) enumeration in Nietzsche's other famous sentence that truth is a "mobile army of metaphors, metonymies, anthropomorphisms," cf. Mainberger (2010).

[33] Cf. Krämer (2008) Tholen (2002) p. 44.

[34] Derrida (2007). On serial aesthetics in Derrida's texts, see also Thomas Rösch (2008) p. 208.

[35] Deleuze (1992) p. 98. In the German translation: "Alles ist Trugbild geworden. Denn unter Trugbild dürfen wir nicht bloß eine Nachahmung verstehen, sondern eher den Akt, durch den noch die Idee eines Urbilds oder einer privilegierten Position angefochten, gestürzt wird. Das Trugbild ist eine Instanz, die eine Differenz in sich schließt, als (zumindest) zwei divergente Reihen, auf denen es sein Spiel treibt, ohne jede Ähnlichkeit, ohne dass es von nun an die Existenz eines Originals und eines Abbilds geben kann."

resolved by Deleuze entirely on the side of difference.[36] Lorenz Engell has already shown how this can be applied to television, which demonstrates the "unrepeatability, the firstness, and even the creativity of each repetition". He finds the "real" series in Deleuze's sense in the "own life of the interval and the non-reducibility of the space in between"[37] in the soap opera.

Nietzsche also forms the hinge to a *linguistic turn* of the concept of media.[38] Linguistics "knows series through Russian formalism with its constructive series and the structuralists with their paradigmatic and syntagmatic series."[39] Saussure's notion of sign is also based on serial repetition and alterity, and here, too, difference (between signifiers and to the signified) produces meaning. Nevertheless, in film and television semiotics, the serial and repetition were and are often considered to solidify meaning.[40] From a media philosophical perspective, Roesler has applied Peirce's triad of sign, object, and interpretant to news broadcasting, emphasizing that meaning is not generated by the medium itself, but from a relationality.[41] The series is therefore to be understood in terms of linguistic theory not merely as a series or sequence, but as "a free production of certain relationality."[42]

A sign- and language-theoretical analysis of the (television) series necessarily remains text-centred, and even in relation to the medium of writing, serial production processes such as letterpress printing are hardly taken into account—the specific medium is lost from view. This brings me to the third strand, which in the true sense of the word is called media theory: the examination of technical means of communication.

---

[36] Engell (1997) p. 477.

[37] Ibid., p. 478.

[38] Mersch (2006) p. 48.

[39] Blättler (2010) p. 8. In the original: "[. . .] kennt Serien durch den russischen Formalismus mit seinen konstruktiven Reih en und die Strukturalisten mit ihren paradigmatischen und syntagmatischen Reihen."

[40] Cf. from a semiotic perspective e.g. Fiske (1990) Others analysed how differential repetition generates (new) meaning or the relationship between syntagmatic and paradigmatic complexity, cf. e.g. Klippel, Winkler (1994).

[41] Roesler (2003) p. 51.

[42] Ibid.

Media Theories

The Canadian School, in particular Harold Innis and Marshall McLuhan, dealt with the mediality of writing and the cultural change caused by the printing press, tracing the process of literacy along with the coding of culture and subjects. The first media theory to be named as such thus initially remained connected to the medium of writing.

While Innis advocated the dissemination and demonopolization of knowledge and the accompanying social changes brought about by the printing of books, he criticized the serialization of language caused by the formation of rows of letters and the accompanying 'mechanization' of culture and subjects, and in turn nostalgically idealized oral cultures. Similarly to the Frankfurt School, he saw a unification of thought through seriality. Summarizing these positions, it can be stated that "under buzzwords such as 'standardization' or 'confection', the serial became the emblem of a mechanical and supposedly soulless form of repetition".[43]

From the perspective of a media philosophy seriality means abstraction and repetition, which entails operationalization, disciplining, fragmentarization, individualization and uniformity. Innis' disciple Marshall McLuhan also followed this line, but saw an almost utopian change brought about by electronic media: "Machine thinking is replaced by a new organicity, the processes of mechanization by those of automation, linearity by cybernetic loops."[44] Moreover, through his thesis that the content of media is other media, another repetitive, non-linear form of temporality emerges, that of circular feedback. This not only changes McLuhan's own linear media historiography towards a different model of the serial. That media 'communicate' something only through other media already involves feedback loops.

It is emphasized that McLuhan not only wrote the history of grammarians, but also places himself in their tradition.[45] "A grammarian, according to McLuhan, searches for [...] fundamental structures in words and things primarily by means of analogical reasoning."[46] Although not a "classification system", this form of analogy-building resembles serial taxonomies, around the creation of relational

---

[43] Köhler (2011) p. 19.

[44] Hartmann (2000) p. 263. In the original: "Das Maschinendenken wird durch eine neue Organizität abgelöst, die Prozesse der Mechanisierung durch die der Automation, Linearität durch kybernetische Schleifen."

[45] Grampp (2011) p. 187.

[46] Ibid.: In the original: „Ein Grammatiker sucht McLuhan zufolge nach [...] fundamentalen Strukturen in Worten und Dingen vor allem mit Hilfe von Analogieschlüssen."

connections that are meant to make visible an underlying order. This relational procedure is in turn also characteristic of McLuhan's utopia of a (re)communalized world in the electronic age. The end of the written culture of the Gutenberg galaxy in fact involves a return to *acoustic space,* a return to thinking in terms of relations and collectivity, and a new "tactility".[47]

Friedrich Kittler criticized McLuhan for not taking digitality adequately into account and for formulating fantasies of redemption from language.[48] Yet both share the analysis of cybernetics as a new paradigm in which humans and machines, technical and psychological apparatuses behave analogously to one another. In contrast to McLuhan, however, Kittler does not understand language and the symbolic as the things to be discarded, but rather, following Lacan, as the things that structure the conscious and the unconscious. Already in Lacan's attempt to grasp the unconscious in terms of cybernetics, repetition is central. However, the extent to which this can also be understood as serial and Lacan's logic of signifiers can be transferred to digital orders would have to be investigated.[49] The unconscious and 'subjects' would thus not only be structured like language, but by series, i.e. definitely serial. However, it is not only the difference between language and computer codes that is cashed in here, but also that between subject and medium.

This position thus resembles conservative television criticism that, which transfers the functioning of television series as redundant repetition of the same to an audience, not interested in the new but in the familiar and bound to television by addiction. Television thereby provides stereotypes that also structure the psyche and patterns of perception and action of the audience.[50]

In the theorization of television, a tension between stasis and change, redundancy and complexity, continuity and interruption can initially be found, as in the aforementioned philosophical literature. In general, the series is seen as a feature of technical reproducibility and mode of production, as well as a formal principle of narrative. Often, no precise distinctions are made between seriality and repetition, with repetition considered a fixed and central component of the serial and of

---

[47]Cf. Hartmann (2000) pp. 264–265.

[48]Kittler (2002) pp. 23–24.

[49]Mersch (2006) p. 193.

[50]Cf. Adorno (1954) Cf. also Faulstich (2008) for a critique of the idea of television addiction see Cavell: "Die Tatsache des Fernsehens". In summary, also Köhler (2011) and Schabacher (2010) pp. 23–28.

television,[51] as well as the serial structural principle of production and programming analogous to the aesthetics and narratology of the products as television series. Depending on the perspective, these were considered redundant and aesthetically worthless to conservative or innovative and open to subversive readings by the audience. Using this distinction, television series can instead be questioned as to whether they aim at identity or difference.

What's Complex About Newer TV Series?

US television series of the last decade, such as *The Sopranos, Lost, Mad Men* or *West Wing,* are characterized by blurring the line between episodic series and serial, among other quality features.[52] This blurring is often associated with the narrative complexity of these series.[53] However, in the 1980s Eco already described a hybrid form of the episodic (recurrence of the same) and the serial (infinite variation), that he also locates in series such as *Bonanza,* that are described as highly episodic. Eco thus insists on a complexity of the serial in television per se, that does not only play a role with the emergence of the quality series. The current tendency to regard the television series themselves as art also partly takes a back seat to Eco's critique of the modernist concept of art. Jason Mittell, for instance, tends to reintroduce the hierarchy between naïve and critical reader that Eco had actually already abandoned. The latter is promoted by the complex narrativity and an operational aesthetic, and is more interested in form than content. David Lavery and Christoph Dreher also refer to the concept of authorial series, and Diedrich Diedrichsen compares the reception of series on DVD with the reading of books.[54] It is not only through this comparison that it can also be determined that cultural and media theory are still strongly influenced by the paradigm of writing.

Finally, using the TV series *Breaking Bad* as an example, I would like to argue for or ask whether other concepts of the serial dominate than those diagnosed in the previous readings. For it is not uniqueness, narration and authorship that dominate

---

[51] On the frequent equation of seriality and repetition, see Blättler (2010) and my text in the volume, Wünsch (2010).

[52] Cf. Thompson (1996) and an update of these 10 characteristics in relation to contemporary series, Blanchet (2011).

[53] Cf. Mittell (2013).

[54] Cf. Dreher (2010) and the contributions by David Lavery and Diedrich Diedrichsen in this volume.

this series, but 'visual effects', a view of things, the popular and the everyday, as well as intermedial and intertextual references. Rancière's previously quoted phrase that "plastic, signifying elements [are] brought into play in such a way as to create a shared sensorium of words, rhythms, ciphers, and images" would apply to this series. Therefore, I would argue that this series does not correspond to a 'new' complexity, but rather recurs to pre-televisual forms of the serial, or to an expanded notion of series.

The opening credits already reveal a level of the serial barely mentioned in this text, mathematical or chemical formulas, which not only point to Crystal Meth cook Walter White's original profession as a chemistry teacher, but also suggest that the things and people that surround us can be traced back to these formulas.

In a flashback, for instance, Walter White and his former research colleague are shown breaking down humans into their chemical components, in another flashback he explains his students the significance of carbon for their existence. One could argue however that formulas are never presented in a linear and progressive way in the series, but relationally. Chemistry is not only brought in as knowledge of the composition of matter, but also as a socio-cultural and economic matter, when it is told that Walter White never profited from his research, only his former colleague and her later partner did. Unlike him, they have earned a fortune from the research they previously conducted together, while he himself has to or cannot pay for his cancer treatment.

However, serialism as a capitalist mode of mass production is negotiated in *Breaking Bad* primarily through crystal meth production. As a good chemist, White becomes a good craftsman who produces excellent drugs and whose work in the laboratory is shown in detail.

Jesse Pinkman also refers to the making of meth as an art several times, or at the abolition of the distinction between art and craft as Eco addressed it. While the lab moves from a trailer in Jesse's basement to a mass production facility with multi-million dollar equipment, and thus changes its manufacturing context, the product of this craft or art remains consistently good.

Another serial element are the various references to popular culture, that is primarily oral or musically influenced, as addressed on the basis of Dyer and Herder, but also Innis and McLuhan. Since illegal drug production must take place in secret, (oral) codes and communication channels are of great importance. Thus White only gains access to the drug scene through his partner Jesse, who as a kind of 'whigger' ('white nigger') embodies hip-hop as music, style and mode of expression. The Mexican drug scene is staged as an almost non-literate community based on handed-down traditions and codes, whose main protagonists do not even speak, but often only send non-verbal or coded messages.

For instance, the opening credits of the seventh episode of the second season consist of a song by the so-called 'Narcocorridos', Mexican bands singing about the drug lords. Besides the focus on music, that is accompanied by a collage-like montage, we learn along the way that White's life is in danger.[55] In any case, the music used in the series often sets the rhythm of the narrative.

One element of the series that stands out is the 'subjective camera shots of things'. This interest in things in *Breaking Bad* leads into the field of media studies, that is increasingly concerned with 'the materially constituted basis of all practice in the production of meaning and knowledge, in technical and aesthetic artefacts'.[56] *Breaking Bad* is indeed characterized by a strong attention to equipment, implicit dramaturgy, style, and thus things and artifacts.[57] This begins with a look at things in Walter White's family home in the first episode, when characters are introduced via the everyday things that surround them. For example, White's wife Skyler is introduced via the color palettes she's hung up to choose from for the nursery renovation, White's 50th birthday is introduced with a vegan faux bacon that's shaped into a 50 from now on to keep his cholesterol low. This focus on style also involves an aesthetic of the ordinary, as elaborated by Herbert Schwaab using the sitcom *King of Queens*.[58] The look *(regard)* at things, however, also means a reference *(égard)*, an opening to the world knowledge and experience of the viewer.

Even when things get a look, they are mostly (serially produced) everyday objects such as the bottom of a pan, a washing machine, a dryer, a refrigerator, a trunk, a cistern, an air vent, a cannula, a pool, a barbecue, and so on. On the one hand, these settings illustrate the difference between the camera's gaze and the human eye and thus point to the media conditions, for they direct the gaze (of the audience) to the possibilities of camera technology (who has ever caught a glimpse of the owner from inside a refrigerator?) and less to the action. On the other hand, they also show the competition between images and things described by Nancy, whereby here the things become subjects (hence, perhaps, the actually misleading term 'subjective setting of things'). As 'subjects' or perhaps rather 'actants' in Latour's sense, however, things do not drive action.[59]

If the 'presence' of images and things in audiovisual representations was previously addressed in relation to Nancy and Rancière, a differentiation should be made

---

[55] Cf. Lang (2011).

[56] Wendler/Engell (2009) p. 38.

[57] Cf. on the importance of implicit dramaturgy and the difference from 'style' Lang: (2011).

[58] Cf. Schwaab (2008).

[59] Cf. Wendler, Engell (2009) p. 46.

at this point. For Nancy, presence is 'not a simple presence', but is based on absence.

> Seen in this light, the entire history of representation, this feverish history of mimesis, image, perception, object and scientific law, of spectacle, art and political representation, is permeated by the split of absence, which in fact splits into absence of *the* thing (the problem of reproduction) and absence in *the* thing (the problem of representation).[60]

This absence is woven into the presence of the image. "The empty place of the absent [is] like a place that is not empty: that is the image".[61] But the image is also essentially one thing: difference, distinction. A thing is not an image and an image is not a thing. "In every respect the image is distinction."[62] This particularity is especially true of the video image, and thus of the television image, which is "particulate, particular".[63]

Engell addresses as well the separating and composing reciprocal basic trait of the process of statement in television in particular: "Every statement is thus equally connecting and separating [. . .]. The double structure of synthesis and diairesis is fundamental to the logos in every form."[64] Television images are created by dividing and reassembling the thing depicted, yet electronic images do not first create this connection, they *discover* it. This discovery function results in the television image not representing, but presenting things "that don't exist outside the image."[65] However, this emergence of the object 'in itself' only ever happens in the context of other things. The point is to make a difference, television is differential and refers to other individual parts.

---

[60] Nancy (2012) p. 66. In the German translation: "So gesehen ist die gesamte Geschichte der Repräsentation, diese fieberhafte Geschichte der von Mimesis, Bild, Wahrnehmung, Objekt und wissenschaftlichem Gesetz, von Spektakel, Kunst und politischer Repräsentanz, von der Spaltung der Absenz durchzogen, die sich in der Tat zerteilt in Absenz des Dings (das Problem der Reproduktion) und in Absenz im Ding (das Problem der Repräsentation)´"

[61] Ibid., p. 116. In the original: „Der leere Platz des Abwesenden [ist] wie ein Platz, der nicht leer ist: das ist das Bild".

[62] Ibid., p. 119. In the original: "In jeder Hinsicht ist das Bild Unterscheidung."

[63] Ibid., p. 125.

[64] Engell (1989) p. 60. In the original: "Jede Aussage ist also gleichermaßen verbindend wie trennend [. . .]. Die Doppelstruktur von Synthese und Diairese ist für den Logos in jeder Form grund-legend."

[65] Ibid., p. 63.

If they are semantically significant, then they still 'symbolise' White's situation and the confrontation of his inconspicuous teacher's existence with that of a feared drug lord, because in some settings these emphatically everyday and ordinary things are combined with objects from the world of crime: Drugs, body parts, bundles of money, axes, revolvers. They are thus also always to be seen in relation to other things, which brings us to the relational concept of seriality.

In this sense, different materials, things and worlds collide instead of creating a linear, continuing inner development. For White as the main character hardly changes, instead his whole life seems determined by meeting the demands of others (his wife, his boss, the lawyer, the dealer), only his sense of responsibility often comes between the demands of others and their fulfilment. Thus, he repeatedly helps his partner Jesse out of self-inflicted situations. In Jesse's case, the compulsion to repeat and the tendency to cling to patterns of behavior is even more evident than in White's. In addition to his own drug addiction, that can also be related to his addiction to television series, it becomes clear that his actions are too much characterized by the repetition of patterns to be able to adapt to a new situation. In this respect, his psyche comes more to the fore, but this does not correspond to a further development of the character, which would possibly culminate in a happy ending. As an example, he tries to cheat the client by diverting drugs from the production in order to sell them himself with disastrous consequences. Here, on the one hand, we find the narrative pattern of the episodic series, according to which "everything remains the same",[66] but this is staged less as a "restoration of an initial state"[67] than as a permanent, repeated failure based on forgetting the experience gained and thus on the principle of the continuing series.[68]

This quasi-Platonic forgetfulness of the medial is reflected when Jesse visits a Georgia O'Keeffe exhibiti on with his girlfriend, where different variations of a door she has drawn are shown. Jesse doesn't understand this serial art, for its form of repetition is based solely on forgetting.

Things, too, are characterized not by a 'full' but by an 'empty' presence, their origin or reason often hidden, like that of the pink teddy bear in White's swimming pool, repeatedly placed in the picture, of which we never learn who it belonged to. The serial images of television here are 'groundless', differential images, taxonomically arranged. Yet they are characterized by a substitutability and

---

[66] According to Günter Giesenfeld, this applies to almost all television series, but especially to the episodic series. Giesenfeld (2001) p. 608.

[67] Hickethier (2001) p. 58.

[68] Cf. Engell (2011).

non-covert manipulability that constitutes the 'metaphoricity of television discourse'.[69] This metaphoricity, as mentioned, involves a transformation in transmission; in repetition, difference emerges. For through the different camera angles things appear "once like this and once different".[70]

Breaking Bad does not side with either repetition or difference, as it is clear that difference is created in repetition. Therefore, the focus on things is also not an 'immediate sensual presence'. In doing so, the series does not disguise its mediality, but rather exhibits it. This also becomes clear in the mix of genres:

> *Breaking Bad* thrives on the virtuoso juxtaposition of different genres: Crime drama against comedy, psychological realism against postmodern comic aesthetics, perfection of craftsmanship against trash.[71]

Through this artificial citationality, the series thus does not pretend to tell about reality or things themselves, but about the different ways in which they can be told about. In this respect, *Breaking Bad* is also a television series that makes visible the characteristics of the media of television.[72]

References

Adorno, Theodor W. (1954) How to Look at Television. In: Quarterly of Film, Radio and Television 3, pp. 23–25

Beil, Benjamin, Lorenz Engell, Herbert Schwaab, Jens Schröter, Daniela Wentz (2012) Die Serie. Einleitung in den Schwerpunkt. In: Zeitschrift für Medienwissenschaft 7 (2), pp. 10–16

Blättler, Christine (2010) Einleitung. In: Kunst der Serie. Die Serie in den Künsten. Munich, Wilhelm Fink Verlag, pp. 7–17

Blanchet, Robert (2011) Quality TV. Eine kurze Einführung in die Geschichte und Ästhetik neuer amerikanischer Fernsehserien. In: Von den frühen Film-Serials zu aktuellen Quality TV und Online-Serien. Marburg, Schüren Verlag, pp. 37–73

Deleuze, Gilles (1992) Differenz und Wiederholung. Munich, Wilhelm Fink Verlag

Derrida, Jacques (1995) Dissemination. Vienna, Passagen Verlag

---

[69] Ibid., p. 34.

[70] Engell (1989) p. 56.

[71] Lang (2011) In the original: "Breaking Bad lebt davon, dass verschiedene Genres virtuos gegeneinander gesetzt werden: Crime-Drama gegen Komödie, psychologischer Realismus gegen postmoderne Comicästhetik, handwerkliche Perfektion gegen Trash."

[72] Cf. Beil (2012) p. 14.

Derrida, Jacques (2007) Sporen. Stile Nietzsches. In: Nietzsche aus Frankreich. Frankfurt, Suhrkamp Verlag, pp. 129–168

Dreher, Christoph (Ed.) (2010) Autorenserien. Die Neuerfindung des Fernsehens. Stuttgart, Reclam Verlag

Dyer, Richard (1997) Kill and Kill again. In: Sight and Sound (Sept. 1997), pp. 14–17

Eco, Umberto (1989) Serialität im Universum der Kunst und Massenmedien. In: Im Labyrinth der Vernunft. Texte über Kunst und Zeichen. Leipzig, Reclam Verlag, pp. 301–324

Engell, Lorenz (1989) Vom Widerspruch zur Langeweile. Logische und temporale Begründungen des Fernsehens. Frankfurt, Suhrkamp Verlag

Engell, Lorenz (1997) Fernsehen mit Deleuze. In: Der Film bei Deleuze. Weimar, Verlag der Bauhaus-Universität, pp. 468–496

Engell, Lorenz (2011) Erinnern/Vergessen: Serien als operatives Gedächtnis des Fernsehens. In: Serielle Formen. Von den frühen Film-Serials zu aktuellen Quality-TV und Online-Serien. Marburg, Schüren Verlag, pp. 115–133

Faulstich, Werner (2008) Grundkurs Fernsehanalyse. Paderborn, Wilhelm Fink Verlag

Fiske, John (1990) Reading Television. London/New York, Routledge

Giesenfeld, Günter (2001) Das Leben in der Schwebe. Potentiale des Serienformats, in: Die Wiederholung. Festschrift für Thomas Koebner zum 60. Geburtstag. Marburg, Schüren Verlag, pp. 603–608

Grampp, Sven (2011) Hundert Jahre McLuhan. In: Zeitschrift für Medienwissenschaft 4 (1), pp. 183–188

Hartmann, Frank (2000) Medienphilosophie. Vienna, Passagen Verlag

Herder, Johann Gottlieb (1966) Abhandlung über den Ursprung der Sprache. Stuttgart, Reclam Verlag

Hickethier, Knut (2001) The Same Procedure. Wiederholung als Medienprinzip der Moderne. In: Die Wiederholung. Festschrift für Thomas Koebner zum 60. Geburtstag. Marburg, Schüren Verlag, pp. 41–62

Hörl, Erich (2010) Die künstliche Intelligenz des Sinns. Sinngeschichte und Technologie im Anschluss an Jean-Luc Nancy. In: Zeitschrift für Medien- und Kulturforschung 2 (1), pp. 129–149

Klippel, Heike, Hartmut Winkler (1994) 'Gesund ist, was sich wiederholt'. Zur Rolle der Redundanz im Fernsehen. In: Aspekte der Fernsehanalyse. Methoden und Modelle. Konstanz, UVK Verlagsgesellschaft, pp. 121–136

Köhler, Kristina (2011) You People are not watching enough television! Nach-Denken über Serien und serielle Formen. In: Serielle Formen. Von den frühen Film-Serials zu aktuellen Quality-TV und Online-Serien. Marburg, Schüren Verlag, pp. 11–37

Krämer, Sybille (2008) Medium, Bote, Übertragung. Kleine Metaphysik der Medialität. Munich, Wilhelm Fink Verlag

Krämer, Sybille (2003) Erfüllen Medien eine Konstitutionsleistung? Thesen über die Rolle medientheoretischer Erwägungen beim Philosophieren. In: Medienphilosophie. Beiträge zur Klärung eines Begriffs. Frankfurt, Suhrkamp Verlag, pp. 78–91

Lang, Christine (2011) Implizite Dramaturgie in der Fernsehserie BREAKING BAD, URL: http://www.kinoglaz.de/archives/35#_edn3. Accessed 05 Jul 2019.

Mittell, Jason (2013) The Qualities of Complexity: Vast versus Dense Seriality in Contemporary Television. In: Television. Aesthetics and Style, pp. 45–57

Kittler, Friederich (1986) Grammophon, Film, Typewriter. Berlin, Brinkmann & Bose

Kittler, Friedrich (2002) Optische Medien. Berliner Vorlesung 1999. Berlin, Brinkmann & Bose

Mainberger, Sabine (2010) Enumerative Praktiken der Philosophie: zu Nietzsche. In: Kunst der Serie. Die Serie in den Künsten. Munich, Wilhelm Fink Verlag, pp. 73–87

Mersch, Dieter (2006) Medientheorien zur Einführung. Hamburg, Junius Verlag

Nancy, Jean-Luc (2005) Evidenz des Films. Abbas Kiarostami. Berlin, Brinkmann & Bose

Nancy, Jean-Luc (2000) Bild und Gewalt. Von absoluter Offenbarung und dem unendlich Bevorstehenden. In: Lettre International (Summer), pp. 86–89

Nancy, Jean-Luc (2012) Am Grund der Bilder. Zürich/Berlin, Diaphanes Verlag

Margreiter, Rainer (2003) Medien/Philosophie: Ein Kippbild. In: Medienphilosophie. Beiträge zur Klärung eines Begriffs. Frankfurt, Suhrkamp Verlag, pp. 150–172

Rancière, Jacques (2015) Die Filmfabel. Berlin, Diaphanes Verlag

Roesler, Alexander (2003) Medienphilosophie und Zeichentheorie. In: Medienphilosophie. Beiträge zur Klärung eines Begriffs. Frankfurt, Suhrkamp Verlag, pp. 34–53

Rösch, Thomas (2008) Kunst und Dekonstruktion. Serielle Ästhetik in den Texten von Jacques Derrida. Vienna, Turia + Kant

Schabacher, Gabriele (2010) Serienzeit. Zu Ökonomie und Ästhetik der Zeitlichkeit neuerer US-amerikanischer TV-Serien. In: Meteling, Arno, Gabriele Schabacher, Isabell Otto, Ludwig Jäger (Eds.) "Previously On. . .". Zur Ästhetik der Zeitlichkeit neuerer TV-Serien. Munich, Wilhelm Fink Verlag, pp. 19–41

Schwaab, Herbert (2008) Stanley Cavell, King of Queens und die Medienphilosophie des Gewöhnlichen, Dokumentation der Textbeiträge zur Tagung „Ästhetik und Alltagserfahrung", Homepage der Deutschen Gesellschaft für Ästhetik in Jena, https://www.dgae.de/wp-content/uploads/2008/09/Herbert_Schwaab.pdf. Accessed 28 Feb 2019

Schwarte, Ludger (2011) Jacques Rancière. In: Därmann, Iris, Kathrin Busch (Eds.) Bildtheorien aus Frankreich. Ein Handbuch. München, Wilhelm Fink Verlag, pp. 347–363

Seel, Martin (2003) Eine vorübergehende Sache. In: Münker, Stefan, Alexander Roesler, Mike Sandbothe (Eds.) Medienphilosophie. Beiträge zur Klärung eines Begriffs. Frankfurt, Suhrkamp Verlag, pp. 10–15

Tholen, Georg Christoph (2002) Die Zäsur der Medien. Kulturphilosophische Konturen. Frankfurt, Suhrkamp Verlag

Thompson, Robert J. (1996) Television's Second Golden Age: From Hillstreet Blues to ER. New York, Continuum

Wendler, André, Lorenz Engell (2009) Medienwissenschaft der Motive. In: Zeitschrift für Medienwissenschaft 1 (1), pp. 38–49

Wünsch, Michaela (2010) Serialität und Wiederholung in filmischen Medien. In: Blättler, Christine (Ed.) Kunst der Serie. Die Serie in den Künsten. Munich, Wilhelm Fink Verlag, pp. 191–205

Michaela Wünsch, Dr. phil, cultural scientist, psychoanalyst and publisher at b_books, teaches at the Heinrich-Heine-Universität Düsseldorf, Germany. Dissertation on serial killers as a medium of the unconscious of white masculinity (2010). Research interests: Critical Race Studies, Queer Theory, psychoanalysis, media philosophy, seriality, television. Recent publications: "'I decided not to use my color as a handicap.' Zur Notwendigkeit, Ambivalenzen aufrecht zu halten", in: Race und Genre. Neue Perspektiven der Medienästhetik. Ed. by Irina Gradinari/Ivo Ritzler, Springer 2021, pp. 243–262; "Between Minority and Mainstream. 'Jewish Sitcoms' before and after Quality Television", in: Before Quality. Ed. by Lukas Förster/Thomas Morsch/Nikolaus Perneczky. Münster 2019, pp. 218–235.

Television's Representations of Play in *Black Mirror: Bandersnatch*

Kim Carina Hebben

(Re)Start: Remediations as Variations of Play

Play, as a *medium of variation*, is a phenomenon entirely based on seriality. In the following, I will take a closer look on play in relation to other media, whereby the focus of these considerations is on repetitive and cyclical forms such as seriality. Due to its repetitive structure, television seems predestined to be examined more closely in the context of playfulness. *Playful television series*,[1] and their transmedia environments are therefore used as examples with which to approach the interrelationship between television, game, and play. In particular, the special episode of the anthology series *Black Mirror: Bandersnatch*, which aired in December 2018, presents itself as an excellent example, as it represents variations of games and play on various levels in terms of content and structure.

The term restart intends to emphasize that it would be wrong to assume a single point of origin, but rather that constant remediations, variations, and the playful *and thus transformative use of media*, contribute to its figurations. Content-related adaptations of game aesthetics and structures represent only one level of play since aesthetic interactions between other media and games become apparent in

---

[1] The figure of thought of *Playful Television* (cf. Hebben (2019) pp. 50–65) refers to special forms and practices of transmedia television series that provide a high degree of participation and invite viewers to play along through their structure, whereby a transformation of the viewers as players can be observed. The following argumentation is based on this figure of thought.

K. C. Hebben (✉)
Institut für Medienwissenschaft, Ruhr-Universität Bochum, Bochum, Germany
e-mail: kim.hebben@tu-dortmund.de

© The Author(s), under exclusive license to Springer Fachmedien Wiesbaden GmbH, part of Springer Nature 2024
D. Newiak et al. (eds.), *Television Studies and Research on Series*,
https://doi.org/10.1007/978-3-658-42915-7_12

them. But the most significant characteristic of play, *joining in* and thereby *playing along*, can in this case only be touched superficially and in an abstract form. I will use cinema or film only in the periphery of this argumentation to investigate the interaction of play and audio-visual media, as their transmedia extensions are of more relevance for consideration as variations of play.

In addition to the narrative forms of film or series, their dispositifs and media practices play a significant role, as these go beyond the narrative adaptation of game motifs to capture *how* playing along a (trans)media narrative is enabled. The interplay between game motifs and playful structures and practices, which is presented strikingly in the genre of *mind game movies*, takes place on various levels. On the one hand, in experimental modes: playing with conventions and forms, trying out new strategies to address the audience, which are adapted to their new needs and demands to use and explore media narratives. Especially the openness of complex narrations allows for "playful readings",[2] meaning variations, interpretations, and trying out different solutions and readings that can be applied in the course of the narrative. These can be modified and revised with new insights, creating a playful interaction with the content. There is a certain pleasure in navigating complex texts, and Tosca notes that it is the performance of remembering that is a "rewarding activity" in decoding these rich narratives.[3] On the other hand, this refers to narrative adaptations of play as well as recurring game motifs and mechanisms (e.g. within the films *eXistenZ*, *The Matrix*, or *Butterfly Effect*). As an aesthetically remediated form, the ludo-narrative tradition can be mentioned here, which is titled by Rauscher, among others, as a "cineludic form".[4] The aesthetic exchange between computers, games, and film is striking—characterized by a digital aesthetic—which in turn is also referred to as a ludo-aesthetic.[5] Films, for example, adopt sequences and aesthetic patterns familiar from (digital) games,[6] such as loops and *restarts (Groundhog Day, Butterfly Effect)*, walking simulators and secondary realities (*The Matrix, Ready Player One*), or arenas (*Hunger Games, Maze Runner*), to name but a small selection.[7] Likewise,

---

[2] Rauscher (2017) p. 200.

[3] Tosca (2017) p. 125 f.

[4] Rauscher (2017) p. 199.

[5] Cf. Schmerheim (2018) p. 42.

[6] In the following, a distinction will be made between *Play as a figure of thought*, which is characterized by variation, movement, and creation (cf. Deuber-Mankowsky (2017), pp. 215–220) and the rule-based *game* or the free *play*.

[7] An overview and systematization of movie adaptations that incorporate game motifs and structures is offered, for example, by Stiglegger (2007) pp. 103–114.

film technology has a decisive influence on digital games: elaborate camera and perspective settings, *cutscenes*, all the way to games that are so narratively comprehensive that they are misjudged as playable films instead of computer games due to their rather minor game mechanics (e.g. games in the *Telltale series* or simulations such as *Dear Esther* or *Gone Home*).

Even early arcade game machines refer to scenery and iconography familiar from classic Hollywood cinema. Literary motifs such as the hero's journey (with its specific *quests*) are of course not game-specific but are often staged to emphasize the digital game aesthetic.[8] In the second part of the *Hobbit series*, for example, Legolas' chase along a river is very reminiscent of a scene familiar from *platform games*.[9] Elsaesser also questions the mind game movie as "a sub-category of games"[10] and thereby predicts the "ludification of cinema"[11]—but what is meant here are mainly adaptations in terms of content and aesthetics, not playing along or playing with the dispositif.[12] While viewers of complex narratives such as *mind game movies* naturally feel agency or immersion[13] through their cognitive performance in deciphering the plot, no direct influence is possible. One form of opening narratives to interaction are *Alternate Reality Games* (ARGs), which are preferably represented in transmedia environments of audio-visual media and become accessible to a broader mass audience, especially as extensions of motion pictures.[14] ARGs

---

[8] Cf. Ibid.

[9] Cf. *Hobbit: The Desolation of Smaug*, "Barrel Scene" [1:00:00–1:08:40].

[10] Elsaesser (2017) p. 61.

[11] Rauscher (2017), p. 200.

[12] However, significant experiments can be mentioned here that enabled the cinema's audience during the viewing to play along and make decisions that directly influence the plot's outcome. Ex: *Late Shift*, an interactive film in which the audience can make decisions via app and thus choose the next plotline. The interactive film was subsequently also released for game consoles and addressed as a *game* or *interactive adventure* (like the aforementioned *Telltale Games, Dear Esther* or *Gone Home*). The line between playable motion picture and digital game is blurred here.

[13] Cf. Murray (2017) pp. 98, 123. Murray places the two concepts in a close, reciprocal relationship. The more immersive an environment, the more intense the desire to participate, i.e. to experience agency as a "satisfying power". Like Tosca, Murray describes movement in virtual environments as "pleasures of navigation" and "participatory pleasure" (Ibid., p. 125).

[14] ARGs are immersive games that blend the boundaries between reality and fiction through hybrid gaming experiences within online and offline mechanisms and that take place in real-time. They can appear as autonomous transmedia games, but often they are used as marketing tools for promotion. They are particularly characterized by the interlocking use of digital platforms and real locations, they convey narrative and playful experiences to the same extent,

are capable of extracting subplots from films and allowing viewers to exert influence over the course of their narration so that the 'Promethean impulse'[15] of the audience to actively participate is fulfilled. It is noticeable that the dispositif and above all the spatial arrangement of cinema is very stable in its form, but film techniques as well as storylines experiment with (narrative) forms and modify these new techniques accordingly. The outsourcing of narrative fragments to other media, i.e. transmedia extensions, will therefore be presented as a variation on making narratives playable.

Using the example of the interactive special episode *Bandersnatch*, the following section will demonstrate precisely the different layers that make it possible to interact with the story and play along. As an introduction, the figurations of television and the associated *playfulness* and experiments will be briefly discussed. *Bandersnatch* is to be considered as a current rash on the seismograph of television's figurations, as a possible appearance of the continuously transforming medium. At the same time, a multiplication of variations of the play element can be shown in the example. I will also highlight seriality, which I consider especially in the form of transmediality, as a crucial factor shaping the relationship between representations of play and television. In the relationship between play and television, constellations of power that move in a constant negotiation of the modes of *playing or being played* become explicit and tangible using the example of *Bandersnatch*.

Television's Figurations

Television can best be described as "always already new",[16] as it has always eluded a designated form and come up with constant transformations. Although all media are subject to constant change and innovation and undergo continuous processes of modification and remediation, television seems to be determined by specific stations in its development and especially the eras attributed to it. But it is difficult to define a specific era, for example, television at the turn of the millennium since the various

---

and they are largely played collaboratively and online. In the process, game masters (so-called *puppet masters*) react to the actions individually, which means that, for example, hints can be conveyed in the game without clouding the illusion of real-world consequences, thus contributing to the credo of ARGs *(this is not a game)*. This creates an alternative reality in which nothing should be addressed as fiction (cf. Bakioglu (2015) pp. 14–22).

[15]Cf. Stiglegger (2007) p. 108.

[16]Keilbach, Stauff (2011) pp. 157, 159. The authors refer to Lisa Gitelman's book of the same name, which fundamentally questions the novelty of media, see Gitelman (2008).

forms and figurations coexist and mutually influence each other. Some trends prevail and others do not—television can always be improved. The expectation of technical improvement has always accompanied television.[17] Nevertheless, clear differences between past and present forms of the medium can be noted, without, however, proclaiming one of these manifestations as *the* distinct form of television, from which in turn other or more recent transformations might deviate.

The following argumentation will use the example of television to illustrate representations of play that emerge from the interactions between its form and content. Here, play is not only to be considered in terms of its narrative content but is ascribed a significant role in the formation of the structures described in more detail.

Overall, television as a medium can be said to have been in a mode of perpetual change since its introduction.[18] The continuous evolutions in television are significantly influenced and motivated by technical achievements, but also the developments of television infrastructure, such as the multiplication of TV networks and the range of channels and programs, initiate and require new techniques and practices that counter the respective figurations of the medium. The remote control and the practice of *zapping*, for example, were the answer to the increasing diversity of programming. The possibilities of the video recorder, such as multiple viewing, stopping and rewinding, and thus the close examination of the narrative, are results of the increasingly complex series and formats; at the same time, this technical concession creates a demand for complexity.[19] Another phenomenon is evident in the design of streaming platforms such as *Netflix*, which evokes a different form of attention and desirable reception behavior by cutting off the credits and automatically starting (via a countdown) the next episode.[20] Many such technical achievements and figurations of television initially appeal primarily to a particularly affine niche audience, while the mass audience may dismiss them as a playful

---

[17] Cf. Keilbach, Stauff (2011) p. 172.

[18] In this context, the authors plead for a re-conceptualization of television and distinguish it from established explanatory models of historical development by defining change and transformation as fundamental characteristics of the medium. Cf., p. 156.

[19] Cf. Schabacher (2010) pp. 35–39; cf. Mittell (2009b) n.p. The authors address aspects such as the interrelationship between technical achievements and narratives that are increasingly complex as a result (Schabacher), or the explicit search for and expectation of complexity in transmedia texts (Mittell). Viewers expect complexity and master it with increased confidence, which makes new challenges necessary to maintain interest.

[20] Cf. Zündel (2019) p. 305 f.

add-on or gimmick *[Spielerei]*.[21] They are trends that briefly gain traction, where the boundaries of the medium are stretched, tried out, but then replaced or changed, as happened with 3D glasses, for example. These then gave way to VR glasses, whose applications are in turn now served by *augmented* smartphone apps.[22]

All these extensions of the television text and its dispositif are still accessible, the decision whether to interact is left to the viewers. However, there are differences in accessibility: while 3D or VR glasses require an expensive technical setting and also only work in combination and on certain receivers, apps or extensions in social media are easily accessible to anyone with a smartphone and internet access, which is why these forms of televisual extensions occur and are received en masse. Additionally, these examples are resembling concepts of play, as on the one hand, they enable immersion, i.e. immersing oneself into a narrative. On the other hand, they extend the television dispositif with additional technologies that are reminiscent of game arrangements with controllers. What these technical extensions have in common is that they offer not only other forms of reception but also participation.

Another interesting aspect is the connection between play and broadcasting. Whether radio quizzes or the Saturday night family game show on television—play as a format and subject matter is just as anchored in the tradition of broadcasting as play (in the sense of experimentation) with new forms and techniques. Television is and always has been a participatory medium, yet the transmedia extensions of what is proclaimed as *Television 2.0* are often postulated as the culmination of "television as an engagement medium".[23]

One could claim that television is in a crisis since as a result of the manifold television technologies and modes of use it is no longer even certain whether television is still a distinct medium.[24] Yet it is precisely these figurations and

---

[21] This text is a translation from a German paper. The German term *Spiel* combines the English concepts of *play* and *game* and includes a broader spectrum of phenomena and topics, which will be elaborated on in the next chapter. The term *Spielerei* is a diminutive. The literal sense of the term *Spielerei* is also very interesting for the following argumentation and means, according to the German dictionary Duden (pejorative), a constant playing, something that is easy and makes little effort and (often pejorative) something additional, dispensable, which is unimportant for the actual thing.

[22] Examples of this are *companion apps*, such as those offered by the series *The Walking Dead*. Or *360-degree apps*, which are also available from AMC as transmedia extensions. These apps, which are also often available as less elaborate Facebook posts, present filming locations, for example, as 360-degree rotatable imagery that can then be rotated via touch gesture and explored from all angles. 3D glasses are therefore not necessary for a virtual tour.

[23] Askwith (2019) p. 101.

[24] Cf. Keilbach, Stauff (2011) p. 156.

diversity that are to be grasped in play and characterized as constituting features of television.

Experiments in Play and Television

It is not productive to reduce television to one concept or definition but to examine its processuality and continuous transformations more closely.[25] Through the lens of cultural studies the concept of play is in many respects appropriate to describe the changes and figurations of television since this observation is closely related to experimentation,[26] as Walter Benjamin already formulated it for the relationship between humanity and technology:[27]

> The results of the second are wholly provisional (it operates by means of experiments and endlessly varied test procedures). The origin of the second technology lies at the point where, by an unconscious ruse, human beings first began to distance themselves from nature. It lies, in other words, in play.[28]

It is precisely this arrangement of "endlessly varied test procedures"[29] that Keilbach and Stauff attest to television as an "ongoing experiment",[30] which constantly reinvents itself and thereby seems to undermine a coherent definition of the medium. In contrast to the model of (re)mediation, however, it should not be assumed that a medium changes (only) through the emergence of new media and their practices, but that transformation is an inherent attribute of media in general. The continuous adjustments, reorganization, and, reflection[31] of technologies

---

[25] Cf. Keilbach/Stauff (2011) p. 155; Piepiorka (2017), pp. 245–278.

[26] I refer to the remarks of Deuber-Mankowsky (2015), who convincingly presents Benjamin's approaches to a theory of play and therefore combines play, experiment, and habit to form a media anthropology of play (cf., p. 52 f.).

[27] Benjamin distinguishes between the first and the second technology. The first technology is characterized by the "once and for all". Benjamin (2008) p. 26. The second technology is directly related to experimentation, variation, and the expansion of the field of action [Spielraum]. Benjamin (1991a), p. 359 f.

[28] Benjamin (2008) p. 26.

[29] Ibid.

[30] Keilbach, Stauff (2013) p. 90.

[31] Cf. Keilbach, Stauff (2011), p. 161 f.

contribute precisely to their productivity and aim to produce new technological or participatory possibilities.

One condition of this "experimental system" as which television is analyzed by Keilbach and Stauff is that new tools and ambivalent objects are constantly integrated into the arrangement.[32] Further, the authors argue that the competing demands and desires that manifest as new practices as well as "the unforeseen effects of the re-arrangements of complex television constellations, guarantee the endlessness of this process."[33]

This interpretation can be examined regarding the play element. Where there is play, there is also experimentation. Play means trying things out, practicing, pretending, usually without real consequences, in a safe, prearranged field of action [Spielraum] in which its own rules apply.[34] Not only is "a climate of continuous experimentation"[35] attributed to digital games but also the German term *Spiel* in its most original meaning[36] refers to a back and forth movement, a wandering undirectedness, a floating flickering[37] as well as a pendulum-like, thus repetitive movement behavior.[38] Play is recursive, but at the same time creates an experienceable or explorable space through its expansive movement. *If there is play, there is also space [Zwischenraum]*—Deuber-Mankowsky and Görling introduce their reflections on the mediality of play and add that play brings things into relation and thereby changes them. No joint functions without play. Play means movement: spatial, temporal, and modal.[39]

This space is created through the act of playing, or rather it is constituted through the constant negotiation of its rules. Beyond this, too, play is characterized by its ambivalences. Krämer specifies this by arguing that whatever falls under the term 'play' moves between two extremes, and is itself of antithetical structure.[40] This

---

[32] Keilbach, Stauff (2013), p. 83.

[33] Ibid., p. 90.

[34] Huizinga calls this prearranged space the *magic circle*. He describes the element of play in culture as a free action, which is decidedly delimited from ordinary life and entails no consequences for everyday life—once it is over, real life continues. It is as temporally closed and limited as it is spatially and arbitrarily repeatable. Its rules create order for the duration of the play. Cf. Huizinga (1950), pp. 14–22.

[35] Gasteier (2017) p. 520 f.

[36] Cf. on the derivation of the etymological discourse: Deuber-Mankowsky (2017) p. 221 f.

[37] Cf. Krämer (2007) p. 240.

[38] Cf. Ibid., p. 241.

[39] Cf. Deuber-Mankowsky/Görling (2017) p. 7.

[40] Cf. Krämer (2007) p. 240.

refers to dichotomous structures inherent in play, such as the tension between autonomy and control, which on the one hand arise from the voluntariness and creation [Schöpfung] of play, but at the same time is at least kept in shape by its rules and the boundaries of the field of action [Spielraum]. But this field of action [Spielraum] is not rigid, as I will argue that its boundaries are perforable and can be modified through play. Play is thus equally rule-bound and unpredictable.[41] And principles of seriality that occur in media figurations are also closely connected to forms of ritualization, schematization, and stabilization, which, according to Harth, are only produced by rules of play.[42]

Due to its textual extensions and fluid transgressions across media boundaries, the consideration of transmedia storytelling as spatialized narration has become established.[43] The spatialization (and thus creation) of experienceable and explorable serial narratives takes place through the interactions of the audience and will be interpreted in the following as an act of play.

This is also where Huizinga's figure of *Homo Ludens* comes from, literally the playing and thus creating human being.[44] Only through the movement of the viewers, that is, their playing with the text by following the scattered text fragments back and forth does their sphere of action [Spielraum] expand. Play means creation. On the one hand, it means the creation of (free) space, which comes into being through variation and movement.[45] On the other hand, play is the creation of habit. Through rhythm and rules, the *law of repetition*, as Benjamin calls it, media can inscribe themselves into space and become habitual.[46] This view is also found in Huizinga's work when he says: "Play casts a spell over us; it is 'enchanting', 'captivating'. It is invested with the noblest qualities we are capable of perceiving in things: rhythm and harmony."[47]

Tosca writes about the role of repetition in transmedia narrations: "[. . .] fans of transmedial worlds do want to keep coming back". And further: "[w]e see the ripples as all our attempts to revisit, reenact and recreate the worlds that were so

---

[41] Cf. Ibid., 238 f.

[42] Cf. Harth (2017) p. 3.

[43] Elsewhere I have already provided an overview and an introduction to this thesis: Cf. Hebben (2017) p. 38 f.; Cf. Hebben (2019) p. 57 f.

[44] Duden: *Homo Ludens.*

[45] Cf. Deuber-Mankowsky (2015) p. 52 f.

[46] Cf. Benjamin (1991b) p. 131; Benjamin (2005) p. 120.

[47] Huizinga (1950) p. 10.

compelling. The 're' prefix very tellingly indicates repetition, coming back".[48] Only by visiting transmedia extensions several times, by playing with the text and movement, do the scattered extensions become an interconnected network through which the viewers navigate. In the process, it becomes apparent that transmediality evokes specific viewing habits, as will be explained below using various examples. Schwaab describes appropriately for the television series that transmedia narratives make it possible to engage with new media practices that they also demand at the same time.[49] And so, for Benjamin, play, as constant movement and variation, becomes the "mother of every habit",[50] for it is through play that any situation can be mastered and mastered through tireless repetition. Deuber-Mankowsky concludes that in this connection with habit, play proves to be an ambivalent medium of change, transformation, and repetition.[51]

Television is thus to be regarded as being through and through playful, which since its introduction has been characterized by its constant variation and whose practices are internalized in play, whereby the constant modification of the medium is also negotiated. A routine emerges from this constant repetition and experimentation with the medium. Through playfulness, this process happens seemingly naturally, new rules and moves are internalized and accepted, but without being explicitly presented and understood as elements of play.[52] Similar to an ARG played under the premise that *this is not a game*, the appeal comes from the intertwining of oppositions: Reality and fiction, autonomy and control.[53] The immersive experience of following a trail, solving a puzzle, and being on a mission is the desired goal. The players are aware of the design of the game, even if it is disguised as best as possible. No player truly feels fear of consequences. The game, which declares not to be a game, can be played or ended at any time. Similarly, the interactively engaging viewers are aware of their actions, but without feeling like being within a game.

---

[48] Tosca (2017) p. 165.

[49] Cf. Schwaab (2013) p. 48.

[50] Benjamin (2005) p. 120.

[51] Cf. Deuber-Mankowsky (2015) p. 53.

[52] Cf. Neitzel (2010) p. 110 f.; cf. Nohr (2008) p. 111.

[53] Cf. Krämer (2007) p. 244; cf. Salen/Zimmermann: *Rules of Play*, p. 304.

The Seriality of the Play Element in Media Narratives

Seriality is a constant feature when considering television, play(ing) and experimentation, and ongoing media configurations. It is the most important characteristics that put play and television in relation to each other that are characterized by seriality: Rhythm, repetition, and variation. Seriality is generally regarded as a paradigm of cultural and media history[54] and is to be interpreted here in the context of the previously presented way of thinking of play (as a driving force of remediation).

Television, as a serial and playful phenomenon, seems to encompass the entire range of play. Play appears as a narrative topic, structure, and aesthetics. A look at recently acclaimed TV series shows a clear tendency towards ludo-narrative play with remediations.[55] At the same time, digital games borrow from film and camera techniques, and audio-visual productions adapt the patterns and aesthetics of digital games. Such a "game-like mise-en-scène"[56] is significant in *Lost*, for example: whether a massive clockwork that moves the whole island in time and space, numerous *Easter Eggs* or *quests* that must be completed by the protagonists, *Lost* offers a template that can be adapted almost identically to a *level design*[57]—or represents it in itself. In the mini-series *Heroes Reborn*, an important subplot adapts a computer game: a protagonist, who is a computer game character, can teleport herself into a digital game using a sword as a portal. The plot then takes place entirely in the game's diegesis, and as the story develops, the fictional real and secondary worlds[58] increasingly converge until they merge.

Another variation of the play element (which is a common motif in digital games) can be seen in the Netflix series *Russian Doll:* the protagonist experiences her personal *Groundhog Day* in an endless loop, dying again and again (*Game Over*) and starting one and the same day all over again (*Restart*). Similar forms of such "ludic architecture"[59] can be found in series like *The Walking Dead* or *Game of Thrones*. On the one hand, the gameplay is represented both as an element within the story (for example competitions or quests that the characters need to complete), and as a narrative vehicle that drives the story forward (for example an increase in

---

[54] Cf. Schlicker (2016) p. 193.

[55] Cf. Schmerheim (2018) p. 41.

[56] Rauscher (2017) p. 200.

[57] Cf. Ibid., p. 201.

[58] Cf. Schmerheim (2018) p. 44.

[59] Rauscher (2017) p. 210.

strength to defeat opponents that grow exponentially stronger with every new challenge or the arrival at a new location that resembles reaching a new level).[60] Here, however, it is not possible for the audience to play along. On the other hand, it is precisely the transmedia extensions that turn the series into playable environments that can be experienced: "The author is not really dead but his or her work comes closer to the task of a game master"[61]—in this context Rauscher describes above all developers of transmedia narratives as game masters. Looking at one of the numerous transmedia offerings of *The Walking Dead*, the *Companion App Story Sync*, one can only agree. During the broadcasting of an episode, an app designed for *second-screen viewings* becomes active, guiding through the plot with aesthetics strongly reminiscent of that of games. The application is *gamified*, in that, for example, quiz-like questions about the story are asked or predictions regarding the development of the plot are requested. Props or details are prepared similarly to a game inventory and resemble the digital aesthetics of video games. Using the second screen app parallels a videogame arrangement, too. The viewer holds and interacts with a device in their hands. Within the *Story Sync App*, there are highlighted elements that guide the user through the narrative. The extension of the television text through dispersive media and the modification and participation that manifest, for example, through the connection of the text fragments, come close to the element of play in the sense of its recursive movement and creation of (game) space [*Schöpfung von Spielraum*] through rules. In addition, various other transmedia extensions of the series (such as 360-degree videos, a graphic novel game, a Telltale game series, browser and casual games, the *Dead Yourself app*, comics, or conventions, among others) allow for immersive experiences within the series universe and represent variations of play and diverse opportunities to play along.[62] The narrative, however, remains unchanged.

A recent modification of interactive television will serve as a prime example to demonstrate different representations of play in television. In the latest special episode of the anthology series *Black Mirror*, the element of play becomes the actual protagonist. It significantly determines the plot, is brought into focus in

---

[60]Mittell explains this very well with the example of the TV series *The Wire* and describes the interaction and the aesthetics between *the game* (meaning drug trafficking, corruption, etc.), in which the protagonists are involved, and the *playful narrative design*, that focuses on a new perspective in every season. Cf. Mittell (2009a) pp. 429–438.

[61]Rauscher (2017) p. 197.

[62]Elsewhere I have analyzed in more detail how *companion apps* and transmedia extensions offer opportunities to play along while establishing a field of action that is characterized by its interrelation between autonomy and control: Cf. Hebben (2017) pp. 33–53.

various ways, and runs like a thread through the entire narrative structure of *Bandersnatch*. Stefan, the protagonist, and the viewers that play along share numerous experiences between autonomy and control. One difference to the examples briefly touched upon earlier, however, is the opportunity to modify the narrative by playing with the plot. Precisely because of its topicality, *Bandersnatch* is, therefore, to be understood as an indexical phenomenon of remediated and thus playful processes, since this example not only paradigmatically demonstrates variations of play, but also allows conclusions to be drawn about implications for modes of reception and media structures, which will be brought together in the final consideration.

Sugar Puffs or Frosties?: Game Mechanisms, Creation & Limits

> Yes. This is a Black Mirror interactive movie where YOU make decisions for the lead character. And with only a few days of bad decision making left before all your 2019 resolutions start, you can help him make some pretty terrible choices. #bandersnatch[63]

With this announcement, *Bandersnatch* is advertised by Netflix and described as "a mind-bending tale with multiple endings".[64] The mode of decision-making and thus agency over the course of the plot is strongly emphasized. The *Bandersnatch* special episode has a duration between 60 and 300 min. There is a total of 5 h of footage from which, depending on the choices the viewers make, a story path emerges that has an average feature length of 90 min. The episode has a unique technical setting: There is no progress bar, as the length depends on the choices made. When selecting the decision options, technical requirements are of importance, so that not all end devices enable to play along and the feature of interactivity is also met with rejection or dismissed as a gimmick by a significant part of the audience. The viewers playing along in front of the screens find themselves in a spatial arrangement reminiscent of a computer game setup. With controllers[65] in

---

[63] Netflix: "Black Mirror Bandersnatch", *Instagram post* from Dec. 28, 2018.

[64] Netflix: "Black Mirror Bandersnatch", *Netflix*.

[65] *Bandersnatch* could be played with controllers, as long as the viewer chooses a game console with access to the Internet and a Netflix app to stream the episode. A particularly interesting observation here would be the extent to which *Bandersnatch* sets itself apart from experimental games (that are very much focused on narration, such as *Dear Esther)* as an interactive film or playful series episode, and what role the media environment plays in this constellation.

their hands, they wait for moments of action in which they can make a decision. The first decision is made after a few minutes and seems banal in terms of content: *Sugar Puffs* or *Frosties*? The protagonist's father holds out two boxes of cereal for his son to choose from; the decision about Stefan's breakfast is made by the viewers in front of the screen.

With the making of this first decision, the structure of the plot path begins, as can be seen in Fig. 1. The map created by an engaged viewer represents all possible decisions, crossroads, exits, and (hyper)links in the form of a *decision tree*,[66] at the same time it shows heuristically the spatial and temporal aspect of the playable narrative. What is more, the map illustrates the cognitive performance, i.e. the path the viewer chooses by playing along, that creates this field of action.

This includes following the different narrative paths across media. In transmedia environments, the mode of choice and navigation continues. Rauscher notes "[transmedia] patchworks allow their audience members to choose between navigating narrative elements as well as wandering around and playing with the setting"[67] and thereby locates the handling of the transmedia storytelling in play. Rauscher also emphasizes the spatial aspect which results from the movement of the players:

> You can follow a series of quests with some alternative branches and experience a narrative similar to a guided tour through the simulated world, but you can also go exploring for yourself and compose virtual snapshots of the landscape or take a walk to find out what can be seen around the next corner.[68]

Within the *Bandersnatch* episode, the field of action is much more limited: the option to fast-forward or rewind is extremely restricted and only possible between choices. It is not possible to skip making a decision or to modify a choice in this way. Here, the viewers are moving in a defined space, which gives them agency and the option of choice, but at the same time restricts and directs them. Schematically, this structure resembles a linear level design of a computer game. Within the game's structure, following the rules and being guided can be ascribed to a form of desire. Murray sees this desire in "the satisfying power to take meaningful action and see results of our decisions and choices".[69] This mode of choice is echoed in other interactive narratives and the transmedia extensions of many television series,

---

[66] Cf. Salen/Zimmerman (2004) pp. 230–248.

[67] Rauscher (2017) p. 208 f.

[68] Ibid.

[69] Murray (2017) p. 123.

Fig. 1 Black Mirror: Bandersnatch Outcome Map. (© 2019 Hypebeast Limited, https://hypebeast.com/2019/1/black-mirror-bandersnatch-complete-choices-outcome-map, accessed 04/07/2019)

supporting the question of the relationship between serial narrative and play: "Has a *dogma of choice* slowly evolved when it comes to the current state of interactive storytelling and the fairly established routines of how to interact with the narrative?"[70]

In this context, it is also interesting to mention the habits, which, as already explained, are characteristics of play. Further, Gasteier describes, "[s]omehow interactive storytelling became synonymous with the element of narrative choice

---

[70] Gasteier (2017) p. 511.

Fig. 2 Still/screenshot from *Black Mirror: Bandersnatch*. (© 1997–2019 Netflix, Inc.)

(and the obligation to render decisions)."[71] In *Bandersnatch*, it is impossible not to make a decision. A horizontal bar that visualizes a *quick time event* familiar from computer games appears at each decision point, setting a 10-s countdown (cf. Fig. 2). If no decision is made within this period, the choice always falls on the action in the left column. In some cases, only one choice is available.

Later in the narrative, there is a prompt requesting manual input in which a correct telephone number can be typed in via remote control to reach a specific plot line. The numbers that played a role earlier in the narrative are now repeated here so that the actual puzzle or memory performance is omitted and only dictated numbers are to be entered under time pressure. In this context, Gasteier poses the interesting question of whether our own choices can captivate us as much as a story whose outcome we cannot influence and whose unexpected twists affect us emotionally.[72] Again, a possible answer can be found in Krämer's understanding of play when she formulates that in play, we experience ourselves as the cause of an event, as its sovereign subject. And yet this experience of sovereignty is only half the truth. At the same time, we are playfully involved in a process that grips us more than we grasp it. As we play, we are being played with as well.[73]

---

[71] Ibid.

[72] Cf. Ibid., p. 516.

[73] Cf. Krämer (2007) p. 243.

Fig. 3 Screenshot *Instagram posting from Netflix*. (© 2019 Instagram, https://www.instagram.com/p/BsBIjXVj9IG/, accessed Jan 16, 2019)

Nohzdyve: Intertextuality, Easter Eggs & Gamification

"Everything but make it Bandersnatch"—with this image caption, Netflix presents a series of film stills with pop culture references that are aesthetically adapted to the decision sequences of *Bandersnatch*. An interesting aspect is that the selected option does not correspond with the actual film's plot. Figure 3 shows a film still of the end of the shipwreck scene from the film *Titanic*, but now, in *Bandersnatch style*, viewers are presented with a choice of two possible outcomes: Either "move over or take turns or try literally anything" or "just let him die".[74] As is well known, nothing is done in this scene; protagonist Rose lies on a wooden door floating in the sea while Jack remains up to his shoulders in ice water, freezing to death in the hands of his lover. The choice made by *Netflix* in this image, however, falls on the left column. It expresses the desire to save the protagonist and implies that he could have been saved had the viewers been able to participate in the decision.

On the one hand, *everything but make it Bandersnatch* stands for the desire for agency and participation, but on the other hand, the credo of *gamification* is also strikingly displayed here. *Gamification* refers to the application of elements of game

---

[74]Netflix: "Everything but make it Bandersnatch", *Instagram post* from Dec. 30, 2018.

playing to other non-game fields of activity.[75] The transfer of gameplay elements usually takes place on an aesthetic level that mimics the digital game. The proposed option of *turning everything into Bandersnatch*, i.e. gamifying everything or imposing game aesthetics on everything, which is, however, limited as described in the previous chapter, is thus only supposedly free. In the following, I will examine representations of game and gamification in *Bandersnatch* in more detail.

Concerning interactive narratives, to which Gasteier attributes an "aesthetic of choice",[76] the author notes "layers of interactivity [are] applied to whatever lies beneath, promising author-like control as its own defining, inherent aspect of gaming culture"[77] and thus describes *gamified narrative* structures. Further, he notes, "we cannot deny the paradox of how much fun it is to interact playfully in fictional story worlds regardless of the quality of our narratological influence."[78] The mere implication of agency is thus desirable, which is also related to the previously explained figures of thought of experimentation and play and underlines Krämer's statement of being immersed [*the process that grips us more than we grasp it*] in play. One form of playing along lies in the creation of the playable narrative space. The possibility of creating this space through the mode of choice, as it could be mapped through the *decision tree* (cf. Fig. 1), has already been explained. Two further possibilities to create a playable story world [Spielräume] are the intertextual references and transmedia extensions presented below, which are interpreted as variations of play.

In the course of the plot, the audience encounters numerous references—beginning with the fictional title *Bandersnatch*, a novel that the protagonist adapts and programs as a computer game of the same name. As the plot progresses, there is also a condensation of events: Intertextual references increase, the extent of the choices made has a more far-reaching impact on the outcome of the plot, and the narrative also becomes more complex in terms of content, reflecting on various representations of play at different levels. As can be seen in Fig. 1, the progression of the initial decisions is still quite linear. Nevertheless, intertextual references that act as *Easter Eggs* create numerous nodes that provide access to transmedia extensions and other texts.

At the very beginning of the story, Stefan accepts the invitation of a game developer, is invited to his company, and meets the programmer Colin. He presents

---

[75] Cf. Deterding (2011) p. 9 f.

[76] Gasteier (2017) p. 512.

[77] Ibid.

[78] Ibid.

his current project to Stefan: a game called *Nohzdyve*. This is a direct reference to a previous *Black Mirror* episode (*Nosedive*, S3:E1), which takes place in an entirely gamified dystopian setting. In *Nosedive*, each character is always immersed in their smartphone, their every action posted and rated by each other through a five-star system. The ranking within this system determines one's social status and results in gratifications such as better housing or sanctions up to exclusion from the gamified society and imprisonment. The computer game *Nohzdyve* symbolizes the (social) fall and loss, observed by passive bystanders, and offers in its description a direct reference to the content of another *Black Mirror* episode:

> You're falling fast through the sky! Collect eyeballs and avoid the buildings and other hazards. Perfection is key. This was truly a five star game by none other than Colin Ritman.[79]

This short game description cannot be found within the *Bandersnatch* episode but on the website of the fictional game developer *Tuckersoft*. This is not only a narrative reference but a point of entry into the spatialized transmedia field of action [Spielraum] of the interactive special episode. The interactivity that takes place within the episode by choosing paths is continued in the transmedia storyworld. Discovering and following these *Easter Eggs* requires a high degree of technological know-how and intertextual knowledge that can only be expected from (game) experts. The path to unlocking these bonus materials is complex and downright a variation of play. Through principles of trial and error, a back-and-forth movement between the various choices and paths, this experimental approach opens up further bonus material such as "Secret Endings" and "Playable Games".[80] If the players reach such a secret ending (through an exact sequence of choices), a sound plays which, played through a simulation program, fabricates a QR code, which, for example, scanned through a smartphone, reveals the link to the *Tuckersoft* website. Every *Easter Egg* or transmedia extension can be discovered by playing along. Through *collective intelligence* and the sharing of knowledge provided by experts, the mass audience also gains knowledge on how to access transmedia extensions and intertextual references.

Another direct reference to digital games are meta-reflexive (game) sequences within the episode. The lead-up to a fight scene seems almost contrived. Stefan's psychologist asks him directly: "If this was entertainment, surely you'd make it

---

[79] *Tuckersoft: Nohzdyve.*
[80] Rouse (2019).

more interesting. [. . .] Wouldn't you want a little more action if you were watching this now on telly?"—The viewers have the choice here between "Yes" and "Fuck Yeah", so the fight scene is unavoidable, but not considered further within the diegesis, since after this sequence there is either a conclusion of the episode (*game over*/official end) or a possibility to *restart*. Aesthetically, the sequence is also set apart from the rest of the narrative and strongly emulates the digital game aesthetics or an action movie. But this is precisely what underlines play as the protagonist of the narrative; it is the thread that connects all (story) paths.

Destroy Computer?: Loss of Control, Dead Ends & Game Over

Further variations of play occur as self-references. These include, for example, the protagonist's loss of control, as he feels himself to be externally controlled and addresses the viewers personally and interacts with them. The representation of play lies on the one hand in the experimental narrative mode and the viewer's participation, and on the other hand in the problematization of the gamelike situation. *For who is being played with here?* Their choices guide the spectators through the text, but textual dead ends also reveal a strong steering. Either there is only one option left, which in case of doubt activates itself when the viewers are inactive, or the viewers find themselves in loops, constantly restarting from a previous scene until they take the path or answer that leads further[81] (cf. Figs. 1 and 2). Thus, at a point when the protagonist is controlled by others, "Netflix" is the only option that can be clicked on, which now also invites the viewers to reflect and rethink their role within this game structure [Spielgefüge].

Stefan becomes an avatar, clearly straining to resist the chosen actions of the viewers, asking directly "Who's doing this to me?", "I know there is someone there" and "Just give me a sign". If the viewers have previously selected "Netflix" as their option, "I am watching you on Netflix. I make decisions for you" appears on the protagonist's tube monitor, and viewers can communicate with Stefan in a limited way and choose which information about Netflix they want to reveal to him. But

---

[81] However, in this context it is also interesting to consider the effect of not following these suggested choices. Consciously playing against the rules or refusing to make a choice could be interpreted in the context of *cheating* as playing by one's own rules.

viewers also reach their limits (and those of their playing field or the filmed material). Through limited choices, loops, and dead ends, viewers experience themselves as similarly eternally controlled and lose control over the narrative as the protagonist does. This becomes clear in Fig. 2: a meta-reflexive dead end can be seen, which marks the action experienced so far as constructed and part of a designed storyworld and visualizes it within two old-fashioned monitors. To leave the loop, a different path than before must be taken, otherwise, the players end up again (and endlessly) in front of this dead end.

This is reinforced by other meta-reflexive statements that can be heard as background noises on the protagonist's television, such as "You're just a puppet. You're not in control". Even if other outcomes or actions were desired, the viewers are left with preconceived choices, dead ends, or the end of the game. This is where the peculiarity of *Black Mirror: Bandersnatch* comes in: The deliberately media- and technology-critical message of the series shows viewers the limits of their agency in this interactive environment. The players find themselves caught between determinism and autonomy:[82] "free movement within a more rigid structure".[83] By repetitive scenarios of trial-and-error, and the selection of their path through the (transmedia) narrative, the viewers explore the playing field [Spielraum] (and the technological possibilities of the medium), define and modify boundaries, discover *Easter Eggs*, and become aware of themselves as media participants, because as Benjamin puts it for the concept of play: "a 'doing the same thing over and over again', the transformation of a shattering experience into habit – that is the essence of play".[84] And what could be more shattering than the realization of being part of a larger play scheme? Accurately, Krämer defines that while playing, playing and being played with become inseparable. We experience ourselves as creators and observers, between empowerment and loss of control.[85]

The numerous references to gamification can also be read in this context: The designed and restricted agency indicates the viewer's experience. Through its various representations of play, *Bandersnatch* virtually holds up a mirror to its

[82] Cf. Harth (2017) p. 4.

[83] Salen/Zimmermann (2004) p. 304.

[84] Benjamin (2005) p. 120. In addition to this, Deuber-Mankowsky notes with reference to Benjamin's concept of habit that Benjamin expresses this ambivalence by bringing together childlike play with the neurosis of the adult. Happiness and horror become indistinguishable (Cf. Deuber-Mankowsky (2015) p. 53).

[85] Cf. Krämer (2007) p. 244.

fellow players and makes clear how deeply they are immersed in media ubiquity and how deeply these structures are anchored in their media practices.

Conclusion: Save and Reload

The testing and probing that is carried out during a run-through of the *Bandersnatch* episode to explore the spatiality of the plot can be seen as an adaption of the concept of *trial-and-error* established in the digital age. Through repetition, all options can be experienced and grasped, which is why Harth also speaks in this context of a *cultural technique [Kulturtechnik] of control*[86] that is accompanied by the effects of optimization. Techniques familiar from computer games such as *save*, *load*, and *reload*[87] are also employed in *Bandersnatch* and are sometimes used explicitly to modify the outcome of the plot because the possibility of reloading invites us to solve the same situations in different ways.[88] The function of saving decisions is automated in *Bandersnatch*, however, decisions made can only be changed by *restarting* the episode. This practice allows bad decisions to be overturned and started over. But the viewer's action is not free of consequence as a result but is reflective and well-thought-out through prior trial and error. A reciprocal effect can be seen: the *Save* and *Reload* techniques influence the game architecture, as interruption and continuation are modified by them. Difficult situations can be practiced and perfected infinitely, only the most satisfactory result is saved and accepted.[89] This technique, common to computer games, represents the figurations of television on another level. Keilbach and Stauff see great significance precisely in these variations of the experimental system because the 'power of television' results in part from the constant process of transformation that entails not only a perpetual rearrangement but also a permanent reflection on the 'appropriate' use of television.[90]

---

[86]Cf. Harth (2017) p. 9.

[87]*Reload* means to delete a certain game sequence and to repeat it from a previously saved starting point, thus experiencing a different outcome. *Restart* means to reset to the beginning; all actions are erased, and the game starts again.

[88]Cf. Harth (2017) p. 1.

[89]Ibid.

[90]Cf. Keilbach/Stauff (2011) p. 175.

The example of *Bandersnatch* makes it evident that play is found on various levels in connection with television. It is only heuristically possible to systematize this since play is not only ambivalent but also activating and creative. It is not only the explicit operation of a controller or direct intervention in an event that makes play(ing along) possible; even a content-related or aesthetic adaptation can be an entry point into a larger, interactive game structure [Spielgefüge] and open up agency and immersion within a playful extended narrative [*erweiteter Spielraum*]. Play is not only revealed as an integral part of television but also as a productive figure of thought that has always been associated with television. In the constant back-and-forth movement and practices that use trial and error, however, the desires and needs of the players are not only satisfied but also constructed in the first place. Playing along is therefore just as inherent to television as its perpetual variations of play. This modification, which is inherent in media structures, is equally evoked and constantly renegotiated by the element of play, which always has been and will be a driving force in the formation of new media technologies and their practices.

List of Sources

References

Askwith, Ivan (2019) Television 2.0. Reconceptualizing TV as an Engagement Medium. Master Thesis Massachusetts 2007. https://cmsw.mit.edu/television-2-0-tv-as-an-engagement-medium/. Accessed 16 Jan 2019

Bakioglu, Burcu (2015) Alternate Reality Games. In: Mansell, Robin, Peng Hwa Ang (Eds.) The International Encyclopedia of Digital Communication and Society, Vol. I. Chichester, John Wiley & Sons, pp. 14–21.

Benjamin, Walter (1991a) Das Kunstwerk im Zeitalter seiner technischen Reproduzierbarkeit. Zweite Fassung. In: Tiedemann, Rolf, Hermann Schweppenhäuser (Eds.) Walter Benjamin. Gesammelte Schriften Band VII. Frankfurt, Suhrkamp, pp. 350–385.

Benjamin, Walter (1991b) Spielen und Spielzeug. Randbemerkungen zu einem Monumentalwerk. In: Tiedemann-Bartels, Hella (Ed.) Walter Benjamin. Kritiken und Rezensionen. Gesammelte Schriften Band III. Frankfurt: Suhrkamp, pp. 127–131

Benjamin, Walter (2008) The Work of Art in the Age of Its Technological Reproduction. Second Version. London: Penguin

Benjamin, Walter (2005) Toys and Play. In: Jennings, Michael W., Howard Eiland, Gary Smith (Eds.) Walter Benjamin. Selected Writings Volume 2, Part 1, 1927-1930. Cambridge Mass., Harvard University Press, pp. 117–121

Deterding, Sebastian, Dan Dixon, Dan, Rilla Khaled et al. (2011) Form Game Design Elements to Gamefulness: Defining ‚Gamification'. In: MindTrek '11 Proceedings of the 15th International Academic MindTrek Conference: Envisioning Future Media Environments, Tampere. New York: Association for Computer Machinery, pp. 9–15

Deuber-Mankowsky, Astrid, Reinhold Görling (2017) Einleitung. Zur Medialität des Spiels. In: Deuber-Mankowsky, Astrid, Görling, Reinhard (Eds.) Denkweisen des Spiels. Medienphilosophische Annäherungen. Wien/Berlin. Turia und Kant, pp. 7–19

Deuber-Mankowsky, Astrid (2017) Variationen des Spiels. *Seeing Red* von Su Friedrich mit Deleuze, Guattari und Benjamin. In: Deuber-Mankowsky, Astrid, Reinhold Görling (Eds.) Denkweisen des Spiels. Medienphilosophische Annäherungen, Wien/Berlin, Turia und Kant, pp. 213–237

Deuber-Mankowsky, Astrid (2015) Spiel und zweite Technik. Walter Benjamins Entwurf einer Medienanthropologie des Spiels. In: Voss, Christiane, Lorenz Engell (Eds.) Mediale Anthropologien. Paderborn, Wilhelm Fink Verlag, pp. 35–62

Elsaesser, Thomas (2017) Cinema and Game Spaces. Contingency as Our New Causality. In: Clash of Realities (Eds.) Clash of Realities 2015/16. On the Art, Technology and Theory of Digital Games. Proceedings of the 6th and 7th Conference. Bielefeld, transcript, pp. 57–76

Gitelman, Lisa (2008) Always Already New. Media, History, and the Data of Culture. Cambridge, MIT Press

Gasteier, Klaus (2017) The Aesthetics of Choice. A Question from the Outside. In: Clash of Realities (Eds.) *Clash of Realities 2015/16. On the Art, Technology and Theory of Digital Games. Proceedings of the 6th and 7th Conference.* Bielefeld, transcript, pp. 509–522.

Harth, Jonathan (2017) Save, Load & Reload – Über den Umgang mit Kontingenz und Serialität in der Praxis des Computerspielens. In: Paidia. Zeitschrift für Computerspielforschung. Sonderausgabe: Gespielte Serialität, March 22, 2017. https://www.paidia.de/save-load-reload-uber-den-umgang-mit-kontingenz-und-serialitat-in-der-praxis-des-computerspielens/. Accessed 16 Jan 2019

Hebben, Kim (2017) How To Watch TV: Die Spielregeln des Transmedialen. In: *ffk Journal* 1, p. 33–53. https://www.ffk-journal.de/?journal=ffk-journal&page=article&op=view&path%5B%5D=4. Accessed 4 April 2019

Hebben, Kim (2019) Verspieltes Fernsehen – Spiel und Spieler_innen im Transmedialen. In: ffk Journal 4, p. 50–65. https://www.ffk-journal.de/?journal=ffk-journal&page=article&op=view&path%5B%5D=68. Accessed 20. Mar 2019

Huizinga, Johan (1950) Homo Ludens. A Study of the Play Element in Culture. Boston, The Beacon Press

Keilbach, Judith, Markus Stauff (2011) Fernsehen als fortwährendes Experiment. Über die permanente Erneuerung eines alten Mediums. In: Elia-Borer, Nadja, Samuel Sieber, Georg Christoph Tholen (Eds.) Blickregime und Dispositive audiovisueller Medien. Bielefeld, transcript, pp. 155–181

Keilbach, Judith, Markus Stauff (2013) When old media never stopped being new. Television's history as an ongoing experiment. In: Valck, Marijke de, Jan Teurlings (Eds.) After the Break. Television Theory Today. Amsterdam: Amsterdam University Press, pp. 79–98.

Krämer, Sybille (2007) Die Welt – ein Spiel? Über die Spielbewegung als Umkehrbarkeit. In: Niehoff, Rolf, Rainer Wenrich (Eds.) Denken und Lernen mit Bildern. Interdisziplinäre Zugänge zur Ästhetischen Bildung. München, kopaed, pp. 238–253

Mittell, Jason (2009a) All in the Game: The Wire, Serial Storytelling and Procedural Logic. In. Harrigan, Pat; Noah Wardip-Fruin (Eds.) Third Person. Authoring and Exploring Vasts Narratives, Cambridge/London, The MIT Press, pp. 429–438

Mittell, Jason (2009b) Forensic Fandom and the Drillable Text. Web exclusive Essay. In: Spreadable Media. https://spreadablemedia.org/essays/mittell/#.WFaakrbhBuV. Accessed 16 Jan 2019

Murray, Janet (2017) Hamlet on the Holodeck, The Future of Narrative in Cyberspace. Updated Edition. New York, The MIT Press, pp. 123–147.

Neitzel, Britta (2010) Spielerische Aspekte digitaler Medien – Rollen, Regeln, Interaktion. In: Thimm, Caja (Ed.) *Das Spiel. Muster und Metapher der Mediengesellschaft*. Wiesbaden 2010, Springer VS, pp. 107–126.

Nohr, Rolf (2008) Die Natürlichkeit des Spielens. Vom Verschwinden des Gemachten im Computerspiel. Münster, LIT Verlag, pp. 104–129

Piepiorka, Christine (2017) Lost in Time & Space. Transmediale Universen & Prozesshafte Serialität. Bochum, tredition, pp. 245–278

Rouse, Isaac (2019) Here's How To Unlock the 'Bandersnatch' Secret Ending & Playable Game. In: *Hypebeast*, January 4, 2019. https://hypebeast.com/2019/1/black-mirror-bandersnatch-secret-ending-game. Accessed 7 April 2019

Rauscher, Andreas (2017) A Game of Playful Art. Transmedia Auteurs, Genre Setting, and the Cineludic Form. In: Clash of Realities (Eds.) Clash of Realities 2015/16. On the Art, Technology and Theory of Digital Games. Proceedings of the 6th and 7th Conference. Bielefeld, transcript, pp. 195–215

Salen, Katie, Eric Zimmermann (2004) Rules of Play. Game Design Fundamentals, Cambridge, The MIT Press.

Schabacher, Gabriele (2010) Serienzeit. Zu Ökonomie und Ästhetik der Zeitlichkeit neuerer US-amerikanischer TV-Serien. In: Meteling, Arno, Isabell Otto, Gabriele Schabacher (Eds.) "Previously on..." Zur Ästhetik der Zeitlichkeit neuerer TV-Serien. München, Königshausen & Wustermann, pp. 19–40

Schmerheim, Philipp (2018) Remediationen des digitalen Spiels in *Offline* – Das Leben ist kein Bonuslevel. In: Schmid, Johannes, Andreas Veits, Wiebke Vorrath (Eds.) Praktiken medialer Transformationen. Übersetzungen in und aus dem digitalen Raum. Bielefeld, transcript, pp. 41–60

Schlicker, Alexander (2016) Serialität – Spiel – Games Studies. Zu Formen, Distinktionen und Potenzialen der Game-Serie. In: Henning, Martin, Hans Krah (Eds.) Spielzeichen. Theorien, Analysen und Kontexte des zeitgenössischen Computerspiels, Glückstadt, Werner Hülsbusch, pp. 193–211.

Schwaab, Herbert (2013) Transmedialität und Mediatisierung. Formen und Motive der Expansion serieller Welten und neuer Medienobjekte, In: Maeder, Dominik/Wentz, Daniela (Eds.) Navigationen. 13 (1) (Der Medienwandel der Serie, 13/1. Siegen, Universitätsverlag Siegen, pp. 85–103

Stiglegger, Marcus (2007) Promethischer Impuls und Digitale Revolution? Kino, Interaktivität und Reißbrettwelten. In: Leschke, Rainer, Jochen Venus (Eds.) Spielformen im Spielfilm. Zur Medienmorphologie des Kinos nach der Postmoderne, Bielefeld, transcript, pp. 103–116

Tosca, Susana (2017) Time, Memory, and Longing in Transmedial Storytelling. In: Clash of Realities (Eds.) Clash of Realities 2015/16. On the Art, Technology and Theory of Digital Games. Proceedings of the 6th and 7th Conference. Bielefeld, transcript, pp. 159–173

Zündel, Jana (2019) Der Episodenabspann zwischen rezeptivem Mehrwert und dispositiver Einschränkung. In: ffk Journal 4, pp. 298–311. https://www.ffk-journal.de/?journal=ffk-journal&page=article&op=view&path%5B%5D=84. Accessed on 20 March 2019

Internet Sources

Duden: „Spielerei", https://www.duden.de/rechtschreibung/Spielerei (Accessed on 15.03.2019).

Duden: „Homo Ludens", https://www.duden.de/rechtschreibung/Homo_ludens (Accessed on 15.03.2019).

Netflix: „Black Mirror Bandersnatch", *Netflix*, 28.08.2019, https://www.netflix.com/title/80988062 (Accessed on 16.03.2019).

Netflix: „Black Mirror Bandersnatch", *Instagram*, Posting vom 28.12.2018, https://www.instagram.com/p/Br7sRYfjRBo/ (Accessed on 16.03.2019).

Netflix: „Everything but make it Bandersnatch", *Instagram*, Posting vom 30.12.2018, https://www.instagram.com/p/BsBIjXVj9IG/ (Accessed on 16.01.2019).

Tuckersoft: Nohzdyve, https://www.tuckersoft.net/ealing20541/nohzdyve/ (Accessed on 07.04.2019).

Movie Directory

Bress, Eric/Gruber, J. Mackye (Drehbuch und Regie): *The Butterfly Effect*, USA 2004.

Cameron, James (Drehbuch und Regie): *Titanic*, USA 1997.

Cline, Ernest/Penn, Zak (Drehbuch); Spielberg, Steven (Regie): *Ready Player One*, USA 2018.

Cronenberg, David (Drehbuch und Regie): *eXistenZ*, USA 1999.

CtrlMovie (Studio); Wales Interactive (Publisher): *Late Shift – Your Decisions are You*, UK 2016.

Jackson, Peter (Drehbuch und Regie); Walsh, Fran/Boyens, Phillipa/del Toro, Guillermo (Drehbuch): *The Hobbit: The Desolation of Smaug. Extended Edition*. [dt. *Der Hobbit: Smaugs Einöde*], USA 2013.

Oppenheim, Noah/Myers, Grant Pierce (Drehbuch); Ball, Wes (Regie): *The Maze Runner* [dt. *Maze Runner – Die Auserwählten im Labyrinth*], USA 2014.

Ross, Gary (Drehbuch und Regie); Collins, Suzanne/Ray, Billy (Drehbuch): *The Hunger Games* [dt. *Die Tribute von Panem*], USA 2012.

Rubin, Danny (Drehbuch); Ramis, Harold (Drehbuch und Regie): *Groundhog Day* [dt. *Und täglich grüßt das Murmeltier*], USA 1993.

Wachowski, Lana/Wachowski, Lilly (Drehbuch und Regie): *The Matrix*, USA 1999.

Series Directory/Episode Directory

Abrams, Jeffrey Jacob/Lindelof, Damon/Lieber, Jeffrey (Idee): *Lost*, ABC, USA 2004–2010.
Benioff, David/Weiss, Daniel Brett (Idee): *Game of Thrones*, HBO, USA 2011–
Brooker, Charlie (Idee): *Black Mirror*, Channel 4, UK 2011–
Bandersnatch (Sonderfolge), 28.12.2018
Nosedive (S3:E1), 21.10.2016
Darabont, Frank/Kirkman, Robert/Moore, Tony (Idee): *The Walking Dead*, AMC, USA 2010–
Kring, Tim (Idee): *Heroes Reborn*, NBC, USA 2015–2016.
Lyonne, Natasha/Poehler, Amy/Headland, Leslye (Idee): *Russian Doll*, Netflix, USA 2019–
Simon, David (Idee): *The Wire*, HBO, USA 2002–2008.

Interactive Applications/Online Videos

AMC: „The Walking Dead Story Sync" (Companion App), *AMC*, © 2010–2019, https://www.amc.com/shows/the-walking-dead/story-sync/ (Accessed on 07.04.2019).
FOX International: „The Walking Dead – VR 360° video!", *YouTube*, 20.10.2016, https://www.youtube.com/watch?v=nRQsn_qd2Vs (Accessed on 16.01.2019).

Game Directory

Telltale Games (Publisher und Studio): *The Walking Dead. The Game*, Android, iOS, Mac OS, Windows, PlayStation 3, PlayStation Vita, Xbox 360, Xbox One, PlayStation 4 2012.
The Chinese Room (Publisher und Studio); Curve Digital (Publisher): *Dear Esther*, PC 2012; PlayStation 4, Xbox One 2016.
The Fullbright Company/Merge Games/Headup Games (Publisher und Studio); The Fullbright Company (Studio): *Gone Home*, Windows, Mac OS, Linux, PlayStation 4, Xbox One, Switch 2013.

Kim Carina Hebben, M.A., is working on her doctorate at the Institute of Media Studies at Ruhr University of Bochum. In her research project, she investigates playful structures and practices of television. Since 2017, she has been working as a research assistant at the Institute of Diversity Studies and since 2022 at the Division of Academic Teaching and Faculty Development at TU Dortmund University. Further research interests are transmediality, convergence, and transformations of media and participation, as well as game studies, digitalization, and media didactics.

Limited Animation, Unlimited Seriality: The Configurations of the Serial in the Anime Series *Haha o Tazunete Sanzenri, Akage no An* and *Tanoshî Mûmin Ikka*

Herbert Schwaab

This paper aims to address a particular form of seriality associated with 'classic' Japanese anime series. At first glance, these programmes seem to be overly accurate and uninspiring adaptations of classic children's books. A typical and defining example of this would be the 1974 anime series *Arupusu no Shōjo Haiji* which as *Heidi* made it as one of the first animated programmes from Japan to German television in the 1970s. It will point to a close coupling of aesthetics and narration that produces its own temporality, which can be captured with terms and approaches of so-called *limited animation*. *Limited animation* is at the same time thought of as the starting point of an 'unlimited seriality', as an intensification of the serial or as a purist form of serial narration. *Limited animation*, however, also contains stasis, a stretching of time and interruptions, as the following three examples will make clear.

Haha o Tazunete Sanzenri

This Japanese anime series from 1976 known as *From the Apenines to the Andes*, broadcast in Germany under the title *Marco* in the 1980s, is characterized by an excessive form of expansiveness. The literary model is a short novella of about

H. Schwaab (✉)
Institut für Information und Medien, Sprache und Kultur, Universität Regensburg, Salzburg, Austria
e-mail: Herbert.Schwaab@ur.de

40 pages by the Italian author Edmondo de Amicis, published in 1886 in the then very popular but now mostly forgotten novella collection *Cuore*.[1] In tells the story of a boy from Genoa looking for his mother who has emigrated to Argentina. In Nippon Animation's version, directed by Isao Takahata and with background art by Hayao Miyazaki, not only is the search extended to quite a few episode: It takes 14 of the 52 episodes for Marco to even set out on the journey. That relatively few pages are extended to 52 episodes here not only means that a lot has to be added in the anime series version of the book, but also explains a particular perspective on the everyday that comes with not having to shorten plots. Thus, Marco is shown taking on various jobs to earn money for his poor family. The performance of the jobs (delivering mail, cleaning bottles) sometimes takes up entire episodes. An important role is also played by collages of cityscapes and landscapes, which also fill a great deal of time and are not intended to show connections between scenes, but help to constitute a space of their own in the narrative. Miyazaki, who would later found Studio Ghibli with Takahata, made studies on a trip to Italy for drawing the backgrounds, which he also did travelling to Switzerland in his collaboration on the *Heidi* series 2 years earlier.[2] Miyazaki stresses that in both series it was important for him to depict the reality of the time. In *Arupusu no Shōjo Haiji* it was the mountain landscapes and everyday life of the alpine world, and in *Haha o Tazunete Sanzenri* he took an interest in the process of industrialization and change in the reality of the urban population in the nineteenth century.[3] Creating backgrounds to montage sequence of still images is an important aspect of the aesthetics of anime, which goes back to the close relationship between television anime and manga.[4] In this case, the design of the backgrounds as still images also intensifies the approach to the everyday, but it seems to come at the expense of a narrative dynamic: This series dwells on countless incidental details.

Happy Moomin Family

Tanoshî Mûmin Ikka (Japan 1990) by Hiroshi Saitóh, published in Germany under the title *Die Mumins*, represents a film adaptation of Tove Jansson's stories that is faithful to the work of the Swedish speaking Finnish author. It was more strongly

---

[1] De Amicis (1947).
[2] Lamarre (2009) p. 58.
[3] Miyazaki (2009) p. 330.
[4] Cf. Steinberg (2012) p. 74.

geared towards transmedia exploitation strategies than *Marco* and contributed to the popularity of the characters from the Mumins universe in Japan.[5] The 52 episodes of the German version represents the accidental product of ZDF's purchasing policy, as there are other episodes in the Japanese version that were never aired in Germany. *Tanoshî Mûmin Ikka* does not actually tell an ongoing story as a whole, but refers to several novel-like collections of stories in a series of individual volumes, some of which show traces of narrative progression.[6] The series is nevertheless an example of a very peculiar serial order: it is oriented towards the rhythm of the seasons, with stories set in winter and dealing with the annual hibernation of the Moomin family, with stories about the dawning of spring, summer and autumn, and the annual farewell and return of characters such as Snufkin. This programme thus offers an extremely flexible, open model of serialization, which, like the other objects discussed here, seems to be immune to a televisual order of the episodic, to the division into segments and the rhythmic composition of climaxes within and at the end of episodes. It tells its stories in the way that is demanded, to put it briefly, by the original stories and the characters that appear in them. This order is consistent with the nature of the Moomins, who are biological life forms, subject to the changing of the seasons and who, with minor exceptions, become inactive in winter. The early airings of *Tanoshî Mûmin Ikka* actually still adhered very closely to the weekly rhythm and distribution over a year, which suits this series very well. The Moomins are inert creatures and the equally inert, slow narrative style is in sync with the Japanese animation style, even though *Tanoshî Mûmin Ikka is* not really a representative of limited animation, the characteristics of which are much more pronounced in *Haha o Tazunete Sanzenri*. But both series avoid drama, preferring to describe gradual processes of steady change. For example, episode 9 "The Invisible Child" tells the story of orphan Ninny. She is given over to the care of the Moomin family because the unloving behavior and sarcasm of a relative who had taken her in has left her shy and literally invisible. With the Moomins, she recovers and slowly becomes more confident and courageous, which is traced in great detail as a process of gradually becoming visible. The deserted space of the image of this absent character can also be understood as an effect of this slow narrative form associated with Japanese anime series. Most series favor distinct state changes (like drama series), have them occur episodically (like in sitcom), or have

---

[5] Clements, McCarthy (2015) p. 547.

[6] The original version of this collections of stories was published as *Trollkarlens Hatt* in 1948 in Swedish. An English version was published in 1950 as *Finn Family Moomintroll*. Some chapters from this volume are adapted and arranged in the series in a similar way.

them occur constantly (like in soap opera). In contrast to these dominant expressions of sericality there aren't necessarily many series that can really trace gradual processes and changes as well as *Tanoshî Mûmin Ikka*.

Akage no An

The final example that will be examined in more detail in this paper also highlights the tendency towards immobility of this narrative form. The first episodes of the anime series *Akage no An* (JP 1979), an adaptation of Lucy Montgomery's *Anne of Green Gables*, broadcast in Germany under the title *Anne mit den roten Haaren* and also released on DVD, feature very little narrative progression per episode and are predominantly about how orphan Anne (mistakenly) ends up with sibling Matthew and Marilla on the Green Gables farm in eastern Canada at the end of the nineteenth century. The first episode shows Matthew preparing to pick up an orphan at the train station in a carriage and his irritation at the station that it is not a boy but a girl. It ends with a long—indeed a very long—carriage ride back to their farm. This carriage ride, its slow, unhurried rhythm enriched only by the lively child's many tales, extends to the second episode, in which Anne finally arrives at the farm, meets the stern Marilla, and spends a first night there. The next day, Anne, who Marilla feels cannot be used as a worker on the farm, is driven back to the orphanage, but this time by Marilla. This ride back is again extended to two full episodes, which the series uses to have Anne tell her life story. After arriving at the orphanage, Marilla decides to keep the unusual but exhausting child, and episode 6 finally shows Anne being brought back by carriage.

This redundancy and slowness becomes apparent in comparison to how the evolution of film language is often told. It is based on the development of editing that conveys sequences of movement, connections and transitions, but condenses them into the necessary number of shots. Film scholar Thomas Elsaesser refers to *Rescued by Rover* (GB 1905) as an example for this evolution and as an early representative of the cinema of narrative integration that presents the little journey of a dog briefly and comprehensibly in short shots. However, he also points out that this development of an economic form of narration is unfinished, as the film repeats these sequences of shots in almost exactly the same order as the dog's returns on his rescue mission of a stolen baby.[7] These repetitions place the film in a primitive form of cinema, what has been defined as a cinema of showing vs. telling, or, to use

---

[7]Cf. Elsaesser (2002) p. 83 f.

another concept, a cinema of attractions, in which spectacular views (of a city and its various milieus visible along the way) and spectacular movements (of a dog) are more important than narrative efficiency.[8] *Akage no An* might similarly be considered primitive, as the series stretches and repeats what could be briefly summarized and edited together. It doesn't even gain anything in this stretching, since it can't simply film a few nature views inexpensively, as live-action series do, then show them at length and fill time with them. After all, the many nature views that are stitched together but never repeated must all be equally painstakingly drawn. Realism in anime and animation is always a laboriously constructed realism that lacks immediate access to a pre-filmic reality.

It may become apparent that we are indeed not dealing with redundancy and a sparse form of narration. For the impression of redundancy only arises from the fact that this retelling of the first episodes is on the level of a pure summary of content and still has little to say about the images, their composition and their temporality. In this case, the coupling of content with recurrent stylistic features of this animated series is interesting: there is little movement in the images themselves, and if there is such a thing as dynamism, it is generated by the montage, image composition and the auditory level, the sound of horses' hooves and the carriage. Sound design always plays a very important role in this type of series and leads to a peculiar form of realism or realistic staging: The soundtrack—music, noises, dialogue—as Daniel Kothenschulte elaborates, is very lovingly and precisely designed in series like *Arupusu no Shōjo Haiji*, also to compensate for the apparent stasis and lack of movement in the setting.[9] Sophisticated and intricately designed backgrounds also play a crucial role.[10] They evoke the impression of landscape paintings and watercolors, intensify an emotional relationship between the viewers and the characters, and replace the lack of movement in the images with a movement of the viewers through the images. The montage of backgrounds and landscape images establish connections to Anne and, in this case, mostly accentuate the longing and transfiguring view of an idyll in which the girl hopes to find a home.

---

[8]Cf. ibid.

[9]Kothenschulte (2008) p. 56.

[10]Nieder (2008) p. 104.

The 'Unlimited Seriality' of the Television Anime of the *World Masterpiece Theatre*

Akage no An and *Haha o Tazunete Sanzenri* are part of a series of animated programmes produced annually under the title *World Masterpiece Theatre* by Nippon Animation since 1975 and broadcast on one of Japan's major channels Fuji TV.[11] These programs were created in the wake of the great success of the anime adaptation of *Heidi* as *Arupusu no Shōjo Haiji*.[12] This series of productions adapted great works of European and American children's literature in the form of animation, spanning 50 or 52 episodes, until 1996. Originally sponsored by soft drink manufacturer Calpis, the series began in 1975 with *Dog of Flanders* and went on to adapt such diverse works as *Tom Sawyer*, *Little Women*, *Rascal the Raccoon*, and *The Sound of Music*.[13]

The annual rhythm of mostly 52 episodes, which the German airing of *Tanoshî Mûmin Ikka* also follows, although it is not part of the *World Masterpiece Theatre series*, establishes, as is often the case with series, a contingent order that affects the form of the adaptation and thus represents a typical feature of television seriality. However, this is neither a miniseries, nor a typical season length of two dozen or so episodes, nor the endlessness of a soap opera. This format, which has similarities to the narrative progression of a serial, mainly gives the show a lot of time to tell its stories and defer the endings. For many, especially viewers in Europe, *World Masterpiece Theatre* series have been the first contact with Japanese anime series, but often without awareness of their origin,[14] although these series offered a completely new viewing experience of accurate but still plesasurable adaptations of works of children's extended to a large number of episodes.[15]The programmes became a staple of German public television in the 1980s and 1990s,[16] which was a good way for the broadcasters to fill a lot of airtime with relatively cheap programmes.[17]

The literary adaptations are rather ambitious works, accordingly the *World Masterpiece Theatre* had a great importance in the Japanese animation industry

---

[11] Clements, McCarthy (2015) p. 932.

[12] Ibid.

[13] Ibid.

[14] Treese (2007) p. 14.

[15] Göhlen (2008) p. 237.

[16] Ibid., p. 236 f.

[17] Ibid., p. 236.

and enjoyed, for example, high esteem among the cartoonists involved compared to other productions: "[. . .] many animators regarded WMT as the only work really worth doing."[18] The importance of this series is also evident from the fact that acclaimed anime artists such as Takahata and Miyazaki, who was later very critical of television anime,[19] were involved in the production. Miyazaki in fact took inspiration from World Masterpiece Theatre programmes for his first anime in the 1980s.[20] The importance of these series also has to do with the relationships many viewers have with their media childhood. Authors such as Daniel Kohtenschulte fondly describe the intense memories of series such as *Kimba—Der weiße Löwe (Janguru Taitei*, English title: *Kimba, The White Lion)* and *Heidi* as programs that seemed to come out of nowhere and were not yet associated with Japan or the genre of anime.[21] This article shares the same enthusiasm and starts from the view that this is not just a nostalgic, sentimental memory of old children's series: The intensity of the memory also has to do with the contributions these series made to the concept of television seriality.

The fact that *Akage no An*, for example, takes 50 episodes to tell the first novel in the *Anne of Green Gables* series by Lucy Maude Montgomery, published in 1908, in anime form, not only means a series time of about 1250 min (which the DVD advertises on its cover). It also leads to a very precise, seemingly less standardized and paced way of filming literary originals, which creates a peculiar rhythm. It remains a serial narrative, but it progresses very slowly, yet avoids any appeal to the episodic, which probably challenges the patience of many recipients.

At first glance, this narrative form seems naïve, ponderous, and spare. The narration drags along to fill 50 episodes, it seems to be based on efficiently translating every line of the original into moving images approaching the condition of immobility. In fact, there's a great contrast between adapting a literary work into a feature film, which is always looking to tighten and condense the plot and draw out the essence of a book, and the expansive serializing of *Akage no An* into a television series of 50 episodes that can take all the time in the world to put all the words into its audiovisual equivalent. It doesn't have to spend time selecting and identifying the essential moments of a work. At first glance, it doesn't seem like the original is being interpreted or adapted in any way at all. There's also no noticeable effort to establish cliffhanger structures. Movements and development tend to be

---

[18] Clements, McCarthy (2015) p. 932.

[19] Cf. Miyazaki (2009) p. 76.

[20] Lamarre (2009) p. 57.

[21] Kothenschulte (2008) p. 56.

interrupted by each episode. Instead, an off-screen voiceover attempts to create a small moment of suspense when a preview of the next episode is offered at the end of each episode. But this preview rarely has much to do with the upcoming episode or just picks out a few events that aren't essential to it—more like mock cliffhangers that create false expectations. These aspects sum up a naive form of narration and seriality that seems disorganized and lacking in dynamism. But it can also be thought of as a consistent abstraction of seriality, a pure form of steady advancement that pays no heed to the order and rhythm of television and its segmented nature. This type of series avoids the schemata of televisual formatting and allows the original story alone to impose its form on the audiovisual text. In the process, however, other serial regimes emerge, which have their origins in forms of representation that are closely linked to the Japanese anime industry and which will be presented in more detail here.

These aesthetic regimes of the Japanese anime series from the *World Masterpiece Theatre* series are to be defined here as the concept of limited animation, in order to make it clear that this seriality is not only manifested in how the story is told (how quickly or how slowly, for example), but that this seriality also reveals itself in the aesthetics, the images, the montage and the sounds. Story, plot, narration, aesthetic form and seriality enter into a close but also unusual relationship. This is not a seriality of progression, nor one of repetition and variation, creating the familiar and unfamiliar in equal measure, but rather a seriality of stretching, of steady progress, of continuous but undramatic change. It should be described here as an unlimited seriality because it does not allow itself to be limited by the specifications of television; it avoids the schemata of the serial as repetition.

Limited Animation **and Seriality**

This unlimited seriality is closely linked to the concept of *limited animation*, which characterizes many, but not all, aspects of Japanese animation culture. Thomas Lamarre describes *limited animation* as an alternative aesthetic of the generation of movement in which movement results from, among other things, its combination of seemingly static images, or in which only a few elements in a single image are moved: "What remains to be noted is that in *limited animation* movement is shifted, on the one hand, to movement between images and, on the other, to movement between the planes of an image."[22] Basically, *limited animation* is about reducing

---

[22] Lamarre (2008) p. 112.

the number of frames to be drawn for cheaper production on television, so instead of the approximately 24 frames in cinematic representations, and the 12 frames per second common in classical animation, animation is reduced to 8 frames per second or less, which prevents fluid impressions of movement.[23] However, *limited animation* applies techniques to compensate for the apparent lack of motion impression. Lamarre mentions, among other things, frequent changes of setting and the montage of static images, the animation of only one part of the face or only one element in the image, movement created by shifting the slides, the emphasis on dialogue and soundtrack, which can also be staged more intensely because *limited animation* dispenses with synchronicity with lip movements. However, this is not just a more efficient form of animation born out of necessity and lack of money. Lamarre refers to the Japanese animation theorist Mori Takuji, who points out that *limited animation* was first used in experimental film before it appeared on television.[24] Above all, Lamarre emphasizes that this aesthetic, following Deleuze's examination of the movement image and the time image, can be thought of as an alternative treatment of cinematic images that creates new spaces and times, but also new perceptions, and can point to a crisis of the action image in which the actions of the protagonists come to a halt or movements seem to become uncontrollable and explosive.[25] Thus affects and emotions become representable in a state of inactivity.[26] This means that anime finds dynamic representations for the ambivalence and inactivity of their protagonists, that the narration and animation allow themselves to let nothing happen or to give themselves time to express emotional states.

Steinberg also points to a potential of *limited animation*, as opposed to 'full animation', to create impressions of movement through immobility, primarily through the composition of a montage of images and a rhythmic alternation between the unmoving and the moving.[27] Steinberg's work seeks to explore transmedia dynamics, which he connects to the context of the birth of anime and *limited animation*. The rationale behind the design principles of *limited animation* is closely linked to the work of Tezuka Osamu, who is known as a manga artist, for experimental animated films, and for television series such as *Tetsuwan Atomu* (*Astroboy*) or *Janguru Taitei* (Eng. title *Kimba, the White Lion*). The founding myth of the Japanese variation of *limited animation* can be told as follows: Osamu wanted to

---

[23] Ibid., p. 108.

[24] Ibid., p. 111.

[25] Ibid., p. 116.

[26] Ibid., p. 118.

[27] Steinberg (2012) p. 5.

produce an animated series for television with *Tetsuwan Atomu* in the 1960s, but the deal with a network offered him far too limited resources for the endeavor. Therefore, he not only applied the procedures of *limited animation* already known from American cartoon productions of UPA,[28] but coupled this procedure with manga aesthetics and developed strategies that made it possible to link advertising, merchandise and anime, which Steinberg calls the birth of the Japanese media mix: "The drawn image of Atomu [...] enabled a convergence of media and objects around it and contributed to the formation of a particularly systematic image-thing network around anime."[29] The *limited animation* provided the rationale for the collaboration with a Japanese chocolate producer that ultimately ensured the anime's success. But this collaboration was based on the specific transmedia qualities of anime, already revealed in the fact that it has a very close bond with the aesthetics of manga and its montage of different points of view.[30] There is already movement in the sequencing of immobile images of the manga that anticipates the principle of montage in anime. All these developments, such as the reduction of movement already named by Lamarre, the montage of different shots of rooms and faces, the sliding of planes of images, but also the looping of movement and the drawing on 'cell banks', an archive of already used images, leads to a "moving stillness economy" that not only makes it possible to reduce the 18,000 drawing needed for 25 min of an episode to an astonishing 1500.[31] The reduction and abstraction also creates the foundations for not only creating transmedia connections between the manga and anime, but also for creating an alternative representation of movement, thus expanding the possibilities of audiovisual representations. The characters of the anime, such as *Tetsuwan Atomu*, are thus given an existence that no longer limits them to the anime and that spills over into everyday life. Steinberg's intention is not only to make clear that Astroboy was able to acquire an omnipresence in reality through the clever cooperation with the chocolate company and its products, but also that the possibilities of transmedial exploitation in merchandise are also based on aesthetic properties of manga and anime and the design of *Tetsuwan Atomu*, which, for example, produces the property of 'stickerability': Astroboy lends itself to becoming a sticker, giving all items it is stuck to the exact same property that the character possesses in the anime. His movement frozen into a pose is the same movement on a sticker as it is in the

---

[28] cf. Lamarre (2009) p. 188.

[29] Steinberg (2012) p. 39.

[30] Ibid., p. 9 f.

[31] Ibid., p. 16.

anime, thus continuing its existence outside of the anime. The sticker gives the character mobility and portability, it makes the character attachable so that it can transform other surfaces into the surface of the anime, and it thus naturally makes the character ubiquitous.[32]

Lamarre also refers to this aspect of a transmedial connection between the world and anime when he speaks in *The Anime Machine* of a power of the audiovisual objects of anime that generate perceptions and affects in the viewers in a variety of ways. He claims that the special expression of movement and the resulting affects of a dynamic relationship between things and people are the reason for the diverse activities of the recipients such as 'cosplay', 'dojinshi' (fan fiction) or 'fansubbing'.[33]

Lamarre names another aspect that marks a difference between *full animation* and *limited animation*, which he illustrates with a scene from *Tenkū no Shiro Rapyuta* (*The Castle in the Sky*, Japan 1986) by Miyazaki. Lamarre speaks of the quality of 'animetism' that is found whenever *limited animation* fundamentally deals with image and movement in a different way. 'Animetism' is revealed, for example, in an "open compositing" the creation of movement by moving slides.[34] The moving of layers thus creates an irritation and deviation from a live-action film design that cannot resort to this means, but it also creates a sense of openness. The film does not pull the viewers immersively into the film, but the film opens up to the viewers through clouds that are pulled apart on the layers *in The Castle in the Sky*:

> While the view is supremely panoramic, the sequence is not constructed to impart a sense of moving into the image world. There is a sense of a world opening up, a world with various layers that invite exploration. . .and awe.[35]

In addition to this opening, Lamarre names another effect of the uncontrolled and unpredictable, which results precisely from the fact that anime very often offers moments of stasis, but also explosive movements that can suddenly arise in intense montage sequences independently of a movement of the characters and refer to their

---

[32] Ibid., p. 79 f.

[33] Lamarre (2009) p. XIII.

[34] "Animetism begins when you allow some degree of play or openness to appear between the layers of the image, or when you flatten the layers to make them look and feel like a single layer. Animetism puts less emphasis on compositing the image tightly, on hiding the gaps between the different layers of the image as the camera (or viewing position) moves." Cf. Ibid.: p. 37.

[35] Ibid., p. 38.

inner states.[36] Animation thus creates the movement of the unmoving, which brings about a different temporality of anime.

What are the effects of *limited animation* on the serial narrative that characterizes the anime examined here? The first thing to note is that Lamarre, referring to the film philosophy of Deleuze, tends to associate *limited animation* with the time image, while *full animation* is assigned to classical cinema and the movement image.[37] This strict classification is softened somewhat by Lamarre himself when, for example, he identifies in Miyazaki's work an interplay between the processes of *limited animation* and *full animation*, which enter into a dialogue in his work.[38] This dialogue is also found in *Akage no An*, for example, in a sequence of scenes in episode 48. The precise depiction of the movement of a cow and its calf in a meadow is followed by a scene full of immobility when panning over the unmoving faces of the mourners at a funeral.

In its strongest form, *limited animation* actually leads to a complete immobility and a new image regime. *Neon Genesis Evangelion*, produced by the studio Gainax in the 1990s, is an extreme form of *limited animation* in television series. The last episode of this series which can be assigned to the Mecha genre, offers a reduced therapy-like setting where the main character Shinji is confronted with his past. There is no activity in this depleted space, instead there is a wild montage of still images where icons and words, abstract patterns of lines and sketches and outlines for the storyboard are incorporated into the anime. Dani Cavallaro regards this scene as an embodiment of a "Beckettian minimalism" that takes an extreme form of stylization. She interprets the hero's immobility not only as an embodiment of his ambivalence, but also as conveying the emotions and traumata of a generation paralyzed by the Kobe earthquake, the economic crisis, or the terrorist attacks of the Aum Shinriko cult.[39] Supposedly, another reason for this extreme form of *limited animation* is credited to the fact that the production ran out of funds to lavishly animate the finale. What emerges, however, is a very idiosyncratic interpretation of movement, stasis and seriality, which Lamarre describes as follows:

> [. . .] the action image opens up from within, exploding into anxiety, uncertainty, disorientation, and also reverie, recollection, love, and confidence. But for this to happen you must first lose all sense of where this character is going and even of where the series is going. The action image is not only stretched out, it becomes populated

---

[36] Lamarre (2008) p. 114.

[37] Lamarre (2009) p. 186.

[38] Ibid., p. 189 f.

[39] Cavallaro (2007) p. 69 f.

with affective response, mood swings, and emotional values. We are then shocked into thought and remembrance.[40]

This quote points out a different regime of time and image in anime, which can be used to express something specific and to charge the single image with meaning regardless of movement, action and progression. A common but limited understanding of seriality as a complexity that results from a psychological depth of the characters revealed in the narrative progression of delicately build story arcs are thus redefined to include the possibility of stasis, of ending, or a radical and crude slowness that the television anime may offer unlike any other form of seriality. This potential unfolds not only in *Neon Genesis Evangelion*, which holds a special place in anime culture as a cult series, but also in a series like *Akage no An* and other representatives of a genre of slow and hyper-accurate literary adaptations that assiduously translate page after page into animation. It is the mechanism of anime production or 'animetism' described by Lamarre that inscribes itself in these images, that finds other solutions to the arrangement of images in anime and thus modifies their serial patterns. In extreme cases, these stylistic operations question the very existence of the series. The differences to 'common' forms of televisual seriality are to be addressed on several levels in the context of *Akage no An*.

Rhythm

Referring to anime series such as *Mitsubachi Māya No Bōken (engl. Title: Maya the Honey Bee)* or *Arupusu no Shōjo Haiji*, Daniel Kothenschulte points to the staging of a tension between opulence and restriction as a defining characteristic of anime aesthetic.[41] Restriction is evident, for example, in the immobility of a single image, opulence in the care given to the sound design and music. The alternation that results from this dialectic establishes a perceptible rhythm to the individual anime. In Omar Calabrese's engagement with seriality as an expression of a neo-baroque aesthetics, Rhythm represents an important moment of the serial. He identifies this rhythm not only in the variation of recurring patterns, but also in a neo-baroque virtuosity that is not concerned with a single organizing principle:

---

[40]Lamarre (2009) p. 199.

[41]Kothenschulte (2008) p. 59.

> In every art virtuosity consists in the total flight from a central organizing principle, by means of a closely knit network of rules, towards a vast polycentric combination and a system based on its transformations.[42]

Series differ in the way they organize sequences, what they repeat and retell, which static and which continuous moments they have. They have a rhythm that is perceptible and imprinted on the viewers, but also conditions them, and which is described in series production, as Linda Williams puts it, with the concept of the 'beat':

> When writers create a television script for any network television single-episode series, their first task is to 'break' the story into a moment-by-moment outline (or 'beat-sheet') constituting a series of moments that yield a typical rhythm of six beats before each commercial.[43]

Creating a familiar rhythm is only one possibility of serial composition. Calabrese emphasizes the moment of a "regulated irregularity", which is connected with a baroque understanding of virtuosity. It is not about creating the familiar with the serial repetition, but the unfamiliar.[44] Calabrese supports an understanding that does not teleologically examine how, for example, the episodic series develops into an ongoing series or narrative chronologies are quantitatively enlarged by focusing on more and more characters, but rather how different rhythms are discernible in each series, which can often be decoupled from what is being told.

Akage no An has a rhythm, which can also be experienced as such because the anime seems to tell so little and so slowly. Above all, the anime series has a 'different' rhythm that is not common to television, because this order differs from an order of segmentation and sequencing of the plot that is typical of television[45] and which suits so well to the production logics of following a 'beat-sheet' mentioned by Williams. From segmentation follows an alternation between different story levels, which establishes a familiar rhythm in many series. But the arrangement of scenes in *Akage no An* destroys such a rhythm and the anticipation of a familiar arrangement of shots. The episodes discussed, in which the process of a journey by carriage is extended to more than one episode, can no longer be explained by the segmented and serial order of television; it follows a different

---

[42] Calabrese (1992) p. 40.

[43] Williams (2018) p. 179.

[44] Calabrese (1992) p. 43.

[45] Cf. Ellis (2001).

logic, such as the most detailed adaptation of the original literary work and the extension of a few actions and descriptions to a maximum of series time.

I will refer to a sequence of about one minute from the second episode of *Akage no An* to illustrate how this peculiar rhythm is created. Although *limited animation* seems to imply an efficient design that attempts to operate with repetition of drawings to save time and money, it should become clear with this description of a list of shots that there is no repetition since each shot is a new shot, if sometimes only minimally: The view of the carriage obscured by trees in a forest (1), Matthew and Anne on the carriage (2), a flock of birds against a cloudy blue sky (3), a pan from the sky to a forest path lost in the horizon (4), Anne and Matthew on the carriage drawn from a greater distance (5), the carriage from behind (6), the carriage on a bridge from the front (7), a wheel of a carriage in an isolated shot (8), Anne and Matthew on the carriage, in a shot similar to the second, but still taking a different point of view (9), the carriage on a bridge from the side from some distance framed by a flowering tree (10), and then a composition of five isolated shots with views of nature, which at the end are coupled to Anne's gaze and are intended to make it clear that she sees her home in the Green Gables farm and the nature surrounding it (Fig. 1).

Similar compositions of views can also be found in *Marco*. with arrangements of shots in which there is sometimes more, often less, and some times no movement at all, and which above all have nothing alternating or repetitive about them. Through the arrangement of the animated (mobile) and non-animated (immobile) shots, and in the minimal variation of these shots, a specific rhythm is created that seems highly organized and in a strange way both redundant and familiar, and non-redundant and unfamiliar. What at first glance seems like a stretching of time and efficient use of repetition actually follows no familiar pattern other than its own and that of many other unwiedly told stories in anime series. This difference to standard serial production is even more noticeable when the anime series is compared to a more recent television adaptation of *Anne of Green Gables*. Co-produced in Canada by Netflix, *Anne with an E.* delivers a live-action, modernized, very carefully crafted version of this story that also attempts to address the darker aspects of Anne's marginalization as an orphan or the inability of people in the Victorian age to express their feelings. But as complex, smart, and individually crafted as it may be as a typical Netflix product, unlike the first episodes of the anime version and its endlessly stretched carriage ride, this version falls back on common cliffhanger structures where the actions and movements are capped at the episode's end and the resolution of the search for rejected Anne is not picked up until the following episode. Again, the first carriage ride is relatively long in the live-action version, but compared to the anime pilot episode's length of over an hour, it's just

Fig. 1 Shot from *Anne with the Red Hair*, Episode 2. (DVD © Studio 1,002,016)

relatively long. And it additionally offers some variations by alternating with segments from another time period, which in this series fragmentarily tell Anne's backstory, while the anime version has its own long segment devoted exclusively to that backstory on the carriage ride with Marilla. The staging of the live-action version is much better described by the notion of a televisual division into 'beats' than the design of the anime version, where it is difficult to speak of a 'beat' simply because of its slow rhythm.

Backgrounds and Repetitions

The minimal variation ensures that there is much that looks like a repetition or a redundant element, but on closer inspection turns out to be a new element. The fact that there is no repetition and that markings of segment transitions such as establishing shots are dispensed with has to do with the need to compensate for loss of movement with another form of movement. Lamarre points out that this strategy is a typical element of Miyazaki's films[46] and it also plays a role in his involvement in television works. Since the background drawings, often found as isolated landscape drawings in the series, are extremely dominant and are also the product of intense study by the animation artists involved in the anime,[47] they are not only an important element of rhythmic composition, but they also take on the task of conveying emotions for the viewers—usually but not always associated with the protagonist. Indeed, they are often also carriers of emotions that appear to be decoupled from the narration, which explains the isolated nature of these settings. These shots bear a resemblance to what Noël Burch has called Pillow Shots in the context of Yasuhiro Ozu's films.[48] These shots seem to have no meaning and perform no function of connection, the composition of space and objects strike us precisely because they have no causal relationships to events (but to feelings) and they are not subordinate to the narrative but superior to it.[49] Through their subtle, gentle interruption of the action (because they look like matching cuts connecting the space and the action, but are in fact spaces of the film in their own right), they create a slow and steady rhythm that, in Ozu's work, also always illustrates or embodies a very everyday, melancholic passing of time.[50] These decoupled shots, like the shots of *Tetsuwan Atomu* freezing his movements into a pose in such a way that they create the same impression of movement in the anime as they do in the

---

[46]Lamarre (2008) p. 111.
[47]Cf. Miyazaki (2009) p. 330.
[48]Singer (2016).
[49]Cf. Bordwell, Thompson (1976) p. 46.
[50]Visarius (2007) p. 130.

manga and as stickers, offer opportunities to point beyond the narrative and make connections with the viewers, and therefore contain a moment of communication. That they serve to project emotion into them is abundantly clear in some other recurring composition of images, for example in episode 9 of *Akage no An*. In these compositions that convey Annes admiration for a new companion, fantasy and imaginary beings are mixed with and superimposed on reality, also alluding to a fantasy integrated into everyday life. The individual and artistic design of the backgrounds or of shots that only show landscape is also interesting because it contradicts an essence of *limited animation* that is also named in the works about it, namely the access to a 'cell bank' from which the same images and drawings are taken again and again in order to save time and money.[51] In fact, *Akage No Anne* refrains from helping itself to a 'cell bank'. As mentioned earlier, the seemingly economic design of these anime is not very economic, since it means that trips had to be made to Europe for *Haha o Tazunete Sanzenri* and *Arupusu no Shōjo Haiji* to make studies and sketches that were later transformed into compositions of backgrounds of city and country views. *Akage no An* and many series in the *World Masterpiece Theatre* series consistently eschew repetition as a defining characteristic of seriality. It is always new background drawings that we can see.

Desegmentation

As another feature of a particular seriality, *Akage no An* is characterized by a process of desegmentation, which has already been addressed in connection with the rhythm of the series. *Anne* and other anime series such as *Haha o Tazunete Sanzenri*, *Tanoshî Mûmin Ikka* or even classics such as *Mitsubachi Māya no Bōken* have, in various ways, an indeterminate dramaturgy that does not fit into the patterns of segmentation of television. In the 1980s, John Ellis used segmentation to define a major difference between television and motion pictures, which results from the adjusting of television to the television flow and from processes of serialization.[52] While Raymond Williams defines the regime of flow as rather chaotic, as an overlapping of various and distinct media content,[53] Ellis identifies a specific structure that gives flow and serialization a foothold, the structure of small segments

---

[51] Steinberg (2012) p. 15 f.

[52] Cf. Ellis (2001).

[53] Cf. Williams (2001).

which are separate but can be coupled at the same time.[54] Television consists of units such as individual news items, reports, advertisements, music clips, trailers, signatures (idents), but also short segments in series such as longer scenes in sitcoms or individual scenes that end with a cliffhanger in soap operas and all other melodramatic series. These series support the segmented structure through a large arsenal of characters and the parallel telling of several stories. This results in a relative independence of these elements, which also guarantee the interruptibility of a television text.[55] A melodramatic series or a drama series does not have to be watched from beginning to end because this order does not strive towards an end and is made up of loose ends. We can therefore switch from one channel to another without it having to mean a significant break with our viewing experience. Quality series like to conceal this interruptibility, but they too enable a familiar rhythm through a segmentation that organizes perception.

This structure of segmentation continues, among other media technological and phenomenological characteristics, on the Internet as a kind of hypersegmentation.[56] Platforms such as YouTube can make good use of the segments of television; they emphasize an aggregate state that is connected to the configuration of television but actually leaves the units to stand on their own: The segmentation inherent in the medium of television becomes visible. Series can therefore also be broken down very well into scenes that can be watched on their own on YouTube and other platforms.

Anime series, however, break with this form of segmentation and, although the short episode time of just under 25 minutes seems to suggest otherwise, offer a highly de-segmented subject matter, with only the theme song and credits song, intro and outro commentary offering anything truly recurring (and therefore easy to find on YouTube). *Akage no An* is captivatingly undramatic, even when dramatic stories are told, such as Anne being suspected of stealing a brooch. The sequences of images, however, do not derive from the drama, but from the passage of time and the plot. As a series, unlike a film, it does not constitute a closed, uniform object that is assembled from the individual parts of a montage. It consists of many small, isolated parts (for example, the individual shots of landscape montages), but nevertheless does not break down into identifiable segments and thus appears not only slow but also astonishingly unwieldy for television.

---

[54]Ellis (2001) p. 48 f.

[55]Cf. Modleski (2001).

[56]Cf. Dawson (2007) p. 240.

The Bulkiness of Anime Series

The aspect of desegmentation ensures that anime series do not fit easily into these broadcast structures of television and insist on their own temporality. In the case of *Haha o Tazunete Sanzenri*, for example, this bulkyness means that the series does not tell what it seems to tell. Although its sole content is the completion of the search for his mother, much else is actually told. The series loses itself in views of the landscape and the detailed depiction of events, the images and movements are repeatedly decoupled from the search for his mother. *Tanoshî Mûmin Ikka* is also a rather desegmented series, its inert creatures seeming to follow a rhythm of the seasons and their own biology much more closely than a televisual beat and rhythm based on segmentation, making it possible to manage stories extremely variably over one or more episodes, while being neither episodic nor ongoing, nor a harmonious blend of the two, a peculiar case of what is also readily referred to as 'flexi-narrative' in the context of recent drama series.[57] These anime series do not offer a harmonious, economical narrative form suited to the needs and beats of television. In their own way they are immoderate and shapeless, but in this way they also leave an impression. It is interesting that these eccentric but somehow advanced forms of series unfold preferentially in children's programming which also tends to disguise their complexity.

These are all attempts to describe the special temporality of these anime series, and thus perhaps explain why these programs leave or have left a special impression on their viewers. While time seems to pass even more slowly in soap operas than in reality[58] or real time series such as *24* create a new experience of what can happen in a day and most series offer the events of a narrative in an organized and condensed form, *Tanoshî Mûmin Ikka*, *Akage no An* or *Haha o Tazunete Sanzenri* represent examples of series in which time seems to pass in the same way as in reality, not overlaid by a television structure. This article may somewhat overemphasize this peculiarity of anime series and underplay how heavily they depend on conditions of televisual production, but it does so in order to put up for discussion the productivity of this seemingly naïve, but ultimately unlimited form of seriality.

---

[57]Cf. Nelson (2013) p. 24.
[58]Cf. Modleski (2001) p. 348.

References

Bordwell, David, Kristin Thompson (1976) Space and Narrative in the Films of Ozu. In: *Screen* 17 (4), pp. 41–73

Calabrese, Omar (1992) Neo-Baroque. A Sign of Times, Princeton, Princeton University Press

Cavallaro, Dani (2007) Anime Intersections. Tradition and Innovation in Theme and Technique. Jefferson North Carolina, McFarland

Clements, Jonathan, Helen McCarthy (2015) Anime Encyclopedia. Berkeley, Stone Bridge Press

Dawson, Max (2007) Little Players, Big Shows. Format, Narration, and Style on Television's New Smaller Screens. In: Convergence: The International Journal of Research into New Media Technologies 13 (3), pp. 231–250

De Amicis, Edmondo (1947) Von den Apenninen zu den Anden. Aus dem Roman ‚Das Herz'. Berlin, Leipzig, Volk und Wissen.

Ellis, John (2001) Fernsehen als kulturelle Form, In: Adelmann, Ralf, Jan O. Hesse, Judith Keilach, Markus Stauff, Matthias Thiele (Eds.) Grundlagentexte zur Fernsehwissenschaft. Theorie – Geschichte – Analyse. Konstanz. UVK, pp. 44–73

Elsaesser, Thomas (2002) Filmgeschichte und frühes Kino. Archäologie eines Medienwandels. München, edition text + Kritik

Josef Göhlen (2008) Suspekt, doch erfolgreich. Der Weg des Anime ins ZDF. In: Ga-Netchū! Das Manga-Anime-Syndrom. Katalog zu den Ausstellungen Mangamania – Comic-Kultur in Japan 1800 bis 2008 und Anime! High Art. Frankfurt a. M, Henschel, pp. 234–239

Kothenschulte, Daniel (2008) Opulenz und Beschränkung. Stile des frühen Anime. In: Ga-Netchū! Das Manga-Anime-Syndrom. Katalog zu den Ausstellungen Mangamania – Comic-Kultur in Japan 1800 bis 2008 und Anime! High Art. Frankfurt a. M, Henschel, pp. 50–63

Nieder, Julia (2008) Südwind aus Fernost. Die Filme des Studio Ghibli. In: Ga-Netchū! Das Manga-Anime-Syndrom. Katalog zu den Ausstellungen Mangamania – Comic-Kultur in Japan 1800 bis 2008 und Anime! High Art. Frankfurt a. M, Henschel, pp. 96–105

Lamarre, Thomas (2008) Full Limited Animation. In: Ga-Netchū! Das Manga-Anime-Syndrom. Katalog zu den Ausstellungen Mangamania – Comic-Kultur in Japan 1800 bis 2008 und Anime! High Art. Frankfurt a. M, Henschel pp. 106–119

Lamarre, Thomas (2009) The Anime Machine. A Media Theory of Animation. Minneapolis, University of Minnesota Press

Miyazaki, Hayao (2009) Starting Point. 1979–1996. San Francisco, VIZ Media

Modleski, Tania (2001) Die Rhythmen der Rezeption. Daytime-Fernsehen und Hausarbeit. In: Adelmann, Ralf, Jan O. Hesse, Judith Keilbach, Markus Stauff, Matthias Thiele Stauff (Eds.) Grundlagentexte zur Fernsehwissenschaft. Theorie – Geschichte – Analyse. Konstanz, UVK, pp. 376–387

Nelson, Robin (2013) Entwicklung der Geschichte: Vom Fernsehspiel zur Hypermedia TV Narrative. In: Eichner, Susanne, Lothar Mikos, Rainer Winter (Hg.) Transnationale Serienkultur. Theorie, Ästhetik, Narration und Rezeption neuer Fernsehserien. Wiesbaden, pp. 22–43

Singer, Leah (2016) The Enigmatic 'Pillow shots' of Yasuhiro Ozu. In: *BFI* December 12, 2016. https://www.bfi.org.uk/news-opinion/news-bfi/features/enigmatic-pillow-shots-yasujiro-ozu. Accessed on 8 June 2020

Steinberg, Marc (2012) Anime's Media Mix. Franchising Toys and Characters in Japan. Minneapolis/London, University of Minnesota Press

Treese, Lea (2007) Go East! Zum Boom japanischer Mangas und Animes in Deutschland. Eine Diskursanalyse. Münster, LIT Verlag

Visarius, Karsten (2007) Die Welt in einer japanischen Familie. In: Frölich, Margrit. Klaus Gronenborn, Karsten Visarius (Eds.) Das Gefühl der Gefühle. Zum Kinomelodram (Arnoldshainer Filmgespräche 25). Marburg, Schüren pp. 126–141

Williams, Linda (2018) World and Time: Serial Television Melodrama in America. In: Gledhill, Christine, Linda Williams (Eds.) Melodrama Unbound. New York, Columbia University Press, pp. 169–183

Williams, Raymond (2001) Programmstruktur als Sequenz oder Flow. In: Adelmann, Ralf, Jan O. Hesse, Judith Keilbach, Markus Stauff, Thiele, Matthias (Eds.) Grundlagentexte zur Fernsehwissenschaft. Theorie – Geschichte – Analyse, Konstanz: UVK, pp. 33–43

Series/Movies

Ai no Wakakusa Monogatari (engl. Titel: *Little Women,* Fuji TV 1987)

Akage no An (dt. Titel: *Anne mit den roten Haaren,* Fuji Television 1979)

Anne With an E. (Netflix 2017–2019)

Araiguma Rasukaru (dt. Titel: *Rascal, der Waschbär,* Fuji TV 1977)

Arupusu no Shōjo Haiji (dt. Titel: *Heidi,* Fuji TV 1974)

Furandāsu no Inu (engl. Titel: *Dog of Flanders,* Fuji TV 1975)

Haha o Tazunete Sanzenri (dt. Titel: *Marco,* Fuji TV 1976)

Janguru Taitei (dt. Titel: *Kimba, der weiße Löwe,* Fuji TV 1965–66)

Mitsubachi Māya no Bōken (dt. Titel: *Die Biene Maja,* TV Asahi 1975)

Shin Seiki Evangerion (dt. Titel: *Neon Genesis Evangelion,* Fuji TV 1995)

Tanoshî Mûmin Ikka (dt. Titel: Die *Mumins,* TV Tokyo 1990)

Tomu Sōyā no Bōken (dt. Titel: *Tom Sawyers Abenteuer,* Fuji TV 1980)

Torappu Ikka Monogatari (engl. Titel: *Trapp Family Story,* Fuji TV 1991)

Tetsuwan Atomu (engl. Titel: *Astroboy,* Fuji TV 1963–1966)

Tenkū no Shiro Rapyuta (*Das Schloss im Himmel,* Japan 1986)

Herbert Schwaab   Dr. phil., teaches as a senior lecturer in the Department of Media Studies at the University of Regensburg. His research focuses on film philosophy and popular culture, sitcoms and reality TV, animals in animation, Japanese media culture, bicycle culture and the mediality of autism. PhD 2006 at the Ruhr University Bochum with a thesis on Stanley Cavell's philosophy of film. Important publications: Ed. (with Benjamin Beil, Daniela Wentz): Lost in Media. Münster: Litverlag, 2017; "Die schwierige Beziehung von Film und Sitcom," in: Thomas Morsch/Lukas Foerster/Nikolaus Perneczky (eds.): Before Quality. Zur Ästhetik der Fernsehserie vor HBO, Netflix und Co. Münster: Litverlag, 2019, 153–181; Erfahrung des Gewöhnlichen. Stanley Cavells Filmphilosophie als Theorie des Populärkultur (Experience of the Ordinary. Stanley Cavell's film philosophy as a theory of popular culture). Münster: Lit, 2010.